I hope that this
proves valuable
and useful to
The students of
Caldwell College.

Marie Mullaney

14 March 1994

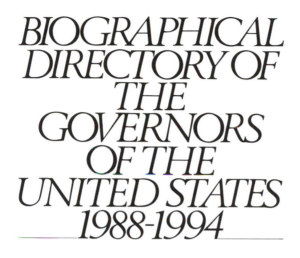

BIOGRAPHICAL DIRECTORY OF THE GOVERNORS OF THE UNITED STATES 1988-1994

BIOGRAPHICAL DIRECTORY OF THE GOVERNORS OF THE UNITED STATES 1988-1994

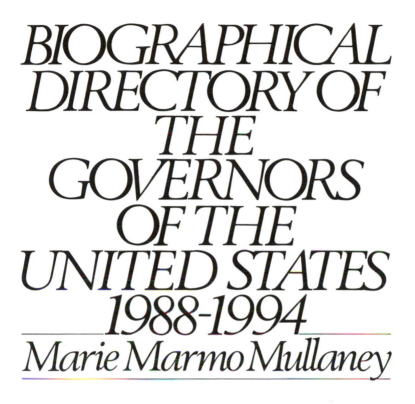

Marie Marmo Mullaney

GREENWOOD PRESS
Westport, Connecticut • London

Library of Congress Cataloging-in-Publication Data

Mullaney, Marie Marmo.
    Biographical directory of the governors of the United States
1988–1994 / Marie Marmo Mullaney.
        p. cm.
    Includes bibliographical references and index.
    ISBN 0–313–28312–5 (alk. paper)
    1. Governors—United States—Biography.   2. Governors—United
States—Election.   I. Title.
JK2447.M86   1994
353.9'1313'0922—dc20   93–37875

British Library Cataloguing in Publication Data is available.

Library of Congress Catalog Card Number: 93–37875
ISBN: 0–313–28312–5

First published in 1994

Greenwood Press, 88 Post Road West, Westport, CT 06881
An imprint of Greenwood Publishing Group, Inc.

Printed in the United States of America

∞™

The paper used in this book complies with the
Permanent Paper Standard issued by the National
Information Standards Organization (Z39.48–1984).

10 9 8 7 6 5 4 3 2 1

Cover photos: W. Clinton (Courtesy of the White House Legal
Counsel), A. Richards (Courtesy of the Governor's Office), L. Weicker
(Courtesy of the Governor's Office), D. Wilder (Courtesy of the
Governor's Office), W. Weld (Courtesy of the Governor's Office),
P. Wilson (Courtesy of Sirlin Studios, Sacramento, Calif.)

CONTENTS

PREFACE

With a former governor sitting in the White House and several other former chief executives serving in his administration, there should be no question as to the value or significance of the governorship to American politics today. This collection of biographies recounting the careers and achievements of all those who have served in their respective statehouses from 1988 through 1994 should be seen as much more than a glimpse at interesting personalities, however. While there are dynamic, charismatic, and effective leaders portrayed herein, a synthetic review of the difficulties faced by governors in these recessionary times yields tremendous insights into the social and economic problems of late 20th-century America and is perhaps the even more valuable benefit of this collection.

Since the 1980s, new responsibilities have been heaped on the statehouses owing to Ronald Reagan's new federalism, which curtailed the flow of federal dollars to state capitals. According to reports issued by the National Governors Association and the National Association of State Budget Officers, the explosion of costs has been particularly acute in the areas of Medicaid and prison construction. Former Missouri Governor John Ashcroft has termed Medicaid "the Pac-man of the state budget because it gobbles up an ever growing share of state revenues,"[1] while many states, under court order to correct severe prison overcrowding, have had no alternative but to resort to new construction. Other factors—the shrinking economy, deteriorating infrastructures, aging populations, the need for new programs in education, and the spiraling costs of courts and prisons due to the drug crisis—all have added to the states' difficulties and required innovative and courageous leadership by their chief executives. Recounted in the pages that follow are stories of bitter legislative sessions nationwide, crises that have culminated in worker layoffs, deeply slashed services, and higher taxes. Other states have scrambled to find enough dollars simply to keep current services operating. Indeed, as the 1990s have unfolded, states that had never before given a second thought to initiating income or sales taxes are debating the issue, whereas others have raised record billions in taxes. In 1991 alone, 33 states were forced to raise taxes, yielding a record $15.1 billion in new revenues. There is much talk about cutting spending and expenses, creating more jobs in the private sector, and even transferring some traditionally public functions to private enterprise. Thirty-six states have recently created commissions to study ways to change and consolidate major state functions.

By all measures, these are difficult times. According to one gubernatorial historian, the period treated by this volume, 1988–1994, has been perhaps "among the most difficult in decades" to take over as governor.[2] California's Pete Wilson has seen his presidential ambitions shattered owing to persistent economic crises, while New York's Mario Cuomo blamed budget woes for his decision to eschew the 1992 Democratic presidential primaries. Michigan's John Engler, Alaska's Walter Hickel, Oregon's Barbara Roberts, and Louisiana's Edwin Edwards have all faced recall drives, while governor bashing became a cottage industry in Connecticut and New Jersey after governors Lowell Weicker and Jim Florio aroused voter ire with record tax increases.

With many governors, particularly in the Northeast, frustrated by growing state budget deficits, ten incumbents chose not to seek reelection in 1990. That same year, voters ousted the governing party in 14 states, while in 1992, of 12 states electing governors, just 4 had incumbents up for reelection.

Voter frustration with politics as usual was also reflected on the state level. Although independents or third-party candidates have rarely won election as governors in this century, two states—Alaska and Connecticut—elected independents for the first time since 1974, when James Longley of Maine won election to the statehouse. Lowell Weicker of Connecticut even drew comparisons between his third-party drive and that of Ross Perot in the White House race of 1992. Only those outside politics as usual, according to Weicker, had the guts to deliver the tough medicine needed to cure budgetary ills.

Other national issues—primarily the divisive problem of abortion rights—took center stage in state races, especially after the 1989 Supreme Court ruling in *Webster v. Reproductive Health Services* invited states to tighten restrictions on the procedure. The abortion issue figured prominently in the 1989 elections of Doug Wilder in Virginia and Jim Florio in New Jersey. Political observers attributed the victory of both men to their prochoice positions. Elsewhere, in Florida, Texas, and California, abortion rights groups pointed to the replacement of prolife incumbents by prochoice challengers.

Wilder's 1989 win in Virginia was even more significant for another reason: With his victory as the nation's first elected black governor, a historic political barrier fell, resonating throughout the nation as other black candidates sought to rise to similar heights. In 1990, for the first time in a century, South Carolina Democrats nominated a black for governor, while in Georgia that same year Atlanta Mayor Andrew Young also sought to duplicate Wilder's feat.

Women, too, have made gains in the years recounted here. In 1990, a record 12 women set their sights on the governorship, while 6 figured prominently in the gubernatorial races of 1992. A total of 7 women have served or are currently serving as chief executives during these six years, with Ann Richards of Texas drawing serious attention as a potential presidential contender at some future date.

Of late, the governorship seems to have become an increasingly viable springboard to the White House, what with the accessions of Jimmy Carter, Ronald Reagan, and Bill Clinton and the aspiring candidacies of former governors Bruce Babbitt of Arizona, Michael Dukakis of Massachusetts, and Bob Kerrey of Nebraska. Political observers believe that Republican governors will be a major supplier to the growing pool of GOP candidates hoping to unseat Bill Clinton in 1996. Already, Carroll Campbell of South Carolina, William Weld of Massachusetts, Tommy Thompson of Wisconsin, and John Engler of Michigan are considering presidential bids, with another former Republican governor, Lamar Alexander of Tennessee, also said to be interested in running.

Also to be noted is the role played by former statehouse executives in the shaping of current national policy. Three highly touted "Education Governors"—Bill Clinton of Arkansas, Richard Riley of South Carolina, and Madeleine Kunin of Vermont—are now serving in Washington and directing federal policy in that area, a presence that should ensure that the role of state leadership and innovation in education reform is recognized and perhaps learned from. In the same area, not to be forgotten is the role played by former Tennessee Governor Lamar Alexander as secretary of education in the Bush administration.

Finally, problems plaguing not only American society but also American politics are tragically unveiled in these pages. The escalating costs of campaigning and getting elected to office as well as the temptations of power both find their lamentable traces herein. In August 1990, long-serving West Virginia Governor Arch Moore began a five-year prison term for his conviction on felony charges of extortion, mail fraud, tax fraud, and obstruction of justice, while in April 1993, two-term Alabama Governor Guy Hunt was unceremoniously removed from office after he was found guilty of violating the state's ethics law. Arizona Governor Fife Symington remains embroiled in a controversy over his involvement in a failed Phoenix Savings and Loan from which he had borrowed heavily and on whose board he had served as a director.

All in all, a biographical study of the American governorship provides fascinating insights into the changing face of American politics during a troubled period.

NOTES

1. John Ashcroft quoted in *The New York Times*, 4–7–91.
2. Samuel Solomon, gubernatorial historian at Eastern Michigan University, quoted in *USA Today*, 1–2–91.

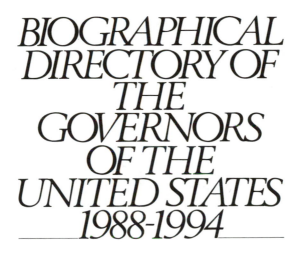

BIOGRAPHICAL
DIRECTORY OF
THE
GOVERNORS
OF THE
UNITED STATES
1988-1994

Guy Hunt (*Courtesy of Governor's Office*)

ALABAMA

GUY HUNT, 1987–1993

Born on June 17, 1933, in Holly Pond (Cullman County), Alabama, Hunt is the son of William Otto Hunt and Frances Holcombe Hunt. A member of the Mt. Vernon Primitive Baptist church, he married the former Helen Chambers on February 25, 1951. They have four children: Pam, Sherrie, Keith, and Lynn.

Hunt graduated from Holly Pond High School in 1950 with intentions of embarking on a career in farming. He was president of the Holly Pond chapter of the Future Farmers of America and later became president of the Cullman County Future Farmers of America. He served in the U.S. Army during the Korean War, in the 101st Airborne Division and in the 1st Infantry Division, and was awarded the Certificate of Achievement for Outstanding Performance of Military Duty.

He began his political career in 1964 when he was elected probate judge of Cullman County. Reelected in 1970, he chose not to seek reelection in 1976, although he remained active in state Republican politics. A supporter of Ronald Reagan's presidential ambitions from the mid-1970s, he was the state chairman of Reagan's presidential campaign in 1976, as well as chairman of the Alabama delegation to the Republican National Convention in Kansas City in 1976. He repeated these roles during Reagan's victorious run for the White House in 1980. His support was rewarded with a presidential appointment as state executive director of the Agricultural Stabilization and Conservation Service (ASCS) under the U.S. Department of Agriculture, a position he held from 1981 to 1985, when he resigned to prepare for the 1986 gubernatorial race.

Alabama politics changed dramatically in 1986 when legendary incumbent George Wallace announced that he would be retiring from the statehouse at the conclusion of his fourth term. Attention quickly focused on who would lead the state into the post-Wallace era. Almost all political observers assumed that it would be a Democrat, since Alabama is a heavily Democratic state that had not had a Republican governor since 1874. Hunt was given little or no chance of victory. In fact, it was widely assumed that he was in the race simply to "show the flag" for the party, especially after several better-known Republicans had chosen not to run.

Hunt had already lost badly once before: In the 1978 gubernatorial campaign, he was defeated by Democrat Fob James, 551,886 votes to 196,963.

The 1986 Republican primary was so small and quiet that it attracted less than 33,000 voters. Hunt won the nomination easily, beating businessman Doug Carter. As had long been standard in traditional southern politics, all assumed that the next governor of Alabama would be whoever won the Democratic primary. That primary, however, turned into a tumultuous battle that badly split the state's Democratic party and paved the way for Hunt's eventual victory. The two leading contenders were Attorney General Charles R. Graddick, a former Republican, and Lieutenant Governor Bill Baxley, a moderate-to-liberal figure in state politics. The campaign stirred racial tensions more overtly than had any other race in years. Graddick chose to spurn the sizable black vote in Alabama, appealing instead to the conservative white vote that had carried the state for Ronald Reagan in 1984. Baxley drew on Wallace's populist coalition of blacks and more liberal whites, as well as union members and public employees.

Although Graddick narrowly defeated Baxley in the June 24, 1986, Democratic runoff (50.3 percent to 49.7 percent), a panel of federal judges stripped him of the nomination because he had violated state and federal voting laws by illegally encouraging Republicans to ignore Democratic party rules and cross over to vote for him in the runoff. As attorney general, Graddick had issued an opinion the day before the election saying such crossover voting was legal. A black couple sued in federal court, accusing Graddick of violating the Voting Rights Act by misusing his office to court Republican voters in order to dilute the strength of black votes. Ruling on the suit, the judges ordered the state Democratic party either to name Baxley the winner or to hold a new election.

State party leaders decided to name Baxley as their nominee, concluding that it was illegal Republican ballots that had provided Graddick with his razor-thin margin of victory. When the Alabama Supreme Court refused to order a new Democratic gubernatorial runoff, Graddick threatened to run as an independent write-in candidate in the fall election. Although the deep divisions in the Democratic party aided Hunt's candidacy, the specter of Graddick's third-party challenge haunted Hunt's campaign in the early months, for both men were aiming their appeals at the same pool of white conservatives and traditional Republicans. When Graddick chose to end his candidacy, Hunt—who had been given no chance of winning—suddenly had a very good chance.

In the campaign, Baxley tried to portray Hunt as unqualified, running ads playing on his lack of a college degree and describing him (a lay Baptist preacher, chicken farmer, and Amway distributor) as a former vacuum cleaner salesman. Hunt was also forced to deny allegations that he had been made to step down from his federal agricultural job in Alabama because he had solicited campaign contributions from government employees.

Hunt based his campaign on the need to create a business climate "second to none" and pledged a range of initiatives to attack waste in government, to revise state laws governing lawsuits for personal injury and property damage, and to improve the state's public school system. He said the task of creating new and better jobs would be the "foundation of his administration," and he spoke of a "philosophical partnership" between conservatives, regardless of party.

Hunt's 56 to 44 percent victory over Baxley in the November 4, 1986, election made him the first Republican governor of Alabama since David Peter Lewis, who served from 1872 to 1874. Political commentators, however, attributed the victory solely to the bitter and divisive battles among Democrats in their struggle to find a successor to the long-serving George Wallace. Hunt's victory appeared to be a lone phenomenon, without discernible coattails or broader effect, since he propelled no local Republicans into office with him.

Surrounded by Democrats in every major executive, legislative, and administrative office, Hunt—it was widely predicted—would be "eaten alive" by the legislature. Moreover, political scientists noted that the executive authority of the Alabama governor's office ranks only in the middle or lower range among states. Interposed between the governor and department heads in many cases are elective boards, and without the cooperation of the legislature, the governor has "only his appointive powers and his powers of public persuasion." Yet Hunt and the Democratically controlled legislature had some conservative beliefs in common: shared views on taxes, spending, and the need to create a more stable economic climate.

In his first inaugural address, Hunt pledged to put to rest the forces that had divided the state since the Civil War and promised a "color blind" administration. Yet within his first month in office, he fought bitterly with an influential group of black Democrats who assailed his appointment record, which included only 1 black among 23 cabinet-level nominees.

During his first term, Hunt proposed sweeping changes in the governance of public colleges, prompting a clamorous debate about how much power the governor should have in setting educational policy. In 1989, the purchase of Montgomery's leading television station by the state's pension fund set off a bitter political feud between Hunt and the state's teachers. Saying that pension fund ownership could undermine WSFA-TV's impartiality in covering statewide news, Hunt asked the Federal Communications Commission (FCC) to stop the sale.

Critics feel that Alabama's tax system, one of the most regressive in the nation, has worked to undermine progress in the direction of educational reform. In 1991, Alabama lost a bid to secure a new Saturn plant, a project that would have brought thousands of jobs and millions in salaries and tax revenues. General Motors executives told state officials that the company lacked confidence that the state was committed to a well-financed educational system that could supply the trained workers needed for the plant. The loss of the plant to neighboring Tennessee confirmed what many in the state had known for years about the effects of low education budgets, racial turmoil in the schools, and depending too heavily on low wages and low taxes to entice new business. Nonetheless, Hunt clung doggedly to his vision of Alabama as a low-tax, low-wage haven for big companies, arguing that he was leading the state into a new era of prosperity.

Competing visions for Alabama marked Hunt's campaign for reelection in 1990. His Democratic opponent, Paul Hubbert, executive secretary of the Alabama Education Association, called Alabama "the equivalent of a third world nation." Hubbert tried to sell voters on the need for a "New South" governor, saying that better leadership on education and economic development was needed to help Alabama catch up with states like Georgia. By contrast, Hunt touted his record on economic development, arguing, as his commercials put it, that Alabama was doing "just fine." Noting his 1987 selection by *U.S. News & World Report* as one of the nation's 11 best governors, Hunt tried to present Hubbert as a candidate of special interests because of his ties to organized labor and teachers' organizations.

The campaign drew close analysis from political commentators who feared a nasty resurgence of racial politics. Democrats contended that Hunt's campaign had a racial component meant to rally his conservative supporters. As evidence, they pointed to Hunt commercials showing Hubbert with black political officials. The slumping economy, white resentment over policies like affirmative action, and a generally angry mood among the electorate seemed to indicate that any proclamations as to the death of the Old South were, unfortunately, premature.

Benefiting from the advantages of incumbency and his own folksy appeal, Hunt won reelection with 52 percent of the vote, becoming the first Republican to be reelected for a consecutive term and only the second governor in Alabama's history to be elected to a consecutive term.

During his second term, Hunt appointed a study group to focus on the state's antiquated tax structure. He also created a new Office of Water Resources in the Alabama Department of Economic and Community Affairs, charged with strengthening Alabama's stance in water negotiations with Georgia and Florida. He urged the legislature to adopt comprehensive water resource legislation to strengthen Alabama's hand during interstate negotiations about water rights. In response to a furor surrounding a gay student group's drive for recognition at Auburn University, Hunt signed legislation prohibiting gay student groups from receiving public money or holding meetings at state university facilities.

Embroiled in a controversy shared by several other southern governors, Hunt insisted on the state's historic right to fly the Confederate battle flag over the state capitol. His refusal to take down the flag that then-Governor George Wallace had first hoisted above the statehouse in defiance of the civil rights movement in 1963 soured his relations with the black community and led to a prolonged court battle that Hunt ultimately lost.

Even more problematic for Hunt, however, was a heightening controversy during his second term over alleged ethical violations of various sorts. As a Primitive Baptist preacher, Hunt used state planes for trips to church meetings where he received cash offerings. In small fundamentalist Primitive Baptist churches, ministers are not paid salaries but are given donations by churchgoers. Consequently, the state attorney general convened a special grand jury to review accusations of ethics violations against him. In response, Hunt wrote the state a personal check to cover the costs of the flights and agreed to stop using state planes to travel to preaching engagements. He charged that he was a victim of politics in a state where Democrats still predominate in important political positions. Trying to block the investigation, Hunt filed suit in 1991, claiming that he was not covered by Alabama's ethics laws because these violate the separation of powers between branches of state government. In 1992, the U.S. Circuit Court of Appeals for the 11th Circuit rejected this claim.

Hunt received even more bad news in September 1992 when the Alabama Supreme Court ruled 8–0 that a taxpayer could sue Governor Hunt for misspending.

The escalating controversy saw Hunt's statewide approval rating plummet, and polls conducted in 1992 showed him to have the lowest approval rating of any sitting U.S. governor.

Even more serious problems emerged in December 1992 when Hunt was indicted on 13 felony charges citing various financial misdeeds. Although 12 of the charges were later dropped as too old to prosecute, the remaining charge accused him of diverting $200,000 from his 1987 inaugural fund for personal use. Insisting that he had done nothing illegal, although admitting that some mistakes may have been made by those overseeing the fund, Hunt characterized the indictment as a political attack directed by Democratic State Attorney General Jimmy Evans.

Nonetheless, the scandal was a severe blow to a state Republican party struggling to reestablish itself and an embarrassment to a state long troubled by a racist past and backward image. With his indictment, Hunt became the eighth state governor in this century to be indicted while in office and the first Alabama governor in modern history to be indicted on felony charges.

Already a lame duck since state law limits governors to two terms,

Hunt was rendered politically impotent by the charges. Claiming that he was unable to exercise effective leadership due to his ongoing legal problems, some Democrats called on Hunt to resign even before his trial began.

Hunt's nine-day trial in April 1993 capped almost two years of controversy over his use of public funds. Although he and his lawyers defended as legal his use of the inaugural fund to cover debts from an earlier unsuccessful gubernatorial campaign, prosecutors countered that part of the $800,000 tax-exempt nonprofit inaugural fund had been spent on furniture, mortgage payments, fencing for Hunt's Holly Pond farm, and a marble shower stall for his home.

After deliberating only two hours over two days, a jury found Hunt guilty of violating the state's ethics law. Under Alabama procedure, the conviction immediately removed Hunt from office, and he was succeeded by Lieutenant Governor James Folsom, a Democrat.

Although he could have been sentenced to up to ten years in prison, Montgomery Circuit Judge Randall Thomas chose to spare Hunt. Saying that he had already been punished enough by the damage done to his good name and reputation, Thomas ordered him to pay $211,000 and to perform 1,000 hours of community service. He was also given five years' probation.

Seeking to clear his name, Hunt has vowed to appeal the conviction. "This is not my battle now," he says. "It's the state of Alabama's battle." If successful, Hunt would be returned to office, but it is not certain whether the Alabama Court of Criminal Appeals will rule on the case before the expiration of his statutory term in January 1995.

According to political scientists, the Hunt case was a critically important one by Alabama standards. The verdict was considered by some to be a much-needed impetus toward clean government in a state with some of the laxest ethics and campaign financing laws in the nation. As for the personal tragedy of Guy Hunt, analysts remain divided over his legacy. Republicans say his probusiness stance was good for the state's economy, which grew at a faster pace than that of the nation while he was in office. Defenders highlight the political nature of the charges raised against him and insist that his conviction reflected the judge's charge to the jury— one that held him to higher standards than were mandated by state law or rooted in common political practice.

Critics, by contrast, insist that the man dubbed "the Accidental Governor" was totally out of his depth in office. They credit him with no real legislative achievements in a state desperate for reform in many areas. Dogged by scandal in his second term, he played virtually no role in the legislative process. In the final analysis, according to University of Alabama historian Bill Barnard, Hunt was "someone from a very humble background who, when he became governor, graced the office with an aura of the imperial."

He remains unrepentant.

Bibliography: Alabama Magazine 51 (Jan.–Feb. 1987); biographical information courtesy of governor's office; *The Chronicle of Higher Education*: 10–22–86; 11–12–86; 1–13–88; 8–28–91; *The New York Times*: 6–29–86; 8–3–86; 9–4–86; 10–2–86; 10–3–86; 10–8–86; 10–25–86; 11–1–86; 11–5–86; 11–6–86; 1–20–87; 2–13–87; 2–7–89; 6–3–90; 6–28–90; 9–26–90; 11–8–90; 11–15–90; 8–25–91; 10–6–91; 5–16–92; 5–17–92; 5–29–92; 9–6–92; 9–14–92; 12–30–92; 4–23–93; 5–8–93; *The Orlando Sentinel*, 8–9–91; Howell Raines, "Alabama Bound," *New York Times Magazine* (June 3, 1990): 40–44, 48, 82, 88; *The Record* (Bergen County, N.J.): 1–21–93; 4–23–93; 5–8–93; *The Star-Ledger* (Newark, N.J.): 6–7–90; 12–29–92; 4–23–93; *USA Today*: 3–7–90; 9–23–91; 12–29–92; 1–4–93; 1–7–93; 4–13–93.

James E. Folsom, Jr. (*Courtesy of Governor's Office*)

JAMES E. ("JIM") FOLSOM, JR., 1993–

Born in Montgomery, Alabama, on May 14, 1949, Folsom is the son of former two-term Alabama governor James E. "Big Jim" Folsom, who served in the statehouse in the 1940s and 1950s. Married to the former Marsha Guthrie of Cullman, Alabama, he has two children.

Educated in the public schools of Montgomery and Cullman, Folsom received his B.A. from Jacksonville State University in Jacksonville, Alabama. Before entering political life, he worked with the Alabama Department of Industrial Relations and as southeastern public affairs representative for the Reynolds Aluminum Company.

A Democrat, Folsom began his political career with election to the state Public Service Commission in 1978. Serving two four-year terms in that office, he went on to be elected lieutenant governor in 1986. Receiving 62 percent of the vote that year, he was reelected in 1990 with over 67 percent of the vote.

During his tenure in the state's number-two post, Folsom was credited with securing legislative passage of the nation's strongest package of tort reform laws. For his efforts, Folsom was honored by the American Tort Reform Association with the Tort Reformer of the Year Award. He also took the lead in educational and environmental initiatives, working to establish the Wallace-Folsom Prepaid Affordable College Tuition Program and playing a key role in the passage of the Forever Wild Land Preservation Program. Other issues with which he concerned himself included workers' compensation, water resources, community corrections, and campaign ethics. In 1989 Folsom was honored by his peers with election to the presidency of the National Conference of Lieutenant Governors.

Folsom ascended to the governorship in tragic and regrettable circumstances after the April 1993 conviction of two-term incumbent Guy Hunt on charges of violating the state's ethics law. Immediately sworn in as the state's 54th governor on April 22, 1993, Folsom is scheduled to serve out the remainder of Hunt's term, which expires in January 1995. Should an Alabama Court of Criminal Appeals reverse Hunt's conviction, the Republican could be returned to office, but it is not certain whether the court could rule on the case before the expiration of his statutory term.

Folsom's accession returned the Democrats to the statehouse after the historic tenure of Hunt, the first member of his party to serve in the capitol since 1874. Immediately after taking office, Folsom announced his objective to work for a smooth transition and to put the state "fully on the path of healing'' after the ordeal of Hunt's trial and removal from office. He also asked Hunt's cabinet officials to remain in their posts for a time as a step in that direction.

One of Folsom's first acts as governor was to ban the Confederate battle flag from the state capitol dome, an issue that had also sparked controversy in Georgia, Mississippi, and South Carolina. His move was hailed by the state's black leaders, who had viewed the banner as an offensive symbol of the state's racist past.

Coming to office owing to the ethical troubles of his predecessor, Folsom soon found himself embroiled in a similar controversy. One month after taking office, he was the subject of four complaints filed against him with the state's Ethics Commission, including one by a former state legislator who told a newspaper that he had given Folsom $25,000 in the hopes of winning a political favor. Folsom claims the charges are politically motivated.

In a state with a sorry history of being highly tolerant of political corruption, the Folsom situation bears watching. Political observers had hoped that the conviction of Hunt might mark a new chapter in state history, serving as an impetus for clean government and much-needed reform.

Bibliography: Biographical information courtesy of governor's office; *The New York Times,* 4–23–93; *The Star-Ledger* (Newark, N.J.): 4–23–93; 4–30–93; 5–23–93.

ALASKA

STEVE COWPER, 1986–1990

Born on August 21, 1938, in Petersburg, Virginia, Cowper grew up in Kinston, North Carolina. He received a B.A. from the University of North Carolina in 1960 and an LL.B., also from the University of North Carolina, in 1963. He served in the U.S. Army in 1960 and in the U.S. Army Reserve from 1959 to 1965. He also spent three years as a maritime lawyer in Norfolk, Virginia. Married to Margaret Stewart Cowper, an attorney and businesswoman, he is the father of three children.

Cowper moved to Alaska in 1968, when he began his political career as an assistant district attorney for Fairbanks and rural Alaska, a post he held from 1968 to 1969. He pursued other interests as well: He was a partner in a Bethel air taxi and cargo business, a political columnist, and author of the script for a highly acclaimed documentary on the history of Alaska lands.

In 1974, Cowper, a Democrat, won the first of two terms in the Alaska House of Representatives. In office from 1974 to 1978, he served as chairman of the House Finance Committee, 1977–1978; chairman of the Steering Council on Alaska Lands, 1978; a member of the Subsistence Committee, 1977–1978; and a member of the Alaska Advisory Committee for the Law of the Sea Conference, 1978.

He has also held numerous business and professional positions: research diver with the Marine Research Team, 1975–1976; a newspaper reporter in Vietnam, 1970; and an instructor at Tanana Valley Community College, 1980.

His first attempt at statewide political office came in 1982. Despite a narrow loss in the Democratic gubernatorial primary to William Sheffield, the man who went on to win the general election and become governor of Alaska, Cowper persisted in his drive for the statehouse. His quest for his party's nomination was aided by the political troubles of incumbent William Sheffield. Sheffield had been badly bruised by state senate hearings during the summer of 1985 on whether he should be impeached on charges of having designed specifications for state office space to benefit a longtime friend and political contributor. Sheffield denied any wrongdoing, and the legislature did not bring formal impeachment charges, but

Steve Cowper (*Courtesy of Alaska Dept. of Education*)

the televised hearings capped three years of controversy over Sheffield's conduct in office. The incumbent was also plagued by a rocky state economy. Plunging oil prices cut the state's income from petroleum taxes and royalties by two-thirds, forcing cuts of $1 billion in the state budget and causing oil companies to cut jobs. Despite being outspent by his opponent, Cowper won the August 26, 1986, Democratic gubernatorial primary by a 2–1 margin.

Cowper faced Republican state Senator Arliss Sturgulewski of Anchorage in the November 1986 general election. To win her party's nomination, Mrs. Sturgulewski led a field of seven that included former state governor Walter Hickel. In the campaign, Cowper stressed economic recovery and redevelopment. He focused on the special development problems of rural Alaska; the need to seek new markets aggressively; and the potential benefits of sharing the state's demonstrated skills in cold-weather engineering and construction, telecommunications, and energy technology. Cowper won the governorship with 48.9 percent of the vote; Sturgulewski gained 43.9 percent, while third-party candidate Joe Vogler of the American Independent party captured 5.7 percent. Minor party candidates split the remaining 1.5 percent of the total.

In office, Cowper called for unity in trying to solve the state's billion-dollar gap between income and spending. With the state continuing to be battered by troubles in the oil industry, he proposed reestablishing the state income tax, abolished in 1979 amid a flood of oil money. Despite the fact that Alaska has neither a sales nor income tax, Cowper's proposal to raise $183 million with the new tax aroused bitter opposition. He also proposed that the Alaska Permanent Fund, a part of the state's income from its vast Arctic oilfields, be tapped to pay part of the cost of state government.

As part of his economic development plan, Cowper advocated the expansion of the University of Alaska's international study programs. In his view, new jobs needed to be developed "from the state's abundant supply of young, well educated immigrants tuned to trade possibilities with the Pacific Rim." He hoped to establish an International Trade Center to bring in people from the business, financial, and governmental sectors of the nations with which Alaska trades. He also placed great emphasis on the teaching of foreign languages and culture, especially Japanese, Chinese, and Russian, in the state's public schools.

In early 1989, Cowper surprised political observers with the announcement that he would not seek a second term as governor in 1990. Although there had been some speculation that he might seek the U.S. Senate seat held by Republican Frank Murkowski, the race never materialized. At this writing, Cowper seems to have retired from political life. Since leaving the statehouse in December 1990, he has been associated with two firms: Steve Cowper and Associates, which does public sector consulting, and

Tradelink Alaska, which participates in international trade as a consultant and principal.

Bibliography: Michael Barone and Grant Ujifusa, *The Almanac of American Politics, 1990, 1992* (Washington, D.C.: National Journal, 1989, 1991); biographical information courtesy of governor's office; *The Chronicle of Higher Education*: 10–22–86; 11–12–86; *The New York Times*: 1–3–86; 2–21–87; 4–6–87.

WALTER J. HICKEL, 1966–1969, 1990–

Born on August 18, 1919, in Claflin, Kansas, Hickel was the eldest in a family of ten children. A 1936 graduate of Claflin High School, he participated in school sports and became the Welterweight Golden Gloves Champion of Kansas in 1938. He came to Alaska in 1940 with—as legend has it—37 cents to his name. He worked a series of odd jobs, from logging to bartending, before making a fortune as a builder and developer. His Hickel Investment Company builds and operates hotels, shopping centers, and other real estate throughout Alaska.

Hickel married Janice Cannon in 1941; the couple had one son, Ted, prior to her death in 1943. In 1945, Hickel married Ermalee Strutz, daughter of pioneer Alaskans Aline and Louis Strutz. Including Ted, the couple has six sons.

During World War II, Hickel served as a civilian flight maintenance inspector for the Army Air Corps. Following the war, he became active in politics, involved in the statehood fight and serving as Republican National Committeeman for ten years, from 1954 to 1964. He was selected to participate in the Hankone Conferences in Tokyo and headed the first Alaska Chamber of Commerce economic trade mission to Japan in 1964.

Hickel served an earlier term as governor of Alaska from 1966 to 1969. In office, he put the state on a sound financial footing, opened the North Slope for oil development, upgraded the court system, and initiated forceful environmental and air pollution efforts.

In 1969, he left Alaska to accept an appointment as secretary of the interior in the administration of Richard Nixon. In that office, he upgraded offshore drilling regulations, established the Parks-to-People Program, reorganized the Bureau of Indian Affairs, and placed all eight species of great whales on the endangered species list. Known as a proponent of development, he surprised his detractors who had originally assumed he would be a strong defender of the oil industry. A short time after he took office as interior secretary, an offshore oil well blew out near Santa Barbara, California. Although he was at first criticized for inaction, he began taking on the oil industry, ordering new safety controls and prosecuting violators with a vigor not previously seen in the department. His career in Washington came to an abrupt end in 1970, however, after he sent President Nixon a letter urging him to listen to antiwar protestors and heed the voices of the nation's youth. Nixon responded by firing Hickel, and for a time, he became an admired symbol of resistance both to the Nixon administration and to the Vietnam War.

Walter J. Hickel (*Courtesy of Alaska Dept. of Education*)

Already a figure of national prominence for his tough stand against big oil, he went on to author a best-selling memoir of his time in Washington and of his vision for a national environmental policy: *Who Owns America?* (Prentice-Hall, 1971).

Hickel made two attempts in the 1970s to regain the governorship of Alaska and tried again in 1986. Each time he lost the Republican primary, once by just 98 votes. Twice he came back to run unsuccessful write-in campaigns.

After this 21-year hiatus from governing, Hickel made a last-minute decision to enter the 1990 gubernatorial race. According to reports, the move was prompted by a disagreement with the Bush White House over Hickel's efforts to get state and federal approval for a pipeline to get Alaska's North Slope gas to market. Hickel, who as chairman of Yukon Pacific Corporation was seeking financing from abroad for the pipeline, reportedly reacted to an implied threat by White House Chief of Staff John Sununu to block the pipeline if Hickel quit the Republican party and ran for governor as an independent. The *Anchorage Times* reported that Hickel became so enraged over Sununu's threat that he became more determined than ever to run. Meeting the filing deadline by less than one hour, Hickel made his decision only seven weeks before the general election.

His independent third-party run came under the banner of the Alaska Independence party. Since its founding in the 1970s by a Fairbanks miner, Joe Vogler, and other conservatives, the party had been best known for its quixotic campaign for Alaskan secession. Although Hickel did not endorse this issue, he did share the prodevelopment theme of the party. The events that followed Hickel's surprise announcement ushered in what the *Anchorage Daily News* called "one of the strangest episodes in Alaska political history" and what retiring Governor Steve Cowper more colorfully termed "the shoot-out at the GOP corral."

The Alaska Republican party was thrown into disarray when its nominee for lieutenant governor, State Senator Jack Coghill, defected to join Hickel's ticket. Republican gubernatorial nominee state Senator Arliss Sturgulewski then had to scramble to find a running mate, ultimately deciding upon Jim Campbell, an Anchorage businessman who had placed a close second to her in the recent party primary. The conservative wing of the party, already angered by Sturgulewski's refusal to adopt their antiabortion and prodevelopment agenda, also abandoned the Republican ticket.

These events were a severe blow to Sturgulewski, a 12-year veteran of the state legislature who, in the opinion of political observers, had stood a serious chance of becoming the state's first female governor. In 1986, she had lost a close gubernatorial race to Steve Cowper, a loss attributed in part to Hickel's presence on the ballot as a write-in candidate.

Somewhat overshadowed by the chaos in Republican ranks, the Democrats nominated Tony Knowles, the former mayor of Anchorage, well known as a liberal environmentalist.

Hickel's bid was at first shrugged off as another of his quixotic quests for the statehouse. Yet he retained a lingering appeal among an older generation of Alaskans who developed the territory after World War II and led it through its boom days during the early years of statehood. Hickel promised to fight for the state's interests—a popular posture among Alaskans fed up with Washington politicians telling them what to do with their land. On the campaign trail, he spoke about trying to find some way other than bureaucratic regulation to protect the environment, a method to make it more expensive for industry to pollute than to conserve. According to pollsters, Hickel's support came from people who thought he could bring industry to the state, create jobs, cut the size of the state bureaucracy, and stand up to Washington, which owns a large portion of Alaska's land. Hickel won the election with 39 percent of the vote to Knowles' 31 percent and Sturgulewski's 26 percent. Minor candidates shared the remaining 4 percent of the vote. Hickel's upset win was seen as one of the real antiestablishment victories of the 1990 campaign season.

At his inauguration, Hickel promised Alaskans a new age of prosperity in which "the battles of the past are going to be the fun of the future." Taking prodevelopment as a theme of his administration, he has called for oil drilling in the continent's biggest wildlife preserve, roads to be built into towns that are presently unreachable by car or truck, and railroad tracks to be laid across central Alaska. He has also proposed construction of two 20-foot diameter pipelines to carry fresh water to parched California. He would also open the Arctic refuge to drilling in order to gain greater access to minerals, timber, and other resources.

One divisive issue in which Hickel has been embroiled concerns the fate of hundreds of state wolves. State wildlife management policies were questioned by many when a proposal was made to kill the wolves as a way to reduce predation and allow numbers of moose and caribou to increase.

Many of Hickel's policies have drawn fire from environmentalists. Angered by his appointment of commissioners with strong prodevelopment backgrounds to two environmental watchdog agencies, they have also criticized his plans for the California water pipeline, maintaining that it would not only cause environmental damage in Alaska but also encourage Californians to continue to waste water.

One year after taking office, Hickel found himself facing a growing storm of political and legal crises that, in the opinion of some, threatened to cut short his administration. Contracting irregularities led to the dismissal of two members of his cabinet, while another administration official resigned after admitting that his claim to have a secret tape recording of reporters plotting against the governor was a hoax. The most serious charges involved Hickel himself, who was accused of seven violations of the state's ethics law for keeping stock in the Yukon Pacific Corporation, which he founded in the 1980s to build a pipeline to carry natural gas across Alaska. An independent counsel for the state said Hickel's efforts to promote the pipeline as governor could be construed as a conflict of interest, and that he had knowingly failed to carry out his pledge to put the stock in a blind trust. Hickel ultimately agreed to give away his stock—valued at $10 million—to a non-profit, charitable foundation in order to settle the ethics case.

Nonetheless, the controversy surfaced in the midst of a recall drive against him, initiated by dissidents of the Alaska Independence party and later joined by environmentalists, women's rights groups, and university students. Although a lawyer hired by the state attorney general has issued an advisory opinion saying the recall grounds are too narrow and don't comply with state law, recall backers insist that Hickel is incompetent.

Some Alaskans are wondering whether the septuagenarian Hickel can cope with the complexities of state government today. His political future bears close watching.

Bibliography: Biographical information courtesy of governor's office; *The Chronicle of Higher Education,* 8–28–91; Phil Duncan, ed., *Politics in America 1992* (Washington, D.C.: Congressional Quarterly Press, 1991); *Newsweek,* 12–24–90; *The New York Times*: 9–22–90; 10–30–90; 11–13–90; 1–27–91; 8–15–91; 12–13–91; 12–14–91; 12–24–91; 1–16–92; *The Star-Ledger* (Newark, N.J.), 1–17–93; *USA Today*: 8–27–90; 8–30–90; 9–24–90; 10–10–90; 11–8–90; 10–1–91; 6–16–92; 8–27–92.

Rose Perica Mofford *(Courtesy of Governor's Office)*

ARIZONA

ROSE PERICA MOFFORD, 1988–1991

Born in the small mining town of Globe, Arizona, on June 10, 1922, Rose Perica is the daughter of Austrian immigrants who settled in Leadville, Colorado, in 1912 and later moved to Arizona. In secondary school, she was a star athlete, winning national honors in softball. She was also a prize-winning typist. Mofford's feminist aspirations were roused by Ana Frohmiller, a suffragist and the first woman ever to run for governor of Arizona. Mofford came to Phoenix in 1940 to work for Governor Bob Jones in the Arizona treasurer's office. At one point, she was sent to take a secretarial post at the state hospital to gather information about patient abuse. The information she gathered was sent to the state capitol, an incident that is said to have "hooked" her on a career in public service.

Moving up through the ranks, she earned a reputation for efficiency and loyalty. In 1947, she became executive secretary to the State Tax Commission but was discharged six years later because Commissioner Thad Mokre said, "We felt it was better to have a man in that job." After she was discharged, she was hired as executive secretary to Secretary of State Wesley Bolin. When he became governor in 1977, he appointed Mofford to be his successor as secretary of state. She ran for that office on her own in 1978, 1982, and 1986 and was elected each time by large margins. Supporters commended her for her honesty, fairness, and even-tempered nature, and she was affectionately known as "Aunt Rosie" in the popular press. Working successfully with 12 governors, she spent hundreds of days periodically standing in for traveling governors.

Her most critical stint as acting governor followed the serious political troubles of Evan Mecham. When Mecham was impeached by the state house of representatives on February 5, 1988, she assumed control of the state government during his six-week senate trial. Because of the agony engendered during Mecham's yearlong administration, she seemed almost reluctant to take over the job. Usually accessible almost to a fault, she secluded herself in her office during the impeachment vote. One of the few state Democrats who had refused to criticize Mecham during his controversial tenure, she lived up to one journalist's characterization of her as "steadfastly noncontroversial." In the immediate aftermath of the house impeachment vote on February 5, Mofford even declined to take over the title of acting governor, waiting over the weekend until she received official notification of the house impeachment vote on Monday, February 8.

Mofford was confident she could be a "healing governor." Hiring some of former governor Bruce Babbitt's top aides to head her transition team, she urged legislators to reinstate Martin Luther King's birthday as a state holiday, a move in direct opposition to Mecham's first controversial decision in office. Although the move drew partisan reaction from legislators, with Republicans calling it a "divisive" reminder of the problems facing impeached Governor Mecham, Mofford defended her decision, saying the furor over the King holiday had been a "national symbol of our disunity." She felt the reinstatement of the holiday was one of the "most decisive things that we can do" and termed it an important part of the healing process in Arizona. In a show of diplomacy, Mofford met with the state's former governors, both Democratic and Republican, and put Mecham's most controversial aide, Administrative Chief Max Hawkins, on a paid leave of absence. Mofford also faced tough decisions while the state legislative process was tied up with Mecham's trial. The state suffered from a $248 million budget deficit, an amount more than 50 times greater than her annual budget for the secretary of state's office.

Mofford formally became governor on April 4, 1988, the moment the gavel fell in Evan Mecham's senate trial. With Mecham's conviction and removal from office, Mofford officially became the state's first woman governor. An official state supreme court declaration canceling a previously scheduled recall election as a result of Mecham's senate trial ended all constitutional debate about the legitimacy of Mofford's succession.

As her tenure began, Mofford won praise for her ability to soothe tensions in the wake of the trauma of the Mecham years. The swearing-in ceremony in the governor's office was deliberately kept low-key to avoid "rubbing salt in the wound" and exacerbating the continuing controversy brought on by Mecham's conviction. In a prepared statement, Mofford declared "the end of some difficult times in Arizona" and urged residents to empty their "hearts of suspicion and hate." Her low-key style was a welcome relief to legislators and voters alike, who sought respite from the ever-swirling controversy of the Mecham years.

Known for her platinum beehive hairdo and heavy mascara, the folksy, fast-talking Mofford drew favorable publicity nationwide. She took pride in her unofficial title as the "Grandmother of Arizona" and served as a refreshing case study of how a secretary could make a career in state government. Mofford frequently stressed that her own career could provide inspiration for other women and insisted that her own experiences with discrimination had made her especially sympathetic to the cause of women's rights. Early polls by the *Arizona Republic* and KPNX-TV put her approval ratings at a whopping 70 percent.

The high expectations that accompanied Mofford's accession, however, were soon dashed. Almost immediately after taking office, Mofford faced some embarrassing financial problems of her own, questions similar to those that had led to the undoing of her predecessor. In late April 1988, she acknowledged that she, too, had not reported some land, loans, and partnerships of her own in the financial disclosure forms that state law annually requires to be filed by officeholders. Existence of Mofford's previously undisclosed holdings, loans, and partnerships was discovered by the Associated Press through interviews and records in the Maricopa County Recorder's Office, the State Corporation Commission, and the Secretary of State's Partnership Office. Mofford attributed the errors to a confused marital situation. Married for ten years to Captain T. R. Mofford of the Phoenix Police Department, she divorced her husband in 1967, but the couple remained close friends until his death in 1983. Mofford explained that she had undertaken most of the financial ventures on behalf of him or his estate and therefore felt no need to report them. Others were of such a minor nature that she felt they did not warrant reporting. Filing amended financial forms, she apologized for what she called an honest mistake, and the matter came to an abrupt halt. In July 1988, she was formally cleared of any wrongdoing after an investigation by the county attorney's office.

Other problems followed. Budgetary haggling with the Republican-controlled legislature caused her to veto a $3.2 billion budget in 1989, the first episode of its kind in 40 years of state history. In December 1989, she was embarrassed by disclosures that she commuted the sentences of two killers without knowing the grisly details of their crimes. Although she eventually reversed the orders, her chief of staff resigned under pressure over the incident. The original decision and her embarrassing reversal became the most politically damaging episode of her political career. Republicans seized upon the issue as proof of her "softness" on crime, while others used the commutation order to question her competence and political savvy. Critics felt she was in over her head and that the demands of running the state government were drastically different from those she had encountered as secretary of state, largely a ceremonial post. Arizona was reeling from the savings and loan crisis, and opponents charged her with doing little to help the sluggish state economy.

Frequently remarking that "my family is my state," Mofford had been expected to seek her own term as governor in 1990. However, her surprise announcement in January 1990 that she wouldn't stand for election threw the governor's race into turmoil. The Democrats had expected her to be their consensus candidate. Although polls testified to her enduring popularity, rumors had persisted for months that she was no longer up to the pressures of the job and that she did not have the stamina to continue to lead her party into a new decade of battles with the Republican-controlled legislature. Although she denied that failing health had anything to do with her decision, she had experienced a series of medical setbacks throughout 1988 and 1989: a concussion after a fall, cataract surgery, and emergency gallbladder surgery.

Announcing her retirement, Mofford explained that she wanted to return to the simple life, as she looked forward to traveling around the state to renew old friendships.

Mofford will be remembered and revered for bringing much needed stability to Arizona during a time of great turmoil. A politician from another era, "Aunt Rosie" always stayed in touch with her constituency and even as governor continued to have her name listed in the Phoenix phone book. In the words of former governor Bruce Babbitt, she was "strong and relentless on the big issues."

Bibliography: "Arizona's 'Rosie' New Boss," *Newsweek* (Feb. 22, 1988); Biographical information courtesy of governor's office; Claudia Dreifus, "The Belles of Recall," *Ms.* (June 1988); *The New York Times*: 2–7–88; 2–9–88; 2–10–88; 4–5–88; 4–6–88; 5–1–88; 7–9–88; 6–7–89; 1–21–90; *The Star-Ledger* (Newark, N.J.), 12–17–89; *USA Today*: 6–13–89; 5–16–90.

J. FIFE SYMINGTON III, 1991–

Born in New York City on August 12, 1945, Symington is the great-grandson of Henry Clay Frick, the founder of U.S. Steel, and the scion of a prominent political family. He attended Gilman Country Day School and earned a B.A. from Harvard in 1968. As a Harvard student, he was an active supporter of Barry Goldwater's 1964 presidential bid. In 1976 he married Ann Pritzlaff, daughter of a former Republican member of the state legislature. He is the father of five children, including two sons from a previous marriage.

Symington first came to Arizona in 1968, when he was assigned to Luke Air Force Base as a U.S. Air Force second lieutenant. A squadron weapons controller, he was assigned to the 621st Tactical Air Command in Thailand. Serving in the air force from 1968 to 1971, he was awarded the Bronze Star for meritorious service.

His military service completed, Symington returned to Arizona in 1976 and founded the Symington Company, a commercial and industrial development company. Active in numerous charitable and civic organizations, he entered politics in the early 1980s. He assumed a variety of roles including precinct committeeman in Legislative District 24, state Republican finance chairman, and campaign adviser to former U.S. House Minority Leader John Rhodes and U.S. Senator John McCain. Although he had never held an elective political office, he decided to seek the governorship in 1990 because of his commitment to the Republican party.

Arizona politics had been in turmoil since 1986. That year, Republican Evan Mecham, widely considered to be a political extremist, won the governorship with only a plurality of the vote. After a tumultuous 13-month administration marred by racial and other controversies, Mecham was ultimately impeached and removed from office on corruption charges. Secretary of State Rose Mofford, a Democrat, acceded to the governorship, but she did not prove to be an activist executive and announced her retirement before the 1990 campaign began. Analysts believed that the state had not really enjoyed the leadership of a strong, active governor for quite some time.

Moreover, the state Republican party had fallen on hard times owing to the unpopularity and constitutional difficulties of the Mecham administration. Although he was the first U.S. governor to be impeached and removed from office in 59 years, Mecham was threatening to seek the Republican gubernatorial nomination again in 1990 in order to obtain

J. Fife Symington III *(Courtesy of Governor's Office)*

personal vindication for himself and his ideas. Saying that "Evan Mecham must be stopped," Symington threw his hat into the ring in order to restore the traditional direction of the Republican party. Having been the first Phoenix business leader to publicly ask for Mecham's resignation as the troubles of his brief administration unfolded, Symington now launched a crusade to rid the Republican party of the stigma of "Mechamism."

After the Arizona Supreme Court unanimously ruled that former Governor Mecham could again seek the governorship despite his earlier removal from office, he and Symington battled it out for the Republican nomination from among a five-candidate field. Although Mecham enjoyed hard-core support from about one-quarter of the party, Symington benefited from the endorsement of former Senator Barry Goldwater, the patriarch of Arizona Republicans, and he went on to win the September 1, 1990, primary.

Going into the general election an underdog, Symington faced Democrat Terry Goddard, the former mayor of Phoenix. Goddard stood to benefit from his strong political bloodlines. His father, Samuel P. Goddard, was currently serving as chair of the Arizona Democratic party and had been governor of the state from 1965 to 1967.

The campaign focused on key issues: increased financing for education, economic development, water supply, and the environment. The candidates also aimed personal attacks at one another's finances and integrity. Presenting himself as a fiscal conservative with deep roots in the private sector, Symington cast Goddard as a "career politician." Goddard countered by painting Symington as a negative campaigner who was stiff and awkward in the political give-and-take. Although the candidates shared similar views on abortion rights and the support of a Martin Luther King, Jr., holiday—the issue that had first undone Mecham—Symington's victory was attributed to his opposition to a costly education referendum that the voters also defeated. Analysts believed that he also benefited from the numerical advantage enjoyed by the Republican party in the state and from his fund-raising ability.

Symington's narrow 4,000 vote margin, however, triggered another constitutional question that was also a direct legacy of the Mecham years. To prevent the future election of minority candidates like Mecham, a 1988 amendment to the state constitution called for a runoff election if no one candidate received 50 percent plus one of the total votes cast. Owing to the write-in candidacy of Mecham, who drew 10,000 votes, Symington polled only 49.7 percent of the total, and the runoff mechanism kicked in. The lame-duck legislature was called into special session by Governor Mofford to finalize all arrangements for the novel contest, and she herself had to postpone her anticipated retirement until the runoff could be held.

Ultimately victorious in the February 26, 1991, runoff, Symington drew 52.2 percent of the vote, a margin considered comfortable but not a landslide in a state where registered Republicans outnumber Democrats by 100,000. After enduring the grueling, three-election campaign, Symington was inaugurated governor on March 6, 1991. In his inaugural address, he promised "fair and competent government" run by ethical people. In a direct reference to the instability of the past years, he said it was time to "turn the page and move on to a brighter future.... We will put the service back in public service."

As governor, Symington faced a myriad of problems: improving the state's image, badly tarnished by the Mecham controversy; voter rejection of a paid holiday for Martin Luther King, Jr.; and the February 1991 indictment of seven state legislators on bribery charges.

One of Symington's first acts as governor was to appoint a committee to develop legislative recommendations for educational reform and financing. He also created a nonpartisan task force on State Long-Term Improved Management ("Project SLIM") to bring total quality management to state government. He has tried to develop trade ties with Mexico and Japan and opened a trade office in Mexico City. Other achievements include a $50 million carry-forward fund for unforeseen emergencies, the resolution of a controversy involving hazardous waste incineration, an agreement to reduce emissions from the Navajo Generating Station near the Grand Canyon, and the creation of the Governor's Council on Economic Development. In 1993, the state legislature enacted a law barring casino gambling everywhere within Arizona, giving Symington the ammunition he had sought to fight the spread of wagering on Indian reservations.

Earning the respect of his peers, Symington has been elected by his fellow governors to serve as vice-chair of the Western Governors Association and chairman of the National Governors Association K–12 Education Committee.

Although Symington has won high marks for both his personal charm and determined drive to return the state to normalcy, he, too, has been beset by a series of political troubles. Three separate controversies emerged during his first year in office: questions about $1.3 million in campaign loans made by his wife and mother, the purchase by the governor's office of $500,000 in Apple computers during a time when the governor was courting the company to locate a facility in the state, and the angry reaction to his surprise November 1991 ouster of two top state officials. With his popularity slipping, even more serious charges were raised about his involvement in a failed Phoenix savings and loan from which he had borrowed heavily and on which he had served as a director. He is presently under investigation by federal regulators for possible self-dealing, accused of improperly using his position as director of the Southwest Savings and Loan Association to obtain loans on very favorable terms. Symington contends that he has done nothing wrong and claims that a political vendetta is behind the allegations.

In the opinion of some analysts, Symington's ultimate political success may hinge less on his legal problems than on his ability to navigate his state through the shoals of economic recession.

Bibliography: Biographical information courtesy of governor's office; *The Chronicle of Higher Education,* 8–28–91; Phil Duncan, ed., *Politics in America 1992* (Washington, D.C.: Congressional Quarterly Press, 1991); Ruth S. Jones and Katheryn A. Lehman, "The CEO Approach of J. Fife Symington III," in Thad Beyle, ed., *Governors and Hard Times* (Washington, D.C.: Congressional Quarterly Press, 1992); *National Review,* May 1989; *The New York Times:* 5–17–89; 1–21–90; 7–14–90; 9–10–90; 9–11–90; 9–16–90; 2–28–91; 9–13–91; 12–16–91; 1–16–92; 2–20–92; 3–7–93; *The Record* (Bergen County, N.J.), 12–17–91; *USA Today:* 4–6–89; 3–8–90; 5–16–90; 10–25–90; 11–8–90; 11–13–90; 2–28–91; 3–21–91; 9–10–91; 12–16–91; 2–21–92.

William Jefferson Clinton (*Courtesy of Governor's Office*)

ARKANSAS

WILLIAM JEFFERSON ("BILL") CLINTON, 1979–1981, 1983–1992

Born in Hope, Arkansas, on August 19, 1946, Clinton is married to the former Hillary Rodham, an attorney. They have one daughter, Chelsea.

Educated in the public schools of Hot Springs, Arkansas, Clinton received a degree in international affairs from the Georgetown University School of Foreign Service in 1968. He attended Oxford University as a Rhodes scholar and received a degree from Yale Law School in 1973. Joining the staff of the University of Arkansas Law School, he also practiced law in Fayetteville before making his first run for public office in 1974. In that Watergate year, he was narrowly defeated for Congress in the Third District, holding incumbent John Paul Hammerschmidt, a Republican, to 52 percent of the vote. Afterward, he continued to teach law; he also taught in the Criminal Justice Program at the University of Arkansas, Little Rock.

Elected Arkansas Attorney General in 1976, Clinton sued to hold down utility rates, fought against 25 cent pay phone calls, and ended bans on liquor and eyeglass advertising. Having established a reputation as an energetic and activist politician—indeed, one reporter noted that Clinton "worked like a madman"—he was elected the nation's youngest governor in 1978. After gaining 60 percent of the vote against four other candidates to win the Democratic nomination without a runoff, he went on to defeat Republican state Chairman A. Lynn Lowe in the general election, winning 63 percent of the vote to Lowe's 37 percent. At 32, Clinton became the youngest man to be chosen chief executive of any state since Harold Stassen carried Minnesota in 1938 at the age of 31.

Boyishly handsome and charismatic, Clinton also had a rather unorthodox background for a rising politician from the Deep South. He had worked as the Texas state coordinator for George McGovern's ill-fated 1972 presidential race and had been a staff attorney for the House Judiciary Committee before the Nixon impeachment hearings. A supporter of the Equal Rights Amendment, Clinton also seemed an anomaly because his wife Hillary was a strong feminist who campaigned for her husband using her maiden name. Clinton also managed to campaign successfully against a rising "Proposition 13" sentiment to cut state taxes. Instead of promising to cut taxes, he asked for new highway taxes and a $132 million spending increase to upgrade the state's school system, which was ranked 49th in quality nationwide. Explaining that he believed the citizens of Arkansas were tired of being ranked last or next to last according to major indices of social and economic welfare, he sought to accelerate the state's economic growth and to make permanent improvements in the quality of life for its residents.

During his first term as governor, Clinton established a strong record in bringing jobs to Arkansas and in selling the state's products abroad. He held down utility rates and curbed utility costs, while working vigorously to improve the state's educational system with programs to test students in basic skills, to increase opportunities for gifted children, to advance vocational education, and to increase teachers' salaries. Clinton also initiated tax cuts for senior citizens by removing the sales tax from medicine and increasing the homestead property tax exemption for the elderly. He worked to eliminate waste in government and sponsored one of the nation's first "workfare" programs, which required that people requesting food stamps also register to work. This requirement eliminated several thousand ineligible people from food stamp rolls. Clinton also led the way in calling for the appointment of women and minorities to cabinet-level jobs. With his activist programs and leadership style, Clinton was able to regain power for the governor's office that had been usurped by the legislature under previous administrations. For all these achievements, *Time* magazine honored Clinton in 1979, listing him as one of America's outstanding young leaders and counting him among "50 faces to watch" in the future.

Nevertheless, Clinton had his critics. He was sometimes lampooned in political cartoons as a brat furiously pedaling a tricycle. Many thought he was more interested in national than in state politics. Conservative opponents tried to use his wife's feminism against him and assailed him for his liberal views by charging him with support for gun control, the Panama Canal treaties, and the decriminalization of marijuana. Most of all, however, Clinton's political stature was damaged by his handling of the Cuban refugee situation. Thousands of Cuban refugees who had left or been expelled from Cuba during Fidel Castro's infamous maneuvers in 1980 were housed at Fort Chaffee, Arkansas, and Clinton was hurt politically by his inability to force the White House to have other states shoulder some of the burdens and costs. His 1980 defeat by Republican Frank White, a businessman and political novice, was widely viewed as a simple case of voter backlash against the Democratic party on both the state and national levels. White won that election with 52 percent of the vote against Clinton's 48 percent. With his loss, Clinton became the first Arkansas governor in 26 years and only the second in this century to fail to win at least a second two-year term.

After leaving office, Clinton joined the Little Rock law firm of Wright, Lindsey, and Jennings, but astute observers knew that his political career was far from over. Indeed, he returned to the governor's mansion two years later, defeating White in his 1982 bid for reelection and becoming the first person in the state's history to be elected to a second, nonconsecutive term as chief executive.

Since that time, Clinton has broken record after record in state politics, capped, of course, by his election to the presidency in 1992. Reelected to the governorship in 1984, 1986, and 1990, he became only the second person in Arkansas history to be elected to five terms as governor. He also achieved a place in the record books as the only Arkansas governor in the 20th century to serve a four-year term, since a constitutional amendment in 1986 extended the governor's term of office from two to four years. By the time of his election to the presidency, Clinton held the record for longest continuous service among the nation's sitting governors.

Clinton's gubernatorial campaigns are interesting case studies, revealing much about the changing vagaries of Arkansas, if not southern, politics. The 1980 loss to Frank White not only shaped and affected Clinton personally but also became a lesson for first-time governors in the dangers implicit in an overly activist and out-of-touch administration. The charge most often heard about Clinton is that after his humiliating defeat he learned the delicate arts of southern *Realpolitik*—compromise and getting along.

To win his third term in 1984, Clinton defeated Republican newcomer Elwood Freeman with 62 percent of the vote, becoming the first chief executive in state history to win a third term since Orval Faubus, who left office in 1966. The tensions between the old and new Arkansas were very much apparent even in 1986, when Clinton sought and won his fourth term. To win renomination by his party, he faced a stiff challenge from Faubus himself. The onetime segregationist, best known for his actions in calling out the National Guard to block black students from entering Little Rock's Central High School in 1957, was making his third comeback bid. Faubus accused Clinton of being a friend and minion of the rich, as well as a champion of the public utilities at the expense of consumers. He charged Clinton with masterminding an unpopular rate increase for Arkansas Power and Light to help the company pay its share of the cost of the $3.5 million Grand Gulf nuclear power plant in Mississippi. Clinton defeated Faubus and W. Dean Goldsby in the primary and went on to trounce his old nemesis, former Governor Frank White, in the general election, garnering 64 percent of the vote.

Despite Clinton's long tenure, Republicans were convinced he was highly vulnerable when he sought reelection in 1990. His biggest legislative initiatives had failed in recent years, and he was accused of shirking his state responsibilities to prepare for a presidential run. He himself admitted that he lacked enthusiasm for the race and was forced to pledge to state voters that he would serve out his full term if elected—obviously a promise not kept. Confident of their chances of unseating Clinton, Republicans staged their first heated primary contest in over a century. The race featured two well-known and well-financed contenders: Congressman Tommy F. Robinson from Little Rock and Sheffield Nelson, a prominent Little Rock lawyer and businessman. The race also generated interest because both candidates had once been prominent Democrats who had only recently switched parties. Despite the high level of interest generated by the contest, political observers theorized that the bruising battle had badly weakened Nelson, the ultimate winner, as he went into the general election campaign against Clinton. Clinton himself had faced a primary challenge from five different opponents. The most vocal, Tom McRae, the former head of the Winthrop Rockefeller Foundation, went on the offensive, blaming Clinton for the state's poor ranking in teacher pay, per capita income, and environmental health. The fall campaign against Nelson was equally cantankerous, with Nelson also assailing Clinton's educational initiatives. Nonetheless, the incumbent pulled out his fifth gubernatorial victory, earning 57 percent of the vote.

Clinton's lengthy administration distinguished itself in several areas, notably education and economic development. Even his critics admitted that he was a master at working with the legislature, that he truly believed in making government work, and that he had a passion for innovative and creative programs. An activist and reformer, he had long attracted public attention both from his fellow governors and from the national press. In a 1986 poll conducted by *Newsweek* magazine, he was selected by his fellow governors as one of the five most effective governors in the nation. The acclaim was repeated in a 1991 *Newsweek* poll, where his fellow governors singled him out as being the most effective governor in the country.

His greatest legacy will probably be in the area of education reform. Both angered and inspired by a brutal indictment of the Arkansas educational system written in 1978 by Dr. Kern Alexander of the Virginia Polytechnic Institute, Clinton called the Arkansas legislature into special session in 1983 to enact new standards for public schools and an increase in the sales tax to support improvements in higher and vocational education. These funds helped put more computers in state schools, contributed to a rise in test scores, and created new jobs. He also engineered a controversial policy requiring all schoolteachers to pass a basic competency test to retain their certification and is credited with significantly lowering the state's dropout rate by requiring students to stay in school to get a driver's license. Other educational initiatives followed later in his administration. These included the nation's second program to allow students to choose the schools they would attend, some mergers of inefficient smaller districts, $1,000 yearly college scholarships for qualifying middle-income and poor students, increases in teacher pay, and a revamping of vocational education programs.

Clinton also made economic development a high priority, introducing comprehensive economic development programs to make Arkansas competitive with other states in the quest for more and better jobs. In 1988, he signed a wide-ranging agreement with the governors of Louisiana and Mississippi to coordinate efforts to improve conditions in one of the nation's poorest regions. The agreement was intended to direct many joint efforts at the counties bordering the Mississippi River, an area scarred by high rates of poverty, unemployment, and illiteracy. Business leaders say that Clinton's economic development efforts, including tax incentives, fostering international trade, and enhancing job training, helped Arkansas outpace both its neighboring states and the nation in terms of employment growth, growth in manufacturing jobs, and income growth.

Because of his strong record on hiring blacks and women in his administration, Clinton drew consistent support from black voters. In 1991, he pushed a bill through a reluctant legislature that committed the state to make a good-faith effort to reach a 10 percent goal of purchasing from and utilizing black-owned businesses. He also established a Minority Business Advisory Council to oversee the law.

He also drew high marks for his efforts to improve health care, especially in poor areas. In recent years, Arkansas has allocated $15 million for early childhood education and begun new programs in prenatal and health care for poor children.

Despite these successes, Clinton has long had his critics. The biggest complaint against him is that he often tries so hard to please both sides that he can leave his listeners uncertain as to where he really stands. The charge was immortalized during the 1992 presidential campaign under the sobriquet "Slick Willie," a term originally coined in the mid-1980s by Paul Greenberg, an editorial writer for the *Pine Bluff Commercial*, a 22,000 circulation daily 50 miles southeast of Little Rock. The charges of untrustworthiness, broken promises, and waffling to please all comers have long been lodged against him and continue to be so.

Concerns have also been raised about his environmental record. Critics charge that Clinton allowed industries to run roughshod over the environment during his gubernatorial tenure. They complain that waste from the poultry and hog industries contaminated the groundwater and fouled streams; that toxic waste sites weren't cleaned up; and that, until recently, representatives from industry dominated the state's environmental control board. In a 1992 study, the World Resources Institute gave Arkansas low marks for solid waste management and drinking water protection, and the Institute for Southern Studies, based in Durham, North Carolina, ranked Arkansas 50th in the nation for its record of addressing environmental problems.

Clinton has also been vulnerable on the issue of taxation. Taxes increased repeatedly and became more regressive during his tenure, with Arkansas being 1 of only 18 states to tax food at the same rate as other retail sales.

Nonetheless, astute Clinton watchers had long been aware of his presidential ambitions. As early as 1980, state voters feared he was more interested in national politics than in the provincial concerns of a small southern state, a charge that followed him throughout his long gubernatorial tenure. One wag joked that Clinton's star had been rising for three decades, while he himself traced his presidential ambitions to a fateful Rose Garden meeting with Jack Kennedy when he was 16.

Owing to his heightened visibility as chair of the National Governors Association in 1987, Clinton had been widely expected to seek the Democratic presidential nomination the following year. He surprised pundits, however, by withdrawing his name from consideration, citing family obligations, the needs of his then-seven-year-old daughter, and the desire for a "more normal life." Still, Clinton remained in the national spotlight. In July 1988, he gave the major nominating address for fellow governor Michael Dukakis at the National Democratic Convention that bestowed its presidential nomination upon the Massachusetts Democrat. From 1985 Clinton had been a key player in the Democratic Leadership Council (DLC), a group of centrist and conservative Democrats primarily from the South and West who attempted to move the national party closer to their constituency and ideals. Traveling throughout the country during 1990–1991 as chairman of the group, Clinton explained that the very future of the Democratic party depended upon its ability and willingness to alter its focus, to move away from the fringes and more toward the mainstream of American concerns. The themes he articulated as chairman of the DLC emphasized traditional values like individual and corporate responsibility as a condition for government help. As such, Clinton posed as a new-age Democrat seeking to help his party recapture the presidency by focusing on its traditional blue-collar and middle-class base. He also struggled to resist ideological labels by crafting a populist message.

Clinton formally entered the 1992 presidential race on October 3, 1991, with a stinging indictment of 12 years of Republican rule and a promise to restore the American dream for the forgotten middle class. He offered himself as someone who could "reinvent government" and infuse it with the values that Americans hold dear, using it as a positive force for change to address the problems plaguing the country—crime, economic decline, hopelessness, and limited access to health care. He explained that as governor of a small state he knew firsthand how cutbacks in federal programs had affected state residents. Indeed, he contended that this was one of the main reasons for his presidential run: He was aware that state problems were only a piece of a larger national crisis requiring a national response from a sympathetic government in Washington. With his announcement, Clinton became the first presidential candidate from Arkansas since the short-lived run of former Congressman Wilbur Mills in 1972.

Clinton's campaign was on the verge of floundering several times during his 14-month run. It was stung by numerous highly publicized allegations that he had used marijuana as a college student, that he had acted improperly to avoid being drafted during the Vietnam War, and that he had been unfaithful to his wife. Old charges of his alleged "womanizing" reappeared, as did basic questions about his character and integrity. Even the role to be played in a future administration by his activist and feminist wife became an issue. Closer to home, he also had to acknowledge that he was indeed breaking a 1990 pledge made to Arkansas voters that he would serve out his full four-year gubernatorial term.

The heart of Clinton's campaign was a detailed platform covering issues including college scholarships, community service, health care reform, job creation, and economic growth. Targeting middle-class voters and disaffected "Reagan Democrats" who had deserted the Democratic party during 12 years of Republican rule, he excoriated the Bush administration for its brutal neglect of domestic concerns.

Riding voter anger over the sour economy to an electoral landslide, he ran strongly in all regions of the country and among many groups that had been key to the Republican domination of the 1980s. The election was also noteworthy for its record voter turnout of 100 million and for the presence of third-party candidate H. Ross Perot, who made the strongest third-party showing since Teddy Roosevelt's Bull Moose run in 1912.

With his election to the White House, Clinton formally resigned the Arkansas governorship on December 12, 1992. He was succeeded by Lieutenant Governor Jim Guy Tucker.

In the opinion of many political observers, Clinton is the most formidable and commanding all-around politician that the Democrats have produced since Robert Kennedy. He also bears watching as the first baby boomer to sit in the Oval Office, living testimony to the fact that the torch has again been passed to a new generation of Americans. At 46, Clinton became the third youngest president in American history.

Bibliography: Charles F. Allen and Jonathan Portis, *The Comeback Kid: The Life and Career of Bill Clinton* (New York: Birch Lane Press, 1993); Peter Applebone, "Bill Clinton's Uncertain Journey," *New York Times Magazine* (March 8, 1992): 26–29, 36, 60, 63; *The Chronicle of Higher Education*: 8–28–91; 4–29–92; *Newsweek*: 3–24–86; 5–13–91; 9–30–91; 1–20–92; 4–13–92; 5–4–92; *The New*

York Times: 2–12–89; 5–23–90; 5–31–90; 10–31–90; 11–7–90; 5–8–91; 8–14–91; 8–16–91; 12–22–91; 12–27–91; 1–24–92; 1–28–92; 3–31–92; 4–1–92; 4–2–92; 4–3–92; 4–4–92; 4–21–92; 4–27–92; 4–29–92; 9–28–92; 11–4–92; *The Philadelphia Inquirer*, 4–19–92; *The Record* (Bergen County, N.J.), 10–4–91; *The Star-Ledger* (Newark, N.J.): 8–18–91; 10–4–91; 4–5–92; *Time*, 8–6–79; *USA Today*: 5–2–90; 8–14–91; 10–4–91; 1–9–92; 1–28–92; 2–7–92; 3–18–92; 5–18–92; 5–26–92; 11–4–92; 11–6–92.

JIM GUY TUCKER, 1992–

Born in Oklahoma City on June 13, 1943, Tucker grew up in Little Rock, Arkansas, and attended city schools. He is a graduate of Harvard College and the University of Arkansas School of Law. He and his wife Betty, also an attorney, are the parents of four children.

A member of the U.S. Marine Corps Reserve, Tucker worked as a civilian war correspondent in South Vietnam between 1965 and 1967 and went on to author one book on the Vietnam War, *Arkansas Men at War* (1968).

A Democrat, Tucker entered political life early, becoming a prosecutor in Little Rock at age 27 and state attorney general at age 29. Elected to Congress in 1976 as part of a freshman class that included Al Gore and Dan Quayle, he was succeeded in the attorney general's office by the young Bill Clinton, whose political path would frequently cross with Tucker's in the years ahead. Serving in Congress from 1977 to 1979, Tucker was a member of the powerful House Ways and Means Committee.

His political career took a wrong turn in 1978 when he decided to seek the U.S. Senate seat opened up by the death of senior Senator John McClellan, long a powerhouse in state politics. Perceiving the vacancy to be "the last opening in my politically viable lifetime of a U.S. Senate seat from Arkansas," Tucker abandoned his congressional post to make the ill-fated run. According to political observers, the race attracted the most outstanding collection of contenders of any single electoral contest in the modern history of the state. Besides Tucker, the other candidates were Governor David Pryor and three-term Congressman Ray Thornton, a Yale-educated lawyer who achieved prominence as a member of the House Judiciary Committee considering the impeachment of Richard Nixon. Although Tucker won 32 percent of the vote in the three-way Democratic primary, he lost to Pryor in the runoff contest—tantamount to victory in solidly Democratic Arkansas.

Four years later, Tucker again found himself engaged in a losing battle, this time for the Democratic gubernatorial nomination. He lost the bid to Bill Clinton, who himself was making a successful comeback after the defeat that followed his first gubernatorial term.

These back-to-back defeats prompted Tucker to retire from public life. Besides serving as senior partner in his private law practice, he became chairman of a cable television management company that owned and operated cable television systems in the United States and abroad. Although he was financially successful, Tucker longed to return to the po-

Jim Guy Tucker *(Courtesy of Governor's Office)*

litical life he so loved. According to the reports of friends, a near-fatal illness caused Tucker to reprioritize his life's goals, and in 1990 he made the decision to launch a comeback bid. Feeling that long-serving Governor Bill Clinton might step down from the statehouse to plan a presidential run, Tucker had his eyes on the governor's mansion. When Clinton opted again for reelection, however, Tucker was unwilling to challenge his old nemesis. Making a run instead for the lieutenant governorship, he won that office in 1990. As lieutenant governor, Tucker chaired the Corrections Resources Committee, worked to strengthen the state criminal justice system, and was instrumental in drafting new insurance legislation.

Although the Arkansas lieutenant governorship is largely a ceremonial and politically invisible post, it assumed new significance when Bill Clinton entered the presidential race in October 1991. As lieutenant governor, Tucker became acting governor in Clinton's absence. The arrangement was a difficult one, as Tucker struggled to make his mark on the day-to-day operations of state government, and the peripatetic Clinton worked to maintain some measure of oversight over his constitutionally mandated functions. Over the course of Clinton's 14-month campaign, the balance was tough to maintain. According to political observers, Clinton's staff often viewed Tucker as too eager to assume power, while Tucker's supporters criticized the campaigning Clinton for being overly protective of the prerogatives of the office. Others traced the friction to the duo's earlier competition in the mid-1970s. Regardless of its causes, however, the power vacuum left Tucker without the authority he needed to govern effectively.

Clinton's victory in the presidential election of 1992 only further confused Tucker's status. Two quirky constitutional issues delayed his formal accession to the governorship. The first involved the legal question as to whether Tucker could serve out the remainder of Clinton's term absent a special election. According to one reading of the Arkansas constitution, a special election was required within 60 days of a vacancy occurring in the governor's office. Tucker and others, however, insisted that the 1913 constitutional amendment creating the office of lieutenant governor had superseded that passage. Others disagreed. Both Republican Sheffield Nelson, whom Clinton had defeated in 1990, and Democrat Winston Bryant, a former lieutenant governor, went to court to clarify the constitutional provisions for succession.

The problem was directly related to another controversy—the exact date of Clinton's formal resignation. Because he and his wife owned no property, they were reluctant to leave the governor's mansion before their January 20 move to the White House. Tucker had promised Clinton that even after resigning he could continue to live in the mansion, with his blessing. If Tucker could not accede to the governorship without an election, however, he would not be able to make such a promise: He would not be entitled to any perks of the office, including use of the mansion!

Not until early December 1992 did a ruling by the state supreme court clarify the issue. Affirming a lower court ruling, the justices confirmed that Tucker could succeed Clinton without a special election and that he could assume all the perks of the office, including living in the governor's mansion.

With these issues settled, Clinton formally resigned from the governorship on December 12, 1992, paving the way for Tucker's formal accession to power that same day.

Political observers in Arkansas expressed relief that the state would once again have a full-time governor. Tucker's constitutional status as acting governor had been a problem, since it denied him real power either to raise taxes or to order major cuts in medical services, options necessary to balancing the state's critical Medicaid deficit.

Immediately after his accession, Tucker called the legislature into special session to deal with the state's Medicaid shortfall. He also asked the legislature to allow Clinton and his family to continue to live in the governor's mansion for 45 more days.

Yet issues arising out of Clinton's move to the White House continued to dog Tucker. A bitter political dispute erupted in late January 1993 when Tucker left the state to attend Clinton's inauguration. In his absence, the position of acting governor was assumed by Jerry Jewell, the president pro tem of the senate, since the office of lieutenant governor had already been vacated by Tucker himself. Jewell's temporary stint in the state's highest office was a matter of some pride to him and others, since he was the first black ever to hold that position. Jewell's short reign, however, erupted into a fire storm of controversy when he used his power of executive clemency to pardon a drug dealer, a murderer, and two parolees, three of whom were black. Upon his return, Tucker questioned the propriety of Jewell's actions and asked his staff to draft bills both restricting executive clemency powers and limiting the authority of the acting governor.

As governor, Tucker continues to grapple with state budget matters, aiming to cut spending as much as possible before presenting any plans for a tax increase. He has also presented a welfare reform package, similar to those undertaken in Wisconsin and New Jersey, whereby women who have additional children while on welfare would receive no further increase in state benefits.

According to political observers, the Harvard-educated Tucker brings an aura of sophistication to Arkansas government and has the potential to emerge as a New South governor very much in the mold of his predecessor Bill Clinton.

Bibliography: Michael Barone and Grant Ujifusa, *The Almanac of American Politics, 1992* (Washington, D.C.: National Journal, 1991); biographical information courtesy of governor's office; *The New York Times*: 10–13–92; 12–4–92; 1–24–93; 2–1–93; *USA Today*: 11–19–92; 12–4–92; 12–7–92; 12–11–92; 1–25–93.

George Deukmejian *(Courtesy of Governor's Office)*

CALIFORNIA

GEORGE DEUKMEJIAN, 1983–1991

Born in Menands, New York, on June 6, 1928, Deukmejian is the son of C. George and Alice Gairdan Deukmejian. An Episcopalian, he is married to the former Gloria M. Saatjian. The couple has three children.

Deukmejian graduated from Siena College with a B.A. in sociology in 1949. In 1952, he received a J.D. from St. John's University School of Law. He worked briefly for the New York State Department of Audit and Control before entering the U.S. Army. Assigned to the Judge Advocate Corps based in Paris, he served a 16-month tour of duty in France, where his major responsibilities included assisting in the settlement of claims made by French nationals against the U.S. Army.

Returning to the United States in 1955, he moved to Los Angeles. There he worked for the Land and Lease Department of Texaco before being appointed deputy county counsel for Los Angeles County. He also established a successful law practice in Long Beach. His first bid for elective office came in 1962, upon the retirement of Republican Assemblyman Bill Grant. Deukmejian served two terms in the state assembly and was named minority whip by his Republican colleagues in 1965. The following year, when the U.S. Supreme Court ordered the states to implement the one-man, one-vote provision, additional state senate seats were created in Los Angeles County. Deukmejian captured one of the new seats the same year that Ronald Reagan was elected governor of California. Thereafter, he served four terms (12 years) in the senate, where he assisted Governor Reagan in moving his anticrime program and tax reform bills through the legislature.

In 1970, the Republicans gained control of the state senate, and Deukmejian was elected senate majority leader. In 1972, he authored the death penalty initiative, which was overwhelmingly approved by California voters. In 1974, he was elected senate Republican leader and in 1977 drafted California's death penalty statute. The measure was vetoed by Governor Jerry Brown, but Deukmejian led the successful fight to override the veto in the legislature. Also in 1977 he authored the "Use a Gun, Go to Prison" law, which he later successfully defended before the California Supreme Court.

During his 16 years in the legislature, Deukmejian authored more than 180 laws including the Senior Citizens Property Tax Assistance law, the Community Drug Abuse Act, the Career Criminal Act, and the bill mandating establishment of Youth Service Bureaus.

Deukmejian first sought statewide office in 1970, when he lost the Republican nomination for attorney general. He ran again in 1978 and was elected the state's top lawyer, receiving the highest vote total for a Republican constitutional office candidate that year.

As attorney general and head of the Department of Justice, he established a Special Prosecutions Unit, a Crime Prevention Center, and a School Safety Center and strengthened the Bureau of Narcotic Enforcement. He formed a state task force centering on youth gang problems and vigorously prosecuted consumer fraud, antitrust violations, Medi-Cal fraud, and other white-collar crimes. He also successfully argued the constitutionality of the state death penalty statute before the state's highest court.

When he launched his campaign for governor in 1982, he explained that his decision to run for the state's highest office was partially attributable to the fact that "attorneys general do not appoint judges, but governors do." He added that he was uniquely qualified based upon his experience and background to appoint the tough judges that the state desperately needed.

His opponent in 1982 was Democrat Tom Bradley, mayor of Los Angeles, who hoped to become the nation's first black governor. Deukmejian won the election by one of the narrowest margins in state history, 93,345 votes, 1.2 percent of all cast, after some experienced analysts had predicted a Bradley victory. Bradley's defeat was attributed primarily to a strong turnout by conservatives, whose election day showing may have been enhanced by the presence of a gun control measure on the ballot. Gun control opponents spent some $5 million opposing the registration proposal, which Bradley supported. Deukmejian's opposition to the measure probably contributed to his victory. Actually, Deukmejian lost the vote at the polls but won the election because of a vast and expensive Republican drive to encourage absentee ballots.

Deukmejian's popularity grew during his first term in office. Gathering around him a group of talented aides and employing an aloof, ceremonial style in stark contrast to that of former Governor Jerry Brown, he dealt successfully and effectively with the state fiscal crisis that confronted him immediately upon taking office. Working with the legislature, he developed a fiscal rescue plan to pay off the deficit he had inherited and balance the budget without raising taxes. In addition to restoring the fiscal integrity of the state, Deukmejian also provided record increases in support for education, transportation, health care programs, and toxic waste cleanup. Over 2 million new jobs were created in the state, and California led the nation in new business expansion. Deukmejian also led efforts to expand the state's foreign trade, including the opening of trade and investment offices in Japan and Europe. He successfully pushed for a workfare program to reduce welfare dependency, sponsored and won passage of a Seniors Initiative to improve vital services for senior citizens, and appointed a record number of women and minorities to state government jobs.

Deukmejian's reelection victory in 1986 was seen as an overwhelming endorsement of his policies and approach to state government. Reelected by one of the largest vote margins in state history, and garnering a higher percentage of the vote than Ronald Reagan ever won in California, Deukmejian again faced Mayor Tom Bradley of Los Angeles. In his campaign against the popular conservative, Bradley strayed from the moderate political stance that had long been his hallmark into more visible, liberal ground. Some analysts interpreted this switch as a decision to play to his strengths with his long-standing urban constituencies, union members, and Jewish, black, and Hispanic voters. Bradley advocated pay equity for women and removal from the city's pension fund portfolio of investments in companies doing business with South Africa. He also drew attention to Los Angeles' passage of a first-in-the-nation ordinance to protest discrimination against victims of AIDS. In the hostile personal race between the two rivals, Bradley accused Deukmejian of endangering children's health through failure to deal with the state's toxic waste problems, citing the governor's ties to big business as the reason for his slowness to act. He also attacked the governor's integrity and character.

The state's overall economic health, however, served the incumbent well. Although Bradley could point to several economic trouble spots, notably the semiconductor portion of California's electronics industry, farming, and logging, the state's general economic condition was good. California's unemployment rate had fallen steadily, and by the time of the election, a record number of Californians were at work. Although colorless and noncharismatic, Deukmejian was generally perceived as stronger on issues of genuine concern to the voters, notably control of drug abuse. His landslide victory over Bradley, 60.5 percent to 37.5 percent, was an even wider margin than most experts had predicted. The remaining 2 percent of the vote was shared by minor candidates.

Deukmejian professed no grand goals for his second term, other than continuing the policies of his first: keeping control of the state budget, appointing a majority on the state supreme court, and strengthening his workfare programs. He spurned those who in 1987 urged him to become a favorite son in the race for the 1988 Republican presidential nomination, but at the same time, he set up his own organization, Citizens for Common Sense, to help him travel around the country to further his goals. Although Deukmejian's name was frequently mentioned as a possible running mate for 1988 Republican presidential candidate George Bush, the governor repeatedly expressed disinterest in the position, because if elected he would be forced to turn over the reins of state government to a Democrat, Lieutenant Governor Leo McCarthy.

State budget problems in 1988 also worked against any aspirations for higher office. Facing a gap between state revenue and expenditures caused largely by miscalculations of the effects of the revision of the federal tax structure, Deukmejian proposed a series of what he called "tax adjustments" to deal with the problem. The proposals were soundly condemned, even by members of his own party, who called them tax increases in disguise and reminded him of his 1986 campaign pledge not to raise taxes. Deukmejian maintained that he would do whatever was necessary to protect the state's fiscal integrity and ability to create jobs.

An increasingly troubled economic climate marred the remainder of Deukmejian's second term. Following a disastrous earthquake that ravaged northern California in October 1989, he was faced with the enormous task of funding emergency relief legislation to help restore businesses, highways, and homes. His response was a temporary sales tax increase to raise $800 million for emergency relief aid.

Faced with mounting problems, Deukmejian took himself out of the running for a third gubernatorial term in 1990. Although Republican leaders insisted that he could easily have won the party's nomination, perhaps Deukmejian had tired of battling with Democrats in the state legislature, with whom his relations had long been rocky. Rumors that Deukmejian would be selected to join the Bush cabinet as attorney general upon the resignation of Dick Thornburgh never materialized.

In assessing Deukmejian's years in office, analysts and commentators view him as having been a low-key, uncharismatic, and passive governor. Although honest, dedicated, and hardworking, he had few clear policy objectives. His approach to government was a reactive one, underscored by his resistance to new taxes. Political observers feel that he left much unfinished business for his successor, fellow Republican Pete Wilson.

Bibliography: Michael Barone et al., *The Almanac of American Politics, 1984, 1986, 1988* (Washington, D.C.: National Journal, 1983, 1985, 1987); biographical information courtesy of governor's office; *The Chronicle of Higher Education,* 11–12–86; *The New York Times*: 10–6–85; 9–15–86; 10–31–86; 11–6–86; 3–24–87; 6–3–88; 6–4–88; 11–7–88; 1–7–89; 6–5–90; *The Star-Ledger* (Newark, N.J.), 11–7–89; *USA Today,* 6–5–91.

PETE WILSON, 1991–

Born in Lake Forest, Illinois, on August 23, 1933, Wilson grew up in St. Louis. He attended the fashionable St. Louis Country Day School, then Yale University, where he majored in English literature. After his 1955 graduation, he came to California as a Marine Corps infantry officer, stationed at Coronado. After his discharge, he earned a law degree at the University of California. Divorced from his first wife, Betty Robertson, he married Gayle Edlund on May 29, 1983.

Wilson became involved in Republican politics in 1962, working as an advance man for the failed gubernatorial campaign of Richard Nixon. He practiced law in San Diego before running for the state assembly in 1966. Rising quickly into the Republican leadership during his legislative tenure, 1967–1971, he left the assembly to run for mayor of San Diego, a post he held until his election to the U.S. Senate in 1982. Defeating former Governor Jerry Brown in a closely watched contest, he went on to win re-election in 1988 with the largest vote total in state history. His opponent in that race was Democratic Lieutenant Governor Leo McCarthy.

Wilson was highly criticized as a political opportunist when he announced his intention to seek the governorship just three months after his victory in the Senate race. Incumbent George Deukmejian's decision not to seek a third term had thrown the race wide open, and Wilson was immediately regarded as the Republican frontrunner for the post. It was an office in which he had long been interested, having run unsuccessfully for the statehouse in 1978 and 1981.

Spared a tough battle for the Republican nomination (he trounced three unknowns in the primary), Wilson faced San Francisco Mayor Dianne Feinstein in the fall campaign. The race received a tremendous amount of national attention for several reasons. As an outspoken proponent of women's issues and causes, Feinstein framed the race as "a historic moment for women." Having first come to national attention as a possible vice-presidential running mate for Walter Mondale in 1984, she had the potential to become not only the state's first female governor but also a serious presidential contender in her own right. Of more immediate concern, the winner of the gubernatorial race would preside over legislative redistricting plans to follow the 1990 census—a prize of potentially great importance in this vote-heavy state.

Other key issues raised by the campaign struck at the heart of contemporary American politics. The race triggered increasing controversy over

Pete Wilson (*Sirlin Studios, Sacramento, Calif.*)

the role of television advertising, critical in a large state like California where political discourse is dominated by 30-second radio and TV spots. A novel twist in the California contest came as the state's newspapers ran the text of each new campaign commercial, accompanied by an analysis that often challenged, clarified, or contradicted points raised by the candidate. A final problem emerged just six weeks before election day, when a federal judge invalidated the state's statutory limits on campaign contributions. Federal Judge Lawrence K. Karlton struck down parts of an initiative passed by voters in June 1988, saying the law unconstitutionally restricted free speech by imposing limits according to the fiscal rather than election year.

Both candidates were centrists by California standards. Each claimed to be protective of the environment, pro choice on the critical abortion issue, tough on crime, pro capital punishment, and supportive of programs to help the underclass break the cycle of drugs and poverty. Because of their ideological similarity, the race turned on issues of style and voter perception of which candidate would be better able to lead the state through a difficult period of economic decline. Interestingly, each had a record as a big city mayor to demonstrate ability and achievement.

Although Wilson's political style was itself an issue—he was frequently described as bland and colorless by reporters and analysts, who also criticized his tendency to waffle on the issues—he was successfully able to raise questions about Feinstein's own political persona. Claiming that she strove to repackage herself as a moderate only to fit the tenor of the times, he drew particular attention to her willingness to increase state income taxes to cover expected budgetary shortfalls. He also made much of her stand on two hot-button ballot issues—one, an anti-incumbent initiative limiting legislative terms, and the other, known as "Big Green," imposing broad and strict environmental controls on oil drilling and air, water, and pesticide pollution. Wilson supported term limits and opposed Big Green, whereas Feinstein did the reverse.

Wilson promised to be an active governor and to lead the state out of its deepening problems with education, pollution, and crime. He targeted the drug problem as his top priority, calling for tougher sentencing for violent crime and drug dealing, and attacking the "arrogant liberals" in the state assembly who had consistently blocked such laws. His education platform called for merit pay for superior teachers, a statewide program to provide adult mentors for poor children, and "alternative credentialing" to allow people without conventional academic backgrounds to teach. He also proposed the establishment of a state program to provide $1,750 worth of prenatal care to pregnant women and another to rehabilitate pregnant addicts.

By contrast, Feinstein presented herself as an energetic candidate of change. She strove to tie Wilson to the outgoing Republican administration of George Deukmejian and its legacy of uncured ills: smog, traffic, and too-rapid growth. In the final analysis, however, Wilson benefited heavily from the growing Republican character of California and the more loyal voting patterns of Republicans. Analysts saw Feinstein's campaign both as unfocused and as hurt by rapidly changing world events. The Persian Gulf crisis, for example, seemed to have made voters more cautious and less willing to make changes in political leadership. Capping a remarkable record of public service, in which he had served Californians on virtually every level of state government, Wilson won the election with 49 percent of the vote. (Minor party candidates kept him from a majority win.) Wilson's victory was the state's first in-party succession since 1930, even though Republicans had held 14 out of 17 state governorships in this century.

Once in office, Wilson faced a roller coaster ride in the court of public opinion. He confronted horrific problems after his inauguration: a budget deficit, recession, unemployment, the effects of a five-year drought, a major earthquake, a disastrous freeze, a population explosion, mounting traffic congestion, an inadequate educational system, and serious social problems. In sharp contrast to his predecessor, however, he proposed an active and ambitious remedial agenda for what he called "preventive government." Hailed as California's first activist governor since Pat Brown in the early 1960s, he was termed the "Golden State's Golden Boy" by nationally syndicated columnists who saw him as a new breed of Republican—a "compassionate conservative" out to remake his party in his own image. *Washington Post* columnist David Broder labeled him "the most interesting and important American politician outside the White House today—and potentially a White House contender." Bringing to the table an ambitious set of programs, he showed his skill as a politician by compromising with the Democrats in the legislature and thwarting his party's own right wing to tackle the largest state budget deficit in U.S. history. The result was a $7.7 billion tax increase, more than one-third of the state's entire budget and the largest in the history of any American state.

Counted at the head of the nation's new crop of governors, Class of 1990, he was widely touted as the GOP's leading candidate for the White House in 1996.

Almost overnight, however, his fortunes changed dramatically. By 1992, his job approval ratings had dropped precipitously since the heady opening months of his term. His rapid fall from grace demonstrates how difficult the job of state government had become over the course of a decade when domestic problems received second billing from Washington and came home to fester in the states.

By 1992, the worsening impact of the recession coupled with national cuts in military and defense spending that hit California hard found the state mired in its worst economic slump since the depression. Since 1990, the state had lost over 700,000 jobs, its bond rating tumbled, and the government was reduced to paying its bills with IOUs. Even with the new tax increase, the state found itself faced with a $10.7 billion shortfall in the new budget, provoking the worst budget crisis in the history of any state. More budget cuts, rather than new taxes, was Wilson's response this time, as he tried to patch relations with his party's right wing, which had harshly criticized his earlier tax increases and half seriously threatened to recall him. This time, Wilson's proposals called for controversial cuts in California's welfare policies, already the most expensive in the nation, and a restructuring of the budgetary process, giving his office more authority to cut spending in financial emergencies.

Another highly publicized controversy adding to Wilson's troubles was his veto of a gay rights bill that would have furnished homosexuals with equal job rights. The bill would have made California the fifth and largest state to add sexual orientation to the laws barring job discrimination on the basis of race, national origin, creed, and other categories. In vetoing the bill, Wilson said it was unnecessary, burdensome on state businesses, and duplicative of protections already in the state constitution. Calling his decision the most emotional political problem he had to face since taking office, Wilson confronted a ferocious reaction from the gay community, who threatened political reprisals against him. The reaction was especially bitter since the moderate Wilson had courted homosexuals in his gubernatorial campaign.

The consensus among political observers was that the veto was a political act designed to shore up Wilson's support within his own party. Conservative antipathy to Wilson dates back to 1976, when he endorsed Gerald Ford's presidential candidacy over that of Ronald Reagan. Although he became one of Reagan's staunchest supporters while in the Senate, Wilson was never trusted by conservatives because of his longtime support for the Equal Rights Amendment and his prochoice position on abortion. His record tax increases did nothing to endear him to state conservatives, who are already threatening to challenge him in his bid for reelection in 1994.

California's continuing budget troubles kept Wilson from traveling to the 1992 Republican National Convention, where Massachusetts Governor William Weld appeared to be overtaking him as the new darling of party moderates.

While supporters say Wilson has demonstrated true leadership by making tough decisions on crucial problems, others doubt that the man once touted as presidential timber will even be able to win reelection as governor of his state. At this writing, the leading contender to succeed him in the statehouse is Democratic state Treasurer Kathleen Brown, sister of ex-governor Jerry Brown and daughter of former Governor Pat Brown.

Bibliography: Biographical information courtesy of governor's office; Phil Duncan, ed., *Politics in America 1992* (Washington, D.C.: Congressional Quarterly Press, 1991); Richard W. Gable, "California: Pete Wilson, A Centrist in Trouble," in Thad Beyle, ed., *Governors and Hard Times* (Washington, D.C.: Congressional Quarterly Press, 1992); Gerald C. Lubenow, ed., *California Votes: The 1990 Governor's Race* (Berkeley: University of California Press, 1991); *Newsweek*: 2–26–90; 5– 28–90; 5–27–91; 8–17–92; *The New York Times*: 11–10–88; 3–21– 89; 11–13–89; 4–29–90; 5–20–90; 6–3–90; 6–7–90; 8–19–90; 8–21– 90; 9–27–90; 10–7–90; 10–9–90; 11–4–90; 11–5–90; 11–8–90; 11– 30–90; 1–8–91; 6–27–91; 7–18–91; 7–25–91; 9–19–91; 11–12–91; 12–18–91; 3–15–92; 4–29–92; 5–3–92; 7–2–92; 8–16–92; 8–30–92; 8–31–92; Robert Reinhold, "The Curse of the Statehouse, *New York Times Magazine* (May 3, 1992): 26–29, 54, 58–59; *The Star-Ledger* (Newark, N.J.): 2–6–90; 6–6–90; 10–28–90; 7–28–91; 12– 15–91; 2–3–92; 7–3–92; Robin Toner, "California Showdown: Dianne Feinstein Takes on Pete Wilson," *New York Times Magazine* (Sept. 30, 1990): 28–31, 63–67, 98; *USA Today*: 5–31–90; 6–7–90; 8–27–90; 10–23–90; 11–2–90; 11–8–90; 1–8–91; 5– 31–91; 7–19–91; 9–10–91; 10–1–91; 10–3–91; 10–11–91; 1–9–92; 8–11–92; 8–13–92; 8–31–92; 9–3–92; 11–18–92; 1–8–93; *The Washington Post*, 7–28–91.

COLORADO

ROY ROMER, 1987–

Born on October 31, 1928, in Garden City, Kansas, Romer and his wife, the former Bea Miller, have seven children. He is a Presbyterian.

Romer grew up in the southeastern Colorado town of Holly, where he moved with his family as an infant. He received a bachelor's degree in agricultural economics from Colorado State University and a law degree from the University of Colorado. He also studied ethics at Yale. Prior to entering public life, Romer was an attorney in private practice, as well as a businessman. From 1942 to 1952, he engaged in dryland farming, irrigated farming, cattle and sheep ranching, and grain elevator operations in Holly, Granada, Dove Creek, and Bristol, Colorado. He has also been owner of a chain of construction equipment stores in Colorado, Virginia, and Florida. He developed a portion of Colorado's Centennial Airport, ran a flying school, and operated a ski area.

Romer, a Democrat, has had a long career in public service. As a member of the state house of representatives, 1958–1962, he served on several important committees. A member of the Joint Budget Committee, he chaired the House Judiciary Committee, the Joint House-Senate Committee on Education Beyond High School, and a legislative task force that recommended creation of Metropolitan State College. From 1962 to 1966, he served in the state senate, rising to the rank of assistant minority leader, 1964–1966. After an unsuccessful campaign for the U.S. Senate in 1966, he dropped out of public life for nearly a decade, to return as a member of Governor Richard Lamm's administration. Chief of staff to the governor from 1975 to 1977 and again from 1982 to 1983, he also served as Colorado agricultural commissioner in 1975 and as state treasurer from 1977 to 1987. Few of the nation's governors had such a long record of experience in their state capitals as did Romer when he assumed the governorship in January 1987.

Richard Lamm's decision not to seek reelection in 1986 left the governor's race wide open. Running in a year when state Republican registration topped Democratic totals for the first time in two decades, Romer's quest to succeed his mentor was assisted by a weak Republican challenger. He was opposed by state Senator Ted Strickland, a controversial Texas

Roy Romer *(Courtesy of Governor's Office)*

native who had lost overwhelmingly to Lamm in 1978. Strickland's campaign was marked by a series of mistakes: He said America should become a "Christian centered" nation and emphasized his strong opposition to abortion. He also ran an advertisement linking Romer with Angela Davis, the once-prominent Communist agitator and black revolutionary. When negative advertising on both sides threatened to alienate voters, Romer offered to take all his negative spots off the air; Strickland declined. In the opinion of political observers, Strickland had defeated himself with a posture voters perceived as decidedly "ungubernatorial." He lost to Romer, 58 percent to 41 percent.

Romer had no difficulty winning reelection in 1990. Extremely popular in the state, he never faced any serious competition, either inside or outside his party. In the general election, he defeated Republican newcomer, businessman John Andrews, with 63 percent of the vote.

During his years in office, Romer's priorities have included stimulating the state's economy, creating new jobs, and encouraging foreign investment in Colorado. Striving to balance his interest in economic development with environmental protection, he has also focused on the need for new and improved highways and other infrastructure modernization.

Romer has a strong record of supporting education and has targeted education reform as a high priority of his administration. In a highly unusual move in 1991, he seized control of the bitter contract talks in the Denver school system after teachers voted to strike. He then became personally involved in writing a contract to overhaul the school system. Several educational analysts as well as spokespersons for the National Governors Association reported that this marked the first time in history that a governor intent on bringing about change in his state's public schools had taken such a direct role in local teacher contract talks. The incident enhanced Romer's national reputation and focused additional attention on his other initiatives in the area of education. He also serves as cochair of the National Council on Educational Standards and Testing, an advisory group of educational and political leaders that has called for voluntary national curriculum standards and national testing for American schoolchildren.

Romer's accession to the chairmanship of the National Governors Association in 1992 gave him another pulpit from which to advance his education agenda. He has created a task force on education to study structural changes in the education system and the adoption of new standards for math and science. Despite stiff opposition, he barnstormed his state asking for a $300 million tax increase to support education.

His Republican critics counter by saying that he really has no new ideas on education other than spending more money. Fiscal issues appeared to be paramount in voters' minds when they handed Romer a serious defeat in 1992. At that time, state voters approved a ballot initiative requiring that all new taxes be approved by popular vote, the nation's most radical tax limitation measure. Romer lobbied hard against the amendment and now must struggle to cope with resulting budget shortfalls. His innovative education agenda is expected to suffer as a result.

Other critics describe Romer as a publicity hound who spends too much time gallivanting around the nation to draw attention to himself. During his tenure, he has also antagonized cattle interests, environmental groups, and labor leaders.

Although Romer repeatedly denies any interest in national office, he is often mentioned in speculation about the Democratic vice-presidential nomination. Since he had served as cochair of the Democratic Platform Committee in 1992 and had worked closely with then-Governor Bill Clinton on National Governors Association committees dealing with education reform, there was strong expectation that he might be named to a cabinet-level post in the Clinton administration.

As current chair of the National Governors Association, Romer continues to involve himself in the national debate on the nation's future. He has encouraged governors to join the federal budget debate and to consider making recommendations to eliminate programs, reduce the eligibility for entitlement programs, and hike taxes.

Generally regarded as a political centrist, he believes the Democratic party needs to "regain its credibility" and spend more time listening to people. While his opponents call him brash, political commentators feel Romer has a refreshing way of saying what he thinks and winning points for it.

Bibliography: Michael Barone et al., *The Almanac of American Politics, 1988* (Washington, D.C.: National Journal, 1987); biographical information courtesy of governor's office; *The Chronicle of Higher Education*: 11–12–86; 5–20–87; 10–31–90; 8–28–91; *The New York Times*: 7–14–87; 6–11–88; 11–5–88; 11–7–90; 3–13–91; 3–29–91; 3–30–92; 11–18–92; 2–26–93; *The Star-Ledger* (Newark, N.J.): 8–5–92; 11–6–92; *USA Today*: 6–10–88; 11–19–92.

CONNECTICUT

WILLIAM ATCHINSON O'NEILL, 1980–1991

Born in Hartford, Connecticut, on August 11, 1930, O'Neill is the son of Joseph and Frances O'Neill. A Roman Catholic, O'Neill married Natalie Scott Damon in 1962. The couple has no children.

Early in O'Neill's life, the family moved to East Hampton, where he attended the local schools and graduated from East Hampton High School. He later attended New Britain Teachers' College and the University of Hartford. A combat flier with the U.S. Air Force from 1950 to 1953, he returned to East Hampton at the end of his military service. His father operated a tavern there, which O'Neill still owns. He worked as a draftsman for a time, then sold life insurance.

His background is a traditionally Democratic one. When he returned from the air force, he got involved in local Democratic politics, serving on the East Hampton Democratic Town Committee from 1954 to 1980. After two unsuccessful bids, he was elected to the Connecticut House of Representatives in 1966. There he was assistant majority leader for the 1971 and 1972 sessions, assistant minority leader for the next two sessions, and majority leader from 1975 through 1978. O'Neill strongly supported Governor Ella Grasso in the 1974 election, and when John M. Bailey, the Connecticut state Democratic chairman and former Democratic national chairman, died the next year, Grasso at first nominated O'Neill to the vacancy. O'Neill accepted, but Grasso later withdrew her support. Relations between the two were strained after that incident. Despite Grasso's unwillingness to endorse a candidate in the primary, O'Neill was elected the state's lieutenant governor in November 1978.

As lieutenant governor, O'Neill assumed the governorship on December 31, 1980, when Grasso formally resigned her office due to ill health. As governor, he steered the legislature through two special sessions, one concerning the budget and the other, flood relief. O'Neill also approved an unpopular tax on incorporated businesses. It was a difficult transition for O'Neill, who claimed he felt like a caretaker.

He was elected to his own full four-year term in 1982, defeating former state Senate Majority Leader Lewis B. Rome in the general election by 578,264 votes to 497,773. O'Neill campaigned on the theme that Con-

William Atchinson O'Neill *(Courtesy of Governor's Office)*

necticut had been relatively prosperous during the recession. Rome drew strong support from normally Republican Fairfield County, but he was unable to overcome the incumbent's advantage in the rest of the state.

During his first term, O'Neill established a more forceful presence, winning enactment of new programs and rebuilding the state's roads and bridges. Although derided by detractors as an amiable but uninspiring leader, O'Neill benefited from a robust state economy that produced large budget surpluses and record tax cuts. Many Republicans said he was merely the beneficiary of an economic boom that they credited the Reagan administration with creating.

In 1986, O'Neill was challenged for renomination by former U.S. Congressman Toby Moffett, who called the O'Neill administration "unprofessional, unprepared, unresponsive, unimaginative, and totally uninspiring." Moffett said he would be an advocate of better programs to aid education and day care, to help laid-off workers start their own businesses, and to protect the environment. He also pledged to have an "accessible" administration that would put "professionalism over politics."

O'Neill rebuffed Moffett's challenge and was renominated by the Democratic State Convention in July 1986. Moffett received 250 delegate votes, short the 20 percent needed to force a September primary. O'Neill received 1,098 votes, 82 percent of all delegate votes cast.

In the general election, he faced Republican Julie Belaga, a 10-year state representative from Westport who had survived a three-way primary fight to win her party's nomination. As the state's first female Republican candidate for governor, she faced a difficult challenge, for the Republicans had elected only one governor in the past 32 years. Making her first bid for statewide office, she campaigned on the theme of bringing "pride and performance" to the state government. She accused the O'Neill administration of being dominated by politicians rather than professional managers and condemned the governor for reacting to events rather than anticipating them. Attributing the state's prosperity to federal economic policies, she charged the Democrats with running an administration "based on cronyism rather than excellence" and called state government "a festering sore," disgraced by frequent "embarrassments" such as the dismissal of bridge inspectors who collected extra pay for work they didn't perform. Presenting herself as a "fresh new face," she called for direct primaries for party nominations, elimination of the state's inheritance tax, and overhaul of the Departments of Motor Vehicles and Transportation to provide better services.

O'Neill stressed his leadership record, claiming that his six years of solid, steady governance had brought the state unparalleled prosperity with high personal income and low unemployment. He also said he was more attuned to the problems of the state's cities and towns than Belaga, whom he termed "a millionaire from Westport." Questioning her record in public service, he charged that she had missed 43 percent of all roll call votes during the 1986 legislative session and had not produced "one piece of meaningful legislation" in her ten years in the general assembly.

In the opinion of political observers, the contest featured more differences of style and personality than major disagreements on issues. Both candidates were political moderates who opposed a state personal income tax and supported the death penalty. Both opposed mandatory drug testing and forcing suburban communities to accept low- and moderate-income housing. Neither candidate made gender a major issue.

In a sweeping reelection victory, O'Neill defeated Belaga by 168,329 votes, more than double his winning margin of 80,491 votes in 1982. The contest had set a spending record for a gubernatorial campaign in the state.

For his second term, O'Neill planned to follow "the same pattern" of his first six years in office, stressing programs to create jobs, protect the environment, and improve transportation. In the area of education, he fashioned sweeping changes. His Education Enhancement Act of 1986 raised salaries of public school teachers. The state was also recognized as one of the nation's leaders in teacher testing and improvement plans. Another noteworthy accomplishment was Connecticut's ranking among the top five states nationally in both its existing program for a clean environment and its climate for economic development. In 1987, the state created a $10 million superfund to clean up hazardous wastes, allocated $409 million to rebuild roads and bridges and to improve commuter service, and returned $1.68 billion in state revenues to cities and towns to cut local property taxes. O'Neill also called for a $6.8 million increase in state programs to help the elderly buy prescription drugs.

While O'Neill's popularity had soared with the economic boom of the 1980s, it plummeted sharply as his second term drew to a close. He suffered a steep drop in support beginning in 1989 after pushing nearly $1 billion in tax increases through the general assembly. The tax increase, the largest in state history, included raising the sales tax to 8 percent, the nation's highest. While O'Neill defended the increase as necessary to counter a decline in revenue caused by the recession in the Northeast, as well as a decrease in federal support to the state, others observed that Connecticut's budget shortfall had become a chronic one. Despite huge spending increases throughout the 1980s for health care, prisons, and road and bridge rebuilding, the O'Neill administration was adamantly opposed to the creation of an income tax, which many were coming to consider necessary.

Even with these problems, however, O'Neill had been expected to seek reelection in 1990. Although he had repeatedly said that only a decline in his health would forestall a reelection bid, he shocked the state with his March 20, 1990, announcement that he wouldn't seek a third full term.

Saying that he had no taste for the negative campaign tactics he feared would be necessary to win, he insisted that he could best serve the people of the state by completing his term in office "unfettered and unimpaired" by the demands of a reelection campaign.

O'Neill also admitted that he was well aware of the "political realities" facing him. Analysts suggested that the tax question was probably one factor in his decision. Another was a looming primary challenge from within his own party. Even before O'Neill's stunning withdrawal, U.S. Congressman Bruce A. Morrison from New Haven had already formed a fund-raising committee to challenge O'Neill at the 1990 Democratic State Convention. Others speculated the voters had simply tired of O'Neill after his long tenure.

O'Neill's surprise exit from the race sent state Democrats scrambling and paved the way for the most tumultuous political contest in 20 years. Although O'Neill declared himself neutral in the race for a successor, he remained curiously involved in the contest, employing tactics that baffled political observers. He kept his name in the political news by expressing doubts that Morrison could win and by praising Morrison's one Democratic challenger, state Representative William J. Cibes, Jr. The public perception of a feud between Morrison and O'Neill was also fed by Morrison's own antics. Even after O'Neill bowed out and was ostensibly no longer a threat, Morrison continued to portray himself as the outsider to the governor's "well-oiled machine." His television ads promised that he would be "a Governor on your side for a change." Other Democrats lamented that O'Neill had given up too soon and that he could have pulled out a victory in the general election. Supporters maintained that he was "one of the most underestimated Governors" in state history. With all the discussion, the spotlight remained on O'Neill even at the July convention that was to choose the new Democratic standard-bearer.

Political scientists saw O'Neill's retreat as the "passing of a generation" in state politics. With the expiration of his term in 1991, he had served as Connecticut's governor longer than anyone since Jonathan Trumbull II, who had died in office in 1809. O'Neill's departure also ended a chapter for state Democrats, who had controlled the statehouse for 36 of the past 40 years. As analysts had predicted, O'Neill would also represent the last in a long line of Connecticut governors who stood firm and fast against the introduction of a personal income tax, that sacred cow of Connecticut politics finally slaughtered by incoming Governor Lowell Weicker in 1991.

Political analysts are divided as to how the O'Neill era will be remembered. Even after many years on the public stage, he remained an elusive figure with few close friends. His stiff public manner, gaffes with language, and modest self-effacing style caused his powerful intellect to be overlooked. He was consistently overshadowed by the more charismatic and telegenic governors of neighboring states, and the economic downturn of the last years of his term caused him to be viewed as a doddering symbol of failure.

Others suggest that O'Neill will be remembered as the man who helped elect the state's first independent governor since the Civil War. His personal feud with Democratic party nominee Bruce Morrison almost certainly eroded Morrison's support and encouraged some Democrats to desert their party for Weicker's independent candidacy.

Many who have watched O'Neill's career say that history will ultimately redeem him. Clearly, he changed the face of state government, leaving it vastly different from how he found it on December 31, 1980. The state budget almost tripled, and the government took on huge new responsibilities as Washington's role in state affairs receded during the Reagan years.

In the waning days of his administration, O'Neill was asked by an interviewer how he hoped he would be remembered. He answered by saying, "I would like, certainly, to be remembered as an honest man . . . a man of very high integrity."

Bibliography: Michael Barone et al., *The Almanac of American Politics, 1984* (Washington, D.C.: National Journal, 1983); *The Chronicle of Higher Education*: 10–22–86; 11–12–86; *The New York Times*: 6–2–85; 11–15–85; 7–20–86; 7–27–86; 9–8–86; 9–10–86; 9–11–86; 9–21–86; 10–17–86; 10–20–86; 10–31–86; 11–5–86; 11–6–86; 2–5–87; 6–2–87; 7–7–87; 2–4–88; 10–8–89; 1–22–90; 3–21–90; 3–30–90; 4–15–90; 7–11–90; 9–7–90; 9–12–90; 1–9–91; *The Star-Ledger* (Newark, N.J.): 7–2–89; 4–4–90; *USA Today,* 3–22–90.

LOWELL P. WEICKER, JR., 1991–

Born in Paris on May 16, 1931, Weicker is an heir to the Squibb pharmaceutical fortune, the company his grandfather helped found in a Brooklyn drugstore after emigrating from Germany more than a century ago. Educated in the nation's best schools, Weicker graduated from the Lawrenceville School in 1949, Yale University in 1953, and the University of Virginia Law School in 1958. He served in the U.S. Army as a first lieutenant from 1953 to 1955 and in the Army Reserve from 1958 to 1964. Married to Claudia Testa Weicker, his third wife, Weicker is the father of seven sons.

One of a vanishing breed of liberal Republicans in the tradition of Jacob Javits, Clifford Case, Mark Hatfield, and Edward Brooke, Weicker began his political career in Greenwich, Connecticut, winning election as first selectman, the town's top official, in 1964. He also served as a state representative from the Greenwich area, and a one-term congressman representing Connecticut's Fourth Congressional District from 1968 to 1970. Elected to the U.S. Senate in 1970, he established a national reputation as a maverick liberal Republican frequently at odds with the leadership of his own party, especially on issues of social policy. He was subsequently reelected in 1976 and 1982.

During his senate career, Weicker became nationally known as a spirited and aggressive member of the Senate Select Committee investigating the Watergate scandal, becoming one of the nation's first Republicans to condemn Richard Nixon and members of his administration for their role in the incident. He also served as chairman and later ranking Republican member of the Senate appropriations subcommittee that funded health and education programs. The author of legislation to protect the rights of the disabled, aid the homeless, and protect small business, he drew praise for his work on behalf of the National Institutes of Health and America's medical research community.

Despite his successes, he tangled with the Reagan White House and battled his party's conservative wing on a range of issues, including abortion and school prayer. Known as the "Republican Rambo" for his tangles with North Carolina's conservative Senator Jesse Helms, he earned the enmity of the Reagan administration by opposing Supreme Court nominee Robert Bork and for fighting against cuts in social programs. One particularly telling gauge of his isolation from his own party was a 90 percent approval rating by the Americans for Democratic Action, a liberal lob-

Lowell P. Weicker, Jr. (*Courtesy of Governor's Office*)

bying group. Weicker was the only Republican in the House or Senate ever endorsed by the group since its founding in the 1940s.

Weicker's maverick style so annoyed Republicans that in 1982 he was briefly challenged for his Senate seat by Prescott Bush, Jr., the president's brother. In 1988, conservative columnist William Buckley and his family launched an effort known as "Buck Pac" dedicated to ridding the Senate of him. Their efforts were successful in 1988, when he was defeated for reelection by Democrat Joseph Lieberman in a major upset. Political analysts and party leaders traced his defeat to several factors, notably the unusually high degree of antipathy against Weicker felt by the conservative wing of his own party. By contrast, Lieberman benefited from a united Democratic party working on his behalf.

After his narrow loss, Weicker retreated from politics, making no speeches and granting few interviews. Teaching law at George Mason University in Fairfax, Virginia, he also served as chairman of a medical research fund-raising group, Research America, based in Alexandria, Virginia. Connecticut politicians regarded his sojourn in Virginia, where he had long maintained a home, as a kind of political exile, and he continued to be shunned by national and state Republicans alike.

In the face of this apparent isolation, Weicker shocked the political world with his 1990 decision to seek the Connecticut statehouse as an independent candidate. Although he had once considered running for governor in 1986, he now had to fend off charges that his independent candidacy was fueled by motives of revenge against state and national Republican leaders. Explaining his decision to seek the statehouse via an independent route, he noted that he felt blocked by his late entrance into the race and by the conservative leadership that had taken over the state Republican party after his defeat by Lieberman.

Weicker's insurgent candidacy worked to solidify his maverick, outsider reputation. Blessed with high name recognition and long-standing popularity in the state, he was also the beneficiary of voter discontent with politics as usual. His "pox on both your houses" candidacy blamed both parties for failing to tackle tough problems and issues because of their narrow-minded concern for how needed solutions would play at the ballot box. By contrast, he pledged that he would "work for the children, not the politicians."

In order to meet a state requirement that any independent bid bear a party label, Weicker christened his venture "A Connecticut party." He promised to infuse state government with nonpoliticians including academics and business people who would have no interest in dispensing political patronage because there would be no party regulars to reward.

Opposing Weicker were Democrat Bruce Morrison and Republican John Rowland. Both retiring congressmen, they labored under the stigma of incumbency in an anti-incumbent year. Yet each insisted that Weicker could not be an effective leader without a party base. While Democrats had to shoulder the responsibility for the economic difficulties that afflicted the state in the last years of incumbent William O'Neill's administration, the Republicans were battered by defections and internal bickering brought on by Weicker's candidacy. Once confident of its ability to recapture the statehouse after 20 years of Democratic control, the Republican party seemed on the brink of being torn apart, as Weicker's candidacy exacerbated the long-running tensions between the party's liberal and conservative wings. The likelihood of imposing a state income tax on wages became a major issue in the race.

Weicker's hard-fought win was heralded as a major personal triumph for him. Since he had received over half his votes from people who called themselves Democrats, his victory was a particular embarrassment to the state Democratic party, whose candidate finished a distant third. With his election, Weicker became the state's first independent governor since Alexander H. Halley of Salisbury was elected in 1857 as the standard-bearer of the American Republican party. He was only the fifth independent to serve as governor of any state since the turn of the century.

Weicker's term in office has been a stormy one. Although during the campaign he had never clearly advocated nor opposed a state income tax, he appointed as his chief budget adviser an earlier gubernatorial candidate, William J. Cibes, Jr., who had sought the Democratic nomination on a platform calling for a state income tax coupled with a cut in the sales tax. Soon the governor himself came to believe that only the historic imposition of a state tax on wages could erase a projected $2.4 billion budget deficit and restore the state's economy by reducing the nation's highest business taxes. Weicker persevered in his daring proposal despite legislative opposition and the catcalls of voters claiming to have been betrayed and misled by his campaign.

Success came to Weicker as a direct result of shrewd political tactics. He proposed the new income tax one month after taking office and then insisted upon its passage through a summer-long deadlock with the legislature. During the dramatic impasse, he vetoed three state budgets and let the government partially shut down for lack of funds. He locked up support from an unlikely coalition—powerful state employee union leaders and much of the business community. With long-term job security in mind, union leaders realized that an income tax levy would provide a much surer and more stable revenue base, while the business community supported the Weicker plan because it promised to reduce business taxes, including sales and corporate income levies. The 1991 tax increase was the biggest in state history and ended the state's historic antipathy to an income tax.

Weicker's victory came at a price, however. After one of the most raucous tax fights in American history, he was hung in effigy by disgruntled state citizens, spat upon by mobs, and bombarded with epithets and obscenities. An October 1991 crowd of 40,000 protestors gathered outside the state capitol was termed the largest and angriest in decades, if not in history. Placards compared Weicker to Adolf Hitler.

By contrast, others hailed him for his courage. *Time* magazine dubbed him "the gutsiest governor in America," and in 1992, he was named the first recipient of the John F. Kennedy Profile in Courage Award by the Kennedy Library Foundation. The citation lauded his willingness to "take a principalled stand for unpopular positions."

The strength of the insurgent H. Ross Perot candidacy in the presidential race of 1992 also seemed to vindicate Weicker. Perot's theme was identical: the irresponsibility of running a budget on borrowing and red ink. At this writing, anger over Weicker's tax policies appears to have subsided, and his popularity has rebounded. The state ended fiscal year 1992 with its first budget surplus in five years.

Besides the tax issue, another critical problem with which Weicker has had to deal involves deep racial divisions in the state's public schools. In a pending court battle, 19 minority students from Hartford have sued the state, arguing that schools segregated by race due to housing and neighborhood patterns violate the state constitution's guarantees of equal education. In response, Weicker has urged the legislature and local school officials to begin a voluntary integration effort that would give urban and suburban school districts roughly equal racial mixes by the 1999–2000 school year. Other elements of his education agenda, however, have drawn fire. One especially controversial proposal presents a cost-containment plan to cut state education aid to wealthier communities.

Throughout his long career, Weicker has had both vehement critics and diehard admirers. In the words of one analyst, he was never one "to bring out the lukewarm in people." Debate continues over what his legacy will be for state politics. Weicker's win transformed Connecticut overnight into a three-party state, with "A Connecticut party" having the guaranteed top position on every election ballot until 1994. Although for the first portion of his term Weicker had to build a working legislative coalition from scratch, without a single member of his own party, that may now be changing. A Connecticut party did hold its first statewide convention in 1992. Drawing together former Republicans and Democrats, Weicker devotees, and a healthy contingent of people fed up with both major parties, the party is presently positioning itself to become more than a vehicle for Weicker's personal agenda.

Weicker currently serves as chair of the National Governors Association Committee on Human Resources. He has led the nation's governors in calling for major changes in federal Medicaid laws to relieve state governments of some of the burdens of shouldering costs. An outspoken advocate of efforts to fight AIDS while he was in the Senate, he was considered to be the leading contender for a new federal post created by the Clinton administration to coordinate work in that area. Despite much speculation, however, Weicker's move to Washington never materialized. Ever the maverick, Weicker stunned the political community with his announcement that he does not plan to seek reelection in 1994.

Bibliography: Biographical information courtesy of governor's office; Phil Duncan, ed., *Politics in America 1992* (Washington, D.C.: Congressional Quarterly Press, 1991); Russell D. Murphy, "Lowell P. Weicker, Jr.: A Maverick in the 'Land of Steady Habits,' " in Thad Beyle, ed., *Governors and Hard Times* (Washington, D.C.: Congressional Quarterly Press, 1992); *The New York Times*: 11–10–88; 2–9–90; 3–3–90; 5–17–90; 5–28–90; 6–3–90; 7–11–90; 9–16–90; 10–30–90; 11–5–90; 11–7–90; 11–8–90; 1–7–91; 1–10–91; 2–15–91; 4–2–91; 4–10–91; 7–14–91; 7–15–91; 7–27–91; 8–5–91; 8–8–91; 8–11–91; 8–16–91; 8–23–91; 8–25–91; 9–1–91; 11–19–91; 12–15–91; 3–9–92; 5–29–92; 7–27–92; 8–4–92; 11–2–92; 1–7–93; 2–28–93; Michael Specter, "In This Corner: Connecticut Governor Lowell Weicker," *New York Times Magazine* (Dec. 15, 1991): 40–43, 69–71; *The Star-Ledger* (Newark, N.J.): 10–28–90; 4–28–91; 7–3–91; 8–23–91; 10–6–91; 5–18–92; *Time,* 11–21–88; *USA Today*: 3–6–91; 6–3–92; 10–1–93.

DELAWARE

MICHAEL NEWBOLD CASTLE, 1985–1993

Born in Wilmington, Delaware, on July 2, 1939, Castle is the son of J. Manderson Castle, Jr., and Louise B. Castle. A Roman Catholic, he is a bachelor.

A graduate of Hamilton College (B.A., 1961) and Georgetown Law School (J.D., 1964), Castle, a Republican, has been an attorney in private practice as well as a longtime state government official. State deputy attorney general from 1965 to 1966, he served in the state house of representatives from 1966 to 1967, as well as in the state senate from 1968 to 1976, where he was minority leader from 1975 to 1976. He served as lieutenant governor under Governor Pierre DuPont from 1981 to 1985. As a close political ally of DuPont, Castle was given major policy jobs. In addition to his duties of presiding over the state senate and Board of Pardons, he headed a study of drunken driving that led to tougher penalties and enforcement procedures. In 1984, he headed a panel that produced more than 70 proposals to improve the state's educational system, resulting in an immediate raise in teachers' salaries totaling $124 million.

Since Governor DuPont was constitutionally ineligible to run for a third term in 1984, Castle was groomed as his successor. Although he was carried along in the election by the tide of affection Delaware felt for DuPont, Castle had been an active lieutenant governor, and he campaigned hard for the right to sit in the statehouse. He held a commanding lead from the start of the campaign. His opponent was former state Supreme Court Justice William T. Quillen, who had won the Democratic gubernatorial nomination against former Governor Sherman Tribbitt. Quillen was the favorite of Samuel Shipley, the state Democratic party chairman, who believed the former justice had the best chance of defeating the Republican ticket in the general election. Quillen, however, in the opinion of political observers, "showed little zest for campaigning." Castle won with 55 percent of the vote in a year when Democrats were winning most of the other state offices in Delaware. One of Castle's main assets on the road to victory was his predecessor's strong support, and his win was seen as a vindication of DuPont's record.

In office, Castle continued DuPont's policies. He presided over a boom-

Michael Newbold Castle *(Courtesy of Governor's Office)*

ing state economy with a healthy budget surplus. Three major cuts in personal income taxes, strict controls on state spending, improved management of state government, and increased state support for public schools were the highlights of his first term. Other achievements included reforms in the state's long-term capital improvement program, a highway improvement program, and increased state involvement in international trade and finance.

Facing the 1988 campaign for reelection, Castle found himself in an enviable position. Having managed to cut taxes and still have funds available for an increase in teachers' salaries and spending for social programs, he was such a sure bet that the Democrats had difficulty finding an opposition candidate. Their choice, retired Wilmington labor lawyer Jacob Kreshtool, focused his campaign on health and environmental issues, since Castle presided over a robust economy. Castle coasted to a lopsided victory, winning easily with 71 percent of the vote, the greatest margin in the history of the state. Castle called the gratifying vote "a referendum on my accomplishments."

With his reelection never in doubt, Castle spent most of his time stumping for his running mate for lieutenant governor, fellow Republican Dale Wolf, a relative unknown. Wolf needed Castle's support since candidates for governor and lieutenant governor are elected separately in Delaware. The tactic caused Castle some unanticipated legal problems, however, when the losing Democratic candidate for the second spot, Gary E. Hindes, sued Castle, accusing him of illegally diverting campaign funds to his personal choice for the post. Hindes charged that Castle took advantage of his own popularity by raising far more money than he needed and then using it to benefit Wolf. This, according to the accusation, violated the state's election finance laws because it amounted to illegal contributions.

During his years in office, Castle played a key role in the reform of national welfare policy, serving as chairman of the National Governors Association Task Force on Welfare Prevention and working as liaison with the White House and Congress to win passage of a comprehensive welfare reform package. Delaware's successful welfare reform program, "First Step," was designed to provide education and training to long-term welfare recipients. Other priority issues for him included education and the environment. He created "Delaware 2000," the first state plan to restructure education at the grass roots to meet visionary national education goals as designed by the Bush administration. He supported teacher salary increases, higher classroom standards, and the development of a pilot program to increase the role of teachers in curriculum development.

His administration also developed a comprehensive "Environmental Legacy" plan to address environmental issues in the coming decades, including efforts to preserve Delaware's beaches and to preserve state land for public recreation.

In 1990, Castle drew national attention for an innovative and comprehensive cancer control plan. Trying to make sense of scientific studies saying that Delaware residents were among the least healthy in the nation, Castle offered a solution hailed as a case study in how government officials must deal with a problem and the image created by that problem. Castle's plan called for the State Department of Health to identify where cancers are the most prevalent, to assess the related environmental and behavioral risk factors, and to establish programs for prevention and early detection. These new programs included mobile mammography labs for use in inner-city neighborhoods and the expansion of experimental programs like health clinics in public schools. As part of his public relations campaign to change people's way of living, Castle asked his cabinet to take fitness tests, to improve their diet, and to start exercise programs. Experts in both health and communication praised his initiatives.

The one black mark received by the Castle administration was given by the National Women's Political Caucus, who ranked him last in the country for three straight years in terms of the percentage of women appointed to his cabinet.

Prohibited by law from seeking a third term, Castle turned his sights on the state's lone congressional seat. In an interesting trade-off, he sought the congressional seat being vacated by Congressman Thomas R. Carper, who in turn aimed to succeed Castle as governor. The swap proved successful for both men. Castle defeated former Lieutenant Governor S. B. Woo and moved to Washington, while Carper defeated B. Gary Scott, a retired real estate executive, to replace Castle in the statehouse.

Bibliography: Michael Barone et al., *The Almanac of American Politics, 1986, 1988* (Washington, D.C.: National Journal, 1985, 1987); biographical information courtesy of governor's office; L. J. Davis, "Delaware Inc.," *New York Times Magazine* (June 5, 1988): 28–32, 38, 96, 100; *The New York Times*: 11–6–84; 11–8–84; 1–16–85; 11–9–88; 10–18–89; 1–21–90; 9–14–92; 11–5–92; *The Star-Ledger* (Newark, N.J.), 8–18–91; *USA Today*: 10–11–88; 11–10–88; 11–8–90; 4–8–92.

DALE E. WOLF, January 3, 1993–January 19, 1993

Born in Kearney, Nebraska, on September 6, 1924, Wolf is the son of Harry E. and Mabel Irene Moss Wolf. He married Clarice Elaine Marshall on December 31, 1945, and has four children.

Wolf served in the U.S. Army during World War II, earning Bronze and Purple stars. He received a B.S. in agronomy from the University of Nebraska and a Ph.D. in crop sciences and weed control from Rutgers University. He was also a participant in the Executive Development Program of the Graduate School of Business at Stanford University.

Throughout his career, Wolf has worked as a researcher, professor, and businessman in the agricultural products and biochemical industries. Rising in the ranks of the DuPont Company, he became group vice-president of its Agricultural Products Division in 1979, serving in that position for eight years.

Throughout his long business career, Wolf remained active in civic and community affairs, holding leadership positions with the American Red Cross, the United Way, and the Girls' Club of Delaware. He was also a member of the Board of Overseers of Widener University and a consultant to the College of Marine Studies at the University of Delaware.

A Republican, Wolf began his public service career as director of the Delaware Development Office, where he worked from 1987 to 1988. In 1988, he was elected lieutenant governor of the state, serving in the administration of popular Republican Governor Michael Castle. As lieutenant governor, Wolf had numerous responsibilities: president of the state senate and Board of Pardons; chairman of the Drug Abuse Coordinating Council; chairman of the Delaware Coastal Heritage Greenway Council; chairman of the Interagency Council on Adult Literacy; initiator and chairman of the Delaware Safe Kids Coalition; chairman of the Education Committee for the National Conference of Lieutenant Governors; chairman of the State Conference of Libraries and Information Services; and chairman of the Delaware Aquaculture Council.

Although there had been some speculation that Wolf might himself seek the governorship in 1992, it was not through the ballot box that he ascended to the statehouse. As Castle's lieutenant governor, Wolf served a brief 16½-day stint as governor when Castle resigned on January 3, 1993, to take his seat as a newly elected member of the U.S. House of Representatives. In an interesting swap, the two-term governor chose to run for Delaware's lone congressional seat in 1992, leaving incumbent

Dale E. Wolf *(Courtesy of Governor Wolf)*

U.S. Congressman Thomas Carper to seek the governorship. Both men were victorious in their bids. Wolf, therefore, served as the state's governor in the brief interim between Castle's resignation on January 3 and Carper's inauguration on January 19, 1993. It was the second time in state history that a lieutenant governor had briefly served as interim governor because of a resignation. On December 30, 1960, Governor J. Caleb Boggs had resigned to enter the U.S. Senate, leaving Lieutenant Governor David Buckson to serve as governor for 18 days until the swearing in of Elbert Carvel on January 17, 1961.

At the swearing-in ceremony, outgoing Governor Castle joked that he had run for Congress intentionally so that his friend Dale Wolf would have the opportunity to be governor. During his brief term, Wolf took as his main objective working to ensure a smooth transition between administrations. He also planned to recognize Delaware residents who had worked in civic and community causes that he had championed, such as fighting drug abuse and illiteracy.

Wolf is presently the chairman of the Delaware Foundation for Literacy and a member of the board of directors of the Wilmington Savings Fund Society.

Bibliography: Michael Barone and Grant Ujifusa, *The Almanac of American Politics, 1992* (Washington, D.C.: National Journal, 1991); biographical information courtesy of Governor Wolf; *The Star-Ledger* (Newark, N.J.), 1–4–93.

Thomas R. Carper (*Leo Matkins Photography*)

THOMAS R. CARPER, 1993–

Born in Beckley, West Virginia, on January 23, 1947, Carper grew up in Danville, Virginia. He earned a B.A. at Ohio State University in 1968, attending college on a naval ROTC scholarship. Upon graduation, he completed five years of service as a naval flight officer and served in Southeast Asia during the Vietnam War. Married to the former Martha Stacy of Boone, North Carolina, Carper is the father of two sons.

Following his military service, Carper moved to Delaware where he earned an M.B.A. at the University of Delaware in 1975. A Democrat, he entered public life in his adopted state, elected state treasurer at the age of 29. He was subsequently reelected in 1978 and 1980. In that post, he was credited with improving the state's credit rating, overseeing its rise from worst in the nation to a respectable AA rating in five years.

In 1982, Carper won a seat in Congress by defeating a three-term incumbent. His congressional career spanned ten years, during which he won high marks as an active and effective legislator. He also earned distinction as one of the few members of Congress to belong to a combat-ready Naval Reserve unit, meaning that he risked being called up for service during the Persian Gulf War. After serving nearly two decades as a member of the Naval Reserve, he retired with the rank of captain in 1991.

In Congress, Carper was a member of the Banking, Finance, and Urban Affairs Committee as well as the Merchant Marine and Fisheries Committee. One of the few Democrats to support the conservative fiscal policies of the Republicans, he backed a balanced budget amendment and the line-item veto. His other legislative interests included affordable housing, welfare reform, and environmental protection. He authored legislation to ban sewage sludge dumping in ocean waters and to manage hazardous waste disposal.

Carper's popularity and successful legislative record led to much speculation that he would challenge William Roth for the U.S. Senate in 1988. Declining to make that race, he engaged instead in a unique swap with retiring incumbent Governor Michael Castle. In 1992, Castle sought Carper's congressional seat, while Carper opted to make a run for the statehouse. His gubernatorial opponent was Republican B. Gary Scott, a real estate executive and newcomer to politics. Although Scott was helped by a vast volunteer network and was once thought by pollsters to be ahead in the race, Carper won a landslide 66 percent victory. With his win, he became Delaware's first Democratic governor in 20 years. He also holds the distinction of being elected to statewide office nine times—more than anyone else in state history.

Carper became Delaware's 71st chief executive on January 19, 1993. In office, he has proposed a new scholarship program for college students and a new internship program to attract students to public service careers. He also aims to promote further cooperation among state government, colleges, and businesses.

Bibliography: Michael Barone and Grant Ujifusa, *The Almanac of American Politics, 1992* (Washington, D.C.: National Journal, 1991); biographical information courtesy of governor's office; *The New York Times,* 10–26–92; *USA Today,* 11–4–92.

FLORIDA

ROBERT MARTINEZ, 1987–1991

Born in Tampa, Florida, on December 25, 1934, Martinez is the son of
Serafin Martinez and Ida Carreno Martinez. A Roman Catholic, he mar-
ried Mary Jane Marino in 1954. The couple has two children, Sharon and
Alan.

A lifelong resident of Tampa, Martinez attended local public schools
there. He earned a B.S. from the University of Tampa and a master's
degree in labor and industrial relations from the University of Illinois.
Martinez held a number of jobs before seeking public office. A onetime
restaurant worker, he spent 7 years as a classroom teacher and a total of
12 years in the field of education. During his teaching career, he helped
lead a teachers' union strike against the policies of Governor Claude R.
Kirk, Jr. He also served as a labor consultant, specializing in the area of
employee relations.

After a career in private business, Martinez was elected mayor of Tampa
in 1979. He was reelected in 1983 with 81 percent of the vote. As mayor,
Martinez practiced a conservative approach to government that lowered
property taxes, decreased the number of city employees, and improved
the quality of life. During his tenure as mayor, the city was hailed as one
of ten ''megatrend'' cities of the future in the United States, and its robust,
diversified economy was seen as a model for growth. Futurist John Nais-
bett highlighted Tampa as one of the ten best sites in the nation for small-
business growth and development.

While mayor, Martinez was a member of the U.S. Conference of Mayors, a member of the board of directors of the National League of Cities,
and president of the Florida League of Cities. One of the political highlights of his second term in office was being chosen as a featured speaker
at the 1984 Republican National Convention.

With incumbent Governor Robert Graham constitutionally ineligible to
serve a third term in 1986, the governor's race was wide open. Martinez
resigned as mayor of Tampa in the summer of 1986 to campaign for the
governorship, an office that only one Republican had won in the last
century. From the start, Martinez was seen as the party's best hope of
securing the governorship. The grandson of Spanish immigrants, Martinez

Robert Martinez *(Courtesy of Governor's Office)*

and the Republicans hoped to capitalize on the state's changing demographics: Republican registration had been swelled by newcomers, retirees from the Midwest, and increasing numbers of naturalized Cuban exiles. Martinez drew a good share of his strength from Miami's Cuban population, which had become overwhelmingly Republican. Political observers were unclear, however, as to whether non-Hispanic Republicans outside of his Tampa Bay base would support him in a climate where cultural divisions were pronounced. Old-line Republicans had initial doubts that someone of Hispanic origin could be elected to statewide office. Martinez also had some problems with party regulars due to his late conversion to the Republican party. Since he had officially become a Republican only in 1983, his endorsement of Jimmy Carter in 1980 enabled his opponents to confront him with the fact that he had opposed the election of Ronald Reagan.

Martinez built his campaign around his experience as a public official and reputation as a strong and effective manager. A stern opponent of crime, he pledged to trim $800 million in waste from the state's $16 billion budget and pledged no new taxes. He faced three opponents in the race for the Republican gubernatorial nomination: Lou Frey, a 52-year-old former congressman from the Orlando area; Tom Gallagher, a 42-year-old state representative from Miami; and 40-year-old conservative Chester Clem from Vero Beach. Because no candidate won a majority of the vote, a runoff election was necessary between Martinez and his leading rival, Lou Frey. Martinez missed winning the nomination in the first primary by a few thousand votes. After his narrow miss, he asked his opponent, who had previously lost bids for the governorship in 1978 and for a U.S. Senate seat in 1980, to drop out of the race in the name of party unity. Frey, however, declined. Martinez officially won the Republican gubernatorial nomination in the September 30, 1986, runoff primary, defeating Frey by a 2–1 margin. By defeating Frey, a former five-term congressman whose name was familiar in state Republican circles, Martinez ably demonstrated his appeal both to traditional Republicans as well as to new party registrants.

Martinez was also to benefit from a divisive primary fight among Democrats. Three Democrats sought to succeed outgoing Governor Graham: former state Representative Steve Pajcic, Attorney General Jim Smith, and state senate President Harry Johnston. Smith combined name recognition as the state's chief law enforcement officer with a hefty campaign war chest: He had reportedly spent $1 million of his own money to ignite the campaign. Yet his campaign appeared disorganized and uncertain, and as he lost some of his organization and support to Johnston, a runoff primary was necessary among the Democrats as well. Although Pajcic was the eventual winner of the nomination, he had been badly bruised by his opponents' charges. Leading rival Smith had attacked Pajcic sharply, accusing the Jacksonville lawyer of voting on the wrong side of law and order issues and of masking his liberal ideology behind a moderate image. In the general election, Pajcic continued to be dogged by the labels planted on him by his rivals for the Democratic nomination, who had accused him of being too liberal on such issues as homosexual rights and capital punishment.

The defection of conservative Democrats to Martinez was seen as central to the Republican win. Martinez's victory with 55 percent of the vote heartened those who had worked to establish a viable two-party system in the state.

Inaugurated on January 6, 1987, as the state's 40th governor and the first elected governor of Hispanic ancestry, Martinez confronted numerous problems associated with the state's rapid growth: overcrowded roads, schools, and prisons; a strained budget; and a poor tax base unable to support the growth needs of Florida. With more than 300,000 new residents arriving each year, Florida suffered from a historic inability to raise revenue for deteriorating highways, education, and other social and economic development. The state, despite its affluence, was among the nation's leaders in adult illiteracy, high school dropouts, and infant mortality. The main issue of Martinez's administration was how to finance the ever-pressing needs of this rapidly growing state.

As governor, Martinez developed a reputation as a tough law and order man. Presiding over a significant decline in the crime rate, he signed legislation creating a new gun law that drew national attention. He doubled the number of state prison cells, stiffened penalties for drug dealers, and advocated wider use of American military forces in operations against drug activities abroad. As governor of a state with hundreds of miles of beaches and waterways that offered South American cocaine smugglers routes to North American customers, Martinez made drug-related crime a major focus of his administration. Developing a close relationship with the Bush White House, he became a spokesman for the National Governors Association on drug issues. While governor, he instituted a program of drug testing for high-level government employees, including all members of his staff, and he made a point of being the first state official to be tested. Emphasizing compulsory drug prevention education in the public schools, he was a major promoter of a bill, eventually enacted into law, that mandated the death penalty for convictions of major drug traffickers.

As his first term unfolded, however, Martinez began to suffer from serious image problems. Once very popular, he came to be viewed by many Floridians as a local version of Jimmy Carter, a blundering manager and lackluster public speaker who wavered and seemed to lose stature. Critics said his stormy four years as governor raised questions about his leadership, judgment, and management skills. Although he was able to win passage of a broadened sales tax on services, he ran into a rebellion led by national advertisers and Florida broadcasters. When he called the legislature into special session to approve a substitute tax of lower yield, Floridians grumbled about their "wishy washy Governor" and his lack of political courage. In 1989, after the U.S. Supreme Court had opened the way for tougher state laws on abortion, he called another special legislative session in which each of his five antiabortion measures was swiftly killed in committee. Political observers quickly realized the magnitude of this defeat and what it portended for his already shaky political hold on a state suffering from a $1 billion budget deficit.

Analysts of both parties believed Martinez to be extremely vulnerable after four years of political missteps. Four months before the November 1990 general election, nearly two-thirds of registered voters gave him a performance rating of "only fair" or "poor." He also had to withstand the indignity of being challenged for renomination by a member of his own party, state Senator Marlene Woodson-Howard.

Hoping nonetheless to become the state's first Republican governor ever to be reelected, Martinez ran a lavish and sophisticated campaign, well financed, boasting a highly professional staff, amply backed by the national Republican party, and supported by the White House. Jeb Bush, one of the president's sons, served as Martinez's campaign chairman, and President Bush himself traveled to Florida several times to campaign for him. In the campaign, Martinez sought to bolster his image by depicting himself as a quiet family man ready and willing to learn from his errors. He spent $1 million on TV spots in which he told voters: "I know I've made mistakes. You've told me I've disappointed you sometimes. . . . I've listened and I've learned."

Despite these efforts, Martinez was unseated in his bid for reelection, losing to former U.S. Senator Lawton Chiles, 57 percent to 43 percent. Little separated the two candidates on the issues. Both spoke of tougher measures on crime and drugs and the need to protect the environment, to manage growth, and to improve education. Neither candidate ruled out raising taxes. In the end, however, the personality of the popular Chiles, a legendary figure in state politics, seemed to be the determining factor. He focused his campaign on a general appeal "to return government to the people" and deflect the power of big business.

Martinez's term ended on January 8, 1991. With his defeat, he became the second Republican governor in Florida history to lose a bid for a second term. After his loss, campaign manager J. M. Stipanovich predicted that he did not expect Martinez to seek political office again.

Nonetheless, Martinez was rewarded for his loyalty to the Republican White House with an appointment as federal drug czar, succeeding William Bennett as director of the Office of National Drug Control Policy. At his swearing-in ceremony in March 1991, he indicated that he would give greater emphasis to drug prevention and treatment than had his predecessor.

Bibliography: Michael Barone et al., *The Almanac of American Politics, 1988* (Washington, D.C.: National Journal, 1987); biographical information courtesy of governor's office; *The Chronicle of Higher Education*: 11–12–86; 9–30–87; *Newsweek,* 4–30–90; *The New York Times*: 9–2–86; 9–3–86; 9–30–86; 10–1–86; 10–2–86; 10–12–86; 11–2–86; 11–5–86; 1–6–87; 5–13–87; 10–16–89; 4–25–90; 9–2–90; 9–5–90; 10–30–90; 11–6–90; 11–7–90; 11–11–90; 11–19–90; 11–30–90; *The Star-Ledger* (Newark, N.J.): 10–12–89; 11–19–90; 3–8–91; *USA Today*: 6–23–88; 12–8–89; 6–19–90; 8–20–90; 10–10–90; 3–29–91; 1–28–92.

LAWTON CHILES, 1991–

Born in Lakeland, Florida, on April 3, 1930, Chiles is the son of a Polk
County railroad worker. A graduate of Lakeland High School, he earned
a B.S. from the University of Florida in 1952 and an LL.B. from the
University of Florida College of Law in 1955. He and his wife, the former
Rhea Grafton of Coral Gables, have four children.

Chiles began his professional career practicing law in Lakeland from
1955 to 1971. He also served as an instructor at Florida Southern College
from 1955 to 1958. A Democrat, he served in the Florida House of Representatives from 1959 to 1967 and in the Florida Senate from 1967 to
1971. Making a victorious run for the U.S. Senate in 1970, he drew headlines with a unique grass-roots campaign during which he and his wife
walked the state in an effort to learn firsthand the needs and concerns of
state voters. The highly publicized 1,003-mile walk from Jay in the Florida
Panhandle to Key Largo in the Florida Keys earned Chiles the nickname
"Walkin' Lawton." Reelected in 1976 and 1982, he became the first U.S.
senator from Florida ever to chair a major committee, the influential
Senate Budget Committee. Known as a crusader against special interests
and a champion of campaign finance reform, he served on numerous key
committees: Appropriations; Governmental Affairs; the Special Committee on Aging; and the Democratic Steering Committee. During his Senate
years, he also helped to found the National Commission to Prevent Infant
Mortality, an organization in which he remains active.

Chiles retired from the Senate after 18 years. Citing an increasing frustration with gridlock on Capitol Hill and disillusioned by Washington's
failure to deal with the mounting budget deficit, he also cited his wife's
serious drinking problem as a factor prompting his withdrawal from public
life. After leaving the Senate, he became the first director of the LeRoy
Collins Center for Public Policy, an affiliate of the University of Florida
at Tallahassee. With a longtime aide, Doug Cook, he began to study small
but effective social programs operating in cities and states around the
country. He also came to know and work with policy makers and political
scientists who were championing the application of fiscally responsible,
market-oriented means to accomplish progressive social ends. He held
the Manning Dauer Eminent Scholar chair at the University of Florida,
teaching an honors class in legislative politics.

Chiles was a late entrant into the 1990 gubernatorial race. Explaining
that his return to politics was sparked by the inspirational and freedom-

Lawton Chiles *(Courtesy of Governor's Office)*

seeking voices of Eastern Europe, especially that of Vaclav Havel, Czechoslovakia's new president, he said that he was spurred by a profound sense that the world had changed while America remained mired in the politics of the past. He declared that, as governor, he hoped to keep Florida from a future of slow bureaucracy and big-money politics.

Chiles' surprise announcement in April 1990 almost immediately turned a lackluster campaign into a high-profile contest, and he instantly became the frontrunner in the race to govern one of the largest, fastest-growing, and most politically influential states in the nation. He introduced broad national themes into the race, including a discussion of whether the political system itself needed significant reform. Limiting campaign contributions to $100 in order to show that "this is an election, not an auction," he attacked the "special interests" that dominate electoral politics and promised to repair the "torn fabric of society."

Succeeding in maintaining his popularity among Democratic party regulars by drawing upon the reserves of goodwill built up during his 30-year career in state politics, he easily won his party's nomination by sweeping Congressman Bill Nelson in the primary. Nelson, who was best known for a 1986 trip into space aboard the shuttle *Columbia,* had sought to frame himself as a candidate of new leadership. An early frontrunner for the nomination, he had hoped to benefit from startling new revelations about Chiles' health leaked to reporters on the very day of his announcement for governor. Having cited "burnout" as one of the reasons for his abrupt retirement from the Senate in 1988, Chiles in the current campaign was forced to acknowledge his continuing use of the antidepressant medication Prozac. In stinging personal attacks dubbed the "politics of sleaze" by many, Nelson questioned Chiles' character, health, and will to govern the state. Chiles responded with TV spots accusing Nelson of below-the-belt tactics that robbed voters of a serious discussion of the issues.

Analysts believe that the Chiles' candidacy will be viewed as a watershed, pushing back the limits of voter tolerance on sensitive issues of psychiatric illness. Although Republican campaign rhetoric alluded to the need for a healthy governor to run the state, Chiles' medical history did not become a significant issue in the fall campaign.

By contrast, it was voter dissatisfaction with the Republican administration of incumbent Governor Bob Martinez, as well as Chiles' own inspirational vision of government, that carried the race. Two issues were at the heart of his campaign: a pledge "to restore faith and trust in state government" and the need to "rightsize" government—to decentralize and "provide more competition" in government services. Little separated Chiles and Martinez on the issues. Both promised tougher measures to combat drugs and crime, and stressed the need to protect the environment, to manage growth, and to improve education. Both refused to rule out a tax increase, all the while remaining opposed to the imposition of a new state income tax. In the end, Chiles' landslide victory was attributable to his enduring personal popularity, to his sterling ethical reputation, and to a personalized campaign reminiscent of his initial 1970 run for the Senate. He spent much of this race talking to people at recycling centers, health clinics, and teenage pregnancy programs, as he waged war against special interests and checkbook campaigning. Perhaps the most enduring image to emerge from the race was the contrast between a $1,500 per person Republican fund-raiser starring former President Ronald Reagan and a $1.50 per person wiener roast for Chiles at an Orlando park. His victory over Martinez was a decisive one, as he garnered 57 percent of the vote.

In office, Chiles has striven to institutionalize the populist ideals of his campaign. He has established "With the People Days" in which he visits communities around the state and also has begun a regular radio program from the governor's mansion in which citizens call in and offer tips and opinions on numerous topics.

His greatest obstacle has been a chronic shortage of funds. After cutting $2 billion from the 1991 budget, he proposed a "Fair Share Tax and Budget Reform" that did advocate higher taxes. Admitting the political risks, he took to the road to sell his constituents on the idea of "investing" in the state's future. Having stated upfront that he would limit his tenure to one term, Chiles feels better able to tackle tough political choices.

He has also set about trying to restore public faith in government by passing one of the country's toughest ethics laws and by sponsoring landmark election reform legislation. Perhaps his biggest victory thus far has been a health care reform bill that will make Florida a testing ground for managed competition, the principle behind President Clinton's proposed national health care plan. Chiles has said that his plan should be a model for the federal government and will help Floridians save money by making health care more affordable. The plan will guarantee "full access to quality, affordable health care for every person in Florida" by the end of 1994.

Despite his earlier proclamations, Chiles has not yet formally announced whether he plans to seek reelection in 1994. One possible Republican challenger has already emerged—Jeb Bush, the son of the former president. A Miami real estate developer, he is well known in the state through directing his father's presidential campaign and from being active in the state Republican party.

Bibliography: Biographical information courtesy of governor's office; *The Chronicle of Higher Education*: 10–31–90; 6–10–92; Robert E. Crew, Jr., "Lawton M. Chiles, Jr.: Reinventing State Government," in Thad Beyle, ed., *Governors and Hard Times* (Washington, D.C.: Congressional Quarterly Press, 1992); Phil Duncan, ed., *Politics in America 1992* (Washington, D.C.: Congressional Quarterly Press, 1991); *The Miami Herald*, 8–13–91; *Newsweek*, 4–30–90; *The New*

York Times: 4–15–90; 4–25–90; 9–2–90; 9–5–90; 10–30–90; 11–7–90; 2–27–91; 8–11–91; 6–29–92; 1–5–93; *The Record* (Bergen County, N.J.), 4–30–93; *The Star-Ledger* (Newark, N.J.): 9–2–90; 9–5–90; 1–29–93; *USA Today*: 9–20–90; 10–1–90; 1–8–91; 1–23–92; 6–22–92; 9–10–92.

Joe Frank Harris *(Courtesy of Governor's Office)*

GEORGIA

JOE FRANK HARRIS, 1983–1991

Born on February 16, 1936, in Bartow County, Georgia, Harris is the son of Franklin Grover Harris and Frances Morrow Harris. A member of the Faith United Methodist church, he married Elizabeth Carlock in 1961. The couple has a son, Joe.

Harris received a B.A. in business administration from the University of Georgia in 1958. Following active duty in the U.S. Army, he opened a concrete products business in Cartersville, Harris Cement Products, Inc., and expanded operations to Bartow and Cobb counties. He also served as president of Harris Georgia Corporation, a diversified industrial development company.

A lifelong Democrat, Harris served 18 years in the Georgia House of Representatives before seeking the governorship in 1982. For the last 8 of those years, he was chairman of the House Appropriations Committee, a position that provided him with an intimate knowledge of the state's budgetary process. He is an acknowledged expert on state revenues and expenditures.

To gain the Democratic gubernatorial nomination in 1982, Harris defeated Savannah area Congressman Bo Ginn in a runoff election, gaining 55 percent of the vote to his opponent's 45 percent. Harris made his strong Christian views on issues and his abstemious personal behavior the centerpiece of his campaign. He pledged early and often that he would impose no new state taxes. Early in the primary race, he was attacked for being dominated by House Speaker Tom Murphy, but after winning the nomination, he was able to secure the selection of a strong Democratic state chairman, former federal Budget Director Bert Lance, thereby demonstrating his own political clout and independence.

The 1982 general election was anticlimactic, due to the continuing weakness of the Republican party in state elections. Harris defeated Republican candidate Robert H. Bell with 63 percent of the vote to his opponent's 37 percent.

Despite a lengthy career in state politics, Harris entered office a largely unknown quantity. Yet he became a popular governor, presiding over a state with rapid economic growth. He crafted an orderly and efficient administration, focusing on the improvement of education and the attraction of new business. As a businessman, he injected a businesslike management style and organizational principles into state government. He created the Economic Development Council of state agency and department heads to coordinate economic development at the state level. He placed special emphasis on minority and small-business development, supported the expansion of existing industry, and encouraged international trade.

So popular did Harris' policies prove that he won the 1986 Democratic gubernatorial nomination with 85 percent of the vote, defeating rival Kenneth B. Quarterman. In the general election, he beat Republican Guy Davis with 71 percent of the vote, carrying every one of the state's 159 counties. Expecting a Democratic sweep, state Republican leaders had earlier toyed with the idea of not even fielding a candidate against the popular incumbent.

During his two terms in office, Harris compiled an impressive record in education, economic development, the environment, and health and human services. In the area of education, his Quality Basic Education Act drew national renown, with its key components: equalizing education funding statewide; specifying new student competencies and accountability measures; offering full-day kindergarten statewide; and targeting students with special needs early in their school career. Harris also presided over the largest sustained library construction program in the country and a $1 billion program for the construction and renovation of public school facilities.

As governor, Harris was a member of the Intergovernmental Advisory Committee on Trade, appointed by U.S. Trade Representative Carla Hills. He worked to promote international investment on 18 trade missions to 20 different countries and created a new Trade Division at the Industry, Trade, and Tourism Department. He also worked to develop the state tourist industry. During his tenure, the state budget grew from $3 billion to almost $8 billion, an increase primarily attributable to economic expansion. His fiscal management brought higher bond ratings for the state, and in 1990, Georgia was named among the top 15 best-managed states in the country by *Financial World Magazine*. Also in 1990, Harris received the American Planning Association's Distinguished Service Award for his precedent-setting Growth Strategies Legislation, which required planning at the local, regional, and state levels to facilitate economic development and environmental protection.

In the area of the environment, Harris backed legislation recommended by his Solid Waste Management Task Force that emphasized recycling, reduction, and new solid waste facilities. He established the Environmental Facilities Authority to provide low-interest loans for local water and sewer expansions and for solid waste disposal sites.

Child abuse, drunk driving, and substance abuse became the focus of Harris' human services efforts. Creating the Commission on Children and Youth in 1987 to provide united advocacy on behalf of children's issues, the Harris administration was responsible for passing one of the most comprehensive child protection packages in the country. He also supported creation of a pioneering Child Welfare Training Academy funded by state and private monies to provide professional training for individuals who work with children. To fight the spiraling drug problem, Harris created the Commission on Drug Awareness and Prevention. In 1990, the commission developed and helped pass legislation hailed nationally as the toughest approach by any state to the issue of drug prevention.

Perceived as a serious and dignified leader, Harris was viewed by political observers as a key example of the need for ideological realignments in southern Democratic politics. As governor, he went to unusual lengths to distance himself from the party's more left-leaning national leaders, refusing, for example, to meet with either Walter Mondale or Geraldine Ferraro when they visited Georgia during the 1984 presidential campaign.

Ineligible to seek a third term in 1990, Harris was succeeded in office by Democrat Zell Miller.

Bibliography: Michael Barone et al., *The Almanac of American Politics, 1984, 1986, 1988* (Washington, D.C.: National Journal, 1983, 1985, 1987); biographical information courtesy of governor's office; *The Chronicle of Higher Education,* 11–12–86; *The New York Times*: 6–25–85; 11–7–90.

Zell Bryan Miller *(Courtesy of Governor's Office)*

ZELL BRYAN MILLER, 1991–

Born on February 24, 1932, in Young Harris, Towns County, Georgia, Miller is the son of Stephen Grady Miller and Birdie Bryan Miller, both teachers. His parents' example is said to have inspired Miller's keen interest in education, which has become a hallmark of his administration.

A Methodist, Miller is married to the former Shirley Ann Carver of Andrews, North Carolina. They have two sons.

Miller was educated in the public schools of Towns County and at Young Harris Junior College, from which he graduated in 1951. He later earned bachelor's and master's degrees from the University of Georgia and completed two years of work on a doctoral degree.

An educator and historian, Miller has taught at Young Harris College, the University of Georgia, DeKalb Community College, and Emory University. He is the author of three books about the culture and history of Georgia: *The Mountains Within Me* (1976), a memoir of his childhood; *Great Georgians* (1983), a book profiling the state's most notable historical figures; and *They Heard Georgia Singing* (1984), biographical sketches of the state's greatest musicians.

After a stint in the Marine Corps, 1953–1956, Miller was elected mayor of Young Harris. A Democrat, he was elected to the Georgia State Senate in 1960. He served as an executive assistant to Governor Lester Maddox from 1967 to 1970 and in 1972 was named executive director of the state Democratic party by then-Governor Jimmy Carter. In 1974, he was elected lieutenant governor, a post he held for 16 years—longer than anyone in state history. In 1984, he chaired the National Conference of Lieutenant Governors.

Miller used the lieutenant governorship as a springboard to the state-house. The gubernatorial race of 1990 was wide open due to the lame–duck status of incumbent Joe Frank Harris, constitutionally ineligible to seek a third term. The Democratic primary drew national attention owing to the presence of Andrew Young, former mayor of Atlanta and longtime civil rights leader. Political analysts believed that Young stood a serious chance of becoming the country's second black governor, thereby attracting heavy media interest in a race that might otherwise concern only Georgians.

Miller led a five–man field in the July 1990 Democratic primary, raising a record $3.9 million and outspending all other candidates. A moderate, he campaigned vigorously for a statewide lottery and did much better than expected by making it the linchpin of his campaign. He also ran on a law and order platform, proposing boot camps for drug offenders. Lining up endorsements from local sheriffs to bolster his law and order image, he attacked Young's record as mayor of Atlanta, citing its crime rate, the nation's highest. Young, in turn, attacked Miller's record as lieutenant governor, deriding the fact that in 16 years in office he couldn't get his lottery proposal passed through the legislature.

Despite Young's presence in the race, the primary was free of racial references or personal attacks. Analysts considered it to be the cleanest state Democratic primary ever, with no negative TV ads and candidates sticking mostly to the issues.

By Georgia law, Miller's 41 percent victory margin in the primary was not enough to secure the party nomination. The runoff election between Miller and Young, as mandated by state law when no candidate receives 51 percent of the vote total, drew an interesting legal challenge from state Representative Tyrone Brooks and the American Civil Liberties Union. Brooks contended that the runoff provision discriminated against black voters and black candidates, favoring white candidates because in a runoff they are more likely to attract supporters of their former white opponents.

Despite the challenge, the August 7 runoff went off as scheduled. Although Young was the first black candidate to make a gubernatorial runoff in Georgia, analysts predicted he would need a political miracle to win the party nomination. True to these predictions, Miller drew 65 percent of the runoff vote.

In the general election, Miller faced Johnny Isakson, a state representative and real estate executive, who was widely expected to mount the most serious Republican challenge for the Georgia governorship in the 20th century. Miller, however, benefited from a sizable early lead in the polls and from a state political tradition that places Georgia as the most solidly Democratic state in the South. A relatively strong state economy and the psychological boost of Atlanta's snaring the 1996 Summer Olympics caused analysts to question whether the voter discontent prevalent elsewhere would be a serious factor in the race. Nonetheless, Isakson tried to capitalize on this mood, arguing that Georgia couldn't afford the "same old ways" anymore. He attacked Miller's somewhat shopworn image and criticized him as being part of the state's "good old boy" network. He also drew attention to the ideological twists in Miller's career, reminding voters that he had been tagged with the derisive label of "Zig Zag Zell" in an unsuccessful race for the U.S. Senate in 1980.

These tactics backfired, however. Isakson's low-key demeanor, tenure in the state legislature, and career in real estate did not provide much grist for the mill of a populist, throw-the-bums-out campaign. Miller won comfortably, although Isakson's 45 percent vote tally was the strongest gubernatorial showing in years for a Republican.

A commitment to educational reform has been the hallmark of Miller's administration. His 1990 campaign promise to improve education at all levels was inspired by a report produced by Illinois State University researchers showing that Georgia was 1 of 13 states in which financial support for higher education had dropped in the 1980s. Miller was so angered by the report that he made a special appearance before the Georgia Board of Regents to declare that it was time for the state to reinvest in higher education. He then promised to embark on a campaign to obtain more funds for facilities and salary increases for faculty.

Other educational reforms have included passage of a constitutional amendment authorizing the establishment of a state lottery, the proceeds of which are to be dedicated to programs such as early childhood education, a personal interest of the governor's. Miller pioneered Georgia's first statewide kindergarten program and has made adult literacy programs a priority in his administration. His wife, First Lady Shirley Miller, has become Georgia's chief spokesperson for literacy initiatives. The governor has also been a strong supporter of historically black colleges.

As the recession of the early 1990s unfolded, Miller joined the governors of other states in imposing stringent cost-cutting measures, including a controversial state employee furlough program that required 100,000 state workers to take off one day a month without pay. Imposed as part of his solution to pare a budget deficit approaching $600 million, a Georgia Superior Court judge later ruled that Miller had usurped the legislature's power and had no authority to issue the decree.

Despite this setback, analysts agree that Miller has emerged as one of the South's most progressive state leaders. In a significant break with his predecessors as well as several other southern governors, Miller supported—without success—legislation to eliminate the Confederate battle symbol from the official state flag. The flag had flown as a defiant symbol of the segregationist South since 1956, when the Georgia legislature voted to adopt it in protest against the tide of civil rights changes that were starting to engulf the nation. Since 1987 the National Association for the Advancement of Colored People (NAACP) has attempted to change the symbols of Georgia as well as those of three other southern states. Miller's support, in the opinion of political observers, was an "amazing development" and marked the first time that a southern governor had taken up the cause. In a similar vein, Miller also agreed to appoint at least 25 black judges by 1995 and to adopt a new judicial tenure system, both moves intended to settle federal racial bias lawsuits.

As a sign of his rising prominence within the national Democratic party, Miller was chosen to give one of three keynote addresses at the 1992 Democratic National Convention. The choice was not accidental. Miller had endeared himself to fellow governor, Democratic nominee Bill Clinton by advancing the date of Georgia's presidential primary in March 1992 so as to give Clinton an important show of strength and strong momentum for the Super Tuesday southern primaries that followed.

Miller has also drawn high marks for his ability to advance his legislative agenda. In 1992 the trade magazine *City and State* named the governor as one of the nation's six most valuable public officials. Although Miller had earlier indicated that he intended to be a one–term governor, he has announced his intention to seek reelection in the wake of the successes of his first term.

Bibliography: Biographical information courtesy of governor's office; *The Chronicle of Higher Education*: 8–7–91; 11–20–91; 4–1–92; 9–30–92; 12–16–92; Phil Duncan, ed., *Politics in America 1992* (Washington, D.C.: Congressional Quarterly Press, 1991); *The New York Times*: 1–14–90; 7–8–90; 7–16–90; 11–3–90; 11–8–90; 11–11–90; 7–18–91; 5–29–92; 3–10–93; *The Star-Ledger* (Newark, N.J.), 9–23–92; *USA Today*: 7–12–90; 7–18–90; 7–19– 90; 8–8–90; 7–11–91; 6–19–92; 6–26–92; 7–13–92; 2–26–93; 6–17– 93.

HAWAII

JOHN WAIHEE, 1986–

Born in the small plantation town of Honokaa on the island of Hawaii on May 19, 1946, Waihee is Hawaii's fourth elected governor and the first of native Hawaiian ancestry. He and his wife, the former Lynne Kobashigawa, have two children.

Waihee holds a bachelor's degree in history and business from Andrews University in Michigan. He has also done graduate work at Central Michigan University. He was a member of the first graduating class from the William S. Richardson School of Law, University of Hawaii, 1976.

After graduating from law school, Waihee became an associate with the distinguished Honolulu law firm of Shim, Seigle, Tam, and Naito. Subsequently, he assumed a career in private practice. He has also served as an administrator of community education programs in Michigan and in the Honolulu Model Cities Program, as well as program manager in the Honolulu Office of Human Resources.

His political career began with his election to the 1978 State Constitutional Convention. Serving as majority leader of the convention, he played a key role in its deliberations, helping to draft such essential components of the new document as the water code, the section on preservation of agricultural lands, the establishment of the Office of Hawaiian Affairs, and the provisions of autonomy for the University of Hawaii. Two years later, he was elected to the state house of representatives, in which he served on the Policy, Judiciary, Consumer Protection, and Commerce committees.

In 1982, he ran successfully for lieutenant governor, serving during the third and final term of Democrat George Ariyoshi's administration. During Waihee's term as lieutenant governor, he was involved in a number of complex issues, including a major airline dispute that threatened the Hawaiian economy, development issues on Molokai, the settlement of long-standing liquor tax disputes, and tort reform.

In 1986, with Ariyoshi's retirement, the governor's race was wide open. Since the Democratic party had controlled Hawaiian government since statehood, the September 20, 1986, Democratic primary was widely regarded as one of the most pivotal in Hawaii's 27 years of statehood, with

John Waihee (*Courtesy of Governor's Office*)

seven candidates seeking the party's nomination. Waihee ran as a protégé of outgoing Governor Ariyoshi and as a member of that faction of the Democratic party that has controlled Hawaii since 1962. By 1986, however, there were signs that the electorate had grown increasingly dissatisfied with these so-called Burns-Ariyoshi Democrats, who had come under criticism for purportedly allowing business people with ties to the statehouse to profit excessively from land development. Waihee, who tried to distance himself from organization Democrats by arguing he was very much his own man, was an underdog in the primary. The favorite was Congressman Cecil Heftel, a broadcasting millionaire free of ties to the governor's office. Heftel outspent Waihee by a 4–1 margin. The third major Democrat in the race was Honolulu City Council member Patsy Mink, a former six-term congresswoman and once the best-known Hawaiian politician outside the state. Waihee's 46 percent to 36 percent victory over Heftel (with Mink garnering 16 percent of the vote and minor candidates splitting the remaining 2 percent) was widely regarded as an upset, attributed by some political observers to an unfortunate "smear" campaign launched against Heftel in the last days preceding the election. Although Waihee had no part in the negative advertising blitz—launched by public employee unions and Republicans who hoped to remove the strongest Democratic candidate from contention—he was its direct beneficiary.

In the general election, Waihee opposed D. G. Anderson, a wealthy businessman and former managing director of Honolulu, who won the Republican nomination against token opposition. The Republicans argued that voters wanted change after three decades of Democratic dominance. Waihee countered by repeatedly denying that he was part of any Ariyoshi machine. Calling the politicians who had run Hawaii since statehood "the first wave," he pledged to name his own top appointees and painted his administration as "a new beginning for Hawaii." Despite his emphasis on the new, however, Waihee did enjoy the unofficial support of the Ariyoshi forces as well as the financial backing of many of the state's builders, architects, and developers, who favored the continuation of intensive development in the state. Waihee won the governorship with 52 percent of the vote.

In 1990, Waihee easily won renomination for a second term, coasting past three little-known opponents in the Democratic primary and garnering 88 percent of the vote. In seeking a second term, he faced Republican state Representative Fred Hemmings, a businessman and former world champion surfer. Waihee won an easy victory with 61 percent of the vote, the greatest majority of any gubernatorial candidate since statehood. His party also retained a substantial majority in the legislature.

Concern for education, housing, economic development, and environmental protection has marked Waihee's years in office. He has been a strong supporter of the University of Hawaii's science programs and supported the founding of the university's School of Ocean and Earth Science and Technology. Supportive of efforts to attract more minority and disadvantaged students to university education, he began a tax-exempt bond program to help families save for higher education. In the area of primary and secondary education, he has embraced school/community-based management to provide for local educational decision making and proposed a seven-year, $800 million superfund for construction of new school facilities.

Waihee's interest in affordable housing has drawn praise from the American Planning Association (APA). A comprehensive package proposed to the legislature in 1988 called for the production of thousands of affordable housing units through a new public-private partnership, a program hailed by the APA as "one of the strongest and most fascinating" of its kind.

Waihee has also worked steadily to improve Hawaii's business climate. Early in his tenure, he won legislative approval for a sweeping reform of the state's tax structure, aiming both to make it less regressive and to stimulate business. Tax relief has been a high priority.

Honored by the environmental organization Earthtrust, Waihee created a $40 million land-banking fund to protect public lands and signed into law a wastewater superfund. He has also strengthened funding of the state's natural area reserves, working to protect endangered species and their habitats.

As a member of the National Governors Association Human Resources Committee, Waihee has demonstrated a keen interest in job placement and training programs. Arguing that child care is essential for public assistance recipients to break out of the cycle of dependency, he has seen welfare caseloads drop statewide in response to efforts he has pioneered.

One serious problem for Waihee surfaced after a devastating hurricane ravaged the island of Kauai in September 1992. A dramatic drop-off in tourist revenues posed a challenge for Waihee as he strove to build upon and expand his progressive record.

Bibliography: Michael Barone et al., *The Almanac of American Politics, 1988* (Washington, D.C.: National Journal, 1987); biographical information courtesy of governor's office; *The Chronicle of Higher Education*: 11–12–86; 2–18–87; 10–31–90; 8–28–91; *The New York Times*: 9–20–86; 9–22–86; 9–24–90; 11–8–90; *The Star-Ledger* (Newark, N.J.), 8–25–91; *USA Today,* 9–24–90.

IDAHO

CECIL D. ANDRUS, 1971–1977, 1987–

Born in Hood River, Oregon, on August 25, 1931, Andrus is the son of Hal S. Andrus and Dorothy Johnson Andrus. A Lutheran, Andrus married Carol M. May in 1949. The couple has three daughters.

Andrus attended Oregon State University and served in the U.S. Navy during the Korean War. First elected to the Idaho State Senate at the age of 29, he served there with distinction from 1961 to 1966, and again from 1968 to 1970. As a legislator, he quickly established a reputation as a forceful advocate for education, the environment, and economic development.

After an unsuccessful race for the governorship in 1966, he came back to win that office for the Democrats in the elections of 1970 and 1974. As governor he championed the causes of improved funding for education, the creation of kindergartens, the establishment of child development centers, and the support of programs to assist the elderly. He twice led the effort to reduce property taxes and pushed the "circuit breaker" property tax relief program for senior citizens. Andrus also spearheaded the drive to reorganize state government and was personally involved in the effort to bring new industry and jobs to Idaho. A member of the Executive Committee of the National Governors Association from 1971 to 1972, he chaired the NGA in 1976. From 1971 to 1972, he was also chairman of the Federation of Rocky Mountain States.

On January 24, 1977, Andrus resigned from the governorship to become the first Idahoan ever to serve in a presidential cabinet. Named secretary of the interior by President Jimmy Carter, he strove for a sense of balance in the development and protection of the nation's resources. During his four-year tenure as interior secretary, his leadership was decisive in resolving the bitter Alaska lands dispute. That settlement protected 103 million acres of virgin public land for parks, wildlife habitat, and forest land, as well as opening up more than 250 million acres of federal land for development. Owing to the strength of his record, Andrus is generally regarded to have been the strongest proponent of wilderness preservation to have served in the Interior Department since the legendary Harold Ickes, Cabinet secretary under Franklin Roosevelt, 1933–46.

Cecil D. Andrus *(Courtesy of Governor's Office)*

With the end of the Carter administration in January 1981, Andrus returned to Idaho to establish his own successful natural resources consulting firm. Remaining widely popular, he challenged Republican Lieutenant Governor David Leroy for the governorship in 1986. Characterizing himself as a problem solver and pledging to turn around the state's ailing economy, he won a narrow victory, garnering 50 percent of the vote to his opponent's 49 percent, a margin of just 3,500 votes. Andrus was able to carry heavily the northern panhandle of the state, hurt by layoffs in the mining and timber industries.

Reelected in 1990 with 68 percent of the vote against Republican Roger Fairchild, former majority leader of the state senate, Andrus made history by becoming the first person in Idaho ever to be elected governor four different times. He is now among the senior governors in the United States in length of service.

Several concerns have predominated during Andrus' years in office: environmental protection, child care, education, reform of nuclear waste disposal, and fiscal responsibility. As a sawmill operator's son, he is emotionally attached to the great natural beauty of the Pacific Northwest. His policy-making efforts have striven to balance the competing tensions between conservation and development. He has championed local land-use planning laws and the protection of wild and scenic rivers. Most recently, he has helped to engineer a comprehensive agreement between industry and conservation groups to ensure the protection of Idaho's water quality.

Avowing a commitment to quality of life issues, Andrus has declared the 1990s as the "Decade of the Child." He has championed the development of day care centers, led the fight to enact tougher laws aimed at preventing child abuse, and expanded the availability of prenatal care for expectant mothers. Other achievements include enactment of a state holiday honoring Dr. Martin Luther King, Jr., adoption of ethics in government legislation, and the expansion of services for the elderly and disabled.

Andrus has drawn national attention for his efforts in the area of nuclear waste disposal. In a celebrated showdown with the national government, he took decisive action in October 1988 to close Idaho's borders to nuclear waste destined for storage in Idaho. He has also tried to force Washington to come to terms with the intractable problem of nuclear waste disposal. He has called upon the Energy Department to commit itself to an extensive program of digging up, repackaging, and removing chemical and radioactive wastes that are improperly buried and threatening the Snake River aquifer beneath the Idaho National Engineering Laboratory.

Idaho is also unique among states in the economically troubled 1990s for being one of the few to boast a budget surplus. Having a $30 million surplus and a $36 million rainy day reserve fund, Idaho under Andrus has been a model of budgetary restraint and discipline. Central to its fiscal success, according to analysts, has been the state's policy of spending surplus on onetime only expenses—such as equipping classrooms with computers—rather than on ongoing programs.

Despite all the above, however, one key issue catapulted Andrus to national attention in 1990: the national acrimony over abortion rights. Heavily Mormon and religiously conservative, Idaho became a battleground for the new politics of abortion unfolding that year, when the Republican-dominated legislature passed the country's strictest abortion law and presented it to Andrus for approval. Although an ardent foe of abortion since the earliest days of his political career, Andrus wrestled with his conscience and his constituency. The law, drafted outside the state by the National Right to Life Committee, would have outlawed all abortion except in extreme cases: if the pregnancy resulted from rape and was reported within seven days; if the pregnancy resulted from incest and the victim was under 18; if a severe fetal deformity was present; or if the pregnancy posed a threat to the life or physical health of the mother. In what he termed an "agonizing" decision, and after a week of intense lobbying and threats to the economy of his state, Andrus broke ranks with some of his supporters and vetoed the bill. Forced to defend his actions, he presented the decision not as a change of opinion but as a reaction to what he called the objectionable and overly restrictive provisions of the bill. While abortion foes responded by threatening to work for his political defeat, others hailed him as a "man of enormous integrity" and presented him as an independent westerner strong enough to resist pressures from the outside. The brouhaha over the legislation placed Idaho in the vortex of the rising national storm over abortion, as supporters of abortion rights threatened to boycott potatoes—Idaho's number-one crop—if the measure became law. Right-to-lifers launched an equally unorthodox countercampaign, taking as their battle cry: "If you love life, eat Idaho potatoes."

For Andrus' supporters, the episode served to heighten the governor's reputation. They were quick to point out that he had fought similar battles with the gun lobby, who felt that his own personal interests in fishing and hunting would color his political views. Here, too, they were wrong, as he has tangled with supporters of gun rights. The independent-minded Andrus has called the National Rifle Association "the gun nuts of the world" for opposing legislation that would have outlawed armor-piercing bullets.

For now, political observers consider such integrity and independence to be Andrus' strongest attribute and the hallmark of his administration.

Bibliography: Michael Barone et al., *The Almanac of American Politics, 1988* (Washington, D.C.: National Journal, 1987); biographical information courtesy of governor's office; *The Chronicle of Higher Education:* 11–12–86; 2–18–87; *Newsweek,* 4–9–90; *The New York Times:* 1–6–87; 10–21–88; 12–17–88; 3–23–90; 3–30–90; 3–31–90; 4–2–90; 5–24–90; 2–8–91.

ILLINOIS

JAMES R. THOMPSON, 1977–1991

Born in Chicago, Illinois, on May 8, 1936, Thompson is the son of James Robert Thompson, a Chicago pathologist, and Agnes Swanson Thompson of De Kalb, Illinois. A Presbyterian, he married Jayne Ann Carr of Oak Park, Illinois, on June 19, 1976. Mrs. Thompson, an attorney, was formerly deputy chief of the Criminal Division, Illinois Attorney General's Office, and was employed by the Mid-America Committee of Chicago as executive vice-president and president of the committee's foundation from November 1985 until December 1986. The couple has one daughter, Samantha Jayne.

After attending local grammar and secondary schools, Thompson enrolled in 1953 at the University of Illinois, Navy Pier, Chicago. Two years later, he resided temporarily with his family in St. Louis and attended Washington University. Without receiving his undergraduate degree, Thompson entered Northwestern University Law School in 1956. He served as student editor-in-chief of the *Journal of Criminal Law, Criminology, and Political Science* and received a law degree in 1959. After his admission to the Illinois bar, he served from 1959 to 1964 as assistant state's attorney for Cook County under Republican Benjamin Adamowski and, following the 1960 election, the Democrat Daniel Ward. Thompson argued more than 200 cases before the Illinois Supreme Court and took the lead in prosecuting pornography cases. In 1964, he presented the state's arguments before the U.S. Supreme Court in the case of *Escobedo v. Illinois*. By a 5–4 vote, the Court ruled in favor of Escobedo, thereby broadening the concept of the civil rights of suspects during police interrogations.

Thompson returned to Northwestern University as an assistant professor of law in 1964. He coauthored three criminal casebooks with his former mentor, Fred Inbau, and was promoted to associate professor. While at Northwestern, Thompson in 1966 joined Inbau and former Chicago Police Superintendent O. W. Wilson in founding Americans for Effective Law Enforcement (AELE). Thompson served as vice-president of this organization, which has often acted as amicus curiae for police and prosecutors. He was a member of the committee that revised the

James R. Thompson *(Courtesy of Governor's Office)*

Illinois criminal code from 1959 to 1963 and of a presidential task force on crime in 1967.

Thompson left Northwestern in 1969 to accept a post under William J. Scott as assistant state attorney general for Illinois. The following year he was named chief of the Department of Law Enforcement and Public Protection, and soon thereafter he became assistant U.S. attorney for the Northern District of Illinois. In November 1971, Thompson was appointed U.S. attorney, and during his almost four years in that office he earned a reputation as a prosecutor of corrupt public officials. Under his leadership, some 300 individuals were convicted of various charges of professional misconduct. The most spectacular of these convictions was that of Otto Kerner, a federal appeals court judge convicted of accepting a bribe when he was governor of Illinois.

Thompson received the Republican nomination for governor in 1976 and easily defeated his Democratic opponent—Michael J. Howlett—by a vote of 3,000,395 to 1,610,258. His margin of victory was the largest in Illinois history. During his unique two-year first term, Thompson was instrumental in securing passage of a "Class X" crime law. This provided a mandatory six-year minimum sentence for those convicted of specified violent crimes.

In 1978, Illinois began holding gubernatorial elections in nonpresidential years. Seeking reelection, Thompson defeated Michael Bakalis by a vote of 1,859,684 to 1,263,134. The nearly 600,000 vote margin was a record for an incumbent chief executive in Illinois. During his second term Thompson continued to balance the state budget, despite having no general tax increases with which to work.

In 1982, Thompson faced a fierce challenge from Democrat Adlai Stevenson III in his bid for a third term. Stevenson, the scion of one of Illinois' leading political families, was a formidable opponent. His father had been the Democratic candidate for president in 1952 and 1956, and he himself had been elected to the U.S. Senate in 1970 to serve the unexpired term of Everett McKinley Dirksen. This time around, Thompson's margin of victory—5,074 votes—was the smallest in state history (1,816,101 to 1,811,027). The outcome was not officially recognized until the Illinois Supreme Court ruled against Stevenson's request for a statewide recount. During the campaign, Thompson had presented himself as a "can-do" official, citing his popular $2.2 billion public works program and his role in persuading a Mitsubishi-Chrysler joint venture to build an automobile manufacturing plant in Bloomington.

In 1986, voters saw a rematch of Thompson's tough struggle with Stevenson. Political observers felt Thompson was vulnerable after ten years in office, especially because the state's manufacturing base had been hit hard by imports. Stevenson was preparing to hammer away at Thompson for huge cost overruns on the State of Illinois Center in Chicago. He also accused him of "wheeling and dealing" and of failing to arrest the state's economic decline by buttressing dying industries rather than nurturing new ones. Thompson was prepared to counter by discussing how he brought business and labor together to agree on tax reform; how he got striking Chicago teachers and the board of education together to reach a contract; and how he froze spending, built new prisons, and set up an in-home care program for the elderly.

In the face of such planning, however, an upset in the March 1986 Democratic primary quickly altered the nature of the campaign and elevated it to one of historic dimensions. Stevenson's campaign stumbled badly when two followers of extremist Lyndon H. La Rouche, Jr., the conspiracy theorist, upset Stevenson's running mates for lieutenant governor and secretary of state. Rather than run with people whose philosophy he denounced, Stevenson refused the nomination of the Democratic party and collected nominating petitions to run instead as the head of a new party, Illinois Solidarity. Never before had anyone in Illinois history sought the fourth term Thompson was after, and never before had the Democratic party not had an official candidate for governor.

Stevenson tried to turn the campaign into a referendum on Thompson's three terms as governor. He hammered away at the incumbent over tax increases, soaring utility bills, the loss of one-quarter of the state's manufacturing jobs, and state contracts awarded to friends of the governor. Thompson attacked his challenger for spending more time criticizing him than with presenting his own vision for the state. Throughout the campaign, he often asked how Stevenson could be expected to run the state when he could not even run a winning primary campaign for his running mates. Thompson won his unprecedented fourth term by a margin of 399,220 votes. In the 1986 campaign, he was the first Republican ever endorsed for governor by the Illinois AFL-CIO. With his victory, Thompson became the nation's senior governor in continuous service.

Political observers viewed Thompson as the last big state governor in the liberal Republican tradition of Thomas E. Dewey and Nelson Rockefeller. Governing by accommodating the major interests in the state, he managed to maintain effective working relations with many sectors of Illinois society and politics, including Democrats in state government who were hard hit by the criminal prosecutions he led in the early 1970s. His administration was stamped by tough criminal justice measures, conservative fiscal policies, and substantial doses of social spending.

During his fourth term in office, Thompson played a key role in the passage of landmark school reform, landed the much-sought-after Japanese Diamond Star assembly plant, and won passage of a temporary income tax for education. Other priorities included developing new uses for surplus agricultural products, major changes in state taxes, and welfare reform. He continued to support increases in state spending for higher education. In a controversial 1987 decision, he vetoed a bill that would have ended teenagers' access to contraceptives at public school health clinics. The legislature had approved the contraceptive ban under intense lobbying from antiabortion groups, the Roman Catholic church, and the conservative Eagle Forum. In 1989, he headed a National Governors Association study group that concluded the nation needed to increase its spending on public works programs and capital investment in its infrastructure.

Thompson's unparalleled political achievements fueled much speculation about his future. Although in March 1987 he formally took himself out of the running for the 1988 Republican presidential nomination, his name surfaced as a possible running mate for George Bush. Political analysts believed that Thompson could potentially help Bush in areas where he was politically weak, such as the agricultural and industrial centers of the Midwest. Others speculated that he would be named attorney general or a Supreme Court justice in the Bush administration.

In light of such consistent and optimistic speculation about his future, Thompson shocked political observers with his unexpected announcement in the summer of 1989 that he had ruled out seeking a fifth term as governor. Basing his decision totally on personal matters, he recalled that he had moved his family out of the governor's mansion in 1983 to give them a normal life, and he explained that his decision ruling out an unprecedented fifth term was being made in the same spirit. Over the course of the previous year, his family had been under serious personal strain with his wife hospitalized and needing treatment for alcoholism. At times near tears as he made the announcement, Thompson admitted that he would not rule out seeking another elective office someday and explained that he might consider appointment to a federal position. Remorsefully, he recognized that with this decision, his lifelong goal of being president would never come to pass.

Often called the last of the liberal Republican governors, Thompson had been a commanding figure in the national Republican party. In the wake of defeats suffered by the Republicans in the 1989 gubernatorial races in New Jersey and Virginia, where abortion was a key issue, Thompson challenged his party to reconsider its rigid opposition to almost all legal abortions. As governor, he regularly backed tax increases to increase state revenue and supported state spending on education and other social welfare programs.

Thompson's retirement marked the end of an era in Illinois politics, so completely had he dominated the state both as politician and as campaigner. His decision to retire offered fresh hope not only to Illinois Democrats long chafing under his rule but also to conservative Republicans who, too, had bristled under his longtime domination of state politics.

Bibliography: Michael Barone et al., *The Almanac of American Politics, 1988* (Washington, D.C.: National Journal, 1987); biographical information courtesy of governor's office; *The Chronicle of Higher Education,* 11–12–86; *The New York Times*: 8–20–85; 9–12–86; 9–19–86; 11–5–86; 1–11–87; 7–14–89; 7–30–89; 11–14–89; 3–12–90; *USA Today*: 6–7–88; 7–14–89.

JIM EDGAR, 1991–

Born in Vinita, Oklahoma, on July 22, 1946, Edgar grew up in Charleston, Illinois. He and his wife, the former Brenda Smith of Anna, Illinois, have two children.

After his graduation from Eastern Illinois University in 1968, Edgar became a legislative staff intern in Springfield, where he was a close associate of progressive state Senator W. Russell Arrington. An unsuccessful candidate for the state house of representatives in 1974, he was ultimately elected in 1976 and reelected in 1978.

A Republican, Edgar became Governor Jim Thompson's director of Legislative Relations in 1979. Upon Secretary of State Alan Dixon's election to the U.S. Senate in 1980, Governor Thompson appointed Edgar to fill the vacancy. Winning his own term as secretary of state in 1982, he was reelected in 1986 by the largest plurality of any statewide candidate in Illinois history. As secretary of state, he was successful in getting a mandatory auto insurance law through the general assembly, an effort that had been unsuccessful for the past 17 years. He also led a drunk driving crackdown that earned national recognition.

Other achievements of Edgar's tenure as secretary of state included the creation of an adult literacy program that became a national model, and a focus on library construction and the strengthening of library access for the disabled. He also brought license plate production back to the state, creating additional jobs for the disabled. Edgar's accomplishments received national attention. In May 1986, *U.S. News & World Report* named him one of 30 "rising stars of American politics." He served as president of the National Association of Secretaries of State and was elected vice-president of the Council of State Governments.

In 1989, Governor Jim Thompson's decision not to seek reelection after four terms in the statehouse threw the 1990 gubernatorial race wide open. As his longtime protégé, Edgar was Thompson's first choice as a successor. The two shared the same moderate to progressive political values that have been the hallmark of other successful Republican candidates in the state, including former Governor Richard Ogilvie and former U.S. Senator Charles Percy. All these winning Republicans benefited from an ability to appeal to Democrats.

Edgar won the Republican gubernatorial nomination by a 2–1 margin, defeating Steve Baer, a former executive director of the conservative United Republican Fund. Baer directed his campaign to groups that oppose abortion and higher taxes.

Jim Edgar *(Courtesy of Governor's Office)*

In the general election, Edgar faced Democrat Neil F. Hartigan, state attorney general, who had also served two terms as lieutenant governor. The race featured a curious reversal in stereotypical party lines: an antitax Democrat versus a prochoice Republican who pledged more money for schools and promised to make a temporary 20 percent state income tax increase permanent. The race was also complicated by the presence of the Harold Washington party, which ran a slate of all black candidates in Cook County. Democrats feared that this might siphon black votes away from their traditional Democratic base. Another big question in the race was whether Edgar could draw away enough liberal votes from traditional Democrats or whether the antitax Hartigan would attract conservatives who deserted Edgar.

Although tax and fiscal matters received the most attention in the campaign, Edgar cited educational improvement as his top priority. Insisting that the tax increase was necessary to support education, he made a cap on property tax increases a major part of his fiscal program.

Edgar eked out a narrow victory in the race, winning by 83,909 votes out of 3,420,720 votes cast. His victory margin was 50.7 percent, with a strong showing among independents deemed critical to his win. Edgar's victory marked the first time in 62 years that one governor succeeded another of the same party.

Edgar has brought a new style and tone to the governor's office. Understandably unable to dominate state politics as did his towering and long–serving predecessor, Edgar is seen as a competent, no–nonsense administrator who knows state government. He is not "flashy," nor does he have the national ambitions nor receive the national attention that Thompson did. Downsizing and streamlining the state government has been a top objective. He is fond of saying that "we can't be all things to all people anymore." While making cuts in many areas, including a state welfare program known as general assistance, he has fought successfully to protect funding for education, his self-proclaimed top priority. Early childhood education has been the special focus of his efforts. He has also increased funding for child abuse programs.

In 1992, Edgar signed one of the nation's strictest antistalking bills, making it a felony to harass or repeatedly follow people and barring the release of suspects without bond. Another problematic issue faced by the governor is the call for casino gambling in Chicago, a move supported by city officials. Edgar, who had campaigned for his job on an antigambling plank, insists that the proposed $2 billion casino and entertainment complex would cut into revenues from the state lottery and horseracing operations and spur an increase in crime. The project bears close watching.

Edgar presently serves as chair of the Education Commission of the States and as president of the board of the Council of State Governments.

Bibliography: Biographical information courtesy of governor's office; *The Chronicle of Higher Education,* 8–26–92; Phil Duncan, ed., *Politics in America*

1992 (Washington, D.C.: Congressional Quarterly Press, 1991); Samuel K. Gove, "Jim Edgar, the New Governor for the Old Party," in Thad Beyle, ed., *Governors and Hard Times* (Washington, D.C.: Congressional Quarterly Press, 1992); *Newsweek,* 9–11–89; *The New York Times*: 3–12–90; 11–5–90; 11–6–90; 11–7–90; 11–8–90; 11–11–90; 4–7–91; 4–22–92; 7–28–92; *USA Today*: 3–22–90; 6–1–90; 11–8–90; 7–11–91; 9–10–91; 1–23–92; 7–13–92; 11–17–92; *U.S. News & World Report*, 5–26–86.

INDIANA

ROBERT D. ORR, 1981–1989

Born in Ann Arbor, Michigan, on November 17, 1917, Orr is the son of Samuel Lowry Orr, an industrialist, and Louise Dunkerson Orr. The Orr family has resided in Indiana since 1835 when Samuel Orr, a Scots-Irish immigrant to the United States in 1833, moved to Evansville to establish a mercantile and iron manufacturing business in that Ohio River town. The Orr Iron Company in Evansville continued to be operated by the family until 1974, when it was acquired by the Shelby Steel Company.

Robert Orr grew up in Evansville, attending school there and at the Hotchkiss School in Connecticut, from which he graduated in 1936. His education also included occasional trips abroad, one of which (in 1935) was delightfully described in James L. Clifford's book *From Puzzles to Portraits: Problems of a Literary Biographer* (1970). In 1940, Orr received a B.A. in history from Yale University; he then attended the Harvard University Graduate School of Business Administration. Following America's entry into World War II, Orr enlisted in the U.S. Army, attending Officers Candidate School and subsequently serving on the quartermaster general's staff in the Pacific. He left the service in 1946 as a major and with a Legion of Merit decoration. In 1944, Orr married Joanne Wallace of Springfield, Massachusetts, who had also served in the military during World War II as a Ferry Command pilot with the Women's Air Force Service Pilots. The Orrs have three children.

Following military service, the Orrs took up residence in Evansville and joined in the management of the Orr Iron Company. During the next few years, Robert Orr became active in a number of other businesses in the Evansville community, specializing in the economic development of the region by buying vacant factories, refurbishing them, and finding new owners and industrial uses for the plants. Orr was also chairman of the board of Indian Industries, a manufacturer of recreational products, and a member of the board of several other companies, including Hahn, Sign Crafters, Erie Investments, Sterling Brewers, Evansville Metal Products, and Product Analysis and Research Industries, all of Evansville, and Dixson, Inc., of Grand Junction, Colorado. He played an important role in local civic affairs, serving as deacon and elder in the First Presbyterian

Robert D. Orr *(Courtesy of Governor's Office)*

church of Evansville. He was also a member of the Rotary Club, active in the Evansville YMCA, a director of the Willard Library, vice-president of Evansville's Future, Inc., and president of the Buffalo Trace Council of the Boy Scouts of America. Subsequently, he served as a director of the Indiana Manufacturers Association for eight years and as a trustee of Hanover College. In 1953, when named the Jaycees' Young Man of the Year and given its Distinguished Service Award, he was an officer in 13 service organizations and a director of 12 companies.

Orr, a Republican, began his political career in a modest way, serving first as a member and then chairman of the Center Township Advisory Board in Vanderburgh County (1950–1954) and then as Republican precinct committeeman from 1954 to 1962. From 1958 to 1960, he was treasurer of the Eighth District Republican Committee. In 1965, Orr was elected chairman of the Vanderburgh County Republican Central Committee, a position he held for six years. During this time, he also launched a legislative career, winning election to the Indiana State Senate in 1968. Before his four-year term ended, however, he was named to the Republican gubernatorial ticket in 1972 as the running mate for Otis R. Bowen. Elected lieutenant governor that year, he was reelected in 1976.

As lieutenant governor, Orr presided over the state senate and frequently had to cast tie-breaking votes, particularly when the state tax system was restructured in 1973. Since Indiana's lieutenant governor also serves as commissioner of agriculture and director of the Indiana Department of Commerce, he also had primary responsibility for promoting state economic development and for fostering tourism programs. Orr participated regularly in Governor Bowen's staff meetings and policy discussions, although this had not been a traditional role for lieutenant governors. He received high marks for his loyalty and dedication to the governor's programs.

Endorsed by the popular Bowen to be his successor, Orr easily won the party's nomination in 1980. His campaign stressed the Bowen connection—"Let's Keep a Good Thing Going"—and resulted in a victory over Democratic candidate John Hillenbrand II by the largest plurality in the history of the state.

Despite this auspicious beginning, Orr's first year as governor was marked by difficulties. Not only was the state in the midst of a recession, which turned what had been a comfortable surplus into a large budget deficit, but pent-up demands among various groups of state employees for higher wages and improved working conditions, unmet by Governor Bowen's property tax relief and budget austerity programs, boiled over. Orr's major recommendations to the Indiana General Assembly in 1981 against any tax increases, while popular with the general public, irritated state employees and public school teachers who stood to receive only minimal salary increases as a consequence. The generally poor economic conditions of the early 1980s, highlighted by unemployment rates that exceeded 20 percent in such automotive-related manufacturing centers as Anderson, Kokomo, and Muncie, and that reached 14 percent statewide, exacerbated the traditional needs of the state for improved mental health and correctional facilities and for additional educational, highway maintenance, and construction funding. Budget restrictions meant that little could be done to achieve the governor's desired objectives of strengthening math, science, and computer instruction in the public schools.

In 1982, following the fall general elections that resulted in continued Republican majorities in both houses of the legislature, Governor Orr confirmed Democratic charges that the projected state deficit for 1983 was in excess of $450 million. After he called the legislature into special session in December to deal with the problem, the state income tax was increased from 1.9 to 3 percent, and the state sales tax from 4 to 5 percent. When the regular session of the legislature convened in January 1983, it appeared that the taxation issue had already been handled, but difficult new issues emerged, particularly utility reform legislation.

The most explosive issue of 1983 concerned the huge increase in utility rates particularly natural gas rates, which had climbed 40 to 50 percent within the year. The utility reform bill that emerged in 1983 expanded the number of members on the state regulatory agency and limited the size and frequency of allowable rate increases. As Governor Orr testified before the U.S. Senate Committee on Energy and Natural Resources in March 1983, the state had only limited ability to deal with the issue. Congress, he insisted, was the responsible body in this area, and he urged prompt action.

The Democrats had some hopes of unseating Orr in the election of 1984. Defeating challenger John K. Snyder to win the Republican nomination, he faced veteran state Senator W. Wayne Townsend in the general election. Only the second state governor constitutionally eligible to succeed himself since Indiana's 1851 constitution was amended in 1972, Orr defeated his Democratic challenger by just over 100,000 votes out of about 2.1 million ballots cast, garnering 52 percent of the vote to his opponent's 47 percent. He ran at the bottom rather than at the top of the Republican ticket statewide. The campaign produced an interesting bit of political trivia: The first known MTV commercial for a statewide candidate was cut for Orr. The take showed the silver-haired governor walking through a roomful of youth, pointing toward the future.

Orr made education and economic development the cornerstones of his second term. The governor's "Prime Time" program reducing class size in grades K through 3 became a model for other states. His "A+" Program brought accountability to public education by measuring results and rewarding performance in Indiana's public schools. The law encompassed the most comprehensive set of educational reforms ever adopted by an

Indiana legislature. Emphasizing Indiana's need to compete in the world marketplace, Orr proposed a tax increase to improve public education. The state's economy, once dominated by agriculture and heavy industry, had shifted in recent years, and new jobs, according to Orr, demanded better-educated employees. Increased revenues were needed to finance improvements in public education.

Orr also encouraged foreign investment in the state. In 1988, Indiana bid for and won a new Isuzu/Subaru light truck and auto plant, a controversial issue due to the size of the financial incentive package put together by state officials to lure the operation to Indiana. Despite popular resentment over the plant-site bidding, Orr maintained that the financial benefits of the deal outweighed the political risks.

During his years in office, Orr also served on the executive committee of the National Governors Association (NGA) and was a member of NGA committees on Transportation, Commerce and Communications, and International Trade and Foreign Relations. He also served as president of the Council of State Governments. By appointment of President Ronald Reagan, he represented the nation's governors on the Amtrak Board of Directors.

Despite all his achievements, Orr suffered by comparison with his predecessor Otis Bowen, who is generally regarded to have been one of the most popular governors in state history. Constitutionally ineligible to succeed himself in 1988, he threw his support to Lieutenant Governor John Mutz, who had directed Orr's efforts to encourage economic development in the state. Despite his 12 years in state government, however, and the benefits of Orr's endorsement, Mutz lost his bid, falling to Evan Bayh, son of former Senator Birch Bayh. In selecting Bayh, Indiana voters not only ended the Republicans' 20-year grip on the statehouse but also exchanged the nation's oldest governor, the 71-year-old Orr, for the youngest.

Bibliography: Michael Barone et al., *The Almanac of American Politics, 1984, 1986, 1988, 1990* (Washington, D.C.: National Journal, 1983, 1985, 1987, 1989); biographical information courtesy of governor's office; *The Chronicle of Higher Education,* 2–18–87; *Newsweek,* 5–30–88; *The New York Times*: 5–7–84; 5–10–84; 11–8–84.

Evan Bayh *(Courtesy of Governor's Office)*

EVAN BAYH, 1989–

Born on December 26, 1955, on his family's farm in Shirkieville, Indiana, just outside of Terre Haute, Bayh is the son of former Democratic Senator Birch Bayh, a prominent figure in state politics. He graduated with honors in business economics from Indiana University in 1978 and received his law degree from the University of Virginia in 1981. His wife Susan is also an attorney.

Bayh first entered politics in 1986. After clerking for a federal appeals court judge and working in a private law practice in Indianapolis, he defeated Robert Bowen, son of former Governor Otis Bowen, to become secretary of state, a position he held from 1986 to 1989.

Despite limited political experience, Bayh sought the governorship in 1988 when Republican incumbent Robert Orr was forced to step down after serving the legally mandated two terms. His Republican opponent was Lieutenant Governor John Mutz, who had served 12 years in the statehouse and state senate. In a political campaign described by seasoned observers as "uncharacteristically nasty" for Indiana, Bayh was derided as an inexperienced rich boy who had spent most of his life outside of Indiana and who arrogantly expected a political career to be his as a kind of family inheritance. Other critics charged that his real interest was not the governorship but regaining the U.S. Senate seat that his father had lost to Dan Quayle in 1980. Despite Mutz's own political experience, however, he was criticized even by Republicans for running a dull campaign and for lacking a compelling message.

While Mutz challenged Bayh's experience and his sincerity in seeking office, Bayh ran on a program of fiscal austerity, focusing on such issues as government efficiency and keeping taxes down. Political commentators observed that it was often difficult to detect which candidate was toeing the traditional Democratic line and which the Republican one. Bayh crisscrossed the state, trying to put Mutz on the defensive, denouncing a "bloated" state government, and attacking Mutz for backing tax increases and state subsidies for foreign investors. He also derided his opponent as a product of the stagnant Republican machine. Another issue Bayh exploited successfully was Indiana's recurrent problem with out-of-state garbage. Low fees at the state's landfills, he charged, had led to the illegal dumping of garbage in the state, a dominant concern in Indiana for a number of years.

For all the rhetoric, however, the candidates agreed on many issues.

Both said they would push for more economic growth and for improved roads and education reform. Both favored a constitutional amendment that would permit a state lottery.

In the end, the energetic and telegenic Bayh won handily, becoming the first Democrat to run the state in 20 years and, at the age of 33, the nation's youngest governor. Bayh's victory was also particularly striking because the Republican ticket of George Bush and Dan Quayle took the state in the presidential contest.

Inaugurated on January 9, 1989, Bayh went to work immediately on his hallmark plan to streamline state government. During his first few months in office, he dispatched efficiency teams to state government departments and found $42 million in savings with no layoffs. He also donated his $9,000 salary increase to a new antidrug program centered in the elementary schools.

Improving public education in the state has been Bayh's top priority. Starting with his EXCEL program during his first year in office and continuing through 1991 with a bold package of programs to promote lifelong learning, Bayh has worked to strengthen child care and preschool education, new school restructuring programs, and innovative work force development initiatives. He worked with President Bush and top national education leaders as one of only six governors on the National Educational Goals Panel, charged with assessing the nation's progress toward meeting education goals set for the year 2000. In March 1991, Bayh was named president-elect of the Education Commission of the States, acceding to the office in July 1992. He has also served as vice-chair of the National Governors Association Task Force on Workforce Development.

A major coup for the Bayh administration was winning a hotly contested United Airlines maintenance facility for the state. In 1992, United Airlines bypassed offers from Denver, Louisville, and Oklahoma City to choose Indianapolis International Airport as the site for its new $800 million maintenance facility. The contract is expected to provide Indiana with more than 6,300 skilled jobs. Soon after winning the contract, Bayh announced plans to spend about $6 million over the next three years to expand college and technical training programs in aviation mechanics. Bayh said the new college programs should "send a clear signal to business and industry that Indiana will do what it takes to increase the skills, productivity, and competitiveness of Hoosier workers."

Bayh remains extremely popular in Indiana. He has led a major Democratic comeback in this longtime Republican state by holding the line on taxes and by cutting government spending. Political observers feel that in an era when most states have been particularly hard hit by the recession, the lesson to learn may be the one taught with such success in Indiana. During the middle of a six-year economic expansion in the 1980s—while other states spent money on crime prevention, road building, education reform, and drug prevention—Indiana saved dollars rather than finance pet projects. Although the state has also been hit by the recession, Bayh has been able to hold the line with only selective cuts, enjoying the use of an $825 million reserve account.

In 1992, Bayh was a strong candidate for reelection. His opponent was Linley Pearson, the state's three-term attorney general. The heart of Pearson's campaign was a "no new taxes" pledge. Bayh said the slogan mattered little to him. "I have a record of not raising taxes," he retorted. Bayh also staved off allegations by Pearson that he had "cooked the books" to show a budget surplus. Reelected governor by the largest margin in Indiana history, 63 percent to 37 percent, this rising star bears close watching.

Bibliography: Biographical information courtesy of governor's office; *The Chronicle of Higher Education*: 3–25–92; 8–26–92; 11–11–92; Phil Duncan, ed., *Politics in America 1992* (Washington, D.C.: Congressional Quarterly Press, 1991); *The New York Times*: 10–10–88; 11–8–88; 11–9–88; 8–19–91; 5–1–92; 10–26–92; 11–4–92; *The Star-Ledger* (Newark, N.J.), 11–10–88; *Time*: 11–21–88; *USA Today*: 11–10–88; 1–3–89; 4–7–89; 1–23–92; 5–6–92; 5–12–92; 11–4–92.

Terry E. Branstad *(Courtesy of Governor's Office)*

IOWA

TERRY E. BRANSTAD, 1983–

Born in Leland, Iowa, on November 17, 1946, Branstad is the son of Edward Arnold Branstad and Rita Garland Branstad. A Roman Catholic, he married Christine Anne Johnson in 1972. The couple has three children: Eric, Allison, and Marcus. Marcus made history as the first baby born to a sitting Iowa governor since 1847.

Branstad received a B.A. in political science from the University of Iowa in 1969 and a J.D. from Drake University Law School in 1974. He served in the U.S. Army from 1969 to 1971 and was the recipient of an Army Commendation Medal.

Branstad, a Republican, first entered state politics in 1968, serving as a delegate to district and state Republican conventions. He was first elected to the Iowa House of Representatives in 1972, winning reelection in 1974 and 1976. Winning the 1978 Republican nomination for lieutenant governor on the basis of his record in the legislature, he served as lieutenant governor during the last term of 14-year incumbent Robert Ray's administration, from 1979 to 1983.

In 1982, Branstad won the Republican gubernatorial nomination to succeed Ray. Political observers believe he won the election largely because of the personal problems of his opponent, Democrat Roxanne Conlin, who lost, in part, because she had legally avoided paying state income taxes one year. Despite Branstad's "ultra-conservative" positions on some issues—positions seen as out of step with those of his moderate predecessor Ray—Branstad won the election with 53 percent of the vote to Conlin's 47 percent.

Branstad won reelection in 1986, again thwarting the predictions of political observers. Most felt Branstad would suffer the consequences of a farm economy in dire straits: He himself owed more money on his family farm than its market value. Branstad, however, blamed the Reagan administration for state problems. Highlighting the fact that he had cut business taxes, he pushed for a moratorium on farm foreclosures and also advocated other programs to help farmers. In the campaign, he was also assisted by the unpopular proposals of his opponent, former state senate leader Lowell Junkins. Junkins proposed a plan to issue $400 million in bonds to stimulate new business and trade, to be paid back out of proceeds from a state lottery. Branstad launched a blistering attack on Junkins' programs, pointing out that lottery proceeds in other states had routinely dropped after the novelty of the venture had worn off. Obviously convinced by these arguments and uncertain that government could allocate money intelligently, voters gave Branstad 53 percent of the vote.

Seeking a third term in 1990, Branstad found himself and his state embroiled in the new politics of abortion rights. Because of Branstad's opposition to abortion, abortion rights supporters were determined to replace him with a more sympathetic governor. Prochoice forces entered the Democratic primary with the specific intention of selecting an abortion rights candidate. The state chapter of the Abortion Rights League endorsed Speaker of the House Don Avenson specifically because of his prochoice stance. In so doing, they launched an attack on longtime Democratic Attorney General Tom Miller, an otherwise popular politician who found himself on the wrong side of the abortion issue. Political analysts theorized that the fall of Miller, who saw his standing crumble over the abortion issue, was a cautionary signal to other Democrats about the difficulty of rising in the party these days when one opposes abortion.

Despite the drama on the Democratic side, Branstad retained his hold on the statehouse, winning the general election with 61 percent of the vote.

In office, Branstad has shown a knack for executive leadership and a degree of success with a Democratic legislature that few experts predicted would be possible. To deal with the farm crisis of his first term, he proposed budget cuts totaling $91 million, forcing the state government to do—in his words—what farmers and businessmen had already done, "pare back and adjust to the economic realities of today." He said the spending cuts would force layoffs but not raise taxes.

An interest in education has marked Branstad's tenure as governor. Iowa boasts the highest literacy rate in the nation, and Branstad has been known for his special generosity to higher education in particular. Considered an advocate for public colleges, he has been vocal in demanding that colleges strengthen undergraduate education and make it easier for community college graduates to complete their education at 4-year institutions. Despite its projected cost, a promise to raise teachers' salaries became a central plank in his race for a third term. In that campaign, Branstad pulled off quite a coup—winning the endorsement of the Iowa State Education Association, an affiliate of the National Education Association (NEA). The union had not endorsed a Republican in 16 years and had backed Branstad's opponents in his two previous gubernatorial runs.

As chair of the National Governors Association (NGA) from 1989 to 1990, Branstad led the NGA campaign to push education to the top of the national agenda, and he worked to improve relations between the Bush White House and the NEA. Particular issues he has championed include incentive pay for teachers and allowing parents to choose schools outside of their district. A member of the NGA's Executive Committee, he has also served on its Committee on International Trade and cochaired its Task Force on Jobs, Growth, and Competitiveness.

In addition to his work with the NGA, Branstad has also chaired the Council of State Governments and the Midwest Governors Conference.

Bibliography: Michael Barone et al., *The Almanac of American Politics, 1984, 1986, 1988* (Washington, D.C.: National Journal, 1983, 1985, 1987); biographical information courtesy of governor's office; *The Chronicle of Higher Education:* 11–12–86; 2–18–87; 10–10–90; 8–28–91; 8–26–92; *The New York Times:* 9–20–85; 9–4–86; 5–28–90; 6–3–90; 6–7–90; *USA Today:* 5–14–90; 6–7–90.

Mike Hayden *(Courtesy of Governor's Office)*

KANSAS

MIKE HAYDEN, 1987–1991

Born on March 16, 1944, in Atwood, Kansas, Hayden is a member of the United Methodist church. Married in 1968 to the former Patti Rooney, he and his wife have two daughters.

Hayden attended Kansas State University, receiving a B.S. in wildlife conservation in 1966. He then entered the military, serving in the U.S. Army from 1967 to 1970, including a 13-month stint in Vietnam, where he was promoted from second to first lieutenant. For his actions as a platoon leader and company commander, he was heavily decorated, awarded the Soldiers Medal, two Bronze stars, and the Army Commendation Medal, among others.

Upon completion of his military service, he returned to Kansas and enrolled at Fort Hays State University, where he taught biology on a graduate assistantship and worked toward an M.S. in biology, which he received in 1974. Hayden explains that he entered politics because of his environmental concerns. An ardent hunter and fisherman, he "soon figured out that the people who make the real decisions regarding the environment were politicians."

A Republican, Hayden served in the Kansas House of Representatives from 1972 to 1986, leading his colleagues as speaker from 1983 to 1986. As a legislator, Hayden was known as a tough negotiator.

The 1986 Kansas governor's race was wide open due to the constitutional ineligibility of retiring two-term incumbent John Carlin. Despite being far outspent, Hayden won a seven-candidate primary to gain his party's nomination, carrying most of the state's rural areas and small towns. He was weakest in urban areas, where he ran second to Larry Jones, a business leader.

The general election was one of the year's tightest and most hotly contested races. It was also a contest that presented one of the sharpest contrasts between competing candidates.

Hayden faced Lieutenant Governor Thomas R. Docking, a Democrat from a famous Kansas political family. His father Robert had served as the state's governor from 1967 to 1975, as had his grandfather George from 1957 to 1961. Both governors had been popular, fiscally conservative leaders whose well-known political slogan—maintaining budgets that were "austere but adequate"—was adopted by their political heir apparent. Docking criticized Hayden for urging an embargo on grain sales to South Africa but was put on the defensive when Hayden called on him to sell his stocks in companies that do business there.

The election was a close one. Kansas, although predominantly Republican in registration figures, had had Democratic governors for nearly 20 of the previous 30 years. Although his victory with 52 percent of the vote was not large, Hayden was able to win the governorship despite his party's nationwide association with the crisis on the farms.

In office, Hayden set these priorities for his governorship: improving the quality of state higher education, creating a statewide governing board for community colleges and technical schools, and changing the state financing formula so colleges wouldn't lose state funds when enrollment fluctuated.

Hayden's administration was beset by a stormy relationship with the state legislature and rocked by a tax revolt led by ordinary citizens. A new property tax system enacted under his predecessor John Carlin but falling to him to implement infuriated voters. Although the measure was designed to correct underappraisals, it included tax measures favored by big business and farm interests. Hardest hit were homeowners and small businesses, who used their power at the polls to vent their ire at Hayden.

In his 1990 campaign for reelection, Hayden had difficulty even winning renomination by his own party. He barely survived the GOP primary challenge posed by Nestor Weigand, a leader of the property tax revolt.

In the general election, he faced Democrat Joan Finney, Kansas state treasurer and the first woman in state history to be nominated for governor. Taking advantage of the property tax revolt and anti-incumbent sentiment, she came from behind in the polls to end Hayden's governorship, drawing 53 percent of the vote.

An interesting sidelight of the race was a curious role reversal on the politics of abortion. It featured a prochoice Republican candidate, who happened to be male, and a prolife Democratic candidate who was a woman. Hayden, in fact, had been optimistic about his reelection prospects precisely because of his prochoice stance. He had even drawn the endorsement of Molly Yard, president of the National Organization for Women, who encouraged feminists and disaffected Democrats to cross party lines in defense of the beleaguered governor.

Bibliography: Michael Barone et al., *The Almanac of American Politics, 1988* (Washington, D.C.: National Journal, 1987); biographical information courtesy of governor's office; *The Chronicle of Higher Education*, 11–12–86; *The New York Times*: 9–23–86; 11–9–89; *USA Today*: 5–14–90; 8–8–90; 8–9–90; 9–20–90; 11–8–90.

JOAN FINNEY, 1991–

Born on February 12, 1925, in Topeka, Kansas, Finney is the daughter of Leonard McInroy and Mary Sands McInroy. A Roman Catholic, she married Spencer W. Finney, Jr., in 1957. The couple has three children.

Finney holds degrees from the Kansas City Conservatory of Music (1946); the College of St. Theresa (1950); and Washburn University (1981). She began her political career as a Republican, serving as a top aide to Republican Governor Frank Carlson. Later switching parties, she became Kansas State Treasurer in 1975, a post she held until her accession to the governorship in 1991. Finney confounded the pundits to achieve her stunning capture of the statehouse. Although she had built up considerable name recognition over her 16-year stint as state treasurer, she benefited from voter discontent over tax increases that had hit homeowners and small businesses especially hard. The first woman in state history to be nominated for governor, she won a surprising upset victory in the August 1990 Democratic primary. Her opponent was former two-term governor John Carlin. Taking advantage of a property tax revolt and anti-incumbent sentiment to win, she spent only $43,000 to Carlin's $340,000 and received no major newspaper endorsements.

In the general election, she also came storming from far behind in the polls to defeat incumbent Mike Hayden with 53 percent of the vote. Finney ran as an outsider against political leaders who wanted to make the treasurer's post appointive rather than elective. Her populist appeal also stemmed from her support of a constitutional amendment to make it easier for voters to bypass elected officials and decide issues in ballot measures. Hayden countered by saying that Finney couldn't handle the job.

The race drew national attention in a year when the politics of abortion rights became a decisive factor in numerous contests. The Kansas race featured a curious role reversal. Although Kansas has been one of the nation's most consistently prochoice states, Finney is an ardent right-to-lifer. She appealed to Kansans' celebrated independent streak, portraying herself as an open-minded politician who wouldn't impose her personal views on others. Although she downplayed the abortion issue, Republican Hayden drew support from disaffected Democrats and feminist groups who lauded his prochoice stand. The campaign demonstrated how tricky the politics of abortion had become. Democrats nationwide were reluctant to showcase Finney because of her prolife stand, while National Organization for Women President Molly Yard, by contrast, crossed gender lines to endorse Hayden, encouraging other women to do likewise.

Joan Finney *(Courtesy of Governor's Office)*

With her upset victory and the concurrent reelection of U.S. Senator Nancy Kassebaum, Kansas became the first state ever to have a woman in both offices simultaneously. She also became the only Democrat holding statewide office in mostly conservative Kansas.

In office, Finney seems determined to keep her campaign pledge not to increase taxes. She vetoed a package of sales and income tax increases passed by the legislature in 1991.

The abortion controversy, however, continues to dog her. In 1991, she found herself thrust into the center of the national debate over abortion when the militant antiabortion group Operation Rescue summoned hundreds of abortion foes to Wichita, Kansas, for what became an unprecedented round of protests at abortion clinics. Finney stepped into the fray when she voiced her support to a cheering crowd of demonstrators. In a state that has had one of the least restrictive abortion laws in the nation, she repeatedly promised that she would sign any legislation that restricted abortion in any way. She ultimately did so in April 1992, signing into law a bill that required any woman seeking an abortion to wait eight hours after receiving medical counseling, and any unmarried woman under 18 to first have her doctor notify at least one parent.

Prochoice groups have remained critical of Finney, while others deride her ideas as "warm and fuzzy." Political observers note that her 1990 victory was probably more of a protest against the policies of her predecessor than it was an endorsement of her agenda. According to University of Kansas political scientist Burdett Loomis, quoted in the national press, both Hayden and Finney registered "mammoth negatives" in the polls. She drew additional fire in 1992 for appointing as the state's abortion-reporting compliance officer a paroled former physician who was sent to prison for molesting a 14-year-old girl over an 11-month period.

Bibliography: The Chronicle of Higher Education: 8–28–91; 4–15–92; Phil Duncan, ed., *Politics in America 1992* (Washington, D.C.: Congressional Quarterly Press, 1991); *Newsweek,* 10–8–90; *The New York Times*: 11–8–90; 4–24–92; *USA Today*: 8–8–90; 9–20–90; 11–8–90; 8–5–91; 7–24–92.

Wallace G. Wilkinson *(Courtesy of Governor's Office)*

KENTUCKY

WALLACE G. WILKINSON, 1987–1991

Born in Liberty, Kentucky, on December 12, 1941, Wilkinson is a self-made millionaire. Getting his start in business with a secondhand bookstore in Lexington, he invested the profits wisely and well, diversifying on a large scale. His real estate and business holdings have come to include farms, coal mines, a flying service, and two banks. He and his wife, the former Martha Stafford, have two children.

In a remarkable rise from political obscurity, Wilkinson won the Democratic gubernatorial nomination in the May 26, 1987, primary. It was his first bid for public office. Waging a state-of-the-art media campaign in which he spent $6.3 million, he described himself as a "conservative Democrat" and placed an antiestablishment message at the heart of his campaign. His lack of a political history enabled him to run a campaign that cut across ideological boundaries. Speaking repeatedly against "politics as usual," he promised to bring as much economic success to Kentucky as he had to his own business career. Casting himself as the candidate of new ideas, he proposed the establishment of a state lottery in lieu of raising taxes. The proposal proved especially popular in parts of the state along the border of Ohio, which already had a lottery of its own.

In a surprising upset, Wilkinson soundly defeated four other major candidates for the Democratic nomination: former Governor Julian Carroll; Dr. Grady Stumbo, a member of former Governor John Brown's cabinet who, as a coal miner's son, built his campaign around a folksy, "down-home" image; Lieutenant Governor and former Attorney General Steven Beshear; and former Governor John Y. Brown. For much of the campaign, the race was a contest between Beshear and Brown, who attacked each other unsparingly. The campaign also transformed the state into a lucrative showcase for media consultants. Beshear sought to tarnish Brown's image, using TV ads to attack Brown's extravagant life-style and to suggest that he planned to raise taxes. He also hinted that Brown wanted to be governor only to return to the public spotlight. For most of the campaign, the major issue was Brown and whether he had the drive and motivation to serve a second term: He had dropped from public view after he left office in 1983. Wilkinson painted Brown as part of the history of mediocrity in Kentucky, a history that had it leading the nation in unemployment and trailing in educational achievement. He assailed both Brown and Beshear for their dirty tactics and accused both of them of wanting to raise taxes.

Brown was the frontrunner for much of the campaign, while Beshear had the support of key Democratic groups, including most of the state's union leaders and the state teachers association. Wilkinson's victory was all the more striking since he had registered only 5 percent in public opinion polls conducted early in the race. Relying on a TV and media blitz, he promised to change the way politics was conducted in Kentucky. What was also noteworthy about his victory was that he seemed to have picked up most of his support in the final week of the campaign. Voters, in the opinion of political observers, had grown weary of the negative campaign waged by Wilkinson's opponents and placed little credence in their charge that he was unknown and untested. Their negativism opened the way for his surprising win, with 35 percent of the primary vote. Brown, by contrast, drew only 25 percent. Remaining totals were Beshear, 18 percent; Stumbo, 14 percent; and Carroll, 7 percent. Three minor candidates shared the remaining 1 percent.

According to political analysts, the returns indicated that the power of local politicians to deliver votes was at an all-time low. This proved a further vindication of Wilkinson, who had run against the courthouse crowd.

From the time of his dramatic victory in the primary, Wilkinson remained far ahead in public opinion polls and until the final weekend of the campaign regularly urged audiences to give him the biggest margin of victory in state history. His Republican opponent was John Harper, a respected state legislator from a heavily Democratic district near Louisville who was bidding to become the first Republican elected governor in 20 years. The Republicans' chances of victory, however, were sharply reduced when Larry Forgy, a politically active lawyer who was thought to be the strongest potential nominee, dropped out of the race at the beginning of 1987. Harper entered the Republican primary only after his withdrawal. To his credit, he had experience as a candidate able to come from behind in tough races, winning his first election in 1984 in a district where Democrats outnumbered Republicans 9–1. His campaign, however, was poorly financed from the start. He was able to raise less than $250,000 compared with the $4 million Wilkinson had amassed since the primary. Harper called the size of the Democratic war chest "obscene" and ridiculed Wilkinson's lottery proposal. He claimed his opponent was planning to eliminate the right of counties to remain dry, and to start a chain of state liquor stores—a charge Wilkinson hotly denied. While Wilkinson vehemently ruled out a tax hike, Harper admitted he could not be so optimistic, a reversal of the usual Democratic and Republican positions on this issue. Although neither candidate had much experience in education policy making, Wilkinson promised to make education a priority in his administration.

Wilkinson won the election resoundingly with 65 percent of the vote, giving him the highest victory margin ever recorded in a state gubernatorial contest. He was inaugurated on December 8, 1987.

True to his campaign promises, education was a top priority of the Wilkinson administration. The hallmark of his program was a sweeping overhaul of the operation of the state's schools, an outgrowth in part of a June 1989 ruling by the Kentucky Supreme Court. In that decision, the court ruled that the unequal financial resources committed to each school district were inherently unconstitutional. It also considered the academic results produced by the current system, which left Kentucky with the country's lowest percentage of high school graduates. Wilkinson's reform bill set a minimum spending level for each of the state's 570,000 students and gave principals, parents, and teachers more responsibility for day-to-day decisions involved in running the schools. Wilkinson drew national praise for the program, which also raised taxes $1.3 billion over the succeeding two years. Wilkinson also was a strong supporter of Kentucky Educational Television, and on the national scene, he championed the idea of using telecommunications for distance learning. Despite such successes, however, Wilkinson's reputation in the academic community suffered from charges of political favoritism in his appointments to college governing boards. Many of those he named had been contributors to his political campaigns.

Wilkinson was not a popular governor. By the end of his term, he was beset by numerous problems. Political analysts were quick to point out that Kentucky as a whole had changed much less than its New South neighbors. More than half of state residents continued to live in rural areas; poverty remained rampant in the Appalachian hill country; and tobacco, cotton, and soybean fields still dotted the landscape. With his disapproval ratings rising to a high of 40 percent, Wilkinson could perhaps take solace in the fact that he would be barred by law from seeking a second term.

Nonetheless, Wilkinson committed what many perceived to be yet another serious blunder as the race to name a successor took shape. His wife Martha entered the Democratic primary with intentions to succeed her husband as governor. Although she had no political track record apart from a highly publicized campaign championing adult education and the General Educational Development Program, Mrs. Wilkinson insisted she was not a mere surrogate candidate for her husband. She dismissed any comparison between her intentions and the 1966 Alabama election of Lurleen Wallace to succeed her husband George. Despite these protestations, however, Wilkinson was seen as boosting his wife's ill-conceived campaign, and she herself raised questions as to the couple's motivations with her promise to name her husband as the economic development secretary in her new administration. Martha Wilkinson's short-lived campaign for the Democratic gubernatorial nomination drew much negative press. Her $4 million campaign was funded primarily by contractors doing business with her husband's administration, and she was portrayed as a transparent surrogate of her husband, a man determined to retain personal control over the statehouse.

The sorry affair tarnished Wilkinson's image, as did an even more controversial maneuver during his final days in office. In a move termed a "flagrant abuse of power" by state Attorney General Fred Cowan, Wilkinson appointed himself to a six-year term on the University of Kentucky Board of Trustees during his final week as governor. Wilkinson said that he had appointed himself to the board because he wanted to continue his efforts to reform higher education. He said the university should be accountable for graduation rates and that the faculty should spend more time teaching. The move drew anger and protest from students and faculty alike and triggered a series of state court cases investigating the constitutionality of Wilkinson's actions. Ultimately, however, the state court of appeals ruled that there was no law prohibiting a governor from making such an appointment, a decision upheld by the state supreme court.

Because of the cloud under which he ended his gubernatorial tenure, Wilkinson's future in state politics is uncertain.

Bibliography: Michael Barone et al., *The Almanac of American Politics, 1988* (Washington, D.C.: National Journal, 1987); *The Chronicle of Higher Education*: 9–23–87; 11–11–87; 8–28–91; 12–18–91; *Newsweek*: 6–8–87; *The New York Times*: 5–26–87; 5–27–87; 11–1–87; 11–3–87; 11–4–87; 3–30–90; 4–13–90; 5–11–91; *The Star-Ledger* (Newark, N.J.), 1–28–91; *USA Today*: 7–2–90; 12–31–90; 5–13–91; 5–24–91.

BRERETON C. JONES, 1991–

Born on June 27, 1939, in Gallipolis, Ohio, Jones is the son of Bartow and Nedra Jones. Raised in Point Pleasant, West Virginia, he is a graduate of the University of Virginia. Married to the former Elizabeth Lloyd, he and his wife have two children. In the early 1970s, Jones moved his family to Kentucky, where he established Airdrie Stud Farm, a thriving thoroughbred operation of international renown.

A former Republican leader of the West Virginia legislature who switched to the Democrats after Watergate, Jones drew heavily on his own money to win the lieutenant governorship of Kentucky in 1987. In that post, he drew praise for cutting nearly 25 percent from the expenses associated with the office, setting an example for thrift that would also become the hallmark of his gubernatorial administration.

Jones became governor of Kentucky after a colorful campaign that drew national attention. He was known as an archrival of sitting Governor Wallace Wilkinson, who was limited by law to one term in office. Although both are Democrats, they had rarely worked together during their years in the capital, and it was known that Wilkinson had promised to do whatever was necessary to deny Jones the governorship. Wilkinson actually went so far as to encourage his wife Martha to seek the Democratic nomination to succeed him in office, an ill-conceived plan that ultimately backfired with her withdrawal from the race. Her $4 million campaign was funded primarily by contractors doing business with her husband's administration, and she was widely perceived as a surrogate candidate for Wilkinson himself.

In the subsequent Democratic primary, Jones put together a smooth-running grass-roots organization and an efficient fund-raising team to defeat three other candidates. His central message was campaign financing reform, perceived as necessary in a state where candidates spent more than $19 per vote in the last governor's race, more than in any state but Alaska and Hawaii. His call for positive campaigning was especially effective in a state that has seen much negative campaigning in recent years, and he credited his primary win to his call for unity among Democrats.

His opponent in the general election was Republican Larry Hopkins, a seven-term congressman who had received campaign help from President Bush. His crushing 35 percent to 65 percent defeat by Jones was a big disappointment to the GOP, who, in the opinion of analysts, stood the best chance of winning the governor's mansion in 20 years. Repub-

Brereton C. Jones *(Courtesy of Governor's Office)*

licans had hoped to capitalize on the massive unpopularity of the Wilkinson administration. Yet Hopkins bruised himself when he overstated his military record during a tough primary struggle and further hurt his chances when he became embroiled in the congressional check-bouncing scandal. Hopkins, for his part, tried to make Jones' refusal to release his income tax returns a key campaign issue.

Overall, the race was "one of the least inspiring in the state's modern history," in the opinion of the *Louisville Courier-Journal*. Few issues were discussed, as the race became a contest of negative advertising. Both men were regarded as political moderates.

Jones has promised to make ethics and campaign finance reform the centerpiece of his administration. In the early months of his administration, he supported and signed into law a bill changing the system for selecting members of the state's seven university governing boards by assuring that future appointments would be based on merit, not contributions to political campaigns. He has also sponsored legislation to reform the state's political structure and to reduce the number and costs of elections. Early in his administration, he brought environmentalists, industry representatives, and state and local officials together to resolve a longstanding controversy regarding the protection of Lake Cumberland, one of Kentucky's most beautiful recreation areas. He has also supported a university, business, and state government partnership to share ideas for economic development.

Barred by the state constitution from seeking a second term, Jones has vowed that he is not interested in any other political office. "I want to do this, I want to do it right, and I want to go back to the farm."

Bibliography: Biographical information courtesy of governor's office; *The Chronicle of Higher Education*: 10–16–91; 11–13–91; *The New York Times*: 5–11–91; 5–30–91; 11–2–91; 11–10–91; *The Star-Ledger* (Newark, N.J.), 1–28–91; *USA Today*: 7–2–90; 12–31–90; 5–13–91; 5–24–91; 5–29–91; 11–6–91; 11–7–91.

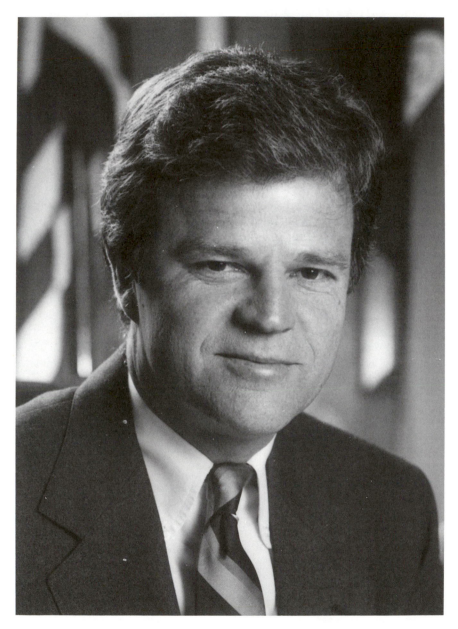

Charles Roemer *(Courtesy of Governor's Office)*

LOUISIANA

CHARLES ("BUDDY") ROEMER, 1988–1992

Born in Shreveport, Louisiana, on October 4, 1943, Roemer is the son of Charles Elson II and Adeline McDade Roemer Elson. The twice-divorced Roemer has three children.

Roemer graduated from Harvard University with an A.B. in 1964 and an M.B.A. in 1967. A former member of the Urban League's Board of Directors, he was a delegate to the Louisiana Constitutional Convention of 1972. From 1981 to 1988, he was a U.S. Congressman from Louisiana's First District and a member of the Banking, Finance, Urban Affairs, and Small Business committees.

Roemer entered a crowded field in the 1987 Louisiana governor's race, seeking to block incumbent Edwin Edwards' quest for an unprecedented fourth term. The flashy and flamboyant Edwards had been a popular governor and effective administrator during his years in office but had fallen on hard times recently due to his own personal legal troubles and the state's plummeting economic fortunes. Louisiana had been hurt badly by the decline in oil revenues and falling prices for oil and natural gas upon which its economy depends. Seen as vulnerable, Edwards was challenged by four major candidates: Secretary of State Jim Brown, Representative W. J. (Billy) Tauzin, Congressman Bob Livingston, and Roemer. Under its unique open primary system, Louisiana chooses its state officials in an unusual manner at an unusual time. Every candidate, regardless of party, runs in a single primary in October. If someone gets 50 percent of the primary vote, he is automatically the winner of the governorship; if not, a runoff is held between the top two vote-getters, irrespective of party affiliation.

As the October 24, 1987, primary approached, Roemer was given little chance of victory. He had placed last in the polls all summer. Other candidates, including Republican Bob Livingston, seemed far more promising contenders. But in the final two weeks of the race, Roemer launched an aggressive TV campaign and vaulted past everyone to win. A Democrat with appeal to conservatives, he cast himself as the champion of those who wanted to take on the state's entrenched political power structure. Denouncing the Edwards administration as corrupt, he ran as a reform candidate who disdained contributions from political action committees and disclosed all financial sources. Roemer's slogan, "A Revolution for Louisiana," obviously attracted large numbers of voters who were convinced the state needed a change. Although Edwards denounced his opponents as enemies of the weak, needy, elderly, and black, most of the state's leading newspapers endorsed Roemer. The fact that Roemer carried a substantial number of parishes in southern Louisiana—Edwards' home base—indicated that the sentiment for change was pervasive. According to political analysts, although voters outside Roemer's home district knew little about him, they were "swept up in a sea of change and voted for the candidate they perceived as being the greatest change for the political system." The election also changed enough seats to turn the state senate in a more conservative direction.

Roemer polled 33.1 percent of the vote to Edwards' 28.1 percent. Other results were Livingston, 18.5 percent; Tauzin, 9.9 percent; Brown, 8.8 percent. Minor candidates shared the remaining 1.6 percent of all votes cast.

Roemer won by drawing on a coalition of college-educated, affluent, under-55 voters, tied into his congressional district base in northern Louisiana. His victory was a historic one, winning as he did without any of the traditional courthouse gang, black or white. Practically no public officials supported him, and he made no deals with other candidates to pull out the victory over Edwards.

What was even more surprising about Roemer's primary victory was the dramatic fashion in which he came into the governor's office. According to Edward Renwick, the director of the Institute of Politics at Loyola University, the campaign was the "most unusual" in the state's recent history. Although Roemer and Edwards, as the primary's two top finishers, were scheduled to compete in a runoff election on November 21, 1987, Edwards astounded friends and enemies alike when he conceded the race to Roemer a few days after the primary bid. When two other major candidates endorsed Roemer, Edwards withdrew from the race rather than face a humiliating result in the runoff.

Roemer's victory was seen as a turning point in state politics. Dr. Joseph Logsdon, a historian at the University of New Orleans, compared Roemer to Huey Long, the populist from northern Louisiana, whose slogan "Everyman a king" swept him into the governorship in 1928. Long, like Roemer, won with just a plurality, and his opponent pulled out, just like Edwards. According to Logsdon, Long and Roemer were similar kinds of candidates. Long, too, was youthful, used the media well, and was a master of radio. Like him, Roemer's pithy slogans calling for a Louisiana "revolution" played well on television.

With more than four months between his victory in the primary and his inauguration, Roemer sought a role in solving the state's budget crisis. In an unprecedented move, he tried to get some control over state policy and spending in this waiting period. He felt he had no choice: If cuts were not made immediately, they would have to be much larger after his March inauguration. In an unusual move, he asked departing Governor Edwards to appoint either him or one of his associates as a commissioner of the administration, with responsibility for the day-to-day operations of government. The move was necessary, Roemer insisted, because Edwards had not moved to avoid a budget crisis.

By the time of Roemer's March 14, 1988, inauguration, state budget projections forecast a $170 million gap between revenue and expenditures. With the decline in oil and gas revenue that enriched Louisiana earlier in the decade, the state also had an estimated $600 million in short-term debt, which began to come due in April.

In his inaugural address, Roemer promised a "new Louisiana," with a new image "as a place where investors, businessmen and women invest and create jobs." He explained that the foundations of his administration would be fiscal responsibility, excellence in education, a drive for economic development, protecting the environment, and ethics in government. He promised to end cronyism in state politics, to revamp the budget and tax structure to eliminate $1.2 billion in cumulative deficits, and to improve the state's educational system. His long-term goals included restructuring the state's tax system so that local government would have more taxing power to pay for services, and diversifying the state's economy to make it less reliant on oil and gas.

Unfortunately, during his stormy four-year tenure as governor, little of Roemer's ambitious agenda was able to pass, and the once-heralded Roemer Revolution did not materialize. Of the "Four E's" around which he focused his 1987 campaign—environment, economic development, ethics, and education—his environmental protection efforts were the most successful. Inheriting probably the most polluted state in the country, Roemer worked hard for a cleanup, trying to impose recycling on cities, to force waste reductions at the source, and to double the environmental protection budget. In this area, the state legislature and voters did follow his lead, making environmental protection a priority. In the spring of 1989, the new legislature ordered the state to halve toxic air emissions by 1994, phase out oil and gas production pits in the wetlands, and start a solid waste reduction and recycling program. In September 1989, a new law, one of the nation's strictest, regulated the disposal of 25 toxic chemicals into the state's waters. In October 1989, voters passed a constitutional amendment establishing a trust fund to preserve the state's wetlands. The state also imposed a new rule tying a company's environmental record to the amount of taxes on business property that the company must pay.

Roemer took action to reduce pollution while trying to collect millions in industrial property taxes from which the same polluters had been exempted.

Yet in the key area of tax reform, the linchpin of his self-proclaimed "revolution," Roemer was much less successful. Arguing that the state's antiquated tax system relied too heavily on oil income that was no longer available, and allowed too many people to avoid property taxes, he campaigned hard for extensive tax changes. Battling a fierce antitax tradition in the state, he tried in vain to convince voters that the days of having some of the nation's lowest taxes were gone. Under his proposal, the tax base would have been shifted by putting more of a load on people through the income tax, reducing the sales tax, and giving businesses an incentive to move to the state and to expand. Opponents condemned the plan, however, as simply a huge tax increase.

Two crushing defeats, one by the legislature and one by the voters, left Roemer badly wounded. As a result, he had to alter his tactics and propose only incremental changes. In October 1989, state voters overwhelmingly approved a gasoline tax increase intended to finance a costly building program and breathe some life into the state's economy. Political analysts saw the result as a sign that the state was moving away, at least a little, from the rigid antitax populism that had been strong since the 1930s when Huey Long enacted high business taxes that forced oil companies to pay the state's bills.

Nonetheless, the state budget continued to grow by $3 billion during Roemer's tenure, and fiscal analysts theorized that additional measures were needed to prevent a projected $1 billion shortfall by the end of Roemer's tenure. Fiscal problems also impaired Roemer's ability to enact his educational agenda, and he was thwarted in his attempts to deal with two of the state's long-standing problems—the segregation of Louisiana's public institutions and the structure of higher education.

Roemer also suffered from a stormy relationship with the state legislature. His campaign pledge to purge the government of the "clubbiness" of the previous administration did not sit well with many legislators who were themselves part of the club, and the state's old political guard did not react well to the "yuppie idealists" who filled Roemer's staff. His driven, sometimes angry style was also an impediment to good relations, as he himself was forced to admit when he went before the legislature in April 1990 and made a startling apology. A midterm change in staff improved relations somewhat, but even his supporters described his style as inconsistent.

By far the biggest controversy of Roemer's tenure came in the volatile area of abortion rights. A self-proclaimed right-to-lifer who had once considered the ministry as a career, he outraged abortion foes by his veto of three stringent antiabortion bills. Although some political observers hailed his decision as "an act of incredible courage," others speculated on the damage done to his reelection prospects. Most Louisianans oppose abortion, and the Orthodox Catholic church of Louisiana even went so far as to excommunicate the Methodist governor for his vetoes. Although his two 1990 vetoes were sustained by the legislature, in 1991 the legislature passed the nation's most restrictive abortion law over his veto, the first time in the 20th century that a state legislature in Louisiana had successfully overridden a governor's veto.

Abortion became a key issue in Roemer's unusual and highly publicized reelection bid. In a move that drew much national attention and was viewed by some with cynicism, Roemer officially switched his party affiliation to Republican in the spring of 1991. His action made him the first incumbent governor in history ever to switch parties. While opponents suggested that the move was orchestrated to reap the benefits of united party support in what was expected to be a difficult campaign, others noted that Roemer had never been comfortable with Democratic politics, Louisiana style. While in Congress, Roemer had often voted with the Republicans and was one of the southern "boll weevil" Democrats who had supported Reagan administration fiscal policies. At odds with former House Speaker Tip O'Neill, he had never been active in Democratic party ranks, ignoring the party machine in his 1987 campaign for governor and feuding with Democrats in the state legislature. The defection was heralded by the Bush White House and hailed as another setback for Democrats, more than 200 of whom had switched parties during the Bush years.

Regardless of its motivation, however, the move appeared to have backfired on Roemer. Hoping to go into the gubernatorial race with the solid support of the state Republican party, he was badly damaged when the state party convention refused to endorse him, throwing its support instead behind U.S. Congressman Clyde C. Holloway. Drawing his support from abortion foes and politically active evangelicals, Holloway was the beneficiary of conservative wrath against Roemer for his controversial abortion votes.

Roemer was clearly in trouble going into his reelection campaign. Louisiana's unusual open primary system, in which candidates of all parties compete together, pitted Roemer against not only Holloway but other even more serious and colorful contenders: former three-term Governor Edwin Edwards, one of the state's most influential politicians, and archconservative David Duke, a former Ku Klux Klan leader whose race-baiting campaign drew national attention. A series of minor candidates also appeared on the October 19, 1991, ballot.

Roemer's third-place showing surprised political analysts and quashed his reelection hopes. His loss came despite the fact that his campaign was managed by professional Republican organizers dispatched from Washington and featured personal appearances by both President Bush and Vice-President Quayle. His problem illustrated the limits of what national Republican leaders have been able to do for southern Democrats who switch parties. Backing from Washington couldn't mask or undo the serious local challenges Roemer faced. According to analysts, many voters simply felt that Roemer lacked leadership ability. Edwards hammered away at what he called the unfulfilled promises of Roemer's last campaign, and Duke was widely credited with putting his message into language that had a potentially broad appeal among white voters. Roemer lost the election in the state's major metropolitan areas, where he ran more poorly than expected.

Roemer left his successor a host of serious problems. The state faced a $1 billion deficit for fiscal year 1992–1993 and chronic problems with low literacy rates and low high school graduation rates. Louisiana's fiscal recovery was hampered by a failure to diversify the state's oil-based economy, and high unemployment rates prompted many residents to leave the state in search of a better future.

After his defeat, Roemer was rumored to be considering a job at the Harvard Business School, from which he received his M.B.A. in 1967. His political career appears to be over.

Bibliography: Michael Barone et al., *The Almanac of American Politics, 1986* (Washington, D.C.: National Journal, 1985); *The Chronicle of Higher Education*: 9–23–87; 11–4–87; 4–27–88; 8–28–91; 10–16–91; 12–11–91; Wayne King, "Bad Times on the Bayou," *New York Times Magazine* (June 11, 1989): 56–59, 120–125; *The New York Times*: 2–28–87; 3–31–87; 6–27–87; 10–22–87; 10–26–87; 11–3–87; 11–20–87; 3–15–88; 3–27–88; 5–14–88; 2–12–89; 5–1–89; 9–27–89; 10–9–89; 11–19–89; 7–7–90; 7–8–90; 7–10–90; 7–13–90; 1–20–91; 2–15–91; 2–27–91; 3–12–91; 3–17–91; 3–19–91; 5–4–91; 6–17–91; 6–19–91; 7–19–91; 9–24–91; 10–21–91; *The Record* (Bergen County, N.J.), 9–6–90; *The Star-Ledger* (Newark, N.J.): 7–2–89; 3–12–91; 7–28–91; 1–13–92; *USA Today*: 3–14–88; 4–14–89; 7–6–90; 3–29–91; 6–5–91; 6–7–91; 6–19–91.

EDWIN WASHINGTON EDWARDS,
1972–1980, 1984–1988, 1992–

Born in Marksville, Louisiana, on August 7, 1927, Edwards is the son of Clarence W. Edwards and Agnes Brouillette Edwards, French-speaking sharecroppers. A Roman Catholic, he married Elaine Schwartzenburg on April 5, 1949. The couple had four children before divorcing in 1989.

After serving in the Naval Air Corps during World War II, Edwards received an LL.B. from Louisiana State University School of Law in 1949. In private practice with a Crowley, Louisiana, law firm from 1949 to 1964, he first entered public service when he was elected as a Democrat to the Crowley City Council in 1954. He was reelected to a second term in 1958. Edwards first captured statewide attention when he ran for the state senate in 1963. Surprising the experts, he defeated the president pro tem of the senate, an incumbent of 20 years. As a floor leader in the senate, Edwards played an active part in the passage of key legislation. Following the death of Seventh District Congressman T. A. Thompson in an auto accident in 1965, Edwards defeated four other candidates to win election to the U.S. House of Representatives. He remained in Congress for almost 7 years, winning reelection in 1966, 1968, and 1970. Edwards served on the Public Works, Judiciary, and Internal Security committees. The Democratic whip for the Louisiana and Mississippi delegations for 4 years, he played a key role in increasing U.S. exports of Louisiana farm products. He was also considered by experts to have a rather liberal voting record for a congressman from the Deep South.

Edwards bested 17 other candidates to win the Democratic nomination for governor in 1971 and narrowly defeated state Senator J. Bennett Johnston of Shreveport in the primary runoff by a vote of 584,262 to 579,774. In February 1972 he defeated Republican David Treen in the general election, gaining 57 percent of the vote to Treen's 43 percent. As a French-speaking Cajun, Edwards won by an especially wide margin in the "Cajun country" along the Gulf of Mexico, outside New Orleans in the bayou country south of Alexandria, and west of the Mississippi River. He also gained a majority of the black vote.

Inaugurated on May 9, 1972, Edwards became Louisiana's first French-speaking chief executive in more than a century and one of the state's few public officials to have served at the city, state, and national levels. He was fortunate to inherit a state that seemed to have put racial issues behind it, a state ready to reap the benefits of economic prosperity as the

Edwin Washington Edwards *(Courtesy of Governor's Office)*

price of oil rose. In 1973, Edwards called a special "energy crisis session" of the state legislature, which doubled the severance tax on natural gas and changed the levy on oil from a volume to a value basis, thus adding $169 million a year to the treasury. He also received a measure of national attention as a spokesman for the oil industry. Graced with a special ability to dominate the legislature, Edwards was considered to be a highly successful administrator in his first term and had little trouble winning re-election in 1975. That election was the first to be conducted under a new open primary law, which the governor himself had engineered. The new system required candidates from all parties to enter an October primary. If any candidate polled 50 percent of all votes cast for the office, that candidate was elected; if not, the top two candidates faced each other in a runoff election. Thus, Edwards faced five primary opponents in 1975, all Democrats: Robert G. Jones, Wade O. Martin, Jr., Ken Lewis, A. Roswell Thompson, and Cecil M. Pizzi. He gained 62 percent of the vote to Jones' 24 percent and Martin's 12 percent. The other candidates split the remaining 2 percent.

Edwards eventually came to dominate state politics as had no governor since the legendary Huey Long. Major achievements of his earlier administration included the calling of a state constitutional convention and an addition to the natural gas tax to finance health, education, and prison improvement. His tenure was also marked by the creation of a plan to simplify state aid to local governments, the establishment of tough policies to fight crime and to aid law enforcement, and the construction of an intrastate highway connecting north and south Louisiana. Edwards represented the state on numerous multistate commissions and committees. Chairman of the Interstate Oil Compact Commission and state cochairman of the Ozarks Regional Commission, he was host governor for the 1975 National Governors Conference held in New Orleans. A member of the Energy Committee of the Southern Governors Conference, Edwards also served on the Committee on Natural Resources and Environmental Management of the National Governors Association (NGA). He was a member of the NGA Task Force on Foreign Trade and Tourism and has served on the NGA's Rural and Urban Development Committee.

One of the most colorful governors Louisiana has ever had, Edwards won widespread popularity because of his ability to appeal to and to work well with various social groups. His popularity stood him in good stead when charges of scandal surfaced in 1976, charges that as a member of Congress he had received gifts from Korean government agent Tongsun Park. Later, in 1980, he was 1 of 13 Louisiana public officials subpoenaed to appear before a federal grand jury investigating allegations of bribery in connection with a major federal undercover investigation in the Southwest. Despite such problems, however, political observers consider Edwards to have been one of the most popular and strongest chief executives in state history, and during his years in office, he has received national attention as a spokesman for the South. He nominated fellow Governor Jerry Brown for president at the 1976 Democratic National Convention, and there were even rumors that he might be offered the vice-presidential nomination that year.

Political observers predicted that he would easily have won a third term had he been constitutionally eligible to run again in 1979. Barred from serving a third consecutive term, he went back to his private law practice until he could run again in 1983, when he won overwhelmingly. He proved his appeal by trouncing the incumbent Republican, Governor David C. Treen, by a margin of 62 percent to 36 percent in the October election, thereby becoming the state's first chief executive to be elected to three terms.

The historic campaign was the most expensive in state history, with Edwards outspending Treen by more than a 2-1 margin. Treen, while a competent and honest executive, seemed dull in comparison with the flamboyant Edwards and himself acknowledged that this was a liability in Louisiana, which has a long tradition of embracing colorful and charismatic leaders. While Treen based his campaign on character issues, promising an honest administration, Edwards offered effective leadership. Frank about his image problems, he pledged to take steps to see that his actions in office did not carry even the appearance of impropriety. He also said he would seek to increase the state income tax and would ask the legislature to approve $200 million in raises for teachers, school personnel, and state employees. He pledged to appoint a representative number of women, blacks, Hispanics, and the disabled to state government posts.

Although Edwards had long been considered one of the ablest administrators in state history, his third term was beset by problems. Louisiana's economy continued to suffer from oil industry problems, and Edwards strained to overcome the revenue drain caused by the oil glut and the slumping production of oil and natural gas. With a moribund economy and a deficit-riddled treasury, the state led the nation in many negative indicators, including unemployment (which rose to a high of 14 percent) and the high school dropout rate (48 percent). Edwards found himself faced with one of the lowest job approval ratings of any incumbent in the nation.

He also continued to be dogged by accusations of scandal and wrongdoing. In March 1985, he was indicted by a federal grand jury on charges of conspiracy and racketeering, alleging that he and associates plotted to use his influence to acquire and sell hospital building certificates that netted them $10 million. His first trial in December 1985 ended in a mistrial; his second, in May 1986, in an acquittal.

Controversy continued to follow him, however. He was also the subject of a federal probe concerning his involvement with Texaco and the sale of state land in northeastern Louisiana to campaign contributors. In October 1986, he testified before a grand jury investigating allegations that state pardons were being sold. His appearance brought to 11 the number of grand juries that had looked into his activities since 1975.

His third term also saw some successes, however. He was credited with rescuing the financially plagued 1984 New Orleans World's Fair, by providing $18 million in loans and guarantees, and with helping the Saints football team stay in New Orleans. A survey by the National Women's Political Caucus found that his administration led the nation in the number of female appointments to cabinet-level positions.

Although Edwards had been considered the favorite to succeed retiring U.S. Senator Russell Long, he chose instead to seek reelection for an unprecedented fourth term as governor in 1987. Counting on the coalition that had always supported him—the Cajun vote in his home base, blacks, and labor—he denounced his opponents as enemies of the weak, needy, elderly, and black. At the center of his campaign were proposals for a state lottery and a casino in New Orleans to buttress state revenues. Casino gambling, he predicted, would cure the state's economic ills, generate 50,000 new jobs and $325 million in public revenue, as well as make New Orleans a resort center. Nonetheless, the proposals drew sharp criticism, denounced by one challenger in colorful, emotional language: "I don't want my children to grow up to be pit bosses and call girls in a casino."

Edwards' opponents in the state's unusual open primary were Congressman Billy Tauzin, a Democrat serving his fourth term; Republican Bob Livingston, a congressman and former prosecutor; Secretary of State James H. Brown, who waged a campaign as a reformer; and Congressman Charles "Buddy" Roemer, a conservative Democrat from northern Louisiana. The theme of all challengers was that the flamboyant Edwards was not the governor to lead the state through difficult economic times.

Under the state's unique system, candidates of all parties run together in the primary. If no one wins a majority, a runoff is held between the top two vote-getters, regardless of party.

The October 24 primary was seen as a historic turning point in state politics. Edwards' second-place finish to Roemer (28.5 percent to 31 percent) marked the first time that he had ever lost an election. Roemer, who had the support of most of the state's leading newspapers, had run TV ads denouncing the Edwards' administration as a "sinkhole of dirty corrupt politics." He ran as a "revolutionary" who promised "a revolution for Louisiana" and as a reformer who disdained contributions from political action committees and who disclosed the names of all financial supporters. According to political analysts, voters knew little about Roemer himself but were "swept up in a sea of change and voted for the candidate they perceived as being the greatest change for the political system.'' Bumper stickers appearing throughout the state attested to the prevalence of such sentiments. Frankly and candidly, voters declared themselves for ''ABE''—Anybody But Edwards. The fact that Roemer carried a substantial number of parishes in Edwards' home base of southern Louisiana indicated that sentiment for change was pervasive. With practically no public officials supporting him, Roemer won with a coalition of college-educated, affluent, under-55 voters tied into his congressional base in northern Louisiana.

In the opinion of political analysts, Edwards had lost his longtime constituency. The state's economic troubles had most affected his traditional supporters—minorities and blue-collar workers. Although blacks continued to vote largely for Edwards, their low turnout seemed to indicate disillusionment about the possibility of change in the system. Poll takers noted that Edwards' statewide support began to erode even before his much-publicized trials. The 1984 tax increases mandated by the state's economic malaise cost him the votes of the white middle class. Political writer John Maginnis called Edwards a ''sort of good-times governor,'' whose administration could not survive hard times.

Even more surprising than Edwards' second-place finish was his reaction to his showing. Although a runoff between Edwards and Roemer, as the primary's two top finishers, was scheduled for November 21, 1987, Edwards astounded friends and enemies alike with his postprimary concession to Roemer. After two other major candidates had indicated that they would back Roemer in the runoff, Edwards chose not to continue with the contest.

The man who had never before lost a political contest in his life retired to his private law practice. Yet, according to his son Stephen, Edwards was planning his comeback even before the final vote tallies were in. Two weeks before the ill-fated primary, when it became obvious that the tide was running against him, Edwards began to lay the groundwork for a future gubernatorial run.

Edwards' concession brought Buddy Roemer to the governorship, with high aspirations to start a new era in Louisiana politics. Promising a much-heralded ''Louisiana Revolution,'' Roemer seemed a symbol of the New South and Edwards a sorry symbol of the Old.

Four years later, however, the tables had rapidly turned. Unable to deliver on much of his reform agenda, Roemer faced stiff opposition in his bid for reelection. A much-ballyhooed party switch from Democratic to Republican ranks backfired when he was unable to gain the endorsement of the state Republican convention. Three vetoes of strict anti-abortion legislation hurt him politically in a state with a large prolife constituency, and his battles with the legislature had left him badly wounded. On a personal level, he had alienated many with his stubborn, often abrasive nature. The state faced a $1 billion budget deficit, and its fiscal recovery had been hampered by a failure to diversify its oil-based economy.

Roemer's many failings spurred Edwards to mount an unprecedented bid for a fourth term. His announcement came little more than a week after voters handed Roemer a humiliating defeat, rejecting a tax revision package considered to have been the linchpin of his highly touted "revolution." In seeking the governorship, Edwards told audiences he was running not to avenge his previous defeat by Roemer but to redeem his good name for the history books. Hammering away at what he called the unfulfilled promises of Roemer's last campaign, he depicted him as a "pompous, preachy," and ineffective leader who had been unable to enact much of his agenda. By contrast, Edwards presented himself as an astute master of the legislative process whose economic proposals—the creation of a state lottery and casino gambling for New Orleans—held the answer to the state's economic woes.

Edwards led the field in the state's October 19, 1991, open primary, with incumbent Roemer placing third. The November 16 runoff race drew unprecedented national attention due to the candidacy of David Duke, a former national grand wizard of the Knights of the Ku Klux Klan and founder of the National Association for the Advancement of White People. Duke's second-place finish in the October primary was attributed by some analysts to the nature of Louisiana's unique system. In their view, the open primary gives electoral advantages to extremists, since an array of moderate candidates gobble up the centrist middle.

Intense media coverage catapulted Duke to national prominence, as he sought to rise above his past association with racist groups and present himself as a serious spokesman for the beleaguered middle class. First entering the political spotlight in 1989 when elected state representative from the New Orleans suburb of Metairie, his impressive primary showing—44 percent of the total vote and almost 60 percent of the white vote—was scrutinized by observers for what it might forebode for the future of racist politics. Running as a Republican, Duke hinted at national political ambitions. Rumors of his plans to enter the 1992 presidential primary races threw fear into Republicans nationwide, and from the White House on down, they were quick to distance themselves from him. Nonetheless, Duke's dramatic showing was credited to an ability to craft a message of potentially broad appeal to disaffected voters. He bemoaned excessive government spending, rising taxes, exploding rates of crime and drug trafficking, the high costs of welfare, and affirmative action programs deemed unfair to whites. Addressing himself to Edwards specifically, he bashed his previous scandal-ridden administrations, his record of tax increases, and his reputation as a gambler and womanizer.

Although both candidates tried to convince voters that they had abandoned their sordid pasts and had atoned for previous indiscretions, the Hobson's choice presented to the electorate left many in a strange predicament. Lame duck Buddy Roemer called the contest "my worst nightmare for the state of Louisiana," while others presented the contest as one between "a racist and a rogue" or "a kook or a crook." The good government voters who had supported Roemer found the choice especially painful. Taught since childhood to deride Edwards as a kind of "rapscallion," they now were forced to see him as the sole alternative to Duke. Political analysts believed this Roemer vote held the key to Edwards' ultimate election.

For his part, Edwards ran a brilliant campaign, trying to project an image of stability and maturity while raising concerns about Duke's ability to govern the state. Benefiting from an unprecedented campaign by business leaders who warned of the economic consequences of a Duke win, he was able to forge a unique coalition of blacks, Jews, business leaders, activists, progressives, and disaffected Republicans. He drew 61 percent of the vote and an astonishing 96 percent of the black vote. It was the most scrutinized and most publicized gubernatorial race in history, with turnout a record 78 percent.

Edwards' victory capped the resurrection of a career once left for dead. Hailed as the "Queen Victoria of Louisiana politics" because he had dominated the state for so long, Edwards faced a host of challenges when he took office on January 13, 1992: a $1 billion budget deficit, lingering questions about his ethical standards, and the challenges of keeping together the unusual coalition that brought him into power. Many doubted whether he knew how to mount a real reform agenda or whether he had the will to deal with the state's crucial environmental problems after a dismal record in the past.

The highlight of Edwards' fourth term thus far has been the passage of a bill legalizing casino gambling in New Orleans. Although Edwards claims the casino will provide jobs, attract tourists, stimulate the economy, and help revitalize the city, opponents say his championing of the casino measure is the best proof that he hasn't reformed his "Bad Boy, Fast Eddie" image. Barely in office six months, he faced a recall drive fueled by opposition to the bill. In a state already awash in myriad forms of gambling—horse racing, off-track horse betting and bingo games, a state lottery approved by the legislature in 1991—skeptics challenged Edwards' plans for the state and questioned whether he has a vision that transcends gambling. Others again raised the ethics issue. Leaders of Recall '92 accused Edwards of ramming through a casino bill while accepting a vacation from a Hawaiian developer who won a $415 million casino bid. Despite all the questions, however, organizers faced a daunting challenge to collect the 740,000 signatures needed to force a recall election.

In response to such concerns, Edwards insists upon his determination to leave a positive legacy. Speaking of his fourth term in office, he asserts, "I'm 64 years old now and I want this opportunity to do something for myself and for my state, and I'm not going to blow it."

Bibliography: Biographical information courtesy of governor's office; *The Chronicle of Higher Education*: 9–23–87; 10–16–91; John Maginnis, *The Last Hayride* (Baton Rouge: Gris Gris Press, 1984); *Newsweek*: 3–11–85; 11–25–85; 10–26–87; 11–4–91; 11–25–91; *The New York Times:* 5–16–79; 2–11–80; 2–14–80; 2–15–80; 2–17–80; 11–2–80; 10–23–83; 10–24–83; 11–7–83; 11–13–83; 3–3–85; 3–10–85; 9–15–85; 12–19–85; 3–23–86; 10–14–86; 10–17–86; 2–28–87; 3–31–87; 6–27–87; 10–22–87; 10–26–87; 5–10–89; 5–4–91; 7–19–91; 9–24–91; 10–21–91; 11–4–91; 11–10–91; 11–11–91; 11–14–91; 11–15–91; 11–17–91; 11–18–91; 1–14–92; 5–1–92; 6–12–92; 7–12–92; Anita Schrodt, "Three Days in the Life of That 'Cajun Fella,' " *Biography News* I (April 1974): 398–99; *The Star-Ledger* (Newark, N.J.): 7–28–91; 11–12–91; 11–17–91; 11–9–92; *USA Today:* 10–15–91; 10–23–91; 11–4–91; 11–8/10–91; 11–12–91; 11–15/17–91; 11–18–91; 1–13–92; 6–16–92; 6–18–92; 11–9–92.

John R. McKernan, Jr. *(Courtesy of Governor's Office)*

MAINE

JOHN R. McKERNAN, JR., 1987–

Born in Bangor, Maine, on May 20, 1948, McKernan is the son of John R. McKernan and Barbara Guild McKernan. A Protestant, McKernan is the father of a son, Peter, from his first marriage. In 1989, he married six-term Maine Congresswoman Olympia Snowe after a decade-long courtship. The two had first met in the Maine legislature.

As a teenager, McKernan helped manage his family's Bangor newspaper after the death of his father. He graduated from Bangor High School in 1966, where he was a standout athlete. After graduation from Dartmouth in 1970, McKernan joined the Army National Guard, serving from 1970 to 1973. In 1971 he enrolled at the University of Maine School of Law, from which he graduated in 1974.

While still in law school, McKernan, a Republican, won election to the state legislature from an at-large Bangor district. He served two terms, 1972 to 1976, the last as the assistant Republican floor leader. The highlight of his tenure was authorship of Maine's returnable container law or "bottle bill," which made Maine one of the first states in the country to pass such legislation.

During his years in the legislature, McKernan also practiced law in Bangor. Upon leaving state government in 1976, he joined the Portland law firm of Verrill and Dana.

Deciding to return to public service in 1982, he ran for Maine's First Congressional District seat when the incumbent challenged Senator George Mitchell for reelection. Victorious in his congressional bid, McKernan served on the House Education and Labor Committee, the Merchant Marine and Fisheries Committee, the Government Operations Committee, and the Select Committee on Children, Youth, and Families.

In 1986, McKernan ran for governor upon the constitutional ineligibility of incumbent Joseph Brennan. It was a unique political swap, with Brennan seeking McKernan's congressional seat while McKernan chose to succeed Brennan in the statehouse. As an environmentalist with strong business support, McKernan was seen as the Republicans' strongest contender since they last won the governorship in 1962. McKernan won the race, but with only 40 percent of the vote. The rest was split among three contenders: Attorney General James Tierney, a Democrat with consumerist and environmentalist credentials, who gained 30 percent; independent Sherry Huber, a critic of nuclear power and previously unsuccessful Republican gubernatorial hopeful, who polled 15 percent; and independent John Menario, a former Portland city manager, who drew 15 percent. McKernan based his campaign on leading Maine into a prosperous high-tech future without abandoning environmental concerns. In the opinion of political observers, his views on taxes and services appeared only mildly different from those of retiring Governor Brennan.

His 1990 race for reelection was termed a race between two incumbents, with McKernan facing Congressman and former Governor Joseph E. Brennan. Brennan, who had the advantage of being well known and well financed, excoriated McKernan for his handling of the state budget. McKernan, on the other hand, charged that Brennan had flipflopped on his support for Maine Yankee, the state's nuclear power plant. McKernan emerged victorious, earning 47 percent of the vote to Brennan's 44 percent. Independent Andrew Adam polled 9 percent.

In office, McKernan has won national recognition for his leadership and innovation on education and human resource initiatives. In 1989, Maine was selected "State of the Year" by the National Alliance of Business. McKernan has worked to expand the state's vocational educational system and to improve communications between state government and the university system. He has been a strong supporter of Maine's only nuclear power plant, the Maine Yankee, one of the nation's most reliable and economical reactors. McKernan has served on the Advisory Committee of the Bangor Community College, coordinated a major fundraising drive for Portland's Mercy Hospital, and in 1982 was appointed to the Commission on Presidential Scholars. In 1976, he handled President Gerald Ford's reelection campaign in the state and was active in both the 1980 and 1984 Reagan-Bush campaigns. In 1988, he served as honorary Maine chairman of the Bush-Quayle campaign. McKernan has served as chairman of the National Governors Association (NGA) Human Resources Committee, directing the NGA's work on health care, job training, and education. He has also chaired Jobs for America's Graduates, a national school-to-work transition organization for at-risk youth. A past chairman of the Coalition for Northeastern Governors and the New England Governors Conference, McKernan has also been a member of the executive committee of the Republican Governors Association. In July 1991, he became chair of the Education Commission of the States, a national educational policy group based in Denver, Colorado.

His public life has also been marked by stress and controversy, however. The economic downturn that racked the Northeast in the early 1990s hit Maine hard. McKernan managed to achieve a $3.6 million surplus for fiscal year 1990 but slashed spending, delayed scheduled tax cuts, and used up virtually all his carryover surplus in order to stay in the black. One year later, the situation had changed dramatically, and McKernan came in for sharp criticism for failing to predict the downturn. To deal with a $210 million shortfall in the state's budget by the end of 1990, he delayed scheduled property tax relief for elderly homeowners, postponed some business tax cuts, and set back the starting date for a health insurance subsidy program for which earmarked beer and cigarette taxes had already been collected. He tangled with the Democratic legislature over spending, taxes, and workers' compensation insurance laws.

Sixteen days of intense negotiations over the 1992–1993 budget were even more dramatic, with the government virtually shutting down as the governor and legislature battled over revision of the state's workers' compensation laws. In Maine, where physically hazardous jobs like logging abound, and compensation for injuries is relatively generous, insurance premiums are among the highest in the nation. McKernan and his Republican allies linked passage of a budget to a 35 percent cut in the workers' compensation program. The new budget also included nearly $300 million in increased taxes. Resulting layoffs of state employees, on top of the tax increases, have hurt McKernan's political popularity.

The state continues to face serious economic difficulties. Maine's once booming real estate industry is in depression, and revenue has been shrinking since 1989. In response, McKernan has ordered every department of state government to undergo careful scrutiny and has insisted that every possible spending cut be made. He seems determined to bring about a balanced budget without further tax increases.

McKernan is the 1994 head of the Republican Governors Association. He has taken as his prime objective the task of helping his party get back to basics: "We have got to stop talking like economists," he advises, "and start talking more like the person next door."

Bibliography: Michael Barone et al., *The Almanac of American Politics, 1984, 1988* (Washington, D.C.: National Journal, 1983, 1987); biographical information courtesy of governor's office; *The Chronicle of Higher Education*: 10–22–86; 11–12–86; *The New York Times*: 10–4–87; 2–20–89; 11–7–90; 7–9–91; 7–17–91; 2–26–93; *The Star-Ledger* (Newark, N.J.), 9–2–90; *USA Today*: 7–19–91; 11–18–92.

William Donald Schaefer *(Courtesy of Governor's Office)*

MARYLAND

WILLIAM DONALD SCHAEFER, 1987–

Born in West Baltimore on November 2, 1921, Schaefer is the son of William Henry Schaefer and Tululu Skiffer Schaefer. An Episcopalian, Schaefer is a bachelor.

Educated in Baltimore's public schools, he graduated from Baltimore City College in 1939 and from the University of Baltimore Law School in 1942. His legal career put on hold by U.S. entry into World War II, Schaefer joined the army, achieved officer rank, and took charge of administering military hospitals both in England and on the continent. After his tour of duty, he remained in the U.S. Army Reserves, ultimately retiring with the rank of colonel.

After the war, Schaefer resumed his legal career, practicing real estate law. He went on to earn a Master of Laws degree from the University of Baltimore in 1952 and later formed a general practice law firm with two colleagues. His keen concern for city planning and housing in Baltimore motivated his entrance into the public arena and prompted him to take a leadership role in citizen associations. His community involvement propelled him to a seat on the Baltimore City Council in 1955, where he served until 1967. In 1967, he was elected council president, and in 1971, mayor of the city. Inaugurated as mayor on December 7, 1971, he served four consecutive terms until he was elected governor.

As mayor, Schaefer initiated a highly innovative urban rejuvenation program, which drew upon the resources of federal, state, and local government as well as those of the private sector. These initiatives led to a widespread revitalization of the city's neighborhoods and to its emergence as a major tourist center. Schaefer's restoration of the Baltimore Inner Harbor area with its showpiece "Harborplace" drew national acclaim. He also strengthened the city's diversified local economy, insisted on the delivery of services to neighborhoods, and bridged the gap between black and white. His programs attracted $1.2 billion in new investments that tripled the city's tax base and retained 39,500 industrial jobs.

Schaefer's work as mayor earned him acclaim as one of the nation's most effective urban executives. He was the recipient of eight honorary doctorates, and the U.S. Conference of Mayors bestowed upon him the highest accolades. He was the fifth person in the nation to receive the Distinguished Public Service Award from Brandeis University.

In 1986, Schaefer sought the Democratic gubernatorial nomination to succeed Harry Hughes, constitutionally ineligible to seek a third term. His opponent in the September 9 primary was Attorney General Stephen H. Sachs, an aggressive prosecutor whose oratory and message were reminiscent of John F. Kennedy. Seeking to embrace the traditional Democratic coalition of labor, minorities, and women, Sachs made public education the centerpiece of his campaign. He also argued that the election of Schaefer, a longtime friend of disgraced former Governor Marvin Mandel, would mark a return to political cronyism—a charge hotly denied by Schaefer, who was untouched by the scandals of the Mandel administration. Sachs also tried to spark interest in his candidacy with the selection of a popular black politician as his running mate, Representative Parren J. Mitchell, a civil rights activist who was dean of the state's congressional delegation. Nevertheless, Schaefer won the primary in a landslide.

His opponent in the general election was state Representative Thomas J. Mooney, who had run unopposed for the Republican nomination. Mooney, however, lacked support even from his own party, and the results of the election were never in doubt. Schaefer won by the greatest margin of victory in state gubernatorial history, sweeping Maryland's 23 counties and the city of Baltimore with an unprecedented 82 percent of the vote.

Schaefer began making public policy even before he took office. In December 1986 he learned of the proposed closing of a major corporation in western Maryland. In an attempt to save jobs and to help displaced workers and their families, he immediately marshaled state forces and headed for Allegheny County. Together with his top advisers and the Maryland congressional delegation, he devised a plan of state and federal action to meet the needs of the company and its employees. As a result, the corporation decided to keep its headquarters in Cumberland, saving 600 jobs. The incident is indicative of Schaefer's oft-cited "Do It Now!" approach that is the hallmark of his leadership style.

Major achievements of Schaefer's first term in office included a plan to hold on to the state's windfall from federal tax reform, an increased gas tax, and changes in workers' compensation and medical malpractice policies. He launched a drive for a $200 million complex of two new professional sports stadiums in downtown Baltimore, one for football, one for baseball. In the area of education, he proposed that the state give a financial bonus to parents who save to pay for their children's college education. He also argued for more clearly defined missions for public colleges and universities and expanded research programs in the University of Maryland system. In 1988, he signed into law a bill that made the state the first to ban the sale of some cheap pistols. In a highly controversial move, he threatened to withhold state funds from poverty lawyers unless they promised not to sue the state. Although the governor repeatedly emphasized that he is a strong supporter of the rights of indigent and disabled people to legal representation in civil lawsuits, he wanted to eliminate an inappropriate use of state funds, saying that the state did not have any responsibility to finance long, expensive lawsuits against itself.

Seeking reelection in 1990, Schaefer won renomination with an easy win over Democratic challenger Frederick Griisser and then went on to defeat Republican William S. Shepard, a retired foreign service officer, in the general election. Schaefer earned 60 percent of the vote. An interesting twist in the race was Shepard's choice of his wife Lois, a teacher and political activist, as his running mate.

The controversy over abortion rights also surfaced in the Maryland campaign, as it did in so many other races in the 1990 election year. Schaefer drew sharp criticism for his silence on the issue, with the national press highlighting his position as the nation's only incumbent governor seeking reelection who refused to take a stand on the matter. Supporters insisted that his silence reflected the painful moral dilemma that the issue posed for him, while critics suggested it represented nothing more than a bald-faced political strategy. Schaefer announced his support for abortion rights only after voters ousted four staunch abortion foes from the state senate. Saying he personally opposed abortion, he promised to veto any restrictive legislation that came across his desk. True to his word, in 1991 he signed into law a bill that would protect a woman's right to abortion, should a future U.S. Supreme Court decision move to restrict it. Supporters of the bill described it as one of the most liberal abortion laws in the nation.

In office, Schaefer has been an activist governor, with education reform, economic development, and social service programs among his achievements. He has worked to overhaul higher education, funneling more state aid to community colleges and four-year institutions and making college more accessible to the poor and minorities. Starting with a major reorganization of public higher education in 1988, he has increased financial support for state student aid and for the construction of new facilities at state universities. Public schools adopted new performance standards as part of a multiyear plan to upgrade education.

In the area of economic development, Schaefer has led nine international trade missions, seeking markets for state products, promoting Maryland as an ideal tourist destination, and strengthening ties with Russia, Europe, and Asia. In 1991 the state of Maryland and the government of Kuwait signed an agreement to give Maryland companies an advantage in the competition to rebuild the sheikdom after the devastation of the Iraqi invasion and Gulf War. Schaefer was lauded for his role in winning the agreement, which came as a direct result of his personal efforts.

Domestically, Schaefer has expanded social programs from housing to child care. He started the nation's first state outreach effort for AIDS patients and reorganized state departments to devote more resources to children, juvenile services, and environmental protection. He initiated a compact between Maryland and neighboring Mid-Atlantic states to share information on drug abuse programs and to cooperate in the enforcement of drug laws. Welfare reform has been another objective of his second term. While basic welfare grants have been reduced as part of his overall budget-balancing plans, his administration has attempted to tie welfare aid to greater personal responsibility, giving full public assistance benefits only to family recipients who send their children to school and get preventive health care. In a highly controversial move in 1993, he proposed that the state offer free Norplant implants to women on welfare and vasectomies to men leaving prison. While the idea won praise from some state welfare officials, others condemned it as a clumsy attempt at social engineering.

Although political observers feel that Schaefer looks like the opposite of an ideal politician—he is not photogenic and squirms when interviewed—all agree that he has been the dominant figure in state politics since 1986. Women's groups have been especially pleased with his efforts. For three consecutive years, National Women's Political Caucus surveys have credited his administration for having the highest number of female appointments to cabinet-level positions of any governor nationwide.

Despite his successes, however, Schaefer has drawn bad press and soured relations with some constituencies due to some petty squabbles. A series of peculiar controversies have marred his last few years in office. He enraged residents of Maryland's Eastern shore, for example, by referring to that rural but politically important part of the state as "an outhouse." Angered at the outspokenness and independence of his lieutenant governor Melvin A. Steinberg, he engaged in a highly publicized cold war with his two-time running mate, kicking him off some committees and stripping him of some aides. By far the worst offense, however, in the eyes of state Democrats, was Schaefer's endorsement of Republican George Bush in the 1992 presidential campaign. After some discussion, the state's Democrats decided not to formally reprimand Schaefer for his actions. Even so, a resolution stating that the governor "relinquish his honorary title as titular leader of the party" was only narrowly rejected by the party central committee.

Schaefer may have had enough of statewide politics. There is some speculation that he is considering a return run for mayor of Baltimore upon the completion of his present gubernatorial term.

Bibliography: Michael Barone et al., *The Almanac of American Politics, 1988* (Washington, D.C.: National Journal, 1987); biographical information courtesy of governor's office; *The Chronicle of Higher Education*: 11–12-86; 2–17–88; 10–31–

90; 8–28–91; *The New York Times*: 12–22–85; 7–13–86; 9–8–86; 9–10–86; 11–5–86; 1–22–87; 7–1–87; 7–8–87; 5–24–88; 7–31–89; 9–16–90; 11–7–90; 2–19–91; 3–15–91; 5–4–91; 11–28–91; 12–18–91; 12–28–91; 1–17–93; 2–1–93; *The Record* (Bergen County, N.J.), 11–9–92; *USA Today*: 7–2–90; 9–10–90; 9–24–90; 4–26–91.

Michael S. Dukakis *(Courtesy of Governor's Office; photo By Richard Sobol)*

MICHAEL S. DUKAKIS, 1975–1979, 1983–1991

Born in Brookline, Massachusetts, on November 3, 1933, Dukakis is the son of Panos Dukakis and Euterpe Boukis Dukakis, Greek immigrants. Married to the former Katharine Dickson, he is the father of three children.

Dukakis attended Brookline High School, graduating in 1951. He received his B.A. degree in 1955 from Swarthmore College, where he earned highest honors in political science. He served in the U.S. Army from 1956 to 1958, including duty in Korea. Dukakis received an LL.B. from Harvard in 1960, graduating with honors. After being admitted to the Massachusetts bar, he practiced law. In 1962, Dukakis was elected to the Massachusetts House of Representatives, serving until 1970. There he sponsored legislation for housing, conservation, and consumer protection. He was the first legislator in America to introduce a no-fault automobile insurance bill, which was passed by the state in 1971. In 1970, Dukakis lost in an attempt to become lieutenant governor. He then returned to his private law practice but remained active in public affairs. He served as moderator of "The Advocates," a public television debate program, and helped to monitor state agencies to ensure efficient government.

In 1974, Dukakis ran against incumbent Republican Governor Francis W. Sargent, after winning the Democratic gubernatorial nomination with 58 percent of the vote over Robert H. Quinn. Promising the most open administration in Massachusetts history, Dukakis pledged to reduce the size of the governor's staff, balance the state budget, and reduce spending. Dukakis declared that the first thing he would do upon becoming governor would be "to introduce the idea of productivity and efficiency goals and standards into state government." Helped by an anti-Republican trend in an anti-Republican state, Dukakis took 56 percent of the vote.

As chief executive, Dukakis spent much of his time trying to correct the fiscal problems of Massachusetts. He reduced the number of public employees and made other cuts in state spending that restored Massachusetts to fiscal responsibility. He worked to regulate state agencies, continued to support consumer protection, and was involved in efforts to alleviate the state's energy shortage.

Christened "Jerry Brown East" by the press, Dukakis impressed voters by eliminating many of the trappings of the governor's office. He continued to live in his own modest home, grew vegetables in his garden, and got rid of the state limousine in favor of the Boston subway. Still, though citizens were impressed by his unquestioned honesty and competence, many were turned off by his lack of warmth. Dukakis was hurt most of all by the way he handled taxes. Elected as a liberal reformer intent on stopping the state's spiraling taxes and public spending, he did slash the budget and turn around the nearly bankrupt state. In the process, however, he was forced to approve the largest tax increase in Massachusetts history, after having given the voters a "lead pipe guarantee of no new taxes." In office, Dukakis disappointed many liberals who had supported him by cutting state services and programs. He made enemies and antagonized allies in the legislature, with whom he wrestled over the budget for almost his entire first year in office. He also earned the reputation of being a cold intellectual who could not compromise with legislative interests. In retrospect, his governorship during his first term "cannot be said to have been a success," in the words of one political observer.

Nonetheless, Dukakis' defeat in the 1978 Democratic gubernatorial primary jolted liberals across the nation. His opponent was Edward J. King, the former director of the Massachusetts Port Authority and head of a business promotional group called the New England Council. King campaigned on a pledge to cut property taxes by $500 million, to slash social spending, and to create a probusiness atmosphere. Outspending Dukakis on advertising by a margin of 2–1, he used sophisticated polling techniques to identify voter grievances against Dukakis. Dukakis, on the other hand, did little campaigning, relying on polls that showed him with a wide lead. In a stunning upset, he was defeated by King, 51 percent to 42 percent (with a third candidate garnering 7 percent of the vote). King went on to defeat the Republican Francis Hatch, a moderate state representative, in the general election.

Dukakis' behavior after his defeat served to alienate him from an increasingly divided state Democratic party. He was criticized especially for his failure to support King, a conservative, in the general election. Vulnerable because of his rigid stance against cronyism and his refusal to wheel and deal politically, Dukakis was even rebuffed by the Massachusetts Executive Council, which voted to ask President Jimmy Carter to keep him out of his cabinet.

After leaving office, Dukakis assumed the position of lecturer and director of Intergovernmental Studies at Harvard's John F. Kennedy School of Government, where he taught courses in management at the state and local level and joined a group of faculty members developing studies in the new field of public management.

By 1982, however, Dukakis was ready to make a surprising comeback and reclaim the governorship. In a rerun of their bitter 1978 contest,

Dukakis challenged the incumbent King for the Democratic nomination in a primary billed as an early referendum on Reaganomics. As a conservative Democrat often referred to as "Ronald Reagan's favorite governor," King presented himself as an advocate of the common man and took conservative positions on capital punishment, mandatory sentencing, and drunk driving. King's openly probusiness attitude, with its emphasis on tax cutting, reduction in state regulation, and crackdown on welfare abuse, had pleased many businessmen, but voters were increasingly displeased with what they perceived as his inept handling of the budget and legislature and his scandal-ridden administration. Not only did Dukakis attack King as a "cheerleader for Reaganomics," but he made effective use of the issue of corruption in state government. One of King's cabinet secretaries was convicted and sent to prison for taking money; another old friend, a deputy commissioner in the Revenue Department, hanged himself after disclosure of a scandal over payoffs to revenue officials.

Dukakis hired professionals from Washington, D.C. to help project an image of integrity and competence. Running on the theme of "honest and effective leadership," he put together one of the largest field organizations ever assembled for a statewide race. Expanding the organization of the liberal coalition that had elected him in 1974, he raised $2 million from a broader base of small contributors than did King and with it was able to overpower King's advantages of incumbency and his own substantial war chest. Dukakis was greatly aided by a resounding endorsement from the *Boston Globe,* which described the King administration as "one of the weakest in the modern history of the Commonwealth."

In May 1982, 68 percent of the delegates to the state's first Democratic convention in eight years passed a nonbinding resolution supporting Dukakis for the nomination. In the September 1982 primary, the most expensive in the state's history and one that received extensive national coverage, Dukakis defeated King with 53 percent of the vote. The bitter grudge match drew the largest number of voters in the history of a Massachusetts primary. Dukakis' support had come from liberals, suburban residents, and the state's relatively large number of intellectuals, while King drew upon blue-collar workers in the old industrial cities and in Roman Catholic, Irish, and Italian communities.

In the general election, Dukakis faced Republican John Winthrop Sears, a well-to-do Boston city councilman. The race was billed as a classic contest between a liberal and a conservative, one that pitted an ethnic Democrat against a Brahmin Republican. Dukakis tried hard in his campaign to shed the reputation for humorlessness and arrogance that he had acquired as governor. Properly chastened after his previous defeat, he presented himself as a bridge builder and a seeker of consensus. He stressed his opposition to the death penalty, his support for gun control, and his concern about problems such as mass transit and human services.

In a state where there are three Democrats for every Republican, Dukakis won handily, gaining 59 percent of the vote.

In his inaugural address, Dukakis pledged to "fight Reaganomics and its philosophy of indifference with all the energy I can summon." Serving with Lieutenant Governor John Kerry, he again faced difficult economic circumstances. Achievements of his second term included the development of programs to aid the estimated hundreds of homeless Massachusetts citizens and to create jobs for the thousands of the state's unemployed.

Dukakis won a third term in November 1986, with the biggest victory margin of any Massachusetts governor in this century. He defeated his Republican opponent, George S. Kariotis, with 69 percent of the vote, garnering 1,157,786 votes to his opponent's 525,364.

Since his return to office in 1983, Dukakis made economic development the keynote of his administration. Presenting himself as a new breed of competent, technocratic, managerial governor, he took credit for the state's booming, high-tech economy. In all, more than 300,000 new jobs were created and 54,000 new businesses started in the state during his tenure. He worked to bring strong economic development initiatives to regions of the state suffering from declining industries and the competition of foreign imports. He also signed into law an education reform program for public schools; initiated open-space acquisitions programs to save valuable areas across the state from overdevelopment; signed a workers' compensation reform bill; and led the fight against drunk driving on state highways. Perceived as a classical northern liberal, he signed the nation's first law to guarantee health insurance to all state residents and also enacted the first program in the country to allow AIDS victims to remain at home to die rather than in hospitals. His efforts to win passage of model plant closing and right-to-know legislation helped protect Massachusetts workers.

In New England, Dukakis served as chairman of the New England Governors Conference and as chairman of the Committee on Economic Development for the Coalition of Northeast Governors. Nationally, he was chairman of the Committee on Economic Development and Technological Innovation of the National Governors Association and chairman of the Committee on Industrial and Entrepreneurial Economy for the Policy Commission of the Democratic National Committee. In 1984, he presented the platform to the National Democratic Convention in San Francisco and, in August 1986, was elected chairman of the Democratic Governors Association.

In March 1987, Dukakis entered the race for the 1988 Democratic presidential nomination, saying he had the "experience to manage" and "the values to lead." Surprising even political pundits with his fund-raising ability and organizational talent, he emerged from a field of seven contenders to win the party's presidential nomination, garnering enough delegates by the end of the spring primaries to ensure his coronation by the Democratic National Convention meeting in Atlanta in July 1988.

Selecting Senator Lloyd Bentsen of Texas as his running mate, Dukakis faced a tough election against Republican nominee George Bush. As a candidate, he offered his accomplishments as governor of Massachusetts as models to be followed on the national level and presented himself as a "CEO" who knew how to make government work. Voicing the impassioned concern that has been so much a part of traditional Democratic appeal, he stressed the problems of adult illiteracy, the misery of the homeless, the need for changes in the welfare system, and the responsibility of society toward older Americans.

Despite a last-minute rally in the polls, Dukakis suffered a decisive defeat, with Bush winning a solid 6–5 victory in the popular vote and a commanding majority in the electoral college. With his political future in doubt, Dukakis returned to Massachusetts to deal with a deteriorating economic climate.

The 1988 run for the presidency had wreaked incalculable harm upon Dukakis' political base at home. Massachusetts residents seemed to take his defeat personally, partly because he lost a big lead due to inept campaigning and partly because he allowed Bush to humiliate their state as the home of runaway taxes, profligate spending, polluted harbors, and rampant crime. They also came to resent his election year absences and began to question how much he knew about the state's collapsing economy all the while that he posed as the creator of the "Massachusetts miracle." Although he had pitched himself to the nation on the strength of his financial competence, exemplified by the ten budgets he had balanced during his two and a half terms in office, by 1989 he faced a $600 million budget deficit. Boston pundits then suggested he had a "Massachusetts mess" to deal with, and critics questioned how much he had really known and failed to disclose about the state's red ink problems. The most serious charges suggested that he had artificially propped up the state's finances to advance his political ambitions. By 1990, the state's bond rating had dropped precipitously—"just above junk bond status," in the words of one source—and he was forced to sign a $1.8 billion tax increase that was the largest in the state's history. Aiming to rescue Massachusetts from a $1.4 billion budget deficit and the worst economy in the Northeast, the bill included the first permanent income tax increase in the state since 1975 and also expanded the sales tax to cover certain professional services for the first time. The bill seemed to lend credence to Republican allegations in the 1988 campaign that Dukakis was indeed a big "tax-and-spender" and that his state might be better known as "Taxachusetts," both charges that he of course decried.

Faced with such economic troubles, Dukakis made a stunning announcement on January 3, 1989, less than two months after his defeat in the presidential race. Saying it was time for new blood and new leadership in the statehouse, he pulled himself out of the 1990 gubernatorial race, almost two years before the actual contest. Although he insisted that it would be easier for him to deal with the state's fiscal crisis as a noncandidate, the announcement surprised many in Massachusetts because Dukakis had often said how much he enjoyed being governor. It also fueled speculation that he was considering another presidential run, especially as he continued to raise campaign funds and negotiate with national political consultants.

Viewed with the benefit of political hindsight, the premature announcement proved devastating to the remaining years of Dukakis' gubernatorial term and to his long-term legacy. Once he announced his retirement, he lost any political power he could have mustered to ward off the frustration and anger pointed his way, and he became a defenseless target for politicians and voters alike. The most humiliating example of his fall from grace came at the hands of his own lieutenant governor, Evelyn Murphy. Seeking to distance herself from the unpopular Dukakis and to bolster her own chances for gaining the 1990 Democratic gubernatorial nomination, she defied Dukakis while he was on a trade mission to Europe. Using state laws that allow the lieutenant governor to assume the powers of governor whenever the chief executive is out of the state, she issued a host of financial and executive orders designed to portray herself as a decisive leader. In so doing, she hoped both to contrast herself with the inept Dukakis and to impose her own plan for solving the state's budget crisis.

Although Murphy's "palace coup" won her little new public support, the whole spectacle of the feud between Dukakis and his own second-in-command was seen by analysts as damaging to the Democratic party and reflective of the extent to which state leaders would go to disassociate themselves from him. In the September 1990 Democratic primary, virtually every Democratic candidate who had any connection to the Democratic party establishment or to Dukakis himself went down to a rousing defeat. The sole exception was U.S. Senator John F. Kerry, a popular and independent figure in his own right.

The postelection period was also a difficult time personally for Dukakis. His wife Kitty suffered from problems stemming from alcohol addiction, and she was hospitalized at least twice, once after drinking rubbing alcohol. Her later publication of a best-seller *Now You Know* (New York: Simon & Schuster, 1990) candidly described her addiction to pills and alcohol and outlined how her husband's actions and personality fed into her addiction.

By the time of Dukakis' retirement from office, his disapproval ratings reached almost 80 percent. He was looked upon with contempt, with some press reports even referring to him as "the most hated man in the state." Even the possibility of impeachment was suggested by a longtime opponent. Political analysts explained that they had never seen anything like his ignominious free-fall, and one political scientist termed him probably the most despised man in American politics, alongside Richard Nixon.

With all his problems, Dukakis did bring a sense of honesty to Massachusetts government that no one ever doubted. He counts among his major achievements in office a job training program for welfare recipients, a bill that made health care available to all state residents, and economic incentives that helped keep a boom running throughout much of the 1980s.

Since his retirement from office, Dukakis has embarked on an academic teaching career, encouraging young people to enter public service. Becoming a visiting professor at Boston's Northeastern University, he has also taught and lectured at the University of Hawaii, Florida Atlantic University, and the John F. Kennedy School of Government at Harvard. Saying he wants especially to advance the cause of national health care, which he calls the primary issue of the 1990s, he has never formally ruled out the possibility of another run for public office.

Bibliography: Biographical information courtesy of governor's office; Fox Butterfield, "Dukakis," *New York Times Magazine* (May 8, 1988): 22–25, 86–87, 92–96; *The Chronicle of Higher Education*: 11–12–86; 9–19–90; 6–19–91; 12–18–91; Richard Ben Cramer, *What It Takes: The Way to the White House* (New York: Random House, 1992); Michael S. Dukakis and Rosabeth Moss Kanter, *Creating the Future: The Massachusetts Comeback and Its Promise for America* (New York: Summit Books, 1988); Charles Kenney and Robert L. Turner, *Dukakis: An American Odyssey* (Boston: Houghton Mifflin, 1988); *Newsweek*: 2–22–88; 4–18–88; 1–2–89; 1–8–90; 9–17–90; *The New York Times*: 7–27–86; 9–19–86; 9–21–86; 12–28–86; 1–6–87; 3–1–87; 3–17–87; 4–30–87; 6–3–87; 6–14–87; 11–26–87; 1–10–88; 1–20–88; 4–22–88; 6–2–88; 1–4–89; 1–13–89; 5–21–89; 6–4–90; 7–8–90; 7–10–90; 9–7–90; 9–8–90; 9–11–90; 9–25–90; 10–17–90; 1–1–91; 6–7–91; *The Star-Ledger* (Newark, N.J.): 1–29–89; 8–18–89; 4–4–90; 10–28–90; 12–30–90; 1–4–91; 1–23–92; 3–4–92; *USA Today*: 4–29–88; 4–16–90; 7–19–90; 9–10–90; 6–7–91.

William F. Weld *(Courtesy of Governor's Office)*

WILLIAM F. WELD, 1991–

Weld was born on July 31, 1945, in Smithfield, New York, the scion of an old patrician family. His ancestors first landed in Boston in 1630, and his father was a New York investment banker. He attended the Middlesex School in Concord, Massachusetts, from 1956 to 1962, before entering Harvard College, from which he graduated summa cum laude in 1966. He received a diploma in economics and political science from Oxford in 1967 and earned a J.D. from Harvard Law School in 1970. Weld is married to a law school classmate, Susan Roosevelt, a great-granddaughter of Theodore Roosevelt. The couple has five children.

After serving as a law clerk with the Supreme Judicial Court of Massachusetts, Weld worked for ten years at the Boston law firm of Hill and Barlow. In 1974, he served as associate minority counsel to the U.S. House Judiciary Committee during its Watergate impeachment inquiry.

After an unsuccessful run for Massachusetts attorney general in 1978, he was named U.S. attorney for Massachusetts by President Ronald Reagan. Serving in that post from 1981 to 1986, he developed a reputation as a tough prosecutor, winning convictions against officials of former Boston Mayor Kevin White's administration, as well as members of Boston's organized crime family. His office won convictions in 109 of 111 political corruption cases, imposed fines on several banks engaged in money laundering, and broke up an arson ring that was responsible for 306 fires in the greater Boston area. In 1985, Weld was honored by his fellow U.S. attorneys with his election as chairman of the attorney general's Advisory Committee of U.S. attorneys.

In 1986, Weld was appointed by President Reagan as assistant attorney general in charge of the Criminal Division. During his tenure in Washington, he targeted political corruption, narcotics, and white-collar crime cases. He resigned from office in 1988 to protest the ethical problems of his boss, U.S. Attorney General Edwin Meese, a move that endeared him to independents, liberal Democrats, and maverick Republicans. After his resignation, he served as a senior partner in the Boston law firm of Hale and Dorr, where he worked until his election as governor of Massachusetts in 1990. It was the first public office to which he was ever elected.

Weld's victory seemed unlikely in a liberal state where Democrats outnumber Republicans by 4–1 and where Republicans had not captured the statehouse since 1970. In the final analysis, however, his victory was attributable to the fact that he was not a traditional Republican and that the Democrats had strayed far from nominating a traditional candidate. Also a key factor in the nationally publicized race was enormous public anger over the state's economic decline and a prolonged state budget crisis.

The unorthodox nature of the governor's race already seemed evident in the primary, which drew a record number of voters. Although he had been unable to win the endorsement of the state Republican party convention, Weld won the party's nomination with 60 percent of the vote over convention-endorsed Stephen Pierce, a little-known legislator. In a move destined to have significant impact on the fall campaign, state Democrats gave their nod to protest candidate John Silber, on leave from his post as president of Boston University. Defeating party regular and long-time state pol Francis X. Bellotti with 53 percent of the vote, Silber drew national attention with his outspoken, brash, and ideological attacks on many of the most cherished beliefs of state Democratic leaders. His views offended many key Democratic constituencies—blacks, women, homosexuals, immigrants, and union members. At the same time, however, he attracted many disgruntled voters who rallied to his refreshing and provocative style. Known for a series of controversial statements known as "Silber Shockers"—such as the call to cut off welfare benefits to teenage mothers who had a second child—he rocked the political establishment with his win and caused many independent and liberal Democrats to reconsider the Republican alternative. Even the *Boston Globe,* generally regarded as sympathetic to liberal Democrats, threw its support to Weld.

For his part, Weld distanced himself from many of the socially conservative policies of Republicans, distinguishing himself, for example, by his prochoice stand on abortion, his concern for strict environmental protection, and his support for in-school condom distribution programs to combat the spread of AIDS. Liberals also drew comfort from his earlier separation from the Reagan Justice Department. Putting $1 million of his personal fortune into the race, he also benefited from an amiable and modest personal style that contrasted sharply with that of the tempestuous and argumentative Silber.

Because of their similar positions on economic issues, some commentators saw the race as one between "two Republicans." Both men distanced themselves from the policies of the outgoing Dukakis administration, and both favored the approval of Question 3, a tax rollback referendum that would have slashed state budget revenues but was ultimately defeated by worried voters.

Weld won a 52 percent victory in a race that saw a 70 percent voter turnout, a record for a nonpresidential run. In the opinion of analysts, the large turnout reflected enormous voter anger against Dukakis and the Democratically controlled state legislature, both of whom were blamed for a recession-ravaged state economy and a prolonged state budget mess.

Others interpreted the results not so much as an endorsement of Weld but as a rebuff of the abrasive Silber.

A strong fiscal conservative, Weld outlined a program for a slimmed-down state government. In a stinging rebuke of the policies of his Democratic predecessor, Weld proclaimed sharply that he didn't believe "government should be about the miracle business." He painted a Reaganesque picture of government, hoping to create a "stripped down entrepreneurial state" that in his words "steers but doesn't row." He used his inaugural address to brand Massachusetts a "fiscal Beirut" as a consequence of past Democratic policies.

In office, Weld has won high marks as a "new age" governor, fiscally conservative yet libertarian on social issues. At a time when other governors were being forced by soaring deficits to make unpopular tax increases, Weld held fast to his no new taxes campaign pledge. He introduced a package of tax cut proposals as part of an effort to reinvigorate the state economy and embarked on a complex and controversial program of spending cuts, including the closing of nine state hospitals. Being compared with Ronald Reagan for his transformation of government via tax and spending cuts, he has also won praise from national conservative groups for initiating a plan to contract with business to perform what are normally state functions, and to sell state agencies to private enterprise. There is general agreement that his biggest accomplishment thus far has been the preparation of a balanced 1992 budget without new taxes or borrowing in the bond market. As a result of his leadership, Massachusetts no longer has the worst bond rating of the 50 states. In late 1992, Standard & Poors raised the state's bond rating from BBB to A, prompting Weld to declare that Massachusetts' three-and-a-half-year budget crisis was finally over.

Other important initiatives introduced by Weld include: changes in state abortion laws to make it easier for women to obtain abortions, especially in the event that a future Supreme Court weakens *Roe v. Wade;* legislation to radically change public schools by abolishing teacher tenure and seniority, imposing merit-based standards for teachers, establishing a statewide core curriculum, and allowing state takeover of weak and failing districts; and a death penalty bill that would allow the state to kill certain categories of first-degree murderers 18 and older by lethal injection. Weld has introduced legislation to give state officials vast new powers to track down parents who owe child support payments and to punish those who refuse to pay. Ranking first among the nation's governors in a National Women's Political Caucus report on female appointments to cabinet-level posts—the first time a Republican has led the field—he also has drawn praise for his record on homosexual rights. A supporter of gay rights who has appointed homosexuals to judgeship and subcabinet posts, he created the nation's first Governor's Commission on Gay and Lesbian Youth to study suicide, hate crimes, and other issues of concern to gay youth. For his efforts, Weld has drawn praise from national gay rights organizations, including the Coalition for Lesbian and Gay Civil Rights who have hailed him as the nation's "most pro-gay governor."

Weld has received much national attention for his pioneering and non-traditional policies. Although he is disliked by state Republican stalwarts for his social liberalism, others see him as a potential new leader for Republicans nationally. At the much-maligned Republican National Convention of 1992, he appealed to the GOP Platform Committee to at least make the abortion plank neutral on the subject, in keeping with the idea of making the Republican party a "big tent" inclusive of divergent views. His stance may receive even more attention in the wake of the subsequent Republican loss of the White House, and he is already being touted as a possible Republican standard-bearer in the presidential race of 1996.

Closer to home, there had been talk that Weld, with his escalating popularity, might be interested in challenging Ted Kennedy for the U.S. Senate in 1994. Although he later backed down from the idea, the speculation itself was testimony to Weld's command of state politics and government. Early in 1992, a *Boston Globe* poll showed Kennedy leading Weld for the Senate by only four percentage points—a statistical deadheat. There has even been fearful talk of the "implosion" of the state Democratic party. Weld has won virtually all his legislative initiatives and sustained nearly every veto. He bears close watching.

Bibliography: Biographical information courtesy of governor's office; *The Chronicle of Higher Education,* 8–28–91; Phil Duncan, ed., *Politics in America 1992* (Washington, D.C.: Congressional Quarterly Press, 1991); Dennis Hale, "Massachusetts: William F. Weld: The End of Business as Usual," in Thad Beyle, ed., *Governors and Hard Times* (Washington, D.C.: Congressional Quarterly Press, 1992); Christopher Lydon, "Hostile Takeover: The Republican Raid on Massachusetts," *New York Times Magazine* (Aug. 2, 1992): 32–33, 50–53; *Newsweek,* 3–26–90; *The New York Times:* 4–6–90; 6–4–90; 7–27–90; 9–20–90; 11–1–90; 11–4–90; 11–7–90; 11–8–90; 11–11–90; 12–31–90; 2–1–91; 4–6–91; 10–17–91; 11–19–91; 1–18–92; 3–13–92; 7–5–92; 8–17–92; 9–10–92; 11–11–92; *The Star-Ledger* (Newark, N.J.): 9–19–90; 1–4–91; 8–2–91; 8–15–91; 4–8–92; *USA Today:* 9–19–90; 9–20–90; 1–17–91; 4–11–91; 2–11–92; 5–14–92; 6–3–92.

MICHIGAN

JAMES JOHNSTON BLANCHARD, 1983–1991

Born in Detroit, Michigan, on August 8, 1942, Blanchard is the son of James Robert Blanchard and Rosalie Johnston Webb Blanchard. A Unitarian, Blanchard married Paula Parker in 1966. In 1987, the pair announced their divorce because of long-standing irreconcilable differences. They have one son, Jay. Blanchard later married Janet Fox, a onetime staff assistant.

Blanchard earned his B.A. (1964) and M.B.A. (1965) in business administration from Michigan State University. He holds a law degree from the University of Minnesota (1968).

He began his public service career in 1968 as a legal adviser in the Michigan Secretary of State's Office. In 1969, he became a Michigan assistant attorney general and served in that capacity for five years. He was also a lawyer in private practice with the Bloomfield Hills firm of Beer and Boltz before being elected to Congress in 1974 as a representative from Michigan's 18th Congressional District.

A Democrat, Blanchard served four terms in Congress. From 1976 to 1982, he served as assistant Democratic whip. In Congress, he was a member of the Banking, Finance, and Urban Affairs Committee and the Science and Technology Committee and was chairman of the House Subcommittee on Economic Stabilization. As chairman, he conducted an extensive series of hearings on the revitalization of the U.S. economy, with a focus on the problems facing the industrial sectors of the country. As the author of the Chrysler Loan Guarantee Act, he was best known for getting the Chrysler bailout passed in the House. Besides economic revitalization, his legislative interests included budgeting and government spending, energy, preserving the Great Lakes, cities, housing, and foreign policy. He also served on the President's Commission on the Holocaust.

Blanchard was first elected to the governorship in 1982, defeating Republican conservative R. H. Headlee with 51.4 percent of the vote. Political analysts believe that his role in engineering the Chrysler bailout was central to his victory.

When Blanchard was inaugurated as the state's 45th governor on January 1, 1983, Michigan faced a $1.7 billion deficit, record-high unem-

James Johnston Blanchard *(Courtesy of Governor's Office)*

ployment, and the worst credit rating in the nation. Working with his cabinet, members of the legislature, and leaders of the state's business, labor, education, and local government communities, he tackled the state's finances, upgrading the state's credit rating and launching an aggressive small-business and economic development program. Among his first acts in office was to call for a tax increase. Although he understood that higher taxes might make the state less attractive to business, he felt that with the state's huge deficit, he had no other choice. Although rather unpopular during his first year in office, he rebounded as the state's economic health improved. In less than three years, Blanchard was able to declare solvency day—November 8, 1985—marking Michigan's return to fiscal health and the end of a decade of deficit. During his first term, he helped Michigan outpace the nation in creating new jobs, restored education as a top state priority, and undertook the most aggressive prison construction program in the state's history. He also wooed and won an assembly plant that Mazda decided to build in the United States and encouraged Japanese auto parts suppliers to open operations in Michigan. Putting the state on the road to developing a more diversified private sector economy, he developed strategies to use Michigan's manufacturing expertise to specialize in high-skill, capital-intensive, flexible manufacturing areas.

For all these accomplishments, *Newsweek* magazine credited Blanchard with leading "one of the most dramatic economic turnabouts in the recent history of state government." As the state's economy picked up, Blanchard was able to get rid of the temporary tax hike passed during his first year in office, thus depriving the Republicans of a major campaign issue in his drive for reelection. Identifying himself with the burgeoning pride in the state's economic revival, he and his party reaped benefits from the recovery and growth of Michigan's economy.

His 1986 campaign for reelection drew national attention because of his Republican opponent, William Lucas, who would have made history by becoming the nation's first black governor. Lucas, a former Federal Bureau of Investigation (FBI) agent, Wayne County sheriff, and Wayne County executive, became the center of nationwide Republican efforts to portray the party as open to minorities. In a highly publicized switch, he himself had abandoned the Democrats to join the GOP in 1985. Lucas campaigned on a platform of toughness on crime, efficiency in government, and control of government spending. As executive of Wayne County, which includes Detroit and surrounding suburbs, he had eliminated the county budget deficit of $140 million a year by cutting payrolls, slimming the bureaucracy, and bringing in a private company to manage a debt-ridden county-owned hospital. The health of the state economy, however, deprived Lucas of the economic issue. Although he won the support of antiabortion groups with his outright opposition to abortion, he made little headway with voters in his calls for lower taxes and a tougher stance on crime.

Blanchard, on the other hand, with his economic development theme "Working Together for Michigan," attracted voters who might normally have voted Republican. According to political analysts, race was not a factor in the campaign: Lucas lost few votes because of race, but neither did his candidacy capture the imagination of many black voters. Blanchard's 68 percent to 31 percent victory was the highest margin in a Michigan gubernatorial election since 1928 and the best Democratic percentage since 1835.

During his second term, Blanchard proposed a unique program to assist parents with financing the costs of their children's college education; worked to encourage universities to work more closely with businesses to stimulate economic development; vetoed a bill that would have raised the state speed limit to 65 miles per hour on rural stretches of Michigan's interstate highways; and signed into law the nation's first bill making surrogate parenting contracts for profit a crime. He was chairman of the Democratic Platform Committee for the 1988 Democratic National Convention.

Overall, during his two terms as governor Blanchard received high marks for his efforts to make the state's manufacturing economy more competitive. As his race for a third term approached, Democrats were optimistic, counting on the staying power that incumbents have traditionally enjoyed in Michigan. Two of his predecessors, William G. Milliken and G. Mennen Williams, held office for 14 and 12 years, respectively, before deciding not to run again. Although Blanchard entered the race as a frontrunner with no opposition in the August 1990 Democratic primary, his Republican opponent, John Engler, majority leader of the state senate, proved to be the most formidable opponent that Blanchard had ever faced, and his upset loss was unexpected by analysts.

In retrospect, however, a string of embarrassments and missteps marked his campaign. Critics believed that it came on too strong employing the same kind of race-baiting tactics of which Democrats had accused George Bush in 1988. In a series of TV spots, Blanchard accused his opponent of voting "to let dangerous criminals out of state prisons early." One ad, portraying Blanchard as tough on crime, showed a white drill sergeant issuing orders to a black inmate at a Michigan work camp. Opponents called the commercial racist and said the governor was embarrassing himself.

The race was also noteworthy in that the former wives of both candidates wrote books that documented the breakup of their marriages. Paula Blanchard's book, *'Til Politics Do Us Part* (West Bloomfield, Mich.:

Altwerger & Mandel, 1990) addressed her reaction to rumors that her husband was having an affair with a staff member, Janet Fox, whom he ultimately married.

By far, however, the most damaging factor in any explanation of Blanchard's loss involved his surprise decision to drop his 78-year-old lieutenant governor, Martha W. Griffiths, from his reelection ticket. Griffiths, a former ten-term congresswoman, was something of a legend in Michigan politics. Many political insiders believe that Blanchard would never have won his first term without her on the ticket. In making his agonizing decision, Blanchard explained that he wanted a running mate who could step in to replace him if necessary and that he doubted Griffiths could do so, given her age and increasing frailty.

Blanchard's announcement drew national attention, inciting charges of sex and age discrimination. Political analysts believed that the dismissal could have been handled more deftly, even if it was necessary.

Cynics, however, saw more sordid motives behind the move. Some believed that Blanchard's larger interest was running strongly enough to look like vice-presidential timber in 1992, while others speculated that Blanchard was positioning himself to take the U.S. Senate seat of Donald W. Riegle, Jr., one of five senators under investigation for his role in the savings and loan scandal. Some observers suggested that Blanchard wanted to ensure that the state was in the hands of a reliable successor who would be willing to appoint him to the seat if Riegle were forced out before his term was up in 1994. That scenario could not be guaranteed with the irascible Griffiths at the helm of state government.

Although Blanchard dismissed all these allegations as "Republican gossip," his opponent moved quickly to gain the political advantage. Spotting an opening, Engler promptly announced that his running mate would be a 66-year-old woman, Connie Binsfeld, a state senator who was once named Michigan's Mother of the Year.

After his narrow defeat (1,260,611 votes to Engler's 1,279,744), Blanchard returned to the practice of law. Becoming a partner in the Washington firm of Verner, Lipfert, Bernard, McPherson and Hand, he was also affiliated with the Michigan firm of Jaffe, Snider, Raitt and Hener. He planned to focus on international law and advising clients on public policy strategies.

During his retirement from public life, Blanchard has served as a guest lecturer at Michigan universities and at the John F. Kennedy School of Government at Harvard. He also accepted a position on the board of the Center for the Great Lakes, a nonprofit research group committed to protecting the lakes. For a time, it was rumored that he was interested in being appointed president of Michigan State University.

A key campaign supporter of fellow Governor Bill Clinton, Blanchard was the unofficial leader of Clinton's 1992 presidential campaign in Michigan. As a result, he was tapped by Clinton to become U.S. ambassador to Canada, a job Blanchard has said he always wanted.

Bibliography: Michael Barone et al., *The Almanac of American Politics, 1984, 1986, 1988* (Washington, D.C.: National Journal, 1983, 1985, 1987); biographical information courtesy of governor's office; *The Chronicle of Higher Education*: 10–22–86; 11–12–86; 8–28–91; 6–17–92; *Newsweek*, 9–17–90; *The New York Times*: 5–5–85; 9–26–85; 10–29–86; 11–5–86; 6–17–87; 7–2–87; 7–12–87; 6–27–88; 6–28–88; 7–22–90; 9–5–90; 11–11–90; *USA Today*: 7–24–90; 5–28–93; *The Record* (Bergen County, N.J.), 3–5–91.

JOHN ENGLER, 1991–

Born on October 12, 1948, in Mt. Pleasant, Michigan, Engler graduated from Michigan State University in 1971 and the Thomas Cooley School of Law in 1981. He is married to the former Michelle Dumunbrun. A Republican, Engler is a career politician. Elected to the state legislature right out of college, he served in the state house of representatives from 1971 to 1979 and in the state senate from 1979 to 1991. He held the position of majority leader from 1984 to 1991. Viewed by many as a superb politician and strategist, he was impeded—in the opinion of many—by his lack of a statewide base of support. He was little known outside of Lansing and his rural central Michigan legislative district when he decided to challenge incumbent Governor Jim Blanchard in 1990.

Yet Engler had made a career out of surprising the pundits and being an unlikely giant killer. While a college student, he had written a paper on strategies for toppling incumbents, plans that obviously served him well in his personal political life. In 1970, at the age of 22, he ousted an incumbent state house member by a handful of votes and then repeated the performance in 1978 by defeating an incumbent state senator.

He went on to do the same in his 1990 statehouse bid, although his victory was both unpredicted and seemingly unexplainable. In the opinion of one observer, he was a Republican who lacked significant business support, an ideological conservative in a state long a pioneer in generous social policy, and an antilabor voice in a state dominated by labor interests. Winning the Republican nomination by 87 percent of the vote against perennial candidate John Lauve, he capitalized on the state's weak economy to make a case against the Blanchard administration. His tough campaign promised to allocate half of future state budgets to education; to crack down on crime by putting white-collar criminals in chain gangs and by denying drug offenders school loans, welfare grants, and driver's licenses; and in what was probably his most effective pledge, promising to reduce local property taxes by 20 percent. He was also backed by abortion foes for supporting a bill requiring teenagers to get parental consent for abortions—one vetoed by Blanchard. More than one-fourth of state voters said the perceived need for change was a decisive factor in their vote. Squeaking into office by a razor-thin margin of 19,000 votes out of 2.5 million cast, Engler faced the challenge of delivering on his promises.

Property tax relief and the need to streamline state government are the

John Engler *(Peter Glendinning Photography)*

goals of his administration. True to his campaign promises, he didn't propose raising taxes in the face of projected budget deficits but, by contrast, endorsed a plan to cut them. Confident that he could deal with the deficit by eliminating waste in state government, he immediately began an effort to cut spending in state agencies via a 9.2 percent across-the-board budget cut, a freeze on state hiring, cuts in state contracts, and "downsizing state government." In enacting welfare cuts that were the deepest in the nation, he removed more than 82,000 able-bodied adults from the rolls and cut deeply into other poverty programs.

In the most far-reaching and radical change of his tenure thus far, Engler and Republicans in the legislature have cut the state property tax 20 percent. Wiping out more than $6 billion in revenues, he has appointed a commission to re-design the entire system of funding public schools through property tax revenues.

Political observers feel that Engler's rapid-fire activism polarized the state. Never known as a proponent of consensus politics, he aroused strong opinions. Eight short weeks into his term, in the words of one analyst, he had become known as "the most hated man in the capital." Nine months into his term he faced a recall petition. His 46 percent disapproval rating was among the highest for the nation's 18 new governors.

Yet supporters charged that his programs appealed to a silent majority who had long resented "being pilloried by liberal Democrats." For all the ballyhoo, they noted, his approval rating of 49 percent was triple that of predecessor Jim Blanchard in his first term. Nationally, press reports asked whether Engler was "the taxpayer's best friend" or the U.S.A.'s "most heartless governor."

Some observers feel that Engler bears watching. Now that he has established his agenda and achieved some victories, he may become a more moderate force for change.

Bibliography: Phil Duncan, ed., *Politics in America 1992* (Washington, D.C.: Congressional Quarterly Press, 1991); *Newsweek,* 9–6–93; *The New York Times*: 7–22–90; 11–7–90; 11–8–90; 11–11–90; 11–19–90; 10– 7–91; *USA Today*: 7–24–90; 8–8–90; 11–8–90; 7–19–91; 9–13– 91; 11–20–91; Carol S. Weissert, "Michigan: No More Business as Usual with John Engler," in Thad Beyle, ed., *Governors and Hard Times* (Washington, D.C.: Congressional Quarterly Press, 1992).

Rudy Perpich *(Courtesy of Governor's Office)*

MINNESOTA

RUDY PERPICH, 1976–1979, 1983–1991

Born in Carson Lake, Minnesota, on June 27, 1928, Perpich is the son of Anton and Mary Vukelich Perpich. A Roman Catholic, he married Lola Simic of Keewatin, Minnesota, on September 4, 1954, and is the father of two children.

Perpich attended Hibbing High School and Hibbing Junior College in Minnesota and received his A.A. degree in 1950. He then graduated from Marquette University with a D.D.S. in 1954. Perpich served in the U.S. Army as a sergeant from 1946 to 1947. A member of Minnesota's Democratic-Farmer-Labor (DFL) party, he was on the Hibbing Board of Education from 1952 to 1962, served in the Minnesota Senate from 1963 to 1970, and was lieutenant governor of Minnesota from 1971 to 1976. Perpich first became governor in an interesting and prearranged job swap. On December 30, 1976, Governor Wendell Anderson resigned, and Perpich was elevated to that office, as provided by Minnesota's constitution. Perpich then appointed former Governor Anderson to fill the seat of Walter Mondale, the vice-president-elect, in the U.S. Senate.

Perpich served as the 34th governor of Minnesota from 1976 until January 1979. The son of immigrants from Eastern Europe, he became the state's first governor of that ethnic background, the first to come from the Iron Range of Minnesota, and the first Roman Catholic. His success as a dentist and later as a politician was a classic American success story that endeared him to Minnesota's large Slavic population. Perpich's father Anton had moved to the state from Yugoslavia when he was 20 to work in the ore mines of the Iron Range, and Governor Perpich was later to claim that this background shaped him, leading him to champion the rights of the poor and minorities. His unorthodox personal style also proved to be exceptionally popular. He opened his first inaugural with a Roman Catholic polka mass, and he once dashed off to Austria on the pretext that a castle might make a nice home for the University of Minnesota's foreign studies program. A believer in the work ethic, he vowed to make government more productive and to crack down on waste and inefficiency. Perpich ordered phones removed from state cars, cut down on travel and the use of state vehicles, and once banned coffee from his office in protest over its high price. Committed to providing citizens access to their chief executive, he maintained an open door policy and attracted attention by showing up unheralded and unexpectedly in public places. At one point, he even allowed reporters to rummage through his office drawers when they asked to do so.

Nevertheless, the friendly and easygoing Perpich also had his critics. Some said he acted without thinking and often without heeding the advice of his staff. Others claimed that he had no clear-cut program or vision for Minnesota. His biggest problem, however, was his link to a Democratic-Farmer-Labor party that was drawing increasing criticism in the state. By early 1978 the Republicans had begun to make the point that all of Minnesota's top statewide positions were filled by people who had not been elected to them—a view that the voters apparently shared, judging by the results of the 1978 elections. The DFL suffered some shattering defeats that year. Seeking election to his own term as governor, Perpich was vulnerable because of his role in the controversy that had ensued over the Mondale-Anderson-Perpich job swap. He also faced a strong challenger in Republican Albert H. Quie, a 20-year veteran congressman from Minnesota's First District.

Seizing on the popularity of "Proposition 13" sentiment in a high tax state, Quie advocated a 10 percent across-the-board tax cut and a constitutional amendment limiting state spending to growth in personal income. The voters responded positively, apparently reassured that Quie's reputation as a political moderate would keep him from slashing spending to ridiculous extremes. He defeated Perpich by a margin of 54 percent to 46 percent in an election in which Perpich failed to carry some normally Democratic counties. Perpich attributed his upset defeat to poor campaign organization and to a split between the conservative and liberal wings of his party. Quie's triumph was also widely interpreted as a victory for right-to-life groups in Minnesota. Although both men had taken antiabortion stands, right-to-life groups felt that Quie had done more for them.

Perpich lived in Vienna after he left office in 1979. Working for Control Data Corporation overseas, he became vice-president and executive consultant to Control Data Worldtech, an international trade division of the Minneapolis-based computer concern. Perpich saw his new career as "an opportunity for me to promote Minnesota in international trade, breaking down barriers."

With Quie's retirement from office in 1983 after having served only a single term as governor, Perpich staged a comeback attempt in which he was widely perceived as the underdog. Still, he scored an upset victory in the Democratic primary that year, defeating popular state Attorney General Warren M. Spannaus and airline mechanic Ellsworth Peterson. Perpich earned 51 percent of the vote, winning huge majorities in his home base, the economically depressed Iron Range.

Perpich was a strong favorite in the general election against Republican Wheelock Whitney, a wealthy businessman. The central focus of the 1982 campaign was the financial health of Minnesota. Perpich, who contrasted the prosperous condition of the treasury when he left office to its depleted state four years later, won an overwhelming victory, gaining 59 percent of the vote to Whitney's 40 percent.

With his victory, Perpich became the only person in Minnesota history to hold the gubernatorial post for two nonconsecutive terms. He was sworn in as the state's 36th governor on January 3, 1983.

Seeking reelection in 1986, he faced a tough primary challenger in George Latimer, mayor of St. Paul for an unprecedented six terms. In the campaign, Perpich emphasized his role in creating jobs and cutting taxes, while Latimer focused on leadership issues. Perpich won the nomination of the Democratic-Farmer-Labor party with 57 percent of the vote.

In the general election, Perpich faced former state Representative Cal Ludeman, the candidate of the Independent-Republican party. Perpich promised tax reform and to make Minnesota "the manpower state" so it would be more attractive to business. His policies of wooing business and disciplining but not dismantling Minnesota's welfare state attracted voters, and he won the election, 56 percent to 43 percent. Although this was a solid victory, it was less than he had won by in 1982 and suggested to political observers that the DFL no longer commanded an automatic majority in state elections.

During his years in office, Perpich sought to be called the "jobs governor." Campaigning on the need for job creation in the state, he joined labor, business, agriculture, education, and the private sector in efforts that put 100,000 more Minnesotans to work than ever before in state history and created a total of 200,000 new jobs. A special focus of his efforts was the diversification of the Iron Range economy. Having grown up in the area, Perpich took a personal interest in its development, and he created a separate state agency, the Iron Range Resources and Rehabilitation Board, to funnel state aid into the area. Lured by special incentives, both electronics and wood products companies invested heavily in operations there. A 1984 survey in *USA Today* identified Minnesota as having the best work force in the nation for high-tech development and credited Perpich with being one of the nation's best governors for promoting growth within that area.

Another priority of the Perpich administration was education reform. Upon taking office, he championed a 26 percent increase in the state's investment in elementary, secondary, and postsecondary education. He also initiated a 70 percent increase in grants and scholarships, three new engineering schools, a natural resources research center, new buildings and a new focus for the University of Minnesota, and an investment in up to 100 new endowed university chairs. He also supported a controversial program allowing high school students to take courses at public and private colleges, using school aid to pay tuition.

In fiscal areas, Perpich spearheaded a drive for a $1 billion income tax cut in 1985. He also delivered a simplified tax form, demanded a strong tax compliance program to find and prosecute cheaters, and proposed the creation of a budget reserve, or "rainy day fund." In 1987, Minnesota imposed the highest cigarette tax in the nation, intended not only to raise revenue and to finance health care programs but also to make smoking so expensive that it became prohibitive. Perpich said he hoped to make Minnesota smoke-free by the year 2000.

Despite all these accomplishments, serious problems began to dog Perpich during his third term. Voters came to be impatient with the eccentricity that had once made him such a beloved figure, and foes took to calling him "Governor Goofy." Critics claimed he had peddled influence to big contributors, adopted a regal life-style, and become just plain strange. Highly publicized scandals involving two of his former associates also hurt his popularity. Political rivals in Minneapolis accused him of devoting too much time and state resources to his home base and of neglecting other areas of the state. Finally, his right-to-life stance also raised hackles in a state with an increasingly militant prochoice movement.

By the opening of the 1990 campaign season, polls indicated that more than 70 percent of the electorate wanted a change in the statehouse. A sagging economy and rising taxes also worked to weaken Perpich's chances for reelection. Trailing in the polls, he faced a strong primary challenge from Mike Hatch, a lawyer and former state commerce commissioner who accused Perpich of providing no leadership. He painted Perpich as a governor who started programs and then abandoned them.

Perpich seemed headed for defeat, failing even to make promises to voters for fear they would not be believed. In desperation, he took to reading aloud on television from an out-of-state magazine that described Minnesota as a nice place to live.

Surprisingly, however, Perpich went up in the polls as Hatch mounted a vigorous and negative TV campaign. His ability to survive the primary challenge was attributed by analysts to Hatch's failure to capitalize on what might have been his strongest issue—the abortion controversy. Although Perpich opposed legalized abortion, supporters of abortion rights did not mobilize the kind of national effort for Hatch that they did in other states where opponents of abortion faced supporters of abortion rights.

In the general election, Perpich faced Republican Jon Grunseth, a conservative businessman and abortion opponent. In one of the most chaotic campaigns in U.S. gubernatorial history, however, Grunseth resigned from the race nine days before election day. Stung by allegations that he had frolicked in the nude with teenaged girls and had had an affair that spanned two marriages, he left his party in disarray with his abrupt withdrawal, a move without precedent in U.S. history. Grunseth accused Perpich of orchestrating the charges. As the Republicans scrambled to find a last-minute replacement, it seemed that Perpich might eke out another victory. He had confounded the pundits before. Yet it was perhaps a testament to the depth of anti-Perpich feeling in the state that a hastily organized campaign by state auditor Arne Carlson, who had challenged Grunseth in the GOP primary, could pull off a narrow win, ending Perpich's long gubernatorial career.

Bitter over his defeat, Perpich presented a sullen, sulking image to the public. He refused to work with the new Carlson administration, to talk with reporters, or even to attend the lighting of the state's official Christmas tree.

After his retirement from office, there was much speculation that Perpich, who is of Croatian descent and speaks the language, would become foreign minister of Croatia. Although he ultimately turned down the job for fear it would cloud the status of his U.S. citizenship, he planned to remain an adviser to the government of Croatia. He has also been working as a consultant to deliver U.S. business investment to Croatia.

Bibliography: Michael Barone et al., *The Almanac of American Politics, 1986, 1988* (Washington, D.C.: National Journal, 1985, 1987); biographical information courtesy of governor's office; *The Chronicle of Higher Education*: 11–12–86; 2–18–87; 1–13–88; *The Dallas Morning News*, 8–1–87; "From the 'Dumps' to Governor," *New York Times Biographical Service* 7 (Dec. 1976): 1775–76; *The New York Times*: 12–31–76; 4–10–77; 11–2–78; 1–10–79; 11–1–80; 2–16–82; 9–15–82; 11–1–82; 1–5–84; 9–9–86; 9–11–86; 9–14–87; 11–20–88; 12–10–89; 1–11–90; 9–11–90; 9–12–90; 9–16–90; 10–27–90; 10–29–90; *The Record* (Bergen County, N.J.), 4–25–91; *The Star-Ledger* (Newark, N.J.): 10–30–90; 4–30–91; *USA Today*: 12–27–89; 10–29–90.

Arne H. Carlson *(Courtesy of Governor's Office)*

ARNE H. CARLSON, 1991–

Born in New York City on September 11, 1934, Carlson is the son of Swedish immigrants. He received a full scholarship to Choate, the exclusive Connecticut prep school, from which he graduated in 1952, and a full scholarship to Williams College, from which he graduated in 1957 with a degree in history. He attended graduate school at the University of Minnesota from 1957 to 1958 and served in the U.S. Army from 1959 to 1960. Before embarking on a career in politics, he worked as a computer executive. He and his wife Susan, an attorney, have three children.

A Republican, Carlson began his political career on the Minneapolis City Council, where he served as majority leader from 1965 to 1967. An eight-year stint in the Minnesota House of Representatives yielded numerous accomplishments. Cited by women's groups and environmental organizations for his outstanding work, he was the chief author of a pioneering day care bill, the chief author of legislation providing assistance centers for rape victims, and the chief author of a law providing access for the physically handicapped. First elected Minnesota state auditor in 1978, he was the leading Republican vote-getter in the elections of 1982 and 1986. He remained state auditor until his election to the governorship in 1990. In that office, he also was highly successful and effective: creating the nation's first Fiscal Health Program to provide early warning signs of severe economic change to local governments; creating a uniform accounting plan for cities, counties, townships, and special districts, making Minnesota a leader in uniform accounting; and overhauling the state's multibillion-dollar pension investment portfolio to allow private sector management.

Entering the governor's race in 1990 as the fortunes of incumbent Rudy Perpich were fading fast, he was one of a number of candidates seeking the Republican gubernatorial nomination. Although he began the race as the frontrunner, his opponents, Doug Keeley, a lawyer, and Jon Grunseth, a business executive, weakened his candidacy by depicting him as soft on crime, and Grunseth ultimately went on to win the nomination.

Nonetheless, Carlson was able to reenter the race in the quirkiest of circumstances. In a bizarre turn of events without precedent in national history, Grunseth abruptly withdrew his candidacy just nine days before the general election. His campaign had been severely damaged by allegations of sexual improprieties, including allegations that he had frolicked in the nude with teenaged girls and had carried on an adulterous love affair that spanned two marriages. Carlson had already launched a write-in campaign after Grunseth's personal problems surfaced, but he was officially chosen as the Republican nominee by a 14-member executive committee hastily summoned to make order out of chaos. The last-minute candidate shift forced the state to use paper ballots, requiring hand tabulation and slowing the tallying of results.

Although he had only nine days to campaign and was the longest of longshots, the scrappy Carlson went on to defeat the unpopular Perpich by the narrowest of margins, gaining only 50.1 percent of the total vote. He got most of the votes of the Grunseth backers and won almost 60 percent of the independent vote. Carlson appealed to voter discontent with the political status quo in rallies around the state and dubbed his campaign a "prairie fire" to scorch the political establishment.

Carlson is relatively liberal by Minnesota standards. He is supportive of abortion rights, for example, and is an enthusiastic defender of spending money on programs like child care and Head Start. He says that he doesn't want Republicans "to be portrayed as cold and uncaring, because they are not."

Once in office, however, Carlson got off to a rocky start. Humiliated by a state court decision overturning eight of his vetoes because they were signed a day late, he also faced an increasingly disgruntled electorate. A *Minneapolis Star Tribune* poll conducted in January 1992 gave him a disapproval rating of 55 percent. Voters seemed frustrated by his veto of a health care bill proposed by the Democratic legislature. With his popularity slipping, he seemed ready to work out some agreement on a universal health care plan. Another initiative of his term has been a proposal to create a new Department of Children and Educational Services, a unified division to provide programs for children from birth through higher education.

Bibliography: Biographical information courtesy of governor's office; *The Chronicle of Higher Education,* 1–27–93; Phil Duncan, ed., *Politics in America 1992* (Washington, D.C.: Congressional Quarterly Press, 1991); *The New York Times:* 10–27–90; 2–18–92; *The Star-Ledger* (Newark, N.J.): 10–30–90; 8–5–92; *USA Today:* 11–8–90; 9–10–91.

MISSISSIPPI

RAY MABUS, 1988–1992

Ray Mabus was born on October 11, 1948, in Ackerman, Choctaw County, Mississippi, the overachieving only child of a prosperous timber farmer. His father was an inveterate traveler who showed his son the world beyond Mississippi. By the time Mabus was 19, he had lived in Mexico, seen Tehran, and journeyed on the Trans-Siberian Railroad. He graduated from the University of Mississippi after 3 years, then studied political science at Johns Hopkins on a Woodrow Wilson fellowship. After receiving an M.A. from Johns Hopkins, he graduated with honors from Harvard Law School. He later joined the high-powered Washington, D.C. firm of Fried, Frank, Harris, Shriver, and Kampelman.

Mabus served in the U.S. Navy on a guided-missile cruiser, was counsel to a subcommittee of the Agricultural Commission of the U.S. House of Representatives, and like his father and uncle, has also been a tree farmer in Choctaw County. He and his wife, the former Julie Hines, have one daughter, Elizabeth.

From 1980 to 1983 he was legal counsel to Governor William Winter. In that role, he was instrumental in securing passage of the landmark Education Reform Act of 1982, a strengthened law against drunk drivers, Mississippi's first open records act, and legislation to give low-interest home loans to Mississippians.

In 1983, in his first bid for elective office, he ran successfully as a reform candidate for state auditor. Although the post for generations had been viewed as a backwater in state politics, Mabus used it as a springboard to prominence. He took on the most powerful and entrenched politicians in the state—county supervisors and other local power barons who could dispense county labor and equipment contracts in exchange for political loyalty. Auditing the state's 82 counties, he pressed court action and won $1.7 million in reimbursements for the state. His actions prompted a Federal Bureau of Investigation (FBI) investigation that led to more than 40 indictments of public officials. Mabus' crusade brought him national attention. His role in restoring a favorable credit rating to 5 counties impressed Wall Street bond brokers, and he gained a statewide reputation as a reformer that would become the basis for his gubernatorial campaign.

Ray Mabus *(Courtesy of Governor's Office)*

In 1987, incumbent Governor Bill Allain chose not to seek a second term, although voters, with his backing, had approved a constitutional amendment permitting consecutive terms for governors for the first time since the 19th century. The Democratic race was therefore wide open. In the August 4, 1987, primary, Mabus drew 37 percent of the vote in a multicandidate field that included former Governor Bill Waller (1972–1976). He faced second-place finisher Mike Sturdivant, a Glendora businessman, in the August 25 runoff. The race was an expensive, acrimonious one. Sturdivant, who spent more than $1.6 million on the campaign, was an aggressive opponent, accusing Mabus of accepting contributions from Wall Street bond brokers. Mabus countered with ads criticizing Sturdivant for being a plantation owner, for taping commercials in Texas, and for wrongly implying that all the jobs he had helped to create were in Mississippi. Campaigning against what he called "the old-time politics and old-time politicians," Mabus won the nomination in an overwhelming victory.

In the general election, he faced Republican Jack Reed, a 63-year-old businessman and former chairman of the state board of education who had won his party's nomination by a 7–2 margin. Reed, a formidable campaigner, was hoping to become the state's first Republican governor since General Adelbert Ames left office in 1876. Political observers believed he was his party's best hope in several elections to claim the office for the GOP. Reed, who stumped as an advocate of change, sought to portray Mabus as a man who would raise taxes if he got into office. He criticized Mabus for his pledge to increase teachers' salaries to the average of other southeastern states. While Reed said that he, too, favored raising salaries—then among the lowest in the nation—he believed that this would have to be done slowly. He charged that Mabus' plan would lead to increased taxes, sharp cuts in other state services, or both. Republican strategists said the issue was effective in part because it raised the question of whether Mabus was experienced enough to be governor. National Republican party leaders such as then Vice-President George Bush and Congressman Jack Kemp stumped the state in Reed's behalf.

Mabus, however, fresh from his impressive primary victory, went into the campaign with broad support. He battled back, arguing that his election would offer the state its best chance for change and for improving its image around the nation. Campaigning on the theme "A New Day for Mississippi," Mabus promised "basic drastic change," and he dramatically vowed that Mississippi would "never be last again." His campaign was heavy on imagery. Through two primaries and the general election, he spent a record $2.9 million.

The result was a historic victory for Mabus, who hailed his win as a triumph for a "new generation of leadership." His 53 percent to 47 percent win over Reed was seen as a signal that the South was changing, and political analysts nationwide were quick to publicize the significance of the win. A February 28, 1988 cover story in the Sunday *New York Times Magazine* called the victory of the 39-year-old Mabus (who became the nation's youngest governor at that time) a sign that the "yuppies had taken over Mississippi."

Mabus was seen to be as much a product of change in Mississippi as he was its author. He came back to the state and entered politics when Mississippi was, for the first time, ready to vote for a politician who talked about pocketbook issues and not race. He won significant support from affluent young professionals in urban areas who had been drifting toward the Republicans, as well as winning the black vote by nearly a 9–1 margin. Mabus was viewed as a prototype of a new sort of southern politician, one adept at building black-white coalitions. Emphasizing innovation, he and the new breed of which he seemed to be representative were socially progressive yet fiscally conservative, aware of the relative lack of resources with which to fund programs. The race also indicated that the power of local politicians (the classical courthouse crowd) to deliver votes was at an all-time low. Alongside Mabus, voters swept into office a group of progressive, reform-minded politicians in their 30s who pledged to help the new governor "unravel the status quo."

The main goals of Mabus' administration were educational improvement, economic development, and streamlining the state government. After his inauguration, he immediately enacted the nation's largest teacher pay increase and became the nation's first governor to make a statewide commitment to electronic education. He created a $13 million program to install computer reading programs in primary schools, a $182 million aid program to improve public school curriculums, and an $800 million bond measure to replace aging school buildings and buses. Moving Mississippi from 31st to 21st among the 50 states in financial support for higher education, Mabus authorized more than $100 million for construction, repair, and renovation of community college and university facilities. He was credited with creating more than 60,000 new jobs. The unemployment rate shrank considerably, and state exports rose by 50 percent. He also achieved some successes in reorganizing state government.

Overall, however, political observers agree that Mabus had a hard time making good on his campaign promises to bring modernization and reform to the nation's poorest state. Critics viewed his record as one of image rather than results. As had been predicted, the activist governor faced a showdown with the legislature. After initially getting support for his legislative initiatives, he was not able to win legislative approval for a state lottery to finance them. Moreover, his refusal to raise taxes or compromise on financing sources appeared intransigent and arrogant to many. Even friends like former Governor William Winter, who had brought Mabus into state government in the early 1980s, conceded that his intransigent stance was a major error. Others theorized that Mabus' style may have played well with the national news media but not with the people of Mississippi. Adding to Mabus' problems were harsh economic realities. An $85 million budget surplus before he took office became a $120 million shortfall by his term's end.

Due to a 1986 change in the state constitution allowing consecutive terms in the statehouse, Mabus became the first Mississippi governor in the 20th century to seek reelection. By the time of his reelection bid, however, he suffered both from his own sagging popularity and from the strong revival of the state Republican party. In the end, it seemed that the same young professionals who had invested so much hope and optimism in him as his term began lost patience and confidence and defected to the GOP.

Mabus faced an unexpectedly tight primary challenge from former Congressman Wayne Dowdy, who tried to present Mabus as an arrogant elitist who was out of touch with state citizens. Dowdy's "Save Us From Mabus" theme, while ultimately unsuccessful, reflected the bitterness and hostility toward Mabus that existed among certain sectors of the electorate.

Perhaps the most spirited Republican primary campaign in the state's history foreshadowed the rising fortunes of the party. Although no Republican had been elected governor of the state in this century, Mississippi's two U.S. senators were Republicans, and the state had delivered up to 60 percent of its vote to Republican presidential candidates. Newcomer Kirk Fordice, the Vicksburg construction executive who emerged victorious, championed popular antigovernment themes like term limits and welfare reform and blasted Mabus as a "Kennedyesque liberal." Criticizing Mabus for deficit spending and for what he called an inordinate emphasis on education, he also condemned Mabus' globe-trotting efforts to attract foreign investment, complaining that these initiatives came at the expense of existing business. He also charged that Mabus had bloated the state's payroll as its economy slid downhill. Mabus retaliated by depicting Fordice as an outsider and former lobbyist who didn't understand the state's needs and wouldn't make education his top priority.

It was also a campaign tinged with racial overtones. Although he rejected comparisons with David Duke in nearby Louisiana, Fordice highlighted his opposition to racial quotas and his support for workfare, not welfare. Mabus, too, played the race card. Relying on his heavy support among black voters, who represented approximately one-third of the state electorate, he blasted Fordice in an 11th-hour series of ads, accusing him of secretly planning to shut down black colleges and of hoping to move Mississippi back to its shortsighted and tragic past.

Despite his problems and sinking popularity, Mabus' defeat by Fordice came as a surprise to political observers. The loss brought to a halt the meteoric and nationally publicized rise of the so-called Yuppie Governor and called into question once again the future of progressive, liberal, and activist leadership in the states of the Deep South.

Bibliography: Biographical information courtesy of governor's office; Peter J. Boyer, "The Yuppies of Mississippi: How They Took Over the Statehouse," *New York Times Magazine* (Feb. 28, 1988): 24–27, 40, 43, 76; *The Chronicle of Higher Education*: 9–23–87; 11–11–87; 8–28–91; 10–16–91; 11–20–91; *The New York Times*: 8–26–87; 11–3–87; 11–4–87; 11–5–87; 3–20–88; 5–14–88; 11–7–88; 2–12–89; 1–13–90; 9–16–91; 9–19–91; 11–3–91; 11–7–91; 5–6–92; *The Star-Ledger* (Newark, N.J.), 11–6–91; *USA Today*: 12–1–88; 11–7–89; 3–29–91; 9–17–91; 11–1–91; 11–6–91; 11–7–91.

DANIEL KIRKWOOD ("KIRK") FORDICE, JR., 1992–

Born in Memphis, Tennessee, on February 10, 1934, Fordice is the son of a self-taught construction engineer who in 1948 left his job with the Army Corps of Engineers to start his own construction company. Fordice earned a bachelor's degree in civil engineering in 1956 and a master's degree in industrial management in 1957, both from Purdue University. He and his wife, Patricia, have four children.

After serving two years in the army, Fordice began working with the family business, which specializes in heavy construction and highway bridge construction. Because such work is heavily dependent on federal contracts, Fordice became active in industry trade groups. Beginning in 1974 he became a member of the executive committee of the Associated General Contractors, whose 32,000 member companies representing 3.55 million employees make it the largest trade association in the construction industry. Holding a series of top offices from 1988 to 1991, including the presidency, he was often called to appear before congressional committees to make the industry's case, and he became known as an aggressive defender of the construction industry.

These connections politicized Fordice. He was the driving force behind a ten-year legal challenge to an Army Corps of Engineers program to set aside some contracts for minority and small businesses. At the same time, he was a key player in an even bigger affirmative action case, *City of Richmond v. Croson,* which the Associated General Contractors helped finance. Handing down its ruling in January 1989, the U.S. Supreme Court decided that affirmative action and set-aside programs based on race were unconstitutional if they were not aimed at redressing specific incidents of past discrimination. Speaking of his own feelings about, and involvement in, the controversy, Fordice explained: "It was very personal. They almost put me out of business because of the color of my skin, and that's just plain unfair. You can't make up for past discrimination by making others suffer." While his connection with these efforts was never a prominent feature of his gubernatorial campaign, Fordice the candidate did stress his passionate opposition to quotas and governmental affirmative action programs.

Although he had held only one minor political office before becoming governor, Fordice entered the race after a nearly 30-year struggle to rebuild the Republican party in his overwhelmingly Democratic state. His

Daniel Kirkwood Fordice, Jr. *(Hawkins Photography)*

role had been primarily one of financial backer, and the only elected post he had ever held was county election commissioner. Becoming the state's first Republican governor in 115 years, Fordice could attribute his victory to several factors. Primary was the growing unpopularity of incumbent Democratic Governor Ray Mabus. Christened by the press as the state's "Yuppie Governor," Mabus presided over an administration that in the opinion of most observers was one more of style than of substance. Although he had run as a feisty and progressive reformer in 1988, he was unable to get his reform package through the legislature, and voters soon tired of the consequent bickering and stalemate. The plain-speaking Fordice capitalized both on the anti-incumbent mood and on the state's fundamental discomfort with Mabus' "Harvard, eastern liberal, elitist" background. He criticized Mabus for "deficit spending," for his globetrotting efforts to attract foreign investment at the expense of existing business, and for what he called an inordinate emphasis on education. He also charged that Mabus had bloated the state's payroll even as its economy slid downhill.

By contrast, Fordice championed popular antigovernment themes like term limits and welfare reform. He openly boasted that his political inexperience was his greatest asset: "The great old country has not fared well under career politicians and the people recognize that." Promising to bring his business skills to state government, he was also a strong opponent of tax increases and often invoked Reaganite themes. Despite being a millionaire, he was comfortable with common people, and political observers noted that the voters seemed to appreciate his "rough" edges.

Although Fordice vehemently condemned any attempt to link him with the racist campaign of neighboring Louisianan David Duke, the Mississippi race did have its own racial overtones. The election was marked by a racially polarized electorate, with Fordice's support overwhelmingly white, while Mabus garnered almost all the black vote. Fordice said he opposed racial quotas; pushed a voucher system that would allow school choice; and favored workfare, not welfare. Mabus played the race card late in the campaign, blasting Fordice in an 11th-hour series of ads and accusing him of secretly planning to shut down black colleges—a charge Fordice denied.

Fordice's victory over Mabus and independent Shawn O'Hara made him the first Republican governor of Mississippi since carpetbagger Adelbert Ames left office in 1876. Calling his victory "a mandate for change," he inherited a state fighting recession and budget woes, and one that has historically been one of the poorest in the nation.

Fordice's term in office has been marked by tough sledding and controversy. In a dramatic 1992 defeat, both houses of the legislature voted to override his veto of a bill to raise the state sales tax in order to provide $168 million in new funding for education at all levels. Fordice insisted that the additional funding was not necessary and that the tax increase would hurt the state's economy. Political observers felt that the neophyte Fordice had shown a "lack of sophistication" in negotiating with the Democratically controlled legislature and that his rigid and conservative ideology was causing him to misread voter concerns. Even Lieutenant Governor Edward Briggs, a Republican, said that Fordice had failed to counter the tax increase proposal with an affirmative approach to address the problem of declining education revenues.

Other controversies dogged Fordice as well. In the case of *U.S. v. Fordice,* argued before the U.S. Supreme Court, opponents charged that segregation lingered in the state's eight public universities, with Mississippi's three predominantly black colleges getting proportionately less funding from the state. Fordice countered by saying Mississippi might resist, even to the point of calling up the National Guard, if ordered by courts to raise taxes in order to equalize spending.

In a nationally publicized brouhaha during the fall of 1992, Fordice aroused ire and criticism when he told a meeting of Republican governors that it was a "simple fact of life" that the United States was a "Christian nation." The remark was politically problematic for a Republican party struggling to shed an image of division and intolerance that many observers held at least partially responsible for the party's presidential loss in 1992.

Fordice's unfortunate remark came as no surprise to critics in his home state, where he has developed a reputation for being blunt and outspoken. Supporters, however, praise his courage and his willingness to challenge privileged interest groups.

Bibliography: Biographical information courtesy of governor's office; *The Chronicle of Higher Education:* 11–13–91; 5–20–92; *The New York Times*: 9–16–91; 11–3–91; 11–6–91; 11–7–91; 11–11–91; 5–6–92; 6–27–92; 10–2–92; 11–22–92; *The Record* (Bergen County, N.J.), 1-18-92; *The Star-Ledger* (Newark, N.J.), 11–6–91; *USA Today*: 11–1–91; 11–6–91; 11–7–91; 1–14–92.

MISSOURI

JOHN DAVID ASHCROFT, 1985–1993

Born in Chicago, Illinois, on May 9, 1942, Ashcroft is the son of fundamentalist minister James Robert Ashcroft and Grace Pauline Larson Ashcroft. A member of the Assemblies of God church, he married Janet Elise Roede, an attorney, in 1967. The couple has three children.

Ashcroft graduated with honors from Yale University in 1964 and from the University of Chicago Law School in 1967. Later on, he joined the business faculty of Southwest Missouri State University as an associate professor. He and his wife also practiced law together in Springfield and later coauthored three textbooks, *It's the Law* (Cincinnati, Ohio: South-Western Publishing, 1984); *College Law for Business* (Cincinnati, Ohio: South-Western Publishing, 1986); and *Law for Business* (Cincinnati, Ohio: South-Western Publishing, 1991). Ashcroft also authored numerous articles published in law reviews and other professional journals. In addition to his legal career, Ashcroft developed his musical talents in gospel singing and song writing. He was well known as a gospel singer throughout churches in Missouri.

Ashcroft moved to Jefferson City from Springfield in 1972, when Governor Christopher S. Bond appointed him to fill an unexpired term as state auditor. As the state's 29th auditor, Ashcroft assumed the responsibilities of reviewing the financial records and operational efficiency of all state agencies and most of Missouri's counties. As auditor, Ashcroft recommended new procedures to save millions of dollars for state taxpayers. He was credited with making improvements in the office and with reducing the time span between audits.

Although Ashcroft lost a congressional primary in 1972 and the state auditor's race in 1974, he retained a loyal following among conservatives in the largely rural southwestern part of the state.

In January 1975, Ashcroft was appointed assistant attorney general under John C. Danforth. He served until April 1976 when he resigned to run for attorney general. Successful in his bid, he won reelection in 1980 by more than 580,000 votes. His 64.5 percent vote total was the largest margin and highest percentage by which a Republican had ever been elected to statewide office in the history of Missouri.

John David Ashcroft *(Courtesy of Governor's Office)*

As attorney general, Ashcroft was best known for his opposition to the settlement of a federal desegregation lawsuit in St. Louis, a settlement that would have cost the state more than $100 million. In 1980, he established the Attorney General's Council on Crime Prevention, a forerunner of the Governor's Crime Commission, which Ashcroft directed as chairman. Under his leadership, the Crime Commission pushed legislation through the general assembly and worked to strengthen local law enforcement. Also during his tenure, Ashcroft served as president of the National Association of Attorneys General and was also appointed chairman of its Budget Committee. For four years he represented the 50 state attorneys general in the American Bar Association House of Delegates. In June 1983, the National Association of Attorneys General presented Ashcroft with the prestigious Wyman Award, given annually to the state attorney general who did the most to advance the objectives of the association and who demonstrated exemplary service in office that year.

Ashcroft sought the governorship in 1984, when incumbent Governor Christopher Bond was constitutionally barred from seeking a third term. He won the Republican gubernatorial nomination by defeating Gene McNary, St. Louis county executive, in the August 1984 primary. Ashcroft polled 244,536 votes (67 percent) to McNary's 115,519 votes (32 percent). The race was Missouri's most expensive gubernatorial primary, with McNary spending $1.4 million to Ashcroft's $1.3 million.

In the general election, Ashcroft faced Democratic Lieutenant Governor Kenneth J. Rothman, a veteran legislator from the St. Louis area. The campaign paired two ideological opponents: Ashcroft, a conservative Republican, and Rothman, a moderate-to-liberal Democrat. Ashcroft had built his political career upon being religious, conservative, and family oriented. His positions on issues—against new taxes and for higher educational achievement—were both conservative and popular, and he won a solid victory in the race. Receiving 57 percent of the vote, he won by more than 280,800 votes and carried 107 of Missouri's 114 counties in one of the largest Republican gubernatorial victories in the state's history. Ashcroft was also the first Republican governor since 1928 to succeed another Republican governor.

In his 1988 campaign for reelection, Ashcroft received a landslide 64 percent of the vote—the largest victory margin of any Missouri governor since the Civil War and the first Republican governor in state history to serve consecutive terms. His opponent was state Representative Betty Cooper Hearnes, wife of a former Democratic governor. Hearnes ran hard, trekking the state in running shoes. Her feisty campaign credited the Democratically controlled legislature—not Ashcroft—for the state's prosperity. After his landslide victory, Ashcroft praised Hearnes for waging a good fight but countered that her charges about the state's prosperity didn't "ring true." He pledged to continue his efforts to make the state "a place of opportunity."

Ashcroft made excellence in education and economic development his top priorities as governor. He received high marks for his work from numerous sources. A 1991 survey of the nation's 50 governors conducted by *Newsweek* magazine found him ranked as one of the country's five most effective chief executives. The May 28, 1991, issue of *Financial World Magazine* rated Missouri as second in the nation for excellent financial management. The magazine had previously given Ashcroft high marks for being "unafraid to use the line-item veto to keep the budget on mark." Finally, *Fortune* magazine heralded Ashcroft for his initiatives in education, listing him as one of the nation's top ten "Education Governors" in 1990.

Ashcroft was credited with generating a favorable state climate for economic development. His policies created more than 270,000 new jobs, culminating in a state work force of record-breaking dimensions. When he left office in January 1993, the state boasted a budget surplus, a state unemployment rate of 4.8 percent, and an income tax rate as low as when he was first elected.

In the area of education, Ashcroft promoted a plan to allow families to set up "Family Savings Accounts" in banks and other financial institutions. Appointed chairman of the National Governors Association Task Force on College Quality, he and his team issued a national report in 1985 emphasizing that assessment could improve academic programs and that funding formula incentives could be used to improve undergraduate learning. He also served as chairman of the National Governors Association Task Force on Adult Literacy, leading the governors' national effort to promote action on the problem of adult illiteracy. In 1987, he succeeded Arkansas Governor Bill Clinton as chairman of the Education Commission of the States, an interstate compact to help state political and educational leaders improve the quality of education nationwide.

Another focus of the Ashcroft administration was welfare reform. In 1987, he proposed a plan to require every applicant for welfare to fill out a job application form. If no job were available, or if the applicant needed more education, the person would be required to enroll in free adult education classes and to work toward a high school diploma. If additional education was not required, a system of welfare-to-work provided job training and help in learning how to search and interview for jobs. The program also provided stipends for incidental expenses, day care assistance, and other support services.

Ashcroft's tenure as governor was also noteworthy for an interesting constitutional challenge that resonated in other state capitals. A feud with Democratic Lieutenant Governor Mel Carnahan over the constitutional interpretation of the "acting governorship" went all the way to the state supreme court. Carnahan, who ultimately did succeed Ashcroft as governor in 1993, had argued that he should be named acting governor whenever Ashcroft left the state, a policy that Ashcroft opposed. Ashcroft countered that in an age of supersonic jets, cellular telephones, and fax machines, being away was "just as good as being there." The political dispute between the two, while the first to go to court, was not unique. A similar power play confused relations between Massachusetts Governor Michael Dukakis and his second in command, Lieutenant Governor Evelyn Murphy in September 1990.

During his years in office, Ashcroft also served as chairman of the Republican Governors Association and as vice-chair and later chair of the National Governors Association. In 1992, he was named by President Bush to be cochair of the Republican Platform Committee for the Republican National Convention. As such, Ashcroft supervised the drafting of the party's controversial platform, which included an intransigent anti-abortion plank and staunch opposition to gay rights.

Constitutionally ineligible to seek another term, Ashcroft stepped down from the governorship in January 1993. His future in national Republican politics remains uncertain. At one time, he had been mentioned as a possible successor to Attorney General Dick Thornburgh, but the GOP fall from grace in Washington has put any further national ambitions on hold, at least for the time being.

In January 1993, he waged a highly publicized race for the chairmanship of the Republican National Committee, the first contested race in 16 years. Although a conservative with solid antiabortion credentials and the strong support of the Christian Right, Ashcroft presented himself as a "neutral broker" who could promote a fair debate of ideas and help the party rebuild after its disastrous defeat in the presidential race of 1992. The bid was unsuccessful, however, as Ashcroft lost out to Haley Barbour of Mississippi, a lawyer and political consultant.

Bibliography: Michael Barone et al., *The Almanac of American Politics, 1988* (Washington, D.C.: National Journal, 1987); biographical information courtesy of governor's office; *The Chronicle of Higher Education,* 7–15–87; *Financial World Magazine,* 5–28–91; *Newsweek,* 7–1–91; *The New York Times*: 8–7–84; 11–6–84; 11–8–84; 1–14–85; 2–22–87; 7–12–87; 2–3–91; 6–5–91; 1–13–93; *The Record* (Bergen County, N.J.): 12–31–92; 1–13–93; *The Star-Ledger* (Newark, N.J.), 11–15–89; *USA Today*: 10–11–88; 11–10–88; 6–5–91; 8–16–91; 11–16–92; 1–29–93.

Mel Carnahan *(Courtesy of Governor's Office)*

MEL CARNAHAN, 1993–

Born in Birch Tree, Missouri, on February 11, 1934, Carnahan is the scion of an old political family from the rural Ozarks. He graduated from Anacostia High School in 1951 and from George Washington University in 1954. Following graduation, he joined the U.S. Air Force and served as a special agent for the Office of Special Investigation during the Korean War. Upon his return to Missouri, he earned a law degree at the University of Missouri–Columbia in 1959.

A Democrat, Carnahan learned traditions of public service from his father, A. S. J. Carnahan, who had served as a congressman from Missouri for 12 years. The younger Carnahan first entered public life in 1961 when he was elected municipal judge in his hometown of Rolla. From 1962 to 1966 he served in the state house of representatives where he rose to the rank of majority floor leader. For his contributions to government, he twice earned the prestigious Meritorious Service Award of the *St. Louis Globe-Democrat*.

Retreating from the public eye to raise his family of four, Carnahan joined the law firm of Carnahan, Carnahan, and Hickle. Active in civic and community affairs, he became president of the local board of education, an officer of the Kiwanis Club, and a member of the board of Boys' Town of Missouri.

He returned to politics in 1980 when he was elected state treasurer, a post he held for four years. After an unsuccessful race for the statehouse in 1984, he became lieutenant governor in 1988, a victory he won by almost 100,000 votes. The win made Carnahan the only Democrat holding statewide office in Missouri.

Carnahan used that office as a springboard to the governorship in 1992. His opponent that year was Republican William Webster. State attorney general since 1984, Webster was also the son of a prominent political figure. His father, Richard M. Webster, had been an influential state legislator for 32 years. Attorney General Webster was also a national figure due to his involvement in two pivotal U.S. Supreme Court contests: *Webster v. Reproductive Health Services* (1989), in which he defended Missouri's restrictive abortion law, and *Cruzan v. Director, Missouri Department of Health,* (1990) which gave the states power to limit a family's ability to withdraw life support from comatose patients.

The Carnahan-Webster contest, however, turned on local rather than national concerns. Although Carnahan favored abortion rights, abortion was really not an issue in the campaign. Webster attempted to cast his opponent as a tax-and-spend liberal by focusing attention on Carnahan's call for a tax increase to finance increased education spending. His campaign unraveled, however, due to a scandal swirling around him. A grand jury probe investigating corruption and misapplication of funds in a state injured-workers fund crippled Webster's bid and, according to Carnahan himself, was the ultimate factor in his victory. He won the race with a decisive 59 percent of the vote.

In office, Carnahan has proposed comprehensive plans to improve state schools and to create more jobs. He has proposed a Universal College Revolving Fund to make loans to students at public and private institutions, and he intends to increase funding of vocational and technical education. In April 1993, he signed a bill permitting casino boats on the Mississippi and Missouri rivers.

Bibliography: Michael Barone and Grant Ujifusa, *The Almanac of American Politics, 1992* (Washington, D.C.: National Journal, 1991); biographical information courtesy of governor's office; *The Chronicle of Higher Education,* 11–11–92; *The New York Times:* 10–11–92; 10–26–92; *The Star-Ledger* (Newark, N.J.), 6–3–93; *USA Today:* 11–3–92; 4–30–93.

MONTANA

TED SCHWINDEN, 1981–1989

Born on August 31, 1925, in Wolf Point, Montana, Schwinden is the son of Michael James Schwinden and Mary Preble Schwinden. A Lutheran, Schwinden married the former Jean Christianson, a registered nurse, in 1946. They have three children.

Ted Schwinden began his formal education in a rural one-room schoolhouse. After graduating from Wolf Point High School in 1943, he enlisted in the U.S. Army, serving in both Europe and Asia during World War II. He was honorably discharged as a staff sergeant in 1946. Schwinden then attended the Montana School of Mines in Butte for one year before transferring to the University of Montana in Missoula. There he received a B.A. in 1949 and an M.A. in 1950, both degrees in history and political science. From 1950 to 1954, he did postgraduate work at the University of Minnesota. Schwinden has owned and operated a grain farm in Roosevelt County, Montana, since 1954.

A Democrat, Schwinden began his political career in 1958, when he was elected to the Montana House of Representatives from Roosevelt County. Named to the Legislative Council from 1959 to 1961, he served as house minority whip during the 1961 session. Over the course of the next decade, he held a variety of prestigious administrative positions and appointments. In 1965, he was elected president of the Montana Grain Growers Association, a position he held for two years. In 1968, he was selected by U.S. Secretary of Agriculture Orville Freeman to represent the United States on a wheat trade mission to Asia. Schwinden was named by Montana Governor Forrest Anderson to be commissioner of state lands in 1969. Reappointed by Governor Thomas Judge in 1973, he served until 1976. During this same period, from 1973 to 1976, he also served as chairman of Montana's Bicentennial Advisory Committee.

In 1976, Schwinden was elected lieutenant governor of Montana. Serving from 1977 until 1981, he was responsible for overseeing the state's role in natural resources, agriculture, and energy issues.

Characterized by political observers as a "folksy rancher with few enemies," Schwinden defeated incumbent Democratic Governor Thomas Judge to gain the Democratic gubernatorial nomination in 1980, gaining

Ted Schwinden *(Courtesy of Governor's Office)*

51 percent of the vote to Judge's 42 percent. Two minor candidates shared the remaining 7 percent. Although Judge, as the incumbent, had been expected to win reelection, or at the very least renomination, his liberal reputation may have worked against him. So, too, some said, did his personal style and manner. After two four-year terms, his personality "did not wear well," wrote one analyst. In the general election, Schwinden easily defeated Jack Ramirez, a Republican state legislator, by attracting 55 percent of the vote. Although Ramirez had won some popularity by pushing a tax cut through the legislature, the fact that he was a corporate lawyer from Billings caused him to be viewed by some as a "city slicker and protector of monied interests." Schwinden carried all but a few scattered counties in the state, a testimony to the strength of the Democratic party in Montana, where it is still difficult for a Republican to win statewide office.

Philosophically, Schwinden attributed Democratic victories in the West to an ability to respond, in his words, to a popular desire for progress "coupled with protection." He felt that measured economic development and environmental protection could go hand in hand. In office, Schwinden achieved a certain amount of national publicity as part of a group of western governors anxious to ensure that the states, rather than Washington bureaucrats, had a greater voice in determining the nation's energy and water policies. "We know we have a responsibility to share our resources and be part of the energy solution," he told a reporter for *Newsweek* magazine. "What we don't want to do is turn over control to outsiders—and that means OPEC, Washington, and the East Coast." In 1982, Schwinden received extensive press coverage because of a dispute with Reagan administration Interior Secretary James Watt over mineral development and coal leases in the Powder River Basin of Montana and Wyoming. Schwinden also involved himself in a growing controversy among western states over interstate water sales and transfers. The lack of water is a crucial issue in the arid Rocky Mountain states, yet Schwinden gave his backing to a proposal that cleared the way for Montana to sell some of its own surface water to developers in other states. This, he said, would not only enable the state to earn money but would also help to expand markets for Montana's huge coal reserves. (Presumably, the water would be used in coal slurry lines to move coal across the country.) Some members of Schwinden's own party attacked the plan, however, which they said would touch off a water war in the West.

During his first term in office, Schwinden also vetoed controversial legislation designed to eliminate the U.S. Supreme Court's exclusionary rule in Montana. Despite strong opposition from the insurance industry, he signed a bill that made Montana the first state in the nation to prohibit discrimination based on sex or marital status in all types of insurance and pension plans.

Governor Schwinden won a second term as chief executive in November 1984 by easily defeating Republican state Senator Pat Goodover. Schwinden captured 70 percent of the vote in that election, compared with Goodover's 26 percent, the largest victory margin in Montana history.

Like a number of other Rocky Mountain governors, Schwinden retained his popularity with voters despite years in the political spotlight. During his years in office, tourism went from being a minor industry to the state's second largest employer, just behind agriculture. While he drew praise for his "Build Montana" programs, it was his unique personalized approach to government and his pleasant low-key style that most endeared him to the electorate. He won plaudits for his accessibility and for such gestures as listing his home telephone number in the Helena directory. Some Democratic critics, however, faulted him for relaxing the state severance tax on coal and for not backing unions more strongly.

In August 1987, Schwinden disappointed supporters with his announcement that he would not be seeking a third term in 1988. Although analysts predicted he would have won an easy victory, the governor insisted that after 27 years in public life he and his wife planned "to put our family first."

Schwinden's retirement sparked contests in both parties. His ultimate successor, Stan Stephens, was the state's first Republican governor since 1964.

Since his retirement from public life, Schwinden has devoted his time to a variety of personal and political pursuits. Since 1989 he has served as Distinguished Professor of Public Affairs at Carroll College in Helena, Montana, teaching workshops and seminars there as well as at the University of Montana, Missoula. The cochair of the Clinton presidential campaign in Montana in 1992, he is presently serving as a consultant for the Montana School Boards Association, directing a study to determine the feasibility of consolidating small Montana schools.

Bibliography: Michael Barone et al., *The Almanac of American Politics, 1982, 1986, 1988, 1990* (Washington, D.C.: National Journal, 1981, 1985, 1987, 1989); biographical information courtesy of Governor Schwinden; *Newsweek,* 9–17–79; The New York Times: 11–5–80; 4–23–81; 4–26–82; 11–22–82; 2–18–83; 4–23–83; 6–6–84; 11–8–84; 8–31–87; 6–9–88.

STAN STEPHENS, 1989–1993

Born on September 16, 1929, in Calgary, Alberta, Canada, Stephens graduated from West Canada High School in 1947. Moving to the United States, he served in the U.S. Army from 1951 to 1953. In his over 40 years in Montana, Stephens has been a successful businessman, serving as a radio broadcaster and cable television executive and ultimately becoming the chief executive officer of three Montana cable TV firms and an officer in two broadcast operations. He and his wife Ann have two daughters.

A Republican, Stephens served in the state senate from 1969 to 1987. For many of those years, he held leadership positions: Republican floor whip in 1977; majority leader in 1979 and 1981; president in 1983; and minority leader in 1985.

In 1988, the decision of popular incumbent Governor Ted Schwinden not to seek reelection to a third term threw the gubernatorial contest wide open. Stephen's election marked the first time that the Republicans had captured the statehouse in 24 years. The contest between Stephens and former Democratic Governor Tom Judge (1973–1981) focused on how Montana's dispirited economy could be revived. Judge based his campaign on a 74-page "Job Opportunities and Business Stability" plan—code-named "JOBS." He also stressed his previous experience in office. Stephens countered by criticizing the plan as simplistic. Proclaiming his opposition to government stimulation of the economy, he contended that he could cut taxes by transferring many duties of the government to private contractors. Promising to slim down the size of state government, Stephens opposed a proposal for annual sessions of the state legislature, which currently met every other year. By contrast, Judge favored the reform. The pair also split over measures that would preserve huge tracts of forested land and wilderness from commercial encroachment. Throwing a gauntlet to environmentalists, Stephens was frank: "We have enough wilderness in Montana. What we need is economic development."

Stephens explained his 53 percent victory over Judge in this way: "People realize we represent change." In office, Stephens struggled with economic issues. Proposals before the legislature included a plan to impose a four cent sales tax and lower personal property and income taxes. Despite his philosophical opposition to new taxes, a tax increase was necessary to carry out a state supreme court order to equalize spending among state school districts. During Stephens' tenure, Montana became

Stan Stephens *(Courtesy of Governor's Office)*

the 48th state to enact a paid state holiday in honor of Dr. Martin Luther King, Jr. His term in office, however, was troubled by a rocky relationship with the legislature and by some troubling and embarrassing cabinet appointments. Democratic gains in the legislative elections of 1990 seemed to presage future difficulties.

While serving as Montana's 19th governor, Stephens was also active in national and regional affairs. In 1990, President Bush selected him to serve as one of four governors on the prestigious Advisory Council on Intergovernmental Relations. Active in the Western Governors Association and the National Governors Association (NGA), Stephens was appointed to chair the NGA Agricultural and Rural Development Committee in 1991.

In January 1992, poor health forced Governor Stephens to renounce a bid for reelection. Two weeks after collapsing at the governor's mansion and suffering a possible stroke, he announced his need to withdraw from the race in order to protect his health. His surprise announcement threw the 1992 gubernatorial contest wide open.

Bibliography: Michael Barone and Grant Ujifusa, *The Almanac of American Politics, 1992* (Washington, D.C.: National Journal, 1991); biographical information courtesy of governor's office; Phil Duncan, ed., *Politics in America 1992* (Washington, D.C.: Congressional Quarterly Press, 1991); *The New York Times*: 10–22–88; 11–9–88; 2–1–92; 5–26–92; *Time,* 11–21–88; *USA Today:* 11–10–88; 1–3–89; 4–7–89; 5–12–92.

Marc Racicot *(Third Eye Photo/Graphics)*

MARC RACICOT, 1993–

Born in Thompson Falls, Montana, in 1948, Racicot is the son of Bill and Pat Racicot. A graduate of Carroll College in Helena, Montana, and the University of Montana Law School, he and his wife, the former Theresa Barber, have five children.

After graduation from law school, Racicot served in the U.S. Army from 1973 to 1976. Stationed in West Germany, he worked as an army prosecutor in the Judge Advocate General's Corps. He also taught business and criminal law through a program sponsored by the University of Maryland.

Upon his return to the United States, Racicot took a position as a deputy county attorney for Missoula County. In 1977, he moved to Helena to become assistant attorney general and Montana's first special prosecutor. A Republican, Racicot made his first successful run for office in 1988, when he became state attorney general. His decision to seek the governorship in 1992 was an unexpected one, coming on the heels of incumbent Stan Stephens' sudden retirement for reasons of ill health.

Racicot's Democratic opponent was Dorothy Bradley, a lawyer and 16-year veteran of the state legislature. The race was an extremely close one, focusing on such issues as the imposition of a sales tax and the protection of the floundering cattle industry. Bradley sought to impart a populist note to the campaign by riding around parts of the state on horseback and by publishing a brochure, à la Bill Clinton, highlighting her "People First" economic program. Racicot's campaign, by contrast, sought to draw attention to Bradley's private life. One campaign flyer highlighted the fact that she was divorced, had no children, no military experience, and had spent some years out of college restoring pottery. While political observers were divided on the impact of the negative ads, Racicot pulled out a narrow 51 percent to 49 percent victory.

Racicot was inaugurated governor on January 4, 1993. Certain education issues have dominated the early part of his administration, including cost cutting in higher education, the goal of raising academic standards, and the need for the higher education system to adapt to students who are changing careers. In a move to equalize spending on education in schools statewide and to attain a measure of property tax relief, he persuaded the state legislature to schedule a referendum on the first sales tax in state history. The move has been seen as a tremendous political risk for him.

Bibliography: Biographical information courtesy of governor's office; *The Chronicle of Higher Education*: 11–11–92; 1–13–93; *The New York Times*: 10–26–92; 5–16–93; *USA Today,* 11–4–92.

NEBRASKA

KAY STARK ORR, 1987–1991

Born Kay Stark in Burlington, Iowa, on January 2, 1939, Orr is the daughter of Ralph Robert Stark and Sadie Stark. A Presbyterian, she married William D. Orr, an insurance company executive, in 1957. The couple has two children.

Orr received her public schooling in Iowa and California, and then attended the University of Iowa, where she met her husband. In the early 1960s the family moved to Lincoln, Nebraska, where she began her career in politics working on the 1964 presidential campaign of Senator Barry Goldwater. Beginning with her election as cochair of the Lancaster County Young Republicans in 1967, she was honored with many party positions, including election as delegate to numerous National Republican conventions. She led Ronald Reagan's Nebraska campaign during his ill-fated presidential bid of 1976 and cochaired former Governor Charles Thone's successful 1978 campaign. She then served as the governor's executive assistant until June of 1981, when she was appointed Nebraska state treasurer. She was then elected to that office by a wide margin in 1982, the first woman ever elected by Nebraska voters to a statewide constitutional office. She completed her four-year term as state treasurer on the day she took the oath of office as Nebraska's governor.

In 1984, she became the first person, male or female, other than a member of Congress or a state's governor, to serve as cochair of the Republican National Convention's Platform Committee. She has also served as a member of the Executive Committee of the National Association of State Treasurers. In 1985, she was appointed to the U.S. Department of Agriculture's National Agricultural Research and Extension Users Advisory Board and to the President's Advisory Committee on the Arts for the John F. Kennedy Center for the Performing Arts.

Orr became governor of Nebraska in a race historic for several reasons. In 1986, this conservative but populist farm state became the first ever to nominate women as the gubernatorial candidates of both major political parties. After defeating 1984 senatorial candidate Nancy Hoch to win the Republican gubernatorial nomination, Orr faced Democrat Helen Boosalis, the former mayor of Lincoln. Both Orr and Boosalis were well-known

Kay Stark Orr *(Courtesy of Governor's Office)*

figures in state politics. Boosalis, a former League of Women Voters activist, launched her political career on the Lincoln City Council in the late 1950s. She served 16 years on the council, then two terms as the mayor of Lincoln, from 1975 to 1983. In that period, she became president of the U.S. Conference of Mayors. Her most recent position was director of the Nebraska Department of Aging.

Although the Nebraska campaign became a symbol of women's political progress, neither candidate came out of a feminist tradition. On the contrary, both were party regulars who first entered politics as volunteers and then worked their way up the political ladder. While the race made feminist history, it did not become a feminist crusade. The National Organization for Women, the National Women's Political Caucus, and the Women's Campaign Fund stayed out of the contest because both women opposed abortion. Although Boosalis supported the Equal Rights Amendment, she was personally opposed to abortion except in cases of rape or incest or to save the mother's life. Orr, on the other hand, was opposed both to the Equal Rights Amendment and to legalized abortion in all instances. She did, however, credit the feminist movement with awakening her and other women to new roles and new possibilities.

In the contest between the two women, what are frequently called women's issues stayed in the background. Most of the political debate concerned problems endemic in the Midwest, chiefly the troubled farming sector and the need for jobs and economic development. The race was seen as a referendum on President Reagan's policies and their effect on the state's beleaguered farmers. While Boosalis ran as a harsh critic of federal farm policy, Orr—unlike other farm-state Republicans—made no attempt to distance herself from the president. Rather, her campaign focused on Boosalis' fiscal policies. She portrayed her opponent as a Democrat committed to increased taxing and spending, charges that Boosalis angrily denied. The campaign became a referendum on taxes, with Orr, an opponent of sales tax increases, defeating Boosalis, who said they might be necessary. There was little evidence that state Republicans suffered from the farm revolt apparent elsewhere, in Iowa or the Dakotas, for example. Orr won handily, with 53 percent of the vote, all the while proclaiming her support for Ronald Reagan. All three Republican Congressmen were also easily reelected.

With her election, Orr became the first woman to be elected governor of Nebraska and the first Republican woman governor in the United States. She was also one of the few Republicans elected governor of Nebraska in recent history: Democrats had held the office for 20 of the 28 years preceding her election.

As governor, Orr faced serious challenges. She had to deal with a state whose agriculture-based economy was in trouble, one that faced both a shrinking population and declining state revenues. Serious budget difficulties were brought on in part by the Tax Reform Act of 1986. Because the state's tax system is tied directly to the amount of federal tax paid by citizens, state revenues dropped by $24 million in 1987 and $36 million in 1988. Dealing with the budget issue became the central focus of Orr's administration.

Saying her administration would be "marked by optimism and tempered with realism," Orr outlined her agenda: creating jobs, reforming the state tax system, and improving education. Her program got off to a rough start, however. Early in her administration, she pushed an economic development plan of tax benefits for businesses that moved to Nebraska or expanded there, a plan linked by critics to a threat by one of Omaha's largest employers, Con Agra Inc., to leave the state because of its tax structure. A companion bill cut income taxes at the top and bottom of the scale but left many lower-to-middle-income taxpayers paying more. Opponents charged that these economic initiatives represented a surrender to corporate blackmail, and some, such as the Center for Rural Affairs, a group of farm advocates, said both measures were too probusiness. One month after the economic measures passed, a poll by the *Omaha World-Herald* indicated that only 53 percent of Nebraskans approved of Orr's job performance, while 33 percent disapproved—the worst rating for a Nebraska governor in 17 years. Orr countered that her motives were misunderstood. Within six months after the bill passed, more than 100 Nebraska companies had in fact expanded. Critics continued to charge, however, that the law merely cut state revenue because these were all homegrown businesses that would have expanded anyway.

Throughout the remainder of her term, Orr struggled to overcome low approval ratings that continued to dog her since the revamping of the tax structure. Although she subsequently sponsored legislation to correct what she said was a mistake, many voters in this heavily Republican state remained critical of her, both for breaking her campaign promise not to raise taxes and for later attempting to explain away the increase.

Another controversial issue to plague Orr, at least in some areas of the state, was her support for a nuclear waste dump to be constructed in rural Boyd County. Although tensions over the waste site had less significance the farther one went from Boyd County, the proposal inflamed passions nonetheless. Orr claimed that her life was threatened as a result of her unwillingness to block the construction, and she later refused to campaign for reelection in the bitterly divided county where the warehouse was to be built.

Even Orr's personality became a target of criticism. Opponents pictured her as a tough, hard-edged politician who was not above exploiting any situation to rescue her sinking administration. Some made sarcastic reference to the fact that she appeared with a 20-month-old grandson when she announced her decision to run for reelection. Cynics speculated that this was a calculated ploy to demonstrate a warmth and humanism that she actually lacked. Orr bristled at the theory.

By the start of the 1990 campaign season, Orr was suffering from a record low in public opinion polls, with a 39 percent approval rating. Although she was able to win renomination by easily defeating Mort Sullivan, an Omaha businessman, seven Democrats eagerly lined up to face her in the general election. The ultimate winner, Ben Nelson, an Omaha lawyer, won the nomination with a bare 42-vote margin over his nearest rival. Even so, party regulars united behind his campaign, and his background as an insurance executive appealed to many Republican voters.

Although Orr outspent Nelson by a 2–1 margin, the tax issue appeared central to her defeat. The Democratic strategy in the race was to press Orr hard on the tax question and to depict her as a big spender who couldn't be trusted. Nelson reminded voters that she had broken her previous no-new-taxes pledge and urged them "not to be fooled again."

For their part, Republicans unleashed a barrage of accusations against Nelson, raising questions about his financial and business dealings and criticizing him for refusing to make public his income tax returns. Nonetheless, Nelson eked out a narrow victory over Orr, winning by less than 5,000 votes out of the more than 560,000 cast.

Orr's defeat ended her attempt to become the state's first Republican governor reelected to a second term since 1957. More important, it cut short the career of a rising star in Republican national politics. For four years, Republicans had been proud to point to Orr as the first Republican woman elected governor of any state. With the backing of Bush supporters, she had been named chair of the Platform Committee at the 1988 Republican National Convention, the first woman ever to hold that position. Her name had also been included on a long list of possible picks as George Bush's vice-presidential running mate that same year. With her defeat, her future in national Republican politics remains uncertain.

Bibliography: Michael Barone et al., *The Almanac of American Politics, 1988* (Washington, D.C.: National Journal, 1987); biographical information courtesy of governor's office; *The Chronicle of Higher Education,* 11–12–86; *The New York Times:* 5–18–86; 9–16–86; 10–30–86; 1–9–87; 3–21–87; 2–9–88; 2–9–90; 5–16–90; 9–30–90; 10–10–90; 11–3–90; 11–8–90; 11–11–90; *The Star-Ledger* (Newark, N.J.): 5–16–90; 10–28–90; *USA Today:* 6–7–88; 5– 16–90.

E. Benjamin Nelson *(Photo: David Dale)*

E. BENJAMIN NELSON, 1991–

Born in McCook, Nebraska, on May 17, 1941, Nelson is the son of Benjamin Earl and Birdella Ruby Henderson Nelson. A member of the United Methodist church, he and his wife Diane have four children.

An Eagle Scout as a boy, Nelson achieved distinction with his election as governor of the Hi-Y Model Legislature for Nebraska. Graduating from the University of Nebraska in 1963 with a B.A. in philosophy, he earned an M.A. in 1965 while teaching logic and philosophy at the university. While working for the Consumer Division of the Nebraska Department of Insurance, he pursued a law degree at the University of Nebraska College of Law, ultimately graduating in 1970.

As a lawyer and insurance executive, Nelson was named state director of insurance by Governor Jim Exon in 1975. In that capacity, he developed a reputation as a consumer advocate, fighting effectively against unwarranted increases in health and automobile insurance rates. He drew acclaim for reorganizing the failed Pioneer Insurance Company into Life of Nebraska, successfully reinsuring the company's shareholders and protecting them from economic loss.

In 1982, Nelson became executive vice-president of the National Association of Insurance Commissioners, a regulatory and advisory organization composed of the nation's state insurance commissioners. He became attorney of counsel to Kennedy Holland, one of Nebraska's most prominent law firms, in 1985.

A Democrat who had never previously held elective office, Nelson decided to challenge incumbent Kay Orr for the governorship in 1990. He won the Democratic gubernatorial nomination by only 42 votes—one of the closest elections for a statewide race in modern American history. Although Nelson was well known in political circles as a major bankroller of past Democratic candidates, he made the race himself this time because the Republican administration of Governor Orr had fallen on hard times. Nelson was relentless in attacking her as a budget buster, pointing out that she had increased state spending 40 percent during her term and raised income taxes to pay for it.

It was a highly negative campaign on both sides, with combined spending topping $4.1 million. In the end, independents and moderates favored Nelson, with his promises to revitalize the state economy and to improve the quality of education driving voters to him. He won the election by a narrow margin, 286,776 votes to Orr's 282,118 votes. Independent Mort

Sullivan drew 1,026 votes. Analysts attributed Orr's defeat to a falloff in support in rural areas, a traditional Republican stronghold.

Nelson was inaugurated as the 37th governor of Nebraska on January 9, 1991. In office, he has faced economic problems common to many states—falling revenues and the challenge to fund new and existing programs. He believes that his experience in private industry can help the state through tough times.

Bibliography: Biographical information courtesy of governor's office; Phil Duncan, ed., *Politics in America 1992* (Washington, D.C.: Congressional Quarterly Press, 1991); *The New York Times,* 11–7–90; *USA Today,* 11–8–90.

NEVADA

RICHARD H. BRYAN, 1983–1989

Born on July 16, 1937, in Washington, D.C., Bryan is the son of Oscar W. Bryan and Lillie Pleasants Bryan. An Episcopalian, he married Bonnie Fairchild in 1962. The couple has three children.

A second-generation Nevadan, Bryan displayed his interest in government early, when he served as president of his sophomore and senior classes at Las Vegas High School. He is a 1959 graduate of the University of Nevada–Reno, where he served as student body president during his senior year. After graduation he entered the U.S. Army as a second lieutenant and became a captain in the Army Reserve. He continued his education at the University of California Hastings College of Law where he earned his law degree with honors in 1963.

Bryan served as deputy district attorney in Clark County from 1964 to 1966. In 1966, he was appointed as the first public defender in Nevada, the youngest person in the nation to hold that position. He served in that capacity from 1966 to 1968, when he was elected to the Nevada State Assembly. There he was named outstanding freshman assemblyman. After serving two terms in the assembly, he was elected to the Nevada State Senate, where he chaired the Taxation and Education committees. State senator from 1972 to 1978, he then served as Nevada attorney general from 1978 to 1982.

The attorney general's post became Bryan's springboard to the governorship. In 1982, he mounted a successful challenge to incumbent Republican Governor Robert List, who was blamed for the state's economic difficulties. The recession of 1981–1982 had shattered the prevailing myth that gambling was recession proof. List also had to deal with two other problems that severely affected the state's number-one industry: New Jersey's entrance into competition for legalized gambling dollars, as well as an increase in air fares due to higher jet fuel prices. List was also harmed by his fiscal policies. His reliance on the sales tax as a source of needed revenue did not bring in the projected income he had expected. Bryan, making economic diversification the theme of his campaign, won with 54 percent of the vote.

He won reelection easily in 1986. Winning nearly 80 percent of the

Richard H. Bryan *(Courtesy of Governor's Office)*

Democratic primary vote against businessman Herb Tobman, he faced state Treasurer Patty Cafferata in the general election. He won the race "almost by acclamation," with 72 percent of the vote, becoming a kind of consensus choice as state revenues increased and growth continued.

During his years in office, Bryan supported economic diversification, the promotion of tourism, and an improved educational system. Political observers believed that he ran a competent administration, leading Nevada from the fiscal crisis in which he found it in 1982 to a $100 million budget surplus in 1988. Critics, however, often called him "Wind Sock" Bryan because of a perception that he changed positions on political issues.

Bryan was long rumored to have ambitions beyond the statehouse. In 1986, there had been some speculation that he would seek the U.S. Senate seat of retiring incumbent Paul Laxalt. Foregoing that race, he decided instead to challenge Republican Senator Chic Hecht in November 1988. Never a strong figure in the state, Hecht was a former state legislator and Las Vegas clothing store owner. Winning election to the Senate in 1982 primarily because of the weakness of his opponent, Hecht had been voted by Senate administrative aides as the chamber's least effective member. Although the popular Bryan held a large lead in early polls, the race between the two men was closer than expected, with some voters apparently angered by Bryan's desire to leave for Washington in midterm. A major issue in the race was the Yucca Mountain Nuclear Depository, which Bryan opposed. Bryan's attacks on Hecht for waffling on the issue lost a little of their force, however, when the governor signed a bill creating a new zero-population Bullfrog County on the site. Challenging Bryan's sincerity on the emotional issue of nuclear waste disposal, Hecht also attacked Bryan for leasing a state airplane. He further questioned the leadership of the state should Bryan succeed in making the move to Washington, noting that Lieutenant Governor Bob Miller was not well known. In the end, however, Bryan won the election with 51 percent of the vote. He left the statehouse in midterm, January 1989, to be succeeded in office by the lieutenant governor.

In the Senate, Bryan serves on the Commerce, Banking, and Joint Economic committees. Known as a liberal on social issues and a conservative on fiscal ones, he has been a strong supporter of increasing "CAFE" (corporate average fuel economy) standards to boost energy conservation. He has also worked to encourage the Federal Trade Commission and the Consumer Product Safety Commission to regulate more aggressively. Political observers feel he remains highly popular in Nevada and is well positioned for a reelection bid in 1994.

Bibliography: Michael Barone et al., *The Almanac of American Politics, 1986, 1988, 1990, 1992* (Washington, D.C.: National Journal, 1985, 1987, 1989, 1991); biographical information courtesy of governor's office; *The Chronicle of Higher*

Education: 11–12–86; 2–18–87; *The New York Times*: 12–1–85; 3–29–88; 10–30–88; *Time*: 11–21–88; *USA Today*: 11–10–88; *U.S. News & World Report*, 10–4–82.

BOB MILLER, 1989—

Bob Miller was born in Chicago, Illinois, on March 30, 1945. He graduated from the University of Santa Clara with a B.A. in 1967 and from Loyola Law School in Los Angeles with a J.D. in 1971. His military record includes a stint in the U.S. Air Force Reserve from 1967 to 1973. A Roman Catholic, he and his wife Sandy have three children.

A Democrat, Miller began his political career with a variety of law enforcement positions on the local level. He served as Clark County deputy district attorney, 1971–1973; the first legal adviser to the Las Vegas Metropolitan Police Department, 1973–1975; Las Vegas Township justice of the peace, 1975–1978; and Clark County district attorney, 1979–1986. With his reelection in 1982, Miller became the first Clark County district attorney in modern history to win a second term. Also in 1982, he was chosen by President Ronald Reagan to serve on the nine-member Presidential Task Force on Victims of Crime. In 1984, he was elected president of the National District Attorneys Association.

Miller's climb to the statehouse began with his attaining the post of Nevada lieutenant governor in 1987. From there, he succeeded to the governorship on January 3, 1989, when two-term incumbent Richard H. Bryan resigned from office to take a U.S. Senate seat. Miller served out the remaining two years of Bryan's term before seeking his own term in 1990.

In the gubernatorial election of that year, he survived a primary challenge from five Democratic opponents before going on to face Republican businessman Jim Gallaway in the general election. Gallaway, a lawyer and former marine and a relative newcomer to the state, achieved considerable financial success founding and running a string of his own telecommunications companies. He stressed his probusiness, antitax stance and criticized Miller for his antiabortion position. He also blasted the incumbent for having shown "a total lack of leadership" on the critical issues facing the state.

Miller, for his part, stressed the need to diversify the state's economy and to improve its educational system. He won his bid resoundingly, gaining 66 percent of the vote.

Miller has faced numerous problems as head of one of the nation's fastest-growing states. One of the most serious challenges confronting him upon his accession to office was coming to grips with street gangs from Los Angeles infiltrating Las Vegas. Proposals he has placed before

Bob Miller *(Courtesy of Governor's Office)*

the legislature include the creation of a drug czar, the reduction of average class sizes in public schools by hiring new teachers, and the need to increase salaries for teachers and state employees. He has worked to increase spending for the University of Nevada system, saying that improvements in the system could attract new businesses to the state by providing better-educated employees. In 1991, he found himself locking horns with the Internal Revenue Service (IRS), when he rejected an IRS request to expand information sharing on taxpayers. Although an IRS spokesman argued that Nevada needed closer watching because of its gambling casinos, Miller countered by defending state residents, charging that the IRS allegedly treats Nevada differently from other states. One of the most interesting areas in which Miller has been involved is a proposal to open a $94 million theme park and casino resort in the People's Republic of China.

Feminist groups, however, have given Miller low marks for his record of appointing women to high office. A 1991 survey by the National Women's Political Caucus ranked him at the bottom of all 50 governors, noting that only 1 member of his 19-person cabinet was a woman.

As governor, Miller has also served as chairman of the National Governors Association Committee on Justice and Public Safety.

Bibliography: Biographical information courtesy of governor's office; *The Chronicle of Higher Education,* 10–31–90; Phil Duncan, ed., *Politics in America 1992* (Washington, D.C.: Congressional Quarterly Press, 1991); *Newsweek,* 9–14–92; *The New York Times*: 9–5–90; 11–7–90; 11–8–90; *USA Today*: 1–3–89; 4–7–89; 3–7–90; 4–26–91; 7–31–91.

John H. Sununu *(Courtesy of Governor's Office)*

NEW HAMPSHIRE

JOHN H. SUNUNU, 1983–1989

Sununu was born in Havana, Cuba, on July 2, 1939. A Roman Catholic, he married the former Nancy Hayes in 1958. His wife is a former chairman of the New Hampshire Republican State Committee and a former officer in the New Hampshire Federated Republican Women. The couple has eight children.

Sununu did his undergraduate and graduate work at the Massachusetts Institute of Technology (MIT), where he earned his Ph.D. in mechanical engineering in 1966. From 1965 until his election as governor, he served as president of JHS Engineering Company and Thermal Research, Inc., in addition to helping found and serving as chief engineer for Astro Dynamics from 1960 to 1965. From 1968 to 1973, he was associate dean of the College of Engineering at Tufts University, where he had been an associate professor of medical engineering since 1966. He was invited to join the Advisory Board of Technology and Public Programs at MIT in August 1984.

Assuming the governorship with a background of nearly 20 years' experience as an educator, engineer, and small businessman, he was first elected in 1982, winning reelection in 1984 and again in 1986. A Republican, he defeated incumbent Hugh Gallen in 1982 when Gallen, faced with fiscal difficulties, refused to promise that he would veto any state sales or income taxes. Taking this no-tax "pledge" has long been seen as critical to victory in New Hampshire. Because of Gallen's reluctance to do so, the newcomer Sununu won the election, gaining 52 percent of the vote to Gallen's 46 percent.

In 1984, he won an overwhelming victory against Chris Spirou, the minority leader in the state house of representatives, who accused Sununu of being a "cheerleader" for the controversial Seabrook nuclear power plant. Winning 67 percent of the vote to his opponent's 33 percent, Sununu made no secret of his staunch defense of nuclear power.

Campaign issues were similar in 1986, when an accident at the Chernobyl plant in the former Soviet Union again pushed the issue of nuclear power to center stage. Sununu's opponent, Democratic attorney Paul McEachern, assailed Sununu as "the world's champion proponent of nuclear power.'' He also challenged Sununu's position on a federal proposal to put a nuclear waste dump in central New Hampshire. Sununu, however, focused his campaign on the economy. Under his leadership, New Hampshire moved from a $40 million budget deficit to a surplus of more than $21 million. It also boasted the nation's lowest unemployment rate and strong growth in personal income. Sununu again won handily, 54 percent to 46 percent.

Sununu earned both regional and national recognition for his achievements as governor. That recognition gained him the chairmanship of the Coalition of Northeastern Governors, the chairmanship of the Republican Governors Association, the chairmanship of the New England Governors Association, and the vice-chairmanship of the Advisory Commission on Intergovernmental Relations. Vice-chairman of the National Governors Association (NGA) in 1986, he assumed the chairmanship in 1987. Claiming that there had been a ''drastic overcentralization of power in Washington,'' he took the main task of his chairmanship to be a thorough examination of federal-state relations. Believing that the federal government had usurped too much of the states' authority and hobbled their ability to attack social and economic problems, he even talked of the need for a constitutional amendment to address the problem.

During his tenure as governor, Sununu also served as chairman of the NGA Subcommittee on Energy; chairman of its Committee on International Trade and Foreign Relations; a member of the NGA Committee on Transportation, Commerce, and Communications; and chairman of the New Technology Education Task Force, which issued the 1991 *Governors Report on U.S. Education*. Through his efforts, the National Governors Association and later the New Hampshire legislature endorsed model acid rain legislation. A supporter of aid to education, Sununu requested continued increases in state spending for the University of New Hampshire system. In 1983, he became involved in a serious political debate over the uses of computer technology, the first of its kind in the nation. Asking the state legislature for money to computerize the system by which the state raises and spends more than $1 billion per year, Sununu sparked a controversy with the legislature, which feared that it was creating a pool of information to which the executive branch would have access while it did not.

In 1988, Sununu threw the New Hampshire governor's race wide open with his unexpected announcement that he had decided against seeking a fourth gubernatorial term. He explained his decision by saying that he needed to take a more lucrative position in private business so as to provide for the education of his large family.

Throughout his years in office, Sununu had been known as an advocate of fiscal restraint. He credited his administration with turning the state around economically and with holding down governmental growth. Critics, however, charged that in reality Sununu had passed on a host of problems to his successor, Judd Gregg. Although Sununu claimed to have left office with a $10 million surplus, Gregg projected a $13 million deficit immediately upon assuming office. He also challenged Sununu's claim to have controlled the size of government, charging that his predecessor had allowed state spending to grow "faster than any other governor in the country" during his six years in office. Political observers suggested that Sununu may have deliberately hidden the extent of New Hampshire's fiscal difficulties in order to appear a more credible Republican spokesman during the 1988 presidential campaign, a hallmark of which was an attack on the fiscal policies of Massachusetts Governor Michael Dukakis, the Democratic nominee.

An early and vociferous supporter of Republican candidate George Bush, Sununu was widely credited with delivering the crucial New Hampshire primary to Bush in his race for the nomination against rival Bob Dole. Bush openly attributed his come-from-behind victory to the support of Sununu, who also served as Bush's representative to the platform panel at the 1988 Republican National Convention.

Sununu's reward for his loyalty and support was the position of White House chief of staff in the new Bush administration, a post he assumed immediately upon his retirement from the statehouse in January 1989. Sununu's tenure in Washington, however, was a troubled one. Christened "King John" by his critics for his high-handed, rude, and dictatorial style, he was nonetheless given credit for his efficiency and for the president's historically high approval ratings. While Bush focused on foreign policy, Sununu directed the administration's domestic agenda, pushing bills on child care, clean air, education reform, and crime fighting. His detractors, however, claimed that he seemed at times to be pursuing his own agenda, not that of the president. In the end, what toppled Sununu was a swirling controversy about the propriety of some of his actions, primarily the use of military aircraft for personal travel. He resigned the position in December 1991.

After leaving Washington, Sununu registered as a lobbyist and adviser on behalf of W. R. Grace and Co., the chemicals and health care concern. He also joined the CNN–cable TV debate program "Crossfire," where he continues to serve as the conservative counterpart to the more liberal Michael Kinsley, editor of the *New Republic*.

Bibliography: Michael Barone et al., *The Almanac of American Politics, 1984, 1988, 1990* (Washington, D.C.: National Journal, 1983, 1987, 1989); biographical information courtesy of governor's office; *The Chronicle of Higher Education,* 11–12–86; *Newsweek,* 5–13–91; *The New York Times*: 11–7–84; 5–6–85; 5–11–86; 9–11–86; 10–11–86; 7–6–87; 7–29–87; 5–17–88; 3–8–89; 5–3–91; 5–5–91; 6–17–92; *The Star-Ledger* (Newark, N.J.), 9–2–90; *USA Today,* 6–7–88.

Judd Gregg (*Courtesy of U.S. Senate Office: Judd Gregg*)

JUDD GREGG, 1989–1993

Gregg was born in Nashua, New Hampshire, on February 14, 1947. He graduated from Columbia University with a B.A. in 1969 and from Boston University with a J.D. in 1972 and an LL.M. in 1975. A Republican, he and his wife Kathleen have three children.

Gregg served in the U.S. Congress from 1981 to 1989. A member of the powerful Ways and Means Committee, the state's first representative on the committee since 1853, he was a strong free market proponent.

As the son of former New Hampshire Governor Hugh Gregg, who served one term in office ending in 1955, Gregg entered the race for the statehouse in 1988 once it became clear that incumbent Republican Governor John Sununu was not interested in reelection. His opponent that year was Democratic lawyer Paul McEachern, who based his campaign on opposition to the Seabrook nuclear power plant, a controversial issue of long standing in state politics. Since 1986, when McEachern, a former state legislator, first ran against John Sununu, he had campaigned on this one plank alone. While Sununu was a staunch supporter of the plant, Gregg defused the issue by opposing the start-up of the plant until certain safety and financial requirements were met. Winning election with 61 percent of the vote, Gregg was reelected in 1990 by defeating Democrat Joseph Grandmaison. His victory margin that year was 63 percent to the Democrat's 37 percent.

Key concerns of Gregg's tenure included the pressing need to lead New Hampshire through difficult financial times, as well as protecting the state's prized environment in the face of exploding growth. Confronted with a $13 million deficit in his first year in office, Gregg ordered state agencies to cut spending by 3 percent. In 1990, he again cut state payrolls and spending, as well as signing increases in taxes on cigarettes, gasoline, property transfers, and licenses of several kinds. The state's traditional opposition to general sales and income taxes became the focus of a nationally publicized lawsuit in 1992, when funding shortages for education in poorer towns prompted five school districts to sue Gregg and other state officials. Arguing that the state's refusal to adopt needed broad-based taxes had a disastrous impact on its system of financing public education, critics charged that the state was able to provide only 7 percent of the education budgets for its public schools, compared with a national average of 50 percent. Those numbers placed New Hampshire last in the country in terms of state spending on public education.

Gregg fought the suit vigorously. Publicly he argued that "the quality of education is not defined so much by dollars as by involvement of parents, involvement of teachers, and involvement of principals." He also insisted that New Hampshire's status as the state with the lowest overall state and local tax burden has made it an attractive place to live and do business.

The lawsuit placed Gregg in an awkward position. Critics pointed out that he placed his own children in private, not public, schools. Moreover, as state chairman of the 1992 Bush reelection campaign, he was the chief representative of the self-proclaimed "Education President."

The conservative Gregg also found himself embroiled in other controversies. In 1990, he vetoed an abortion rights bill that would have been one of the most liberal in the nation. In 1991, he called for the ouster of the president of Keene State College because of his decision to hold the college's baccalaureate ceremony off campus to avoid mixing church and state. Gregg excoriated the college's trustees for knuckling under to atheism and lamented that "political correctness" had "raised its ugly head" in the state education system.

Despite such controversies, however, Gregg drew high marks in other areas. Early in his term, he settled a feud between residents and the state legislature over the fate of Pease Air Force Base near Portsmouth. He also created a tax-free bond program to help parents save for college costs. In April 1990, New Hampshire drew recognition from *Financial World Magazine* as one of the nation's top 15 states for excellence in fiscal management.

Deciding against seeking reelection as governor in 1992, Gregg announced instead that he would seek the U.S. Senate seat of retiring Republican Senator Warren Rudman. Seeing "institutional failure" in Washington, Gregg promised to oppose tax increases and to press for a balanced budget amendment. He presented himself as the best candidate to represent the state's values on Capitol Hill, charging that his Democratic opponent, wealthy businessman John Rauh, was a liberal outside the state mainstream. Rauh's calls for drastic cuts in defense spending also hurt him in a state where thousands of local shipyard workers depend on military contracts for employment.

For his part, Rauh sought to gain votes by targeting Gregg's antiabortion stance and by raising questions about his failure to serve in Vietnam. Despite rejecting a sitting Republican president for the first time in 80 years, state voters showed their Republican roots by handing Gregg a narrow victory.

In preparation for his move to Washington, Gregg resigned the governorship on January 2, 1993. He was succeeded by state Senate President Ralph Degnan Hough, who served as acting governor until the inauguration of Governor-elect Stephen Merrill on January 7, 1993.

Bibliography: Biographical information courtesy of governor's office; *The Chronicle of Higher Education*: 10–31–90; 8–28–91; Phil Duncan, ed., *Politics in America 1992* (Washington, D.C.: Congressional Quarterly Press, 1991); *National Review,* 4–13–92; *The New York Times*: 11–9–88; 3–8–89; 4–11–90; 9–12–90; 5–4–91; 1–2–92; 10–1–92; 11–4–92; 11–5–92; *The Star-Ledger* (Newark, N.J.): 4–4–90; 4–11–90; 9–2–90; 1–4–91; 9–9–92; *USA Today*: 11–10–88; 1–3–89; 4–7–89; 4–1–92; 5–12–92; 11–4–92.

Stephen Merrill *(Courtesy of Governor's Office)*

STEPHEN MERRILL, 1993–

Born in Hampton, New Hampshire, on June 21, 1946, Merrill is a graduate of the University of New Hampshire and Georgetown University Law School. An Episcopalian, he is married to the former Heather MacLean.

After serving as a captain on active duty in the U.S. Air Force, Merrill practiced law in Manchester, New Hampshire. A Republican, he began his public service career as legal counsel and chief of staff to Governor John Sununu. Becoming state attorney general in 1985, he established a Victim Assistance Program, the New Hampshire Drug Task Force, and an Elder Citizens Unit during his time in office.

In 1992, the race for the statehouse was thrown wide open due to incumbent Governor John Gregg's decision to seek the U.S. Senate seat of retiring Warren Rudman. The contest to replace Gregg drew national attention due to the presence of strong female candidates in both parties, women who not only were prochoice but also made calls for a state income tax a major linchpin of their campaigns. The primary contest was called "an astonishing turn of events" for conservative New Hampshire, one of only two states that have never elected a woman either to a statewide office or to Congress. The tax call was even more pathbreaking in a state where candidates of both parties have routinely taken "the pledge" not to impose a statewide income tax.

While Democrat Deborah Arnesen survived the primary contest, Republican state Representative Elizabeth Hager lost her bid for the nomination to Merrill, who had the strong support of the influential *Manchester Union Leader*. A strong conservative, Merrill came out both against new taxes and against abortion. Indeed, he said he would support criminal penalties for doctors who perform abortions except in rare situations: cases of rape or incest or to preserve a pregnant woman's health. His 56 percent to 40 percent win preserved the state's conservative traditions and retained the Republican lock on the statehouse. Independent Miriam Luce drew the remaining 4 percent of the vote.

In office, Merrill has promised to control the state budget by vigorous cost cutting, not new taxation. He is stressing a back-to-basics core curriculum in public schools and more evaluative testing to assess student learning.

Bibliography: Biographical information courtesy of governor's office; *The Chronicle of Higher Education*, 11–11–92; *The New York Times*: 9–5–92; 10–26–92; 11–4–92; *USA Today*: 5–12–92; 11–4–92.

Thomas H. Kean *(Courtesy of Governor's Office)*

NEW JERSEY

THOMAS H. KEAN, 1982–1990

Born in New York City on April 21, 1935, Kean is the son of Robert Winthrop Kean and Elizabeth Stuyvesant Kean. He is the descendant of a well-known and influential political family. His father served in the U.S. House of Representatives from 1939 to 1959. His ancestors include William Livingston, who was governor of New Jersey from 1776 to 1790. Married to the former Deborah Bye of Wilmington, Delaware, he is the father of three children.

Kean attended St. Marks School and graduated from Princeton University. He earned an M.A. at Columbia University but abandoned plans to go on for a Ph.D. after joining William Scranton's unsuccessful bid for the Republican presidential nomination in 1964. Kean taught American history and English in high schools for three years, directed a camp for disadvantaged children, and took part in the White House Conference on Youth in 1970 and 1971. He taught political science at Rutgers, New Jersey's State University and worked as a commentator on the New Jersey Educational Network's evening news program. Prior to entering politics, he was president and chairman of the Realty Transfer Company of Elizabeth, New Jersey.

A member of the New Jersey General Assembly from 1967 to 1977, Kean was named speaker of that body in 1972, despite the fact that the Republicans did not hold the majority of the seats. David Friedland, the Democratic minority leader of the previous assembly, had been passed over for the nomination as speaker in favor of a black pastor from Trenton. Friedland and two others retaliated by defecting to Kean, the Republican minority candidate. One disgruntled Democrat noted that "Jesus Christ had his Judas, the Democrats now have David Friedland."

Kean managed President Gerald Ford's campaign in New Jersey in 1976 and in the following year sought the Republican gubernatorial nomination. Losing in the primary to state Senator Raymond H. Bateman, he returned four years later to earn the nomination against seven other contenders. His principal opponent for the nomination that year was Lawrence Kramer, the mayor of Paterson.

In the general election of 1981, Kean faced Democrat James Florio, a long-term congressman from South Jersey. Both men were moderate liberals. Kean, in fact, spent much of his time attempting to disassociate himself from the conservative policies of Republican President Ronald Reagan. The race was extremely close: 1,145,999 votes for Kean and 1,144,202 for Florio. Eleven minor candidates divided the remaining 25,000 votes cast. Although there were allegations that the national Republican party had tried to scare Democratic voters away from the polls by using a "ballot security" force, in the end Florio conceded the election without a court fight.

Despite the closeness of his win, Kean went on to establish himself as one of the most popular governors in the state's history. In his campaign for reelection in 1985, he scored the biggest landslide victory in the annals of state politics, defeating his Democratic opponent, Essex County Executive Peter Shapiro, with over 70 percent of the vote. The final vote total was 1,352,459 for Kean to 574,980 for Shapiro. The strength of Kean's victory also helped the Republicans win control of the state assembly for the first time in 12 years. In the campaign, Kean had received the endorsement of the AFL-CIO, the first time that the union had ever supported a Republican gubernatorial candidate. He also won 60 percent of the black vote, an achievement that made him a national celebrity and a rising star in national Republican party politics. After his win, Kean became a national spokesman for Republicans eager to widen party ranks to include more minority and blue-collar voters. He outlined his strategies and policies for opening up the party in his book *The Politics of Inclusion* (Free Press, 1988).

During his first term in office, Kean signed increases in state income and sales taxes to close a budget deficit exacerbated by the recession of the early 1980s. Taking advantage of economic gains in the state caused by the national recovery that followed, he created more than 350,000 new jobs during his first term, and the state's unemployment rate ran consistently below the national average. The gains of his first term continued during his second, with New Jersey undergoing a rapid transformation into a blossoming state with a thriving, diverse economy. During the Kean years, the state gained 600,000 new jobs, unemployment dropped to 4 percent, and each year the state reported a large surplus.

Kean's two terms in office will be remembered as a time of roaring growth and rising self-esteem for New Jersey. He cultivated his role as the state's promoter, appearing in TV commercials to extol the state's strengths: the casinos of Atlantic City, its seaside resorts, and the sports mecca of the Meadowlands. He took special pride in the transformation of the once-dilapidated Hudson River waterfront into a bustling financial and commercial center, and in the elevation of the arts to a major element in state life. During his years in office, Kean also lowered business taxes, signed a death penalty law, persuaded the legislature to pass a law protecting freshwater wetlands, and oversaw the divestment of state pension funds from companies doing business with South Africa. An adviser to President Reagan on welfare reform, he proposed a state "workfare" program that required all able-bodied welfare recipients either to go to school or to seek employment.

The Kean administration was also distinguished by its style. Unlike many governors, he refused to win support for his programs by promising, threatening, or cajoling the legislature. With statesmanlike detachment, he outlined what he believed to be right and expected rational men and women of good faith and sound judgment to follow. Throughout, he retained his personal popularity, which at its high point generally approached 70 percent in public opinion polls.

Critics, however, saw Kean's role differently. Charging that he deliberately remained distant from unpopular issues like the garbage crisis and auto insurance reform, they complained that he left a host of daunting problems for his Democratic successor to solve.

Nonetheless, Kean will be credited by historians as being the first New Jersey governor since Woodrow Wilson to attain a prominent national role as a spokesman for political reform and innovation. His major achievements were in the area of education. Hailed as the "Education Governor" by the national press, he introduced major reforms in the state's teacher training programs as well as hiking the minimum starting salary for public school teachers. He pushed for regular increases in state higher education spending, launched a competitive grant program that provided money for institutions to carry out special initiatives, helped state colleges lobby for a controversial plan to give them more control over financial matters, and pushed for a $90 million bond issue for higher education construction and equipment purchases. Frequently appearing as a panelist at higher education conferences, he was active in influencing national higher education policy. He served as chairman of the Education Commission of the States, as cochairman of a National Governors Association policy panel on education, and as a member of a special teaching panel formed by the Carnegie Forum on Education and the Economy. He was also a member of Princeton University's board of trustees.

A moderate Republican, Kean supported the Equal Rights Amendment as well as freedom of choice on abortion. Although he was known for his rather liberal stands on certain issues, including civil rights, aid to cities, and environmental protection, he was a firm conservative on others. He vigorously supported President Reagan's large tax cuts and the Reagan plan to build a space-based missile defense system. Chairman of the Republican Governors Association in 1987, he relished using what he called the "bully pulpits" available to him as he traveled around the country promoting both his education reforms and his politics of inclusion. Mentioned as a possible running mate for George Bush in 1988, he was chosen instead to deliver the keynote address at the 1988 Republican National Convention in New Orleans.

Prohibited by the state constitution from seeking a third consecutive term, Kean left office in 1990, widely regarded as having been one of the state's most highly successful governors. Although he was mentioned as a possible secretary of education in the Bush administration, he insisted that he needed a respite from public life and chose instead to return to an academic career. Becoming president of Drew University in January 1990, he has drawn high marks for his accessibility and involvement on the campus of the selective liberal arts institution located in Madison, New Jersey.

The speculation that Kean will one day return to public life never dies. He has remained actively involved in national public service, working as an emissary for progressive Republican policies. He retained close ties with the Bush White House, serving on two presidential commissions and running Bush's 1992 reelection campaign in New Jersey. Even with the Democratic win, there was some talk that the "Education Governor" might be named secretary of education in the Clinton White House. Despite much speculation that he would challenge Democratic incumbent Frank Lautenberg for the U.S. Senate in 1994, he has decided to continue his retirement from politics, at least for the time being. Nonetheless, he has acknowledged an interest in playing some role in the Republican presidential campaign of 1996, probably to steer his party in a more moderate direction in the area of abortion rights.

Bibliography: Michael Barone et al., *The Almanac of American Politics, 1988* (Washington, D.C.: National Journal, 1987); biographical information courtesy of governor's office; *The Chronicle of Higher Education,* 10–14–87; Thomas Kean, *The Politics of Inclusion* (New York: Free Press, 1988); *Newsweek,* 3–24–86; *The New York Times*: 10–26–81; 9–17–85; 10–31–85; 11–1–85; 11–6–85; 11–7–85; 9–10–86; 10–9–86; 4–20–87; 12–27–87; 1–12–88; 1–13–88; 1–22–88; 1–31–88; 12–15–88; 1–12–90; 10–28–92; *The Record* (Bergen County, N.J.): 2–12–92; 3–6–92; 8–18–92; *The Star-Ledger* (Newark, N.J.): 10–24–86; 3–8–87; 7–29–89; 12–31–89; 4–28–91; 7–9–91; 7–18–91; 3–16–92; 4–27–92; 6–24–92; *USA Today,* 6–7–88; *The West-Essex Tribune* (Livingston, N.J.), 7–11–91.

JAMES J. ("JIM") FLORIO, 1990–1994

Florio was born in Brooklyn, New York, on August 29, 1937, the son of a dockyard worker. Struggling against poverty in his youth, he developed tough work habits and a spartan life-style and personal ethic that have stayed with him throughout his life. At 17 he dropped out of Erasmus Hall High School to join the navy, where he fought as an amateur boxer. Facial injuries he received crushed his left cheekbone, leaving half of his face permanently sunken. Upon his return to civilian life, Florio earned his G.E.D. diploma. He graduated magna cum laude from Trenton State College in 1962 with a degree in social studies. Later he took graduate courses at Columbia University on a Woodrow Wilson Fellowship and earned a law degree from Rutgers University in 1967. As a law student, he worked at night as a janitor to support his wife and three children.

A Democrat, Florio entered politics as a district leader with the Camden political machine. Serving in the New Jersey Assembly from 1970 to 1974, he won election to the U.S. House of Representatives in 1974 after a previously unsuccessful run. Defeating conservative Republican Congressman John E. Hunt, he went on to be reelected seven times. Representing a largely blue-collar district centered in Camden, he earned the grudging respect of his colleagues who remembered him as an aloof, driven, and tenacious worker. A bitter opponent of the Reagan administration, he compiled a distinguished record on consumer issues, transportation, and the environment. He is best remembered as the architect of the 1980 Superfund Law that allocated billions of dollars for the cleanup of toxic waste sites. He also helped force the dismissal of Environmental Protection Agency administrator Anne Gorsuch Burford after charges of superfund mismanagement.

Most of the issues Florio championed in Congress were New Jersey issues, and political watchers knew that he was grooming himself to be governor. His base became south Jersey, where in 1979 he led a rebellion against the Democratic machine dominated by Camden Mayor Angelo J. Errichetti. Florio's supporters have dominated politics in the county ever since.

After an unsuccessful run for the Democratic gubernatorial nomination in 1977, Florio faced Thomas Kean for the governorship in 1981. Although many political analysts had expected him to breeze to victory over Kean, he lost by 1,797 votes—a margin so razor-thin that it took a month of recounts to certify Kean as the winner. In the opinion of experts, neither

James J. Florio *(Courtesy of Governor's Office)*

Florio's congressional record nor the issues he championed were responsible for his defeat. Rather, his narrow loss was attributed to his personal style. He too frequently came across as cold, brusque, and aloof. In a supreme irony, the patrician Kean, scion of a wealthy and powerful political family, charmed voters with his folksy style, while Florio, a child of the working class, came across as rigid, formal, and arrogant.

The message was not lost on the politically savvy Florio when he sought the governorship again in 1989. This time he was the beneficiary of an auspicious marriage that friends say brought a dramatic change in him. Legally separated from his first wife Maryanne in 1978, he married Lucinda Coleman on Valentine's Day in 1988. Also divorced, also a former high school dropout, and also the daughter of a shipyard worker, she had all the human qualities he appeared to lack in 1981. Politically, she was a boon in terms of helping him relax and develop a more voter-friendly political style. Two new grandchildren also helped to soften his image.

Defeating Princeton Mayor Barbara Boggs Sigmund and Assemblyman Alan Karcher to win the Democratic nomination, he went on to face Republican Congressman Jim Courter in the general election. A conservative from rural Warren County, Courter presented a sharply contrasting vision of state government from that of the liberal, urban-oriented Florio. Courter promised to extend the politics of Reaganism into the 1990s by fighting big government, taxes, and crime. Florio, by contrast, said that the good times of the 1980s had left in their wake worries about overdevelopment and pollution that required an activist government to solve. Key issues in the race were abortion, automobile insurance, the environment, taxes, crime, and drugs. Each candidate claimed he would cut the fat from the state bureaucracy, keep taxes from rising, and design an auto insurance plan to get high premiums under control.

Despite the array of issues raised, the campaign was widely criticized as the nastiest in the memory of the state. Both men assaulted each other's character. Florio accused Courter of failing to clean up toxic waste on property he owned, while Courter accused Florio of accepting campaign contributions from mob-run labor unions. Florio contributed one of the campaign's most memorable television commercials, attacking his opponent's credibility by comparing him with Pinocchio in a widely run ad.

In the final analysis, Florio's landslide victory with 62 percent of the vote was attributed not only to the flawless nature of his own campaign but also to the ineptitude and missteps of the Courter organization. Waffling on the key issue of abortion, Courter himself traced his defeat to a failure to give the voters a clear picture of who he was or what he stood for.

With his overwhelming victory, Florio became the state's first Italian-American governor. He also carried into office a Democratically controlled assembly.

Once in office, however, Florio's fortunes changed dramatically. In the opinion of most analysts, 1990 will be remembered as the most turbulent political year for a New Jersey governor since Brendan Byrne began the state income tax in the late 1970s. Although during the campaign Florio had said that he saw no need to raise taxes, within his first five months in office he pushed a $2.8 billion tax increase through the state legislature, the largest such increase in state history. Supporters defended the plan as a bold and courageous act necessary to put the state on a firm financial footing, while critics derided both Florio's policies and his tactics. Condemning the massive rise in income tax rates as liberal social engineering and "Robin Hood" economics, conservative economists and others predicted that the tax package would chase away corporate leaders and destroy the business climate with which Florio's predecessors had lured companies and jobs from New York.

More troubling even to supporters was the manner in which Florio had acted to wreak his will on the legislature. Within his first five months in office, Florio had brought so many radical changes to the state that aides bragged they had changed more public policy in five months than other governors had done in the previous decade. Besides huge increases in income and sales taxes, Florio asked the legislature for a ban on assault weapons, an overhaul of the auto insurance system, stiffer penalties for polluters, and a new way to finance public schools that would pump millions into poor and middle-class school districts at the expense of the rich. Most experts now agree that Florio had grossly misread the public's mood in 1990.

Perhaps even more damaging was his failure to communicate his actions and ideals adequately to the electorate. Called aloof, arrogant, and insensitive to people's concerns, he became the target of a massive citizens' revolt that swept across the state. An ad hoc group of antitax protestors, Hands Across New Jersey, gathered more than 800,000 signatures protesting the tax increases and asking for the right to recall Florio, a provision that did not exist under current state law. A tidal wave of anti-Florio sentiment engulfed the state—anti-Florio hats, T-shirts, signs, bumper stickers, even 8 x 10 renderings of the governor as a swastikaed Hitler in Nazi regalia. Already in 1990, the most popular bumper sticker predicted and promised that the state would be "Florio-Free in '93."

Florio's unpopularity extended to others in his party. In November 1990, a political unknown almost defeated Democratic Senator Bill Bradley, who had long been New Jersey's most popular Democrat and who had frequently been mentioned as a future presidential contender. Even though Bradley had had nothing to do with Florio's tax policies, he suffered the wrath of voters eager to send a message to his fellow Democrat. In November 1991, massive Democratic losses in both houses of the state legislature were also seen as voter revenge against Florio. The Republicans won control of the state senate for the first time in 18 years and regained control of the assembly after 20 years in the minority. Both developments were viewed unequivocally as personal repudiations of Florio. Assured of veto-proof majorities in the legislature, Republicans kept a campaign pledge and rolled back the Florio sales tax increase by one penny. Their override of his veto marked the first such legislative victory in a decade. In 1992, they again locked horns with the Democratic governor over the fiscal 1993 budget. Florio's veto of the GOP spending plan marked the first time in state history that a New Jersey governor had vetoed a state budget.

On another level, Florio's tactics have gone down in the political record books as a case study of how *not* to present a tax increase to voters. The lessons of New Jersey were apparently not lost on President Bill Clinton as he made a very public case for his own tax increase proposals in 1993.

While Florio's tax increases remain the dominant legacy of his administration, other important issues and actions marked his term in office. In 1990, he won approval for a state ban on assault weapons that is widely considered to be the nation's toughest gun law. Although the action made him one of the National Rifle Association's prime political targets, it also earned him the prestigious John F. Kennedy Profile in Courage Award for 1993. An insurance reform law designed to protect policyholders and offer insurers a chance to make reasonable profits engendered more controversy, as Allstate, New Jersey's largest insurer of automobiles and homes, pulled out of the state, taking 1,400 jobs along with it. In January 1992, Florio signed a package of welfare reform laws designed to curb long-term reliance on public assistance. The most controversial provision of his plan denied a $64-a-month grant increase to women who had additional children while on welfare. Despite the outcry of critics lamenting the plan's harshness, President Clinton praised Florio's efforts to make much needed changes in welfare policy and named the governor to a National Governors Association welfare reform panel working with Clinton to encourage other such reforms nationwide.

Facing re-election in 1993, Florio squared off against Republican Christie Whitman, who had made opposition to Florio's tax policies the hallmark of her dramatic run against Bill Bradley in 1990. Actually the Republican had never stopped running since her near miss in that race, and early polls predicted a sure defeat for the unpopular governor.

Yet, Florio persevered, striving to be—according to one report—the "phoenix of '93 politics." Defending himself against the massive tax increases that had sparked such public vitriol, he argued that his brand of tough and decisive leadership was badly needed in 1990 and that, by acting promptly, he had helped the state escape the credit-rating problems of states like New York and the budget crises that temporarily shut down governments in Connecticut and Maine. Florio also liked to compare himself with one of the state's former governors, Democrat Brendan Byrne, whose popularity had also plummeted after imposing the state income tax in 1976, yet who nonetheless went on to win reelection handily. Relying on the talents of political consultant James Carville, who had engineered Bill Clinton's successful White House bid, Florio waged a near flawless campaign, deflecting the attention from himself by depicting his challenger as inexperienced and lacking in credibility. Attempting to woo back middle class voters by stressing his tough stands on gun control and welfare reform, he also played the populist card, contrasting his own working class roots with those of the patrician Whitman, the daughter of one of New Jersey's wealthiest and most politically well connected families. Asking voters whether the high-born Whitman really could relate to people like them, he also ridiculed her plan to cut income taxes by 30 percent over three years. He likened her ideas to the failed supply side economics of the Reagan years, policies that in his view had led to massive deficits and much human suffering. Picking up the endorsement of most major newspapers in the metropolitan region, Florio's fortunes showed a dramatic turn around, and one month before election day he was heavily favored in the polls. Press reports spoke of his "resurrection," while others suggested that perhaps the anti-tax furor of the early years of his administration had indeed subsided. Even John Buzdash, the statewide leader of a citizens anti-tax lobby, endorsed the governor.

It was the power of a large undecided voter bloc, seemingly unenthusiastic about either candidate, that decided Florio's future. In the end, the tax issue proved decisive, and newcomer Whitman, despite the polls, pulled off a stunning upset. Her victory over Florio by 33,307 votes was the second narrowest in the last half-century. Interestingly, it was the second razor-thin gubernatorial loss in which Florio had been involved. With his loss, Florio became the first New Jersey governor since the adoption of the present 1947 constitution to be unseated in his bid for a second term.

Claiming that he has no aspirations to return to Washington, where he began his political career, Florio has also quashed speculation that he is interested in joining the Clinton administration. Doubtful that he will ever seek public office again, he has expressed interest in a teaching career.

Bibliography: Biographical information courtesy of governor's office; *The Chronicle of Higher Education,* 8–28–91; Phil Duncan ed., *Politics in America 1992* (Washington, D.C.: Congressional Quarterly Press, 1991); Peter Kerr, "Read His Lips: More Taxes," *New York Times Magazine* (May 20, 1990): 30–33, 51–57; *Newsweek,* 8–6–90; *The New York Times:* 6–7–89; 6–8–89; 7–3–89; 11–8–89; 11–9–89; 6–24–90; 7–13–90; 11–8–90; 1–9–91; 3–28–91; 4–30–91; 8–19–91; 9–22–91; 11–6–91; 11–20–91; 1–15–92; 1–22–92; 4–3–92; 5–4–92; 5–6–92; 5–19–92; 5–22–92; 5–23–92; 6–19–92; 7–28–92; 8–5–92; 1–4–93; 1–17–93; 6–9–93; 9–18–93; 10–17–

93; 11–3–93; *The Record* (Bergen County, N.J.): 8–20–91; 8–31–92; 10–17–93; *The Star-Ledger* (Newark, N.J.): 11–8–89; 12–5–89; 7–13–90; 8–18–91; 11–6–91; 11–10–91; 2–3–92; 3–5–92; 4–8–92; 5–22–92; 6–27–92; 8–5–92; 5–25–93; 10–10–93; 11–3–93; 11–4–93; *USA Today*: 11–19–90; 7–19–91; 9–18–91; 9–10–92; 8–27–93; 10–1–93; 11–3–93.

Christine Todd Whitman *(Courtesy of People for Whitman Campaign)*

CHRISTINE ("CHRISTIE") TODD WHITMAN, 1994–

Born in New York City on September 26, 1946, Whitman is the scion of one of the state's wealthiest and best-connected political families. She is the daughter of Webster B. Todd, a major figure in state and national Republican politics and an Eisenhower appointee to economic posts in Europe. Todd's success as a building contractor responsible for such projects as Rockefeller Center, Radio City Music Hall, and historic Williamsburg left him with not only a personal fortune but also the wherewithal to bankroll the campaigns of Republican candidates. Whitman's mother, Eleanor Schley Todd, was a Republican national committeewoman and a leader of the New Jersey Federation of Republican Women.

Whitman also boasts political connections through marriage. Her husband John Whitman, a financial consultant, is the son of Charles S. Whitman, Jr., a New York circuit court judge, and the grandson of Charles S. Whitman, Sr., governor of New York from 1914 to 1916. The Whitmans have two teenaged children.

Whitman was raised on a farm in Oldwick, New Jersey, where she continues to make her home. After her 1968 graduation from Wheaton College with a degree in government, she worked for a time in Washington, D.C. Serving in the U.S. Office of Economic Opportunity, an anti-poverty program of the Nixon administration, she also worked with the Republican National Committee, attempting to develop relationships with minority groups, senior citizens, and others traditionally outside the mainstream of Republican politics. She also lived for a time in England, where her husband was affiliated with CitiCorp. She has a long record of involvement in civic, community, and volunteer services.

Making her first bid for elective office in 1981, Whitman served two terms as a Somerset County freeholder. In that office, she was instrumental in opening the county's first homeless shelter and its first halfway house for alcoholic teenaged boys. She was also involved in the creation of the county's open space program.

In 1988 Republican Governor Tom Kean appointed Whitman as President of the state Board of Public Utilities (now known as the Board of Regulatory Commissioners). In that office, she fought to keep utility rates low and was given high marks for instituting an ethics code for the board.

Whitman resigned from the board in 1990 to make a run for the U.S. Senate against popular incumbent Bill Bradley. Widely viewed as a sacrificial lamb in the uphill struggle, she stunned the nation with a dramatic near upset win over the former Knicks basketball star and would-be presidential contender. Capitalizing on voter fury over a record $2.8 billion tax increase rammed through the legislature by Democratic Governor Jim Florio—who, only months before, during his bid for the statehouse, had told voters he saw no need to raise taxes—Whitman focused her campaign on Bradley's refusal to comment on the actions of his fellow Democrat. Coming within two percentage points of defeating Bradley, the little-known Whitman was credited with humbling the heretofore popular incumbent and with quashing—at least for the time being—his presidential ambitions. As for her own career, Whitman—the would-be giant-slayer—drew the attention of the Republican party establishment and began laying the groundwork for a campaign to challenge the "taxman" himself. For the next three years she never stopped running, forming her own political action committee, the Committee for an Affordable New Jersey, writing a newspaper column, hosting a radio talk show, and crisscrossing the state winning endorsements from party leaders. In June 1993 she earned the right to challenge Florio by defeating former legislator Jim Wallwork and former attorney general Cary Edwards in the Republican gubernatorial primary.

Yet Whitman did not emerge unscathed from her primary victory. She was stung by charges that she had hired illegal aliens as household workers and then failed to pay taxes on their salaries. Also damaging were disclosures that the patrician Whitman had failed to vote in local school board elections since her own children attend private schools.

Nonetheless, experts at first viewed her as a heavy favorite to trounce the hapless Florio, who registered massive negatives in the polls and whose approval ratings had once dropped to a low of 17 percent in the wake of the tax-hike furor. Whitman, however, failed to build on the momentum generated by her primary victory. She was widely criticized, for example, for taking the summer off, while Florio used his visibility as an incumbent to register gains with voters. As summer turned to fall, the national press began to speculate about the "resurrection" of Jim Florio. He was portrayed as a courageous leader, much like President Clinton, who had had the vision and leadership to make the tough choices necessary to resolve the state's budget woes. Benefiting from the talents of former Clinton strategist James Carville, Florio succeeded in putting Whitman on the defensive, painting her as an inexperienced neophyte with no real agenda for the state. Rather than defining herself to voters, Whitman was left to defend herself against Florio's charges. She was portrayed as an out-of-touch millionaire unable to comprehend the needs of real people, criticized for her ownership of two tax-sheltered farms, and taunted for her failure to disclose her net worth and initial reluctance to release her income tax records. Most serious was Florio's masterful use of negative television and newspaper advertising. Boasting of his successful battle with the National Rifle Association to pass the nation's toughest ban on assault weapons, Florio equated Whitman's opposition to components of that bill with support for the gun lobby.

Even more problematic for Whitman were a series of missteps on the crucial tax issue. Flip-flopping at first on the merits of a possible tax cut, Whitman aroused skepticism with her promise to cut income taxes by 30 percent over three years. Critics charged that the plan would cause property taxes to soar. Others noted that the plan was unrealistic, unworkable, and only served to underscore Whitman's inexperience and lack of credibility as a candidate. Still others suggested that public anger over the tax issue had indeed subsided. By late summer, some polls gave the once-maligned incumbent an astonishing 21-point lead over Whitman.

Nonetheless, Whitman persevered in what turned out to be a roller coaster campaign. A late fall shuffle in campaign staff allowed her to refocus her message on the tax issue. She excoriated the Florio administration for ethical lapses and blamed his high tax policies for New Jersey's high unemployment rate and for the exodus of jobs from the state. Promising to eliminate the sales tax on phone calls and advocating a reduction in some business taxes, she stumped for votes as a reforming outsider, touring the state on a campaign bus appropriately entitled the "Wheels of Change."

Although analysts recognized a turn in political fortunes as election day neared, no one predicted the upset Whitman victory. Although her 26,093 vote margin (out of 2.4 million votes cast) was one of the slimmest ever, it nonetheless demonstrated the unreliability of the polls, the volatility of the electorate, and the centrality of the undecided vote.

With her victory, Whitman became the first challenger in modern state history to successfully oust an incumbent from office. Even more important, she became the first woman governor in the history of the state. Despite her historic candidacy, however, gender was not really an issue in the campaign. While Whitman received endorsements from the National Women's Political Caucus and its state chapter affiliate, as well as a "recommendation" from the National Organization for Women, hers was not a feminist campaign. Nor did she excite women voters, who as a group threw their support to Florio.

The New Jersey race was closely monitored for what it might portend for national politics, and for what messages it might send to other politicians who raised taxes and then faced the voters. Following other Republican victories in 1993, in a special Texas senate race, the Los Angeles mayor's race, the New York City mayoral contest, and the Virginia gubernatorial test, Florio's loss was seen as a major political embarrassment for President Clinton, to whom he had frequently been compared.

One week after Whitman's upset victory, however, a political firestorm erupted over statements made by her former campaign manager Ed Rollins that Republicans had paid $500,000 in "street money" to black ministers and Democratic campaign workers to suppress the black vote. Although Rollins later recanted—attributing his braggadocio to a desire to play a "head game" with Florio political consultant and arch-rival James Carville—Rollins' boast triggered investigations by the U.S. Attorney's Office, the state Attorney General's Office, and the state Election Law Enforcement Commission. National and state Democratic committees even filed suit to overturn the election. These lawsuits were eventually dropped when the Democrats could not uncover any evidence of wrongdoing by her campaign.

Although she vigorously denied the statements from the outset, the scandal slowed Whitman's transition plans. The controversy absorbed the state for weeks after the election and, in the opinion of some observers, may have weakened Whitman's ability to carry out her ambitious agenda. Whitman has promised to make New Jersey "business friendly" and to concentrate on the economic revival of the state insisting on her commitment to her tax cut proposal.

Bibliography: Biographical information courtesy of People for Whitman; *The New York Times*: 6–9–93; 9–18–93; 10–17–93; 11–3–93; *The Record* (Bergen County, N.J.), 10–17–93; 11–14–93; *The Star-Ledger* (Newark, N.J.): 10–10–93; 11–3–93; 11–30–93; *USA Today*: 8–27–93; 10–1–93; 11–3–93; 11–16–93; *The Wall Street Journal*, 9–23–93.

GARREY CARRUTHERS, 1987–1991

Garrey Carruthers was born in Aztec, New Mexico, on August 29, 1939. He and his wife Kathy have three children.

He graduated from Aztec High School in 1957 and two years later served as state president of the Future Farmers of America. He earned a bachelor's degree in agriculture from New Mexico State University in Las Cruces in 1964 and a master's degree in agricultural economics from New Mexico State University in 1965. Earning a Ph.D. in economics from Iowa State University in 1968, he returned to Las Cruces to teach agricultural economics and agricultural business at New Mexico State. His association with the university continued until 1985, when he resigned to run for governor.

In 1974, Carruthers became a White House Fellow under President Gerald Ford. Returning to Las Cruces after the fellowship, he served as acting director of the New Mexico Water Resources Research Institute from 1976 to 1978. He also accepted a 1976 appointment from President Ford to serve on the commission that screens White House Fellows.

In 1977, he was elected chairman of the New Mexico Republican party, a post he held until 1979. In 1981, President Reagan appointed him assistant secretary of the interior, where he served under controversial Secretary James Watt. He served in two key administration positions until 1984, when he returned to New Mexico.

State Republicans were optimistic about their prospects in the 1986 gubernatorial race, thanks to the political troubles of outgoing Democratic incumbent Toney Anaya. The oil and gas crisis had also hurt the economy. Carruthers, as the Republican nominee for the state's top post, was favored over his Democratic opponent Ray Powell, a retired engineer and businessman. The selection of nonpolitical technocrats by both parties was no accident, attributable at least in part to voter displeasure with Anaya and state government. In an ironic move, the Democrats tried to portray Carruthers as a conservative version of the mercurial Anaya, a man as likely to anger voters with his conservative ideology as Anaya did on the opposite side of the spectrum. His office under Interior Secretary James Watt had also been plagued by allegations of irregularities, and

Garrey Carruthers *(State Records Center and Archives, Santa Fe, New Mexico)*

Democrats warned of his tendency toward brash, simplistic approaches. Thus, they tried to convince voters that Powell's calm approach was the only real alternative to the current administration. They also hoped to capitalize on widespread voter dissatisfaction with the state's Republican-controlled house, which they believed could temper the Anaya fallout. In the opinion of pollsters, however, the low-key Powell was not the ideal candidate to wage a dramatic uphill fight.

Carruthers promised to streamline government and to promote economic development. His campaign stressed such issues as educational and managerial competence. Making much of the fact that he was a political outsider and not a member of the legislature, he won with 53 percent of the vote.

Carruthers was sworn in as the state's 24th chief executive on January 1, 1987, the state's first Republican governor in 16 years. In office he disappointed some conservatives with his generally moderate approach to issues, but others hailed the benefits of his go-slow style. One political observer defended Carruthers: "He's following perhaps the most unpopular governor in the state's history. The state probably would have reacted negatively to a more forceful role." Despite lingering economic problems in one of the nation's poorest states, Carruthers drew high marks for his political skills and aggressive travels around the state. He asked for a tax increase during his first year in office, saying that he had no alternative since the state had been chronically short of funds for the previous four years. Although the Democratically controlled legislature reacted coolly to his proposal to revamp the state's welfare system, one of his legislative priorities, he generally received positive acclaim in a state where Democrats outnumber Republicans almost 2–1.

Carruthers also stressed economic development and the reform of higher education. He sought to raise high school graduation requirements, started a competitive grant program to improve academic departments at the state's colleges and universities, and moved all remedial courses from the state's four-year institutions to community colleges. He sought major increases in faculty salaries and tried to change state formulas for financing colleges so they wouldn't depend so heavily on enrollment. Other projects included starting a telecommunications program so professors could teach courses on more than one campus, and developing an initiative with researchers at the state's two national laboratories so as to entice them to teach part-time at public colleges and universities.

One major controversy of Carruthers' term in office involved a dispute with the federal government over nuclear waste storage and disposal. He challenged Washington by insisting that his state would not accept any more radioactive waste at its storage facilities until the Energy Department met its previous commitments to the state, including compensation for road improvements and assurances on safety and environmental protection.

Ineligible to seek a second consecutive term in office, Carruthers retired from the governorship in January 1991. Due to a change in the state's constitution, his successor, Bruce King, will be the first governor in state history allowed to serve two consecutive four-year terms.

Bibliography: Michael Barone et al., *The Almanac of American Politics, 1988* (Washington, D.C.: National Journal, 1987); biographical information courtesy of governor's office; *The Chronicle of Higher Education,* 11–12–86; *The New York Times*: 8–31–86; 9–12–86; 11–21–87; 12–17–88; 6–3–90.

BRUCE KING, 1971–1975, 1979–1983, 1991–

Born in Stanley, New Mexico, on April 6, 1924, King is the son of Molly Schooler and rancher William King. He attended the University of New Mexico between 1943 and 1944 and then served in the Field Artillery of the U.S. Army from 1944 to 1946. A rancher and livestock feeder by trade, King holds a partnership in King Brothers Ranch and King Butane Company. He is married to the former Alice Martin of Moriarty and has two sons.

King's career in state politics has been a long and varied one. He is the only person in New Mexico's history to have been elected to three four-year terms as governor. Interestingly, however, because New Mexico's constitution, until 1991, prohibited incumbent governors from serving consecutive terms in office, King's long tenure in the statehouse has been an interrupted one.

King began his career in state politics as Sante Fe County commissioner in 1954. Holding that post for the next four years, he eventually served as chairman of the board of commissioners from 1957 to 1958. He was a member of the New Mexico House of Representatives for the next decade, from 1959 to 1969, and served as speaker of the house from 1963 to 1969. Positions as state Democratic chairman (1968–69) and president of the New Mexico State Constitutional Convention in 1969 preceded his first run for the governorship in 1970. With the strong support of organized labor, he defeated Republican Pete Domenici, a former chairman of the Albuquerque City Commission who later went on to become a U.S. senator. King was the first chief executive of New Mexico elected to a four-year term, under the provisions of a constitutional amendment adopted in 1970.

King's first administration saw New Mexico pass the Equal Rights Amendment to the U.S. Constitution, organize a department of Corrections, establish a State Capitol Improvement Fund, and create a Children's Court Division of the District Courts. He also served as vice-chairman of the Western Governors Conference from 1973 to 1974.

Retiring to his ranch and cattle investments in 1975, he was succeeded in the governorship by Jerry Apodaca, who had previously been a member of the state legislature. Although Apodaca was a Democrat, the two men were not political allies and were very different governors. King's interest in politics continued during his temporary retirement, and he served as a delegate to the Democratic National Convention of 1976.

Bruce King *(Courtesy of Governor's Office)*

Two years later he returned to politics, seeking his party's gubernatorial nomination in the 1978 primary. Although King soundly defeated his opponent Robert Ferguson, gaining 61 percent of the vote, he had a more difficult time in the general election against Joseph Skeen, a conservative Republican who attacked King on the right-to-work issue. New Mexico Republicans had been gaining strength in statewide contests, and King, a moderate Democrat, just managed to defeat Skeen by a 51 percent to 49 percent margin, gaining only about 1 percent more of the total vote than had Apodaca in 1974. Yet, like Apodaca, he did well in Hispanic areas, and he ran stronger than Apodaca in so-called Little Texas, the southeast corner of the state.

A delegate to the 1980 Democratic National Convention, King was ineligible to seek reelection as governor in 1982. His successor this time was former Democratic Attorney General Toney Anaya, who had served as King's administrative assistant during his first term as governor.

King reentered state politics in 1990, using his high-name recognition and a middle-of-the-road, noncontroversial style to recapture the statehouse for an unprecedented third term. Having defeated three challengers to win the Democratic nomination, he easily defeated Republican Frank Bond, a lawyer and rancher, garnering 54 percent of the vote. In the election, King campaigned on his record, stressing his conservative, businesslike approach to government. The state's poor economy was a key issue in the campaign, and King called for measures to spur economic development, promising to create more growth in the state's private business sector. Exit polls confirmed that those voters most concerned about the economy tended to favor King.

Other priorities set by King for his third term include education and the environment.

While governor, King has served as chairman of several boards and commissions, including the Interstate Oil and Gas Compact Commission, the Rocky Mountain Federation, the Four Corners Regional Commission, the Western Governors Conference, and the Bi-National Governors Commission of Mexico and the United States.

Bibliography: Biographical information courtesy of governor's office; *The Chronicle of Higher Education,* 10–31–90; Phil Duncan, ed., *Politics in America 1992* (Washington, D.C.: Congressional Quarterly Press, 1991); *New Mexico Blue Book,* 1979–1980; *The New York Times,* 11–7–90; *USA Today*: 6–7–90; 11–8–90.

Mario Matthew Cuomo *(Courtesy of Governor's Office)*

NEW YORK

MARIO MATTHEW CUOMO, 1983–

Born in Queens, New York, on June 15, 1932, Cuomo is the son of immigrant parents, Andrea Cuomo and Immaculata Giordano Cuomo. A Roman Catholic, Cuomo has been married since 1954 to the former Matilda Raffia. They are the parents of five children.

An alumnus of Queens public schools and St. John's Prep, Cuomo graduated summa cum laude from St. John's University in 1953 and tied for top of class honors at St. John's University School of Law in 1956. For a brief time, he played professional baseball with the Pittsburgh Pirates, before an injury cut short his career. After a stint as a confidential legal assistant to Judge Adrian P. Burke of the New York State Court of Appeals in 1956, he entered private law practice with the firm of Corner, Weisbrod, Froeb, and Charles. He also taught as a part-time law professor at St. John's Law School for 17 years.

Cuomo first came to public attention in 1972 when he settled the Forest Hills housing controversy at the request of New York Mayor John Lindsay. Having earlier resolved a similar crisis in Corona, Queens, in Forest Hills he worked to preserve a low-income housing project in a middle-class neighborhood. He later wrote a highly acclaimed book, *Forest Hills Diary: The Crisis of Low-Income Housing* (Random House, 1974), which contained his reflections on the dispute. In 1975, he was called upon again to be a fact finder in a nursing home controversy. His actions here led to the creation of the Moreland Act Commission and the appointment of a special nursing home prosecutor.

These activities started Cuomo on the path to a public service career. In 1975, he was appointed secretary of state by Governor Hugh Carey. At the governor's request, he acted as a roving negotiator in statewide crises; he settled the Co-op City rent strike controversy and mediated the Mohawk Indian lands claim dispute. In addition, he was responsible for the first revision in more than 70 years of the state's lobbying law, convened the first statewide arson conference, and fought for new rules for real estate brokers and against blockbusting. In 1978, he was elected lieutenant governor. In his new position, he assumed additional responsibilities as chairman of the state's Urban and Rural Affairs cabinets as well as head of the State Advisory Council on the Disabled. He also assumed leadership as the state's first ombudsman, helping thousands of New Yorkers through the maze of state agencies and regulations.

Entering the 1982 race for governor of New York, he waged a come-from-behind fight to defeat New York City Mayor Ed Koch to win the Democratic gubernatorial nomination. In the September 23, 1982, Democratic primary, he defeated the outspoken mayor by 60,544 votes. His opponent in the general election was Republican Lewis Lehrman, a political unknown who had made millions by building the Rite-Aid drugstore chain. The campaign provided a vivid contrast between two ideological opponents: The conservative Lehrman advocated tax cuts and a stern approach to crime, while the liberal Cuomo, an inspiring orator, defended in uplifting language the classic positions of the welfare state. Cuomo was elected with 51 percent of the vote, capturing the statehouse by a 180,386 vote margin. His day-by-day accounting of his campaign was published as *The Diaries of Mario M. Cuomo: The Campaign for Governor* (Random House, 1984). In 1986, he won reelection with a record 64.6 percent of the vote over opponent Andrew P. O'Rourke, Westchester County executive. He was reelected a third time in 1990, defeating Pierre Rinfret, a political unknown.

Throughout his years in office Cuomo established himself as a caring, committed, hard-working, and thoughtful leader. He has initiated programs to reform the criminal justice system, to improve state budget practices, to ease the burden on counties through assumption of the local share of many Medicaid costs, and to provide permanent shelter for the homeless. His tenure in office includes a long list of accomplishments, including billion-dollar bond issues to rehabilitate roads and to improve the environment; the allocation of $8.6 billion to rebuild New York City's transit system; and the establishment of a new program to subsidize the purchase of prescription drugs among the elderly. He has also supported state spending increases for higher education and efforts to give public universities more authority over their state allocations. In 1988, he proposed a pioneering new program of grants called "Liberty Scholarships" that provided an extraordinary incentive to low-income students to continue their education. The first such effort on a statewide level, the program guaranteed that any poor seventh-grade student who eventually graduated from high school would receive enough money from the state to attend one of its public colleges.

From July 1984 when Cuomo captivated the nation with a stirring and memorable keynote address at the Democratic National Convention, speculation has persisted as to his national ambitions. Widely regarded as one of the most charismatic governors New York State has ever had, he has clung to a liberal vision of government, pressing for a society in which everyone should have a voice and a stake. In the opinion of political observers, one area in which his governorship has been a success is his ability both to articulate a liberal agenda and to educate the public, raising its consciousness, compassion, and awareness. A 1984 address at the University of Notre Dame, "Religious Belief and Public Morality," was highly acclaimed, outlining as it did a philosophy on church-state relations from the perspective of a Catholic governor.

During the Reagan-Bush years, Cuomo drew national attention as a spokesman for the cities and states. He argued that the Republicans had improperly ceded fiscal obligations for national problems to the states and that in the process had made the country's tax structure more regressive. While his persistent use of national themes in his gubernatorial campaigns encouraged speculation about his status as a presidential candidate, he saw his role differently. Because he is the governor of the country's second-largest state, and because he attracts more national attention than other governors, Cuomo says he has an obligation to speak out against federal policies that affect his and other states.

Yet for all his skills as a debater, message maker, and strategist, Cuomo also has a darker side. Questions first surfaced in 1986 as to whether he was temperamentally suited for a presidential race. His refusal to engage his opponent in a genuine campaign and to do the kind of stumping and grass-roots politicking that is a staple of most gubernatorial runs led to charges that he was aloof and arrogant. He also has a reputation for testiness and irascibility. Critics see him as tentative and Hamlet-like. His surprise decision in February 1987 not to seek the presidency in 1988 shocked friends and opponents alike and threw the campaign for the 1988 Democratic presidential nomination wide open. Similar and perhaps even more egregious grandstanding marked his behavior on the eve of the 1992 presidential race. The process of public introspection in which he engaged for ten weeks, from October to December 1991, was unique in the annals of American politics. Finally announcing that the state's fiscal problems forced him to stay out of the race, he nonetheless implicitly endorsed a write-in campaign in the February 1992 New Hampshire primary. Not only was his 4 percent draw underwhelming, but critics charged that he seemed to want to win the party nod without actually campaigning for it.

So much talk of Cuomo's national ambitions seemed to be damaging his political prospects at home. By 1990, the persistent and repeatedly voiced conviction that Cuomo was well positioned for a presidential run caused political observers to suggest that he might even skip a reelection bid and simply prepare for the 1992 presidential race. Although Cuomo did ultimately seek and win a third term, his refusal to commit himself to serving out a full four-year term once again fueled speculation that his days in Albany were numbered.

Yet Cuomo's position in 1990 was markedly different from what it had been four years earlier. Taxes in the state had increased by record amounts in each of the previous two years, at the same time that the state's fiscal condition continued to deteriorate. At the time of the election, New York had its lowest credit rating in history and the third lowest in the nation. Moreover, problems of crime and drugs had grown unabated, and Cuomo's staunch opposition to the death penalty seemed to place him at odds with the very real fears and concerns of state voters.

Despite the possible opportunities presented by this rather dismal scenario, the state Republican party found itself in disarray, unable even to find a prominent Republican willing to face Cuomo. After 19 potential candidates turned down the nomination, the party nod went to millionaire economist Pierre Rinfret, a virtual unknown whose erratic behavior throughout the campaign and open attacks on party leaders alienated members of his own party. Even with such feeble opposition, Cuomo won by a surprisingly small margin. His 53 percent tally was substantially less than what he had received in 1986. Many political analysts concluded that at a time when polls showed a majority of New Yorkers thought the state to be headed in the wrong direction, a stronger challenger might have inflicted substantial damage on Cuomo. His sharply reduced vote total indicated that he, too, had become a target of voter dissatisfaction with government, and observers agreed that he was entering into his third term in what was probably the weakest position, fiscally and politically, that he had ever been in as governor.

One of the greatest challenges currently faced by Cuomo is the need to recast his image and message for recessionary times. Even he has conceded that New York's fiscal condition poses a serious threat to his philosophy of government. While he has announced his third-term agenda to be one of "refocusing, reform, and renewal," others fear that the three Rs will become "retrenchment, retreat, and repeal." Many of his new proposals, such as creating a privately financed loan fund for small-business expansion, changing the state's fiscal year, and requiring private employers to offer family leave benefits, have been measures that would require legislation, not dollars, to enact. His popularity has continued to lag after a 1991 budget fight that ended in a record delay, severe spending cuts, and a broken pledge against raising income taxes yet again.

With a Democratic administration now in Washington, and potentially there until the year 2000 if not beyond, serious questions continue to be raised about Cuomo's future. Prospects for a White House bid appear slim, although hints raised by Bill Clinton in the 1992 race suggest that Cuomo may one day be named to the U.S. Supreme Court. The enigmatic Cuomo, however, quickly quashed such speculation and took himself out of consideration when Justice Byron White announced his retirement from the bench in the spring of 1993.

Others have observed that Cuomo's decision to pass up the 1992 presidential race seriously diminished his popularity and weakened his influence in the state capital. To some, he is even now essentially a lame duck.

Bibliography: Michael Barone et al., *The Almanac of American Politics, 1984, 1988* (Washington, D.C.: National Journal, 1983, 1987); biographical information courtesy of governor's office; *The Chronicle of Higher Education*: 11–12–86; 1–13–88; Elizabeth Kolbert, "The State of the Governor," *New York Times Magazine* (Feb. 10, 1991): 22–25, 32, 36–38; Robert S. McElvaine, *Mario Cuomo: A Biography* (New York: Scribner's, 1988); *The New York Times*: 11–2–86; 11–5–86; 11–6–86; 12–16–86; 2–17–87; 2–21–87; 1–6–88; 5–22–90; 5–31–90; 6–4–90; 6–9–90; 7–13–90; 9–22–90; 9–29–90; 10–7–90; 10–23–90; 11–7–90; 11–8–90; 11–11–90; 1–10–91; 2–10–91; 6–23–91; 7–25–91; 10–27–91; 11–1–91; 12–21–91; 12–22–91; 2–22–92; *The Star-Ledger* (Newark, N.J.): 12–8–89; 12–21–91; *USA Today*: 11–2–90; 5–31–91.

James G. Martin *(Courtesy of Governor's Office)*

NORTH CAROLINA

JAMES G. MARTIN, 1985–1993

Born in Savannah, Georgia, on December 11, 1935, Martin is the son of Arthur M. Martin, a Presbyterian minister, and Mary Grubbs Martin. A Presbyterian, Martin married Dorothy McAulay in 1957. The couple has three children.

Martin graduated from Davidson College in 1957 and received a doctorate in chemistry from Princeton University in 1960. Returning to Davidson as a professor of chemistry, he remained in that post until 1972 when he left for Washington as a congressman. Prior to his election to Congress, he had served three terms as a Mecklenburg County commissioner. During those terms in office, he was elected commission chairman and served as president of the North Carolina Association of County Commissioners.

First elected to Congress in 1972, he served six terms on Capitol Hill, becoming a senior member of the powerful Ways and Means Committee and rising to a position of Republican party leadership as chairman of the House Republican Research Committee. Due to his technical education and background, he became an expert on issues relating to food additives, the environment, and toxic wastes. He successfully led the fight against banning saccharin, the artificial sweetener. As a chemist, he argued that the sweetener was not dangerous and helped more people than it harmed. For his work in this and other areas, Martin was honored with the Charles Lathrop Parsons Award, given by the American Chemical Society for outstanding public service by an American chemist. He was the first elected official ever to receive the award. As a conservative Republican, he received an 86 percent approval rating from the U.S. Chamber of Commerce for his 12 years of service in Washington.

Martin gave up what was considered to be a safe Republican seat to make the run for governor of North Carolina in 1984. An ardent advocate of supply-side economics, Martin argued that President Reagan needed loyal fiscal conservatives like himself at the state level. Never having campaigned statewide before, he began at 30 points behind in public opinion polls. He also had to overcome the higher name recognition of his Democratic opponent, state Attorney General Rufus Edmisten, a onetime assistant to former U.S. Senator Sam Ervin. To combat these obstacles, he visited all 100 of the state's counties on a series of "Jim Martin Listens" tours. He campaigned on a probusiness platform, with special emphasis on economic development. Promising to carry on in the tradition of the state's proeducation governors, he proposed a $300 million pay increase for public school teachers. Noting the economic and political progress made by blacks and women in the state, he departed from the path of other Republican aspirants for state office by refraining from appealing to racism. In that sense, his campaign was viewed by political observers as one more indication of the growing sophistication of voters in both North Carolina and the South in general in recent years.

Martin won the election with 54.3 percent of the vote, becoming only the second Republican elected governor of North Carolina in this century. His victory was due not only to his political talent and skill but also to the Democrats' own troubles. Retiring Governor Jim Hunt had named no heir apparent, missing a chance to endorse House Speaker Carl Stewart in his 1980 primary bid against weak Lieutenant Governor Jimmy Green. The 1984 Democratic gubernatorial primary was therefore a bitter battle among ten contenders. When Edmisten won, second-place finisher Eddie Knox, the former mayor of Charlotte, reacted bitterly because he had not gotten the outgoing governor's support. Members of Knox's own family made a point of publicly endorsing Martin.

Martin won reelection in 1988, becoming the first Republican governor since Reconstruction to be elected to a second consecutive term. Although he faced a strong challenge from Lieutenant Governor Robert B. Jordan, a Democrat, he won handily, garnering 56 percent of the vote to Jordan's 44 percent. Jordan, a millionaire lumber company executive, had portrayed Martin's administration as unethical and incompetent.

In office, Martin focused his efforts on improving the quality of life for state citizens. Better schools, better roads, and better jobs remained at the heart of his political agenda. Inheriting a state economy rapidly on the upswing, he attempted to sustain and upgrade economic growth. To do so, he proposed tax cuts designed primarily to attract more business to North Carolina and to undercut its reliance on the troubled tobacco industry. He also endorsed a road improvement program, more spending on schools, and an accelerated merit pay program for teachers.

Political analysts had predicted that Martin could do a great deal to change the face of state politics. Because he had such broad appeal to middle-income voters, observers hoped he would be able to build a strong Republican party in the state. He was viewed as less doctrinaire and ideological than the state's other leading Republican, U.S. Senator Jesse Helms, and had been widely expected to seek the Republican nomination for the U.S. Senate in 1992. Party hopes were dashed, however, in February 1990 when Martin made a surprising announcement that he would be retiring from politics at the end of his second term. Martin explained that he wanted to preclude any suggestion during the remainder of his gubernatorial term that he was merely positioning himself for future campaigns. Analysts believed, however, that the professorial and scholarly Martin had simply lost his stomach for politics after mean-spirited attacks on him in the press and by state Democrats. He had also had an angry run-in with his own attorney general, Lacy Thornburg, for hinting that a state agency faced an investigation after reports of political misuse.

Since his retirement from the governorship in January 1993, Martin has been seeking to get back into an education-related position. His acceptance in April 1992 of the chairmanship of the Research and Development Board that directs the James G. Cannon Research Center at the Carolina Medical Center was seen as one step in this direction. It is also rumored that he is interested in becoming president of Duke University.

Bibliography: Michael Barone et al., *The Almanac of American Politics, 1986, 1988* (Washington, D.C.: National Journal, 1985, 1987); biographical information courtesy of governor's office; *The Chronicle of Higher Education,* 4–29–92; *The New York Times:* 2–13–84; 5–9–84; 6–6–84; 11–7–84; 11–8–84; 1–6–85; 3–1–87; 11–10–88; 2–26–90; 3–27–90; *USA Today:* 10–11–88; 11–10–88; 5–6–92.

James Baxter Hunt *(Courtesy of Governor's Office)*

JAMES BAXTER HUNT, 1977–1985, 1993–

Born on May 16, 1937, in Greensboro, North Carolina, Hunt is the son of James B. Hunt, a farmer and soil conservationist, and Elsie (Brame) Hunt, a teacher. A Presbyterian, Hunt married Carolyn Joyce Leonard on August 20, 1958. The couple has four children.

Hunt graduated from Rock Ridge High School and attended North Carolina State University, where he received a B.S. in agricultural education in 1959 and an M.S. in agricultural economics in 1962. He received a J.D. from the University of North Carolina Law School in 1964, eventually establishing a law practice in Wilson. Hunt began his political career as a young student activist working for Democratic candidates. He served as chairman of "Young Voters for Terry Sanford" in 1960 and as national college director for the Democratic National Committee from 1962 to 1963. In 1964, he went to Nepal for two years under the sponsorship of the Ford Foundation, where he became an economic adviser to the government. Elected president of the North Carolina Young Democratic National Convention, he was appointed assistant state party chairman in 1969.

In the Democratic primary for lieutenant governor on May 6, 1972, Hunt defeated Roy Sowers, Margaret Harper, Allen Barbee, and Reginald Grazier. Reversing a Republican trend in the state, he was elected lieutenant governor in the November election, defeating John Walker, the Republican candidate, by over 200,000 votes. Four years later, Hunt sought the Democratic nomination for governor, and in the August 1976 primary, he received 52.3 percent of the vote, defeating Edward M. O'Herron, Jr., George M. Wood, Thomas E. Strickland, and Jetter Braker. In the general election, he attracted 1,081,293 votes compared with 564,102 for the Republican candidate, David T. Flaherty.

Hunt was first inaugurated governor on January 6, 1977. In his inaugural address, he called for a "new beginning" that would "eliminate the last vestiges of discrimination" from the state. He advocated a renewed emphasis on the teaching of reading in public schools and supported a new utilities regulation structure that would reflect consumer interests. Hunt named women and blacks to high-level posts and actively promoted the appointment of minorities to judicial positions. In 1978, he was urged by a number of organizations, including Amnesty International, to free the "Wilmington 10"—a group of nine black men and one white woman accused of firebombing a Wilmington, North Carolina, grocery store. The case drew international attention. At the time, the Soviet Union contended that the imprisonment of this group was a human rights violation, and critics of the trials maintained that the defendants had been convicted in a politically charged atmosphere that included tampering with evidence by state officials. Hunt declared that there had indeed been a fair trial, although he decided that the sentences were too long and reduced the terms for the prisoners. All ten were on parole within a year.

In 1980, Hunt, who could succeed himself after the passage of a 1977 constitutional amendment, engaged in a primary struggle with former Governor Robert Scott. Scott asserted that Hunt had failed to deal adequately with mill workers' claims that they had contracted brown lung disease while on the job, but Hunt managed nonetheless to pull out a victory in the primary. Later in 1980 Hunt was the focus of a brief assassination scare while attending the Democratic National Convention. In November of that year, he easily defeated Beverly Lake, the Republican candidate, by 1,847,432 votes to 691,449. Those counties that Hunt failed to carry were located predominantly in the mountainous western region of the state. With his victory, Hunt became the first person since the Civil War to serve two terms in the North Carolina statehouse.

Hunt's eight-year administration was widely regarded as highly successful. During his years in office, the state achieved sustained economic growth with higher wage levels and one of the nation's lowest unemployment rates. Industries invested $15.5 billion in new and expanded plants in the state, producing 250,000 additional jobs. The state work force grew by 15 percent from 1975 to 1985, and by the time Hunt left office, North Carolina was well on its way to recovering fully from the national recession of 1981. By the end of his second term, *Business Week* magazine ranked North Carolina as the nation's top state for business investment.

Hunt also pumped money into education and insisted on competency tests for students and teachers alike. During his two terms in office, he started programs in standardized testing, intensive reading instruction in the primary grades, and dropout prevention. He also established the North Carolina School of Science and Mathematics. In 1983 he served as chairman of the National Task Force on Education for Economic Growth. One of the first governors ever to perceive the relationship between education reform and economic growth, he began the North Carolina Business Committee for Education to bring business leaders to the work of school reform. For all these efforts, Hunt was awarded with the prestigious James B. Conant Award for 1984, a recognition of the public official who has contributed most significantly to educational progress.

Hunt also worked to build a strong Democratic party in North Carolina and had important involvement in party affairs at the national level. In 1981, he chaired the Hunt Commission, concerned with the Democratic party process for presidential delegate selection.

In the opinion of political observers, Hunt's greatest legacy as governor was to change the tone of public life in the state, abandoning old southern traditions of racial segregation and working to create a mood of tolerance and open-mindedness toward individuals of diverse cultures and backgrounds.

In 1984, Hunt waged an especially acrimonious campaign for the U.S. Senate against conservative Republican incumbent Jesse Helms, who was running for his third term as one of the Senate's most outspoken conservatives. The race attracted national attention, for it was seen as a symbolic ideological clash between conservatives and progressives, the Old versus the New South. Liberals and conservatives alike poured millions of dollars of campaign contributions into the state, in a contest Helms christened a "referendum on the conservative cause." It also became the most costly Senate campaign in U.S. history at that time.

Hunt, as a moderate Democrat, became the candidate of all those both inside and outside North Carolina who sought to end Helms' Senate career. He based his campaign on his support for economic and educational reforms designed to make the state more attractive to high-tech industries. Yet he drew criticism even from supporters for some of his political positions. Instead of making Helms defend his record, Hunt adopted positions on military and foreign policy similar to those of the incumbent. Experts believed that Hunt, knowing the power of the conservative vote, sought to minimize his differences with Helms by supporting organized school prayer, the B-1 bomber, the MX missile, and the Stealth bomber and by opposing the nuclear freeze movement. He also favored a gradual increase in military spending. Nonetheless, Helms won an easy victory, attributed by political analysts to the Reagan landslide of that year.

After his defeat, Hunt returned to private law practice, working as a senior partner at Poyner and Spruill, one of the state's largest firms. He also raised beef cattle on his farm in Wilson County.

Despite his loss to Helms, Hunt retained his political popularity in the state and was widely regarded as the Democrats' strongest candidate to win the U.S. Senate seat being vacated by incumbent John P. East in 1986. Although prodded by state and national party leaders to make the race, Hunt declined, explaining that he was reluctant to put his family through the grueling ordeal of another campaign.

Even in retirement, however, Hunt retained an interest in education reform. In May 1987, he was named chairman of the National Board for Professional Teaching Standards, newly created by the Carnegie Foundation. Indeed, it was Hunt's "crusade" to improve public education that caused him to reenter the political fray in 1992. With the race for the statehouse thrown wide open due to the constitutionally mandated retirement of incumbent Jim Martin, Hunt sought an unprecedented third term as governor of North Carolina, campaigning on a platform to raise educational standards and to create jobs.

His opponent was Republican Jim Gardner, the cofounder of the Hardees fast-food chain. Lieutenant governor since 1989 and the first Republican to hold that post since Reconstruction, Gardner had failed in two previous runs for the statehouse.

The race between the two was one of the nastiest in state history. Condemning Hunt's "wornout policies of the past," Gardner called Hunt—among other things—"a bald-faced liar" and even accused a Hunt supporter of eavesdropping on his cellular phone calls. According to political analysts, Hunt won the election by bringing conservative whites back to the Democratic camp. He called his 53 percent victory over Gardner a personal triumph for him after his stinging defeat by Jesse Helms.

Hunt has made continued education reform a goal of his new administration. He wants to make a long-term financial commitment to improving community colleges and proposes to build a Technology Extension Service to serve as a link between university research and manufacturers. Other priorities of his third term include strengthening early childhood education, raising education standards for high school graduates, strengthening the state's manufacturing base, and expanding drug education and prevention programs.

Bibliography: Michael Barone et al., *The Almanac of American Politics, 1984, 1986, 1988, 1992* (Washington, D.C.: National Journal, 1983, 1985, 1987, 1991); biographical information courtesy of governor's office; *The Chronicle of Higher Education,* 11–11–92; *The New York Times:* 12–15–79; 12–8–81; 2–5–84; 4–22–84; 4–29–84; 5–7–84; 5–9–84; 5–27–84; 8–12–84; 11–4–84; 11–8–84; 1–6–85; 9–13–85; 5–16–87; 10–15–87; 10–26–92; 11–5–92; *USA Today:* 5–6–92; 5–12–92; 11–3–92; 11–4–92.

NORTH DAKOTA

GEORGE A. SINNER, 1985–1993

George Sinner was born in Casselton, North Dakota, on May 29, 1928. Married to the former Jane Baute, he and his wife are the parents of ten children.

Sinner graduated from St. John's University in Minnesota with a B.A. in 1950. A prosperous sugar beet farmer, he was active with the Red River Valley Sugar Beet Growers Association, the Northern Crops Institute, and several other agricultural organizations. He is also a partner in Sinner Brothers and Bresnaton, a diversified farming operation in Casselton.

A Democrat, Sinner entered politics in 1962, serving in the state senate from 1962 to 1966 where he was a member of the Education Committee. An unsuccessful candidate for the U.S. House of Representatives in 1964, he was a delegate to the North Dakota Constitutional Convention in 1972. He also served as a member and former president of the state Board of Higher Education. Elected to the North Dakota House of Representatives in 1982, he served as chairman of the Finance and Taxation Committee.

In 1984, Sinner challenged incumbent Republican Governor Allen Olson for the statehouse. He won the Democratic nomination easily, defeating Anne Belle Bourgeois, a supporter of political extremist Lyndon H. LaRouche, Jr., in his party's primary.

Political analysts believe that Sinner's unexpected victory over Olson was due as much to his opponent's gaffes and blunders as to his own political talents. Olson came under attack for frivolous spending such as redecorating his office and buying a state airplane for his own use. Despite Ronald Reagan's landslide presidential victory in November 1984, Sinner managed to beat his Republican opponent by the convincing margin of 55 percent to 45 percent.

The days after the election provided some unexpected moments of colorful political drama, as both men continued to battle over exactly when one's term ended and the other's began. Olson maintained that his four-year term ran at least until January 6 (four years to the day after his 1981 inauguration), and that the new governor customarily has not taken office until even later, when the legislature convened. Sinner, on the other hand, maintained that he signed his oath of office on December 31 and

George A. Sinner *(Courtesy of State Historical Society of North Dakota)*

was preparing to take office the next day. Although Olson did not admit this publicly, at stake in the historic dispute was the authority to fill two appointments to the state's highest court. In addition to the appointments question, Sinner said that he wanted to take office on January 1 to consider the legality of bonuses totaling $20,000 awarded to 100 employees by various state agencies on December 31. He also planned to seek an immediate freeze on hiring. Asked to mediate in the constitutional tug of war, the state's highest court ruled in favor of Sinner, who took office on January 1, 1985.

In 1988, Sinner won a decisive reelection victory against GOP populist and antitax activist Leon Mallberg. Mallberg charged that Sinner had been all talk and no action on economic development, a subject Mallberg wanted to make central to his administration. He also accused Sinner of absentee government and planning to raise taxes. Despite such charges, Sinner polled 60 percent of the vote, breaking a two-election trend in the state of throwing out the incumbent.

In office, Sinner presided over a government in retrenchment as both the agricultural and energy sectors of the economy suffered. Major cuts in state spending as well as increases in both personal income taxes and state sales taxes marked his administration. He also took an active role in promoting economic development.

The politics of abortion, coming to have an increasingly important role across the country in the early 1990s, also entered state affairs. Although Sinner was a devout Roman Catholic who had once considered the priesthood, he vetoed what would have been the nation's strictest antiabortion bill in 1991. Sinner said that the bill, which would have banned virtually all abortions except in cases of rape and incest and to save the mother's life, went "too far," and he explained that "government policy must find a balanced way which respects the freedom of women in this difficult area."

During his years in office, Sinner was the Western Governors Association lead governor on water issues. He also served as chair of this largest regional governors' conference in 1989–1990. In addition, he chaired National Governors Association Committees on Energy and Environment as well as Agriculture and Rural Development. Appointed to a two-year term on the Federal Advisory Commission on Intergovernmental Relations, he also chaired the Interstate Oil Compact Commission.

Sinner decided against seeking a third term as governor in 1992. Although he had had heart bypass surgery in 1991, he insisted that his health was fine and didn't play a role in his decision. As a former member of the state Board of Higher Education, he is rumored to be interested in the presidency of the University of North Dakota.

Bibliography: Michael Barone et al., *The Almanac of American Politics, 1988* (Washington, D.C.: National Journal, 1987); biographical information courtesy of governor's office; *The Chronicle of Higher Education*: 8–28–91; 1–15–92; *Fargo Forum* (Fargo, N.D.), 11–9–88; *The New York Times*: 6–13–84; 11–8–84; 1–3–85; 1–5–85; 12–7–89; 4–2–91; *The Star-Ledger* (Newark, N.J.), 7–2–89; *USA Today*: 7–14–88; 10–11–88; 3–29–91; 4–2–91; 11–1–91.

EDWARD T. SCHAFER, 1993–

Born on August 8, 1946, in Bismarck, North Dakota, Schafer is the son of Harold and Marian Schafer. After graduating from the University of North Dakota in 1969, he earned an M.B.A. from the University of Denver in 1970. Schafer is married to the former Nancy Jones and has four children.

A successful businessman, Schafer worked to develop the Gold Seal Company, a consumer packaged-goods marketer founded by his father. He has also been associated with Dakota Classics, an automobile dealership; TRIESCO Properties, a real estate development company in Bismarck; and Fish 'N Dakota, an aquaculture enterprise in Beulah. He has also served as board chairman of the North Dakota Micro Business Marketing Alliance, a nonprofit organization that helps start small businesses.

A Republican, Schafer made his first bid for public office in 1990, running for Congress against incumbent Byron Dorgan. His decisive 65 percent to 35 percent defeat in that race caused political observers to predict that his short-lived political career was over.

Contrary to their analysis, however, Schafer in 1992 made a run for the statehouse, a race thrown wide open by the retirement of incumbent George Sinner. Presenting himself as a business-minded leader who could create jobs in a state with a shrinking economy, Schafer financed his own campaign. He also benefited from the support of a united party.

The Democrats, by contrast, had suffered through an unusually fractious primary fight. The eventual nominee, Attorney General Nicholas Spaeth, defeated state Senate Majority Leader William Heigaard in a bitter primary battle in which Heigaard portrayed Spaeth as untrustworthy and Spaeth bashed Heigaard for voting in favor of higher taxes.

The general election was also a nasty personal race. Spaeth made an issue of Schafer's business ventures on the East Coast and charged that he failed to meet state residency requirements for governor. Schafer countered with an income tax form that he said proved his residency. Analysts believe the tactic may have backfired on the Democrats.

The main issue in the race was the economy and the question of which man could best handle the state's budget deficit. A key concern for state voters was how to keep both jobs and people from leaving the state, which had lost more than 50,000 residents in the last eight years. Pointing to his successful business ventures, Schafer presented himself as someone with creative solutions to the state's economic problems, while Spaeth focused his program on finding broader markets for the state's farm products.

Edward T. Schafer *(Courtesy of Governor's Office)*

Voters were obviously persuaded by Schafer's message, as he racked up an impressive 59 percent to 41 percent win over Spaeth.

In office, Schafer has opposed raising taxes and is searching for ways to involve higher education in economic development efforts.

Bibliography: Michael Barone and Grant Ujifusa, *The Almanac of American Politics, 1992* (Washington, D.C.: National Journal, 1991); biographical information courtesy of governor's office; *The Chronicle of Higher Education,* 11–11–92; *The New York Times,* 10–26–92; *USA Today*: 6–9–92; 11–4–92.

Richard F. Celeste *(Courtesy of Celeste & Sabety Ltd.)*

OHIO

RICHARD F. CELESTE, 1983–1991

Born in Cleveland, Ohio, on November 11, 1937, Celeste is the son of Frank P. Celeste and Margaret Lewis Celeste. A Methodist, he married Dagmar Braun of Vienna, Austria, on August 25, 1962. The couple has six children.

Celeste graduated magna cum laude from Yale University in 1960, where he was selected as a Rhodes scholar. He studied at Oxford University from 1960 to 1962. In 1963, he was appointed executive assistant to Chester Bowles, U.S. Ambassador to India. During his four years in New Delhi, he traveled more than 60,000 miles throughout the subcontinent, taking a special interest in agricultural productivity and community development.

The recipient of several honorary degrees, Celeste is also the author of two books: *It's Not Just Politics, America* (Educational Forum, 1976) and *Pioneering a Hunger Free World* (Friendship Press, 1977).

A Democrat, Celeste began his political career in 1970, when he was elected to the Ohio House of Representatives. Serving two terms in the legislature, he authored bills calling for voter registration reform, improved state employee retirement benefits, adoption reform, and revised pension systems.

Celeste served as lieutenant governor of Ohio from 1974 to 1978. Especially interested in social service programs for children and the elderly, he sponsored several programs aimed at increasing citizen participation in government.

In 1978, Celeste ran an unsuccessful race for the governorship, losing to incumbent Republican James Rhodes. Following his defeat, he was appointed director of the Peace Corps by President Jimmy Carter, a position he held from 1979 through January 1981.

Celeste was first elected governor of Ohio on November 4, 1982, defeating Congressman Bud Brown with 59 percent of the vote. It was an unprecedented victory for a Democrat in an Ohio gubernatorial race. During his first term, Celeste experienced ups and downs in his popularity. In his first year in office, he made permanent a temporary tax increase instituted by his predecessor James Rhodes, enraging voters who had misinterpreted his ambiguous campaign rhetoric on the issue. As his poll ratings plummeted, conservatives put a measure on the ballot to reverse the increase. Celeste fought back shrewdly, making the case for "positive" government that ultimately became his trademark. Ads were run reminding voters that some Ohio communities had been forced to close their schools for lack of funds and suggesting that this would happen again if the referendum passed. It failed by a solid margin, a result seen as a victory for Celeste.

Celeste won reelection in 1986, defeating former Governor Rhodes in a contest seen as a replay of their earlier 1978 battle. The 77-year-old Rhodes, seeking a fifth term as governor, ran an old-fashioned campaign built around one issue—assertions of corruption and mismanagement in the Celeste administration. Celeste was badly damaged by a scandal affecting the Home State Savings and Loan Association in March 1985. While Celeste had received crucial financial support from the institution's owner, Democratic campaign contributor Marvin Warner, an investigation revealed that its affairs had not been properly regulated by the state. Celeste was also plagued by a series of felony indictments against several of his associates and campaign supporters. Rhodes also accused the Celeste administration of failures in economic development, of raising personal and business taxes, and of unethical conduct.

Celeste, however, stuck with his own positive economic themes and capitalized on voter uneasiness with electing a 77-year-old candidate. He won easily, garnering 60 percent of the vote.

Among the achievements of Celeste's years in office were the following: restoring financial stability to the state, initiating a jobs program that put thousands of Ohioans to work, and bringing Ohio's schools and universities to national excellence. Establishing "Operation Jobs" to help create more than a half-million jobs for state residents, Celeste also began the "Buy Ohio" program, which brought thousands of jobs and hundreds of thousands of dollars to Ohio companies. He also initiated a state travel and tourism campaign, "Ohio . . . the Heart of It All," which in two years brought 20,000 new full-time jobs to the state.

Dedicated to educational excellence, Celeste also started a series of programs to improve the quality of the state's colleges and universities. In the area of higher education, his major achievements included keeping tuition costs down, improving academic programs, helping universities create new ties with business, and using his position to promote the state's colleges and universities. He also raised the amount of state funding received by educational institutions, spending 74 cents out of every dollar on schools from kindergarten through college.

Celeste also put a halt to rising utility rates, toughened the Certificate of Need Program to cut medical care costs, and reduced operating expenses for state government by eliminating 2,000 state employees. During his administration, the toughest missing children's law in the nation was signed; a program was put into place creating a health clinic for women, children, and infants in every county in the state; and the Children's Trust Fund for abused and neglected children was established.

Despite his successes, Celeste's administration was also marred by the taint of scandal, the most serious being the 1985 collapse of the state-insured Home State Savings and Loan. Political analysts have suggested that Celeste's decision to take himself out of consideration for the 1988 Democratic presidential nomination may have been attributable at least in part to the lingering cloud surrounding the affair, especially his relationship with Marvin Warner. By contrast, Celeste explained that the run would have been too expensive and would have taken too much time from the administration of state affairs.

Required by state law to step down after serving two consecutive terms, Celeste retired from the governorship in January 1991. A staunch opponent of capital punishment, he drew headlines in the last days of his term by commuting the death sentences of eight prisoners awaiting execution.

Since his retirement from public life, Celeste has operated Celeste and Sabety Ltd. in Columbus, Ohio, a business advisory firm that specializes in providing linkages to world markets. In 1993 he was named chairman of the National Health Care Campaign, the Democratic National Committee initiative to promote President Clinton's health care reform agenda.

Bibliography: Michael Barone et al., *The Almanac of American Politics, 1984, 1986, 1988, 1992* (Washington, D.C.: National Journal, 1983, 1985, 1987, 1991); biographical information courtesy of Governor Celeste; *The Chronicle of Higher Education:* 10–1–86; 11–12–86; *Newsweek,* 6–15–87; *The New York Times:* 11–10–85; 9–21–86; 10–23–86; 6–5–87; 8–26–87; 6–6–88; *The Record* (Bergen County, N.J.), 8–20–93.

George V. Voinovich *(Courtesy of Governor's Office)*

GEORGE V. VOINOVICH, 1991–

Voinovich was born in Cleveland, Ohio, on July 15, 1936. He graduated with a B.A. from Ohio University in 1958 and with a J.D. from the Ohio State College of Law in 1961. He and his wife Janet have three children.

A Republican, Voinovich served in a variety of positions early in his political career: a member of the Ohio House of Representatives, 1967–1971; Cuyahoga County auditor, 1971–1976; Cuyahoga County commissioner, 1977–1978; and lieutenant governor, 1979. He first achieved national prominence upon his election as mayor of Cleveland in 1979. Serving longer in that position than anyone else in the city's 200-year history, he is credited with having turned the city around economically. Spurning a request from GOP leaders that he run for governor in 1986, he did make an unsuccessful run for the U.S. Senate in 1988, losing to incumbent Howard M. Metzenbaum. One of the Senate's most liberal Democrats, Metzenbaum cast himself as the tribune of Ohio's working people and won comfortably, gaining 57 percent of the vote. The campaign drew national attention that year as one of the nation's most expensive, with the two candidates spending a combined $16 million.

Voinovich sought the governorship in 1990 upon the retirement of two-term Democratic incumbent Richard Celeste. Trumpeting both his business experience and the need for change after eight years of the scandal-plagued Celeste administration, Voinovich explained that the state needed to "work harder and smarter" in controlling costs. If elected, he promised to cut state spending through a management audit of state government. His Democratic opponent was Attorney General Anthony J. Celebrezze, Jr., the son of a former mayor of Cleveland. Both candidates were generally viewed as honest and intelligent politicians. Their campaign, however, was a classic ideological battle that played the class warfare card. Celebrezze posed as a populist outsider, running against the Washington establishment and putting himself forward as the man who would fight for the working class. His commercials portrayed Voinovich as part of a Republican party that caters to the elite. Voinovich, by contrast, derided his Democratic opponent as "Tax-Hike-Tony." Seizing upon earlier comments by Celebrezze that suggested he would repeal a 1976 law protecting Ohio homeowners against property tax increases, Voinovich charged that Celebrezze favored a "billion dollar tax increase." While Celebrezze argued that workers and others of modest means were not getting a fair shake from government, Voinovich pointed to his record of reinvigorating the economy of Cleveland and promised that his probusiness stance could do the same for the state as a whole.

The politics of abortion also played a key role in the campaign, with Celebrezze attempting to exploit his rival's antiabortion views. Reversing a longtime antiabortion position, Celebrezze declared his support for abortion rights, a move that critics charged was engineered to contrast with Voinovich's prolife position. Although Celebrezze hoped the policy shift could be a winning issue for him, Voinovich painted him as a waffler, assuring Ohio voters that he did not plan to impose his personal opposition to abortion on the state.

In the end, Voinovich proved popular among voters, both black and white. Using his base of support in Cleveland, a largely ethnic, racially diverse, and heavily unionized city, he ran well ahead of normal GOP performance there and in other urban areas. Throughout Ohio, many voters cited his role in Cleveland's revival as reason enough to entrust him with the governorship. His 56 percent win over Celebrezze was seen as a major coup for the Republican party nationwide.

In office, Voinovich has faced a budget problem that he terms "unparalleled in Ohio history." To deal with it, he has proposed ending the state's general assistance program and replacing it with smaller, less expensive projects. He has also been especially attacked by critics for zeroing in on higher education as a target for his cost–cutting measures.

Bibliography: The Chronicle of Higher Education: 10–31–90; 9–9–92; Phil Duncan, ed., *Politics in America 1992* (Washington, D.C.: Congressional Quarterly Press, 1991); *The New York Times*: 11–10–88; 4–28–89; 12–5–89; 10–18–90; 11–7–90; 11–8–90; 11–11–90; 4–7–91; *The Record* (Bergen County, N.J.), 5–10–90; *USA Today,* 11–8–90.

OKLAHOMA

HENRY BELLMON, 1963–1967, 1987–1991

Born September 3, 1921, on a farm near Tonkawa, Oklahoma, Bellmon is the son of George D. Bellmon and Edith Eleanor Caskey Bellmon. A Presbyterian, Bellmon married Shirley Osborn in 1947. The couple has three daughters.

Bellmon attended public schools in Noble County and graduated from Billings High School in 1938. He graduated from Oklahoma Agricultural and Mechanical College (now known as Oklahoma State University) with a degree in agriculture in 1942. During World War II, Bellmon joined the U.S. Marines and served with a tank company for more than three years. He participated in four Pacific battles including Iwo Jima. Bellmon received the Legion of Merit and Silver Star for his military service.

A wheat farmer and cattle rancher, Bellmon began his political career at 25, when he was elected to the Oklahoma House of Representatives. He represented the people of Noble County from 1947 through 1949, when he returned to his Billings farm. Chairman of the Republican State Committee from 1960 to 1962, he became the state's 16th governor in 1963, the first Republican to serve in that office. His first administration was well respected for its success in reforming and improving services for Oklahoma citizens. Limited by law to one term in office, he ran successfully for the U.S. Senate, serving two terms from 1969 to 1981. In the Senate he was a member of the Budget Committee. Announcing his retirement from the Senate in 1980, he explained that he had not enjoyed life in this "exclusive club" and did not like Washington.

Returning to his farm in 1981, Bellmon embarked on a series of public service roles. He was cofounder and served as cochairman of the Committee for a Responsible Federal Budget. By appointment in 1983, he became director of the Department of Human Services, the state's largest agency. In 1985, he was appointed receiver of the financially troubled Cowboy Hall of Fame in Oklahoma City. He also joined an organization formed to assist financially troubled farmers avoid foreclosures on their properties. He served as a professor and lecturer at Oklahoma City University, Central State University, the University of Oklahoma, and Oklahoma State University, as well as working as a commentator for an Oklahoma City television station.

Henry Bellmon *(Courtesy of Governor's Office)*

In 1986 when Oklahoma faced tough economic times brought on by a decline in oil prices, Bellmon sought to return to the governorship, claiming that the state was in a jam and couldn't afford to elect a "greenhorn." Widely respected by the voters for his personal integrity, Bellmon presented himself as the safest bet for a state in trouble.

His Democratic opponent was David Walters, a 34-year-old businessman who campaigned as a newcomer and political outsider. He was the surprise winner of the Democratic primary, having survived a divisive six-way fight as well as a runoff race against Attorney General Mike Turpin. Walters hoped that voters would see him as a fresh and youthful face against the veteran Bellmon. Although he had never held elective office before, he had worked in state government and was backed by some supporters of outgoing Governor George Nigh. Walters was harmed, however, both by his positions on issues and by his campaign practices. In a curious role reversal, it was the Democratic Walters who stood firmly for a "right to work" law, hated by unions because it would ban the closed shop. His campaign was badly damaged by a mid-October court case in which he was accused of violating the campaign finance law by accepting $162,000 in loans from four supporters.

Bellmon's campaign focused on an aggressive program of economic development. He proposed a number of measures to encourage business expansion, including reducing the corporate income tax rate from 5 percent to 4 percent and lowering workers' compensation payments for businesses. While a fiscal conservative, Bellmon was not opposed to expanding spending on social services, such as providing medical care for poor pregnant women not on welfare. He hoped to attack the root causes of poverty through vocational education and expanded, accessible, and affordable health care programs. One of these proposed the establishment of an indigent health care fund that would be distributed to hospitals all over Oklahoma. Bellmon was also unequivocal in his promises not to cut education budgets and called for a referendum on the state's proposed right to work law—both proposals expected to gain him the backing of labor unions throughout the state.

State voters, obviously fearful of the austerity ahead, rejected both major party nominees. Bellmon won with only a plurality of the vote, 47 percent to Walters' 45 percent. Two minor party candidates split the difference.

With his inauguration on January 12, 1987, Bellmon became only the second governor in the state's history to serve more than one term. In office, he proposed a six-cent rise in the gas tax, across-the-board cuts in all spending except for education, and abolition of pension reserve funds. Citing the need for a smaller, more efficient state government, he proposed sweeping plans for the restructuring of many government agencies. In view of the drastic decline in the state's oil revenue, he also outlined a dramatic revamping of public higher education that included closing some colleges, merging others, and establishing new governing boards for most remaining institutions. He also proposed a major study of the financial management of public higher education, as well as urging Oklahoma's public colleges and universities to start a variety of programs to assess student learning and to raise academic standards.

An "old-fashioned" Republican who dislikes supply-side deficits and New Right cultural conservatives, Bellmon found himself extremely unpopular as his second term unfolded. As state economic troubles worsened, Bellmon announced that he was retiring from public life and would not seek another term in office. Political analysts believe that Bellmon would probably have been defeated, had he not stepped aside.

After his retirement, Bellmon joined his alma mater, Oklahoma State University, as its first statesman-in-residence, teaching courses in Oklahoma government and politics. He was also honored by being named one of five finalists for the John F. Kennedy Profile in Courage Award created by the Kennedy Library Foundation in 1989.

Bibliography: Michael Barone et al., *The Almanac of American Politics, 1988* (Washington, D.C.: National Journal, 1987); biographical information courtesy of governor's office; *The Chronicle of Higher Education*: 11–12–86; 2–18–87; 9–23–87; 12–19–90; *The New York Times*: 9–4–86; 9–17–86; 9–30–86; 2–22–87; 4–21–90; 9–20–90; *USA Today*: 3–7–90; 5–30–90.

DAVID WALTERS, 1991—

David Walters was born in Canute, Oklahoma, on November 20, 1951. He graduated from Canute High School in 1969, from the University of Oklahoma in 1973 with a bachelor's degree in industrial engineering, and from Harvard University with an M.B.A. in 1977. A Roman Catholic, he and his wife Rhonda have three children.

A Democrat, Walters' first experience in politics came when he served as a project manager in the administration of former Oklahoma Governor David Boren. He also served as assistant and associate provost of the University of Oklahoma Health Sciences Center, where, at 29, he became the youngest executive officer in the history of the university.

In 1982, Walters joined the Burks Group, a commercial real estate company. In 1985, he was named president of American Fidelity Property Company, a real estate investment leasing and management concern.

During this early professional career, Walters remained active in community and state affairs. He served as chairman of the Oklahoma State Department of Human Services, as well as cochair of the 100-member Governor's Commission on Government Reform.

Walters made his first bid for public office in 1986. Campaigning as a newcomer and political outsider, he was the surprise winner of the Democratic gubernatorial primary, surviving a divisive six-way fight as well as a runoff race against Attorney General Mike Turpin. Although he hoped that voters would see him as a fresh and youthful face compared with Republican nominee and former Governor Henry Bellmon, Walters lost his bid in a close race.

By 1990, however, the political climate in Oklahoma seemed poised for change. The incumbent Governor Bellmon had announced his retirement from public life, and Oklahoma voters were angry over two big tax increases and a state government deadlocked between a Republican statehouse and a Democratic legislature. In the elections of that year, citizens vented their frustration by imposing a 12-year limit on the tenure of legislators, the first state ever to do so.

Walters tied his repeat candidacy to the campaign for term limits. In the Democratic primary, he ran an antigovernment campaign against challenger Wes Watkins, a seven-term congressman. Defeating Watkins with 51 percent of the vote, Walters went on to face Republican Bill Price, a former U.S. attorney, in the general election. Dark horse candidate Thomas Ledgerwood, a lawyer, ran as an independent. In the bitterly

David Walters *(Courtesy of Governor's Office)*

contested race, Walters took a hard line against new taxes and ran as a prochoice candidate in the increasingly volatile area of abortion rights.

In a state boasting a 2–1 margin of registered Democrats over registered Republicans, Walters pulled ahead, carrying 75 of the state's 77 counties and winning with the largest margin enjoyed by a gubernatorial candidate in 32 years. He gained 64 percent of the vote to Price's 36 percent.

In office, Walters struggled to advance his agenda. Using a strong cabinet system, he initiated dozens of review teams to lay plans for significant reform. Focusing on strong fiscal management and on job recruitment efforts, he has also been a strong supporter of education reform. Reallocating state funds to this priority area, he has led the nation in finding increases for education without raising taxes. On the university level, he has supported efforts to raise faculty salaries and to increase the financing of scholarships and university research projects. Nationally, he has achieved recognition as a strong advocate for a more sensible energy policy, winning election as chairman of the Interstate Oil and Gas Compact Commission, chairman of the Southern States' Energy Board, and vice-chairman of the Democratic Governors Association.

Despite these lofty objectives, however, the Walters administration was beset by difficulties from the outset. Dogged by ethical questions involving his campaign's financing practices, he also faced a libel suit filed by his former opponent, Bill Price, who was angered by Walters' campaign allegations that he had been involved in oil price gouging. There were even rumors that Walters was close to resigning due to the difficulties of his early months.

Walters' problems escalated in 1993, when he was indicated following a two-year probe into his 1990 campaign. Pleading guilty to charges of campaign finance violations, he used a plea bargain to escape eight grand jury charges of conspiracy, perjury, and accepting illegal campaign contributions. Walters' plea touched off a furor in the state, with former Governor Henry Bellmon even going so far as to call for Walters' impeachment. Faced with such difficulties, Walters has already announced his intention to withdraw from politics following the completion of his term.

Bibliography: Biographical information courtesy of governor's office; *The Chronicle of Higher Education*: 10–31–90; 8–28–91; Phil Duncan, ed., *Politics in America 1992* (Washington, D.C.: Congressional Quarterly Press, 1991); *The New York Times*: 9–20–90; 11–7–90; 11–23–92; *The Star-Ledger* (Newark, N.J.), 9–19–90; *USA Today*: 8–27–90; 11–8–90; 9–10–91; 10–25–93.

Neil Goldschmidt *(Courtesy of Neil Goldschmidt Inc.)*

OREGON

NEIL GOLDSCHMIDT, 1987–1991

Goldschmidt was born in Eugene, Oregon, on June 16, 1940, the son of Lester H. Goldschmidt and Annette Levin Goldschmidt. He is the divorced father of two children.

After graduating from South Eugene High School, Goldschmidt was student body president at the University of Oregon, where he received his B.A. in political science in 1963. He earned a law degree from the University of California's Boalt School of Law in 1967 and was awarded an honorary doctorate from the University of Portland in 1980.

As a college student, Goldschmidt was a choke-setter and loading dock worker during the summers between 1960 and 1963. In 1964, he was an intern in the Washington, D.C. office of former U.S. Senator Maurine Neuberger of Oregon. In Washington, he was recruited by Allard Lowenstein for voter registration work in the Freedom Summer civil rights campaign in Mississippi in 1964. A legal aid attorney in Portland from 1967 to 1969, he began his political career as a city commissioner there from 1971 to 1973. A Democrat, Goldschmidt was the youngest mayor of a major U.S. city when he became mayor of Portland in 1973 at the age of 32. He served as mayor until 1979 when he was named U.S. secretary of transportation by President Jimmy Carter. He served in that capacity through January 1981, upon the accession of the Reagan administration. As secretary of transportation, Goldschmidt authored "U.S. Automobile Industry, 1980," a report to the president.

At the close of the Carter years, Goldschmidt returned to Oregon where he joined Nike, the running shoe company based in Oregon. Working with Nike from 1981 through December 1985, he became head of its Canadian subsidiary, Nike Canada, in 1986. Goldschmidt has also served on the board of directors of Gelco Corp., Infocel Inc., Kaiser Foundation Health Plan, and National Semiconductor.

In 1986, Goldschmidt entered the Oregon governor's race, which saw him and Republican Norma Paulus locked in one of the state's closest gubernatorial contests in modern times. Elected two times by big margins as Oregon secretary of state in 1976 and 1984, Paulus was striving to become the state's first woman governor.

The campaign was conducted against the backdrop of the state's continuing economic distress and high unemployment. Goldschmidt, campaigning under the handicap that Democrats had held the statehouse for only 10 of the previous 60 years, bluntly summarized that the race was "about jobs." He focused his campaign on a blueprint for Oregon's future and stressed his role as an innovator while mayor of Portland in the 1970s. Hailed as a "public sector risk-taker in the entrepreneurial mold" by the *Portland Oregonian,* Goldschmidt was helped by his support from many businessmen and by his own business experience. He won the race over Paulus, 52 percent to 48 percent. Analysts attributed his victory to his economic program and to his record of cutting crime as mayor of Portland.

During his term in office, Goldschmidt led what has been called the "Oregon comeback," the revival of a state suffering from nearly 8 years of recession associated with the decline of the timber industry. Redesigning and invigorating the state's economy, he worked to develop new economic opportunities: international trade, tourism, agriculture, and the development of hundreds of new businesses, most of them high-tech. He actively pursued international trade opportunities, created an innovative program to promote rural economic development, and produced the state's first long-range economic development strategy. He improved Oregon's business climate through a series of regulatory reforms, including a major overhaul of the workers' compensation system and the initiation of an investment strategy to repair the state's deteriorating infrastructure. As a result of his efforts, the state's unemployment rate dropped from 8.5 percent to 5.4 percent, the lowest in 20 years. By 1990, Oregon was being recognized as one of the best places to do business in the country, hailed as one of only six states not to have slid into the nationwide recession. The state also became somewhat of a haven for people fleeing the urban woes of California for the Northwest.

Because of such accomplishments, Goldschmidt had long been considered one of the rising stars of the Democratic party. Among other awards and honors, he was selected as one of the Ten Outstanding Young Men in the United States by the National Jaycees in 1972 and identified as 1 of the "200 Faces of the Future" by *Time* magazine in 1974. In 1980, he received the International B'nai B'rith Sam Beber Award for Outstanding Leadership.

Having been a dominant force in Oregon politics for 20 years, Goldschmidt shocked political supporters with his surprising decision not to seek reelection in 1990. Although he was under intense pressure to make the race, he explained that his 25-year marriage was breaking up and that he wanted to devote more time to his personal life. "It's certainly no time to be running for governor," he insisted.

Since his retirement from public life, Goldschmidt has devoted his time to his own legal practice, focusing on national policy, international trade, and strategic planning advice.

Bibliography: Michael Barone et al., *The Almanac of American Politics, 1988* (Washington, D.C.: National Journal, 1987); biographical information courtesy of governor's office and Neil Goldschmidt, Inc.; *The Chronicle of Higher Education*, 11–12–86; *The New York Times*: 10–19–86; 5–19–87; 11–10–88; 2–8–90; 5–13–90.

Barbara Roberts (*Courtesy of Governor's Office*)

BARBARA ROBERTS, 1991–

Born in Corvallis, Oregon, on December 21, 1936, Roberts (née Hughey) is a fourth-generation Oregonian, the daughter of a machinist. A graduate of Sheridan High School, she attended Portland State University, Marylhurst College, and the John F. Kennedy School of Government at Harvard University. She and her husband Frank have two sons.

A Democrat, Roberts began her years of community service as an activist seeking help from the state for her autistic son. Known as a tireless crusader for the rights of the handicapped, she sought public office after being frustrated by her unpaid lobbying for the disabled. Winning election to the Oregon House of Representatives, she served two terms, 1981–1985, and in 1983 was chosen its first female majority leader. In 1984, she won election as secretary of state, the state's number-two job, and was reelected in 1988. Her achievements in that office included sponsorship of election reform legislation, policies to ensure handicapped accessibility to polling places, and the construction of a state archives building. In 1987, she chaired Governor Neil Goldschmidt's Workers' Compensation Reform Task Force and served as his representative to the Hanford Waste Board.

Goldschmidt's sudden and unexpected decision to retire from the governorship after one term caused Roberts to jump into the race to succeed him. Unopposed in the Democratic primary, she faced a strong challenge from Attorney General Dave Frohnmayer, who went into the general election as the favorite. She also struggled to overcome a series of personal blows during the course of the campaign: the death of her father, the prolonged illness of her husband, and the problems of her autistic son. Nonetheless, she persevered. By the end of the campaign, she had pulled ahead, the beneficiary of strong name recognition as well as her own effusive campaign style. The Roberts name signifies a near dynasty in state politics. Roberts' husband Frank is a longtime Portland state senator, and his ex-wife Betty is a retired state supreme court justice. Her stepdaughter, Mary Wendy Roberts, is a state labor commissioner. Even more important was Roberts' own charisma as a campaigner. In the words of one analyst, "They don't come much better in campaign style."

Roberts' campaign was also aided by infighting among the Republicans, who protested Frohnmayer's support for abortion rights. Conservative independent candidate Al Mobley, who emphasized his opposition to abortion, eroded the Republican base. Aided by Republican women who crossed party lines to vote for her, Roberts won with 46 percent of the vote, earning 30 percent more votes from women than her GOP challenger. Frohnmayer polled 39 percent of the vote, while Mobley and another independent candidate shared the remainder of the total vote.

With her election as the state's first female governor, Roberts promised change and new social programs. An unabashed liberal, she courageously bucked the timber industry in this most timber-dependent state. Accusing Frohnmayer of pandering to fears about the loss of logging jobs, she insisted that Oregon must build a future on more diversified industries rather than relying so heavily on logging. Taking the opposite tack of the state's two U.S. senators, Mark Hatfield and Robert Packwood, who favor timber industry bills to allow high levels of tree cutting in national forests, she has argued that the solution to the timber crunch is to get mill towns to do more with the state's timber. The state should encourage job retraining and new industry, like making furniture and finished wood products. She has also endorsed controversial initiatives to close Oregon's only nuclear power plant and to mandate recycling.

Early in her term, Roberts drew national attention for her novel approaches to education, social policy, and health care. A bill designed to overhaul the state's elementary and secondary schools included a controversial provision that required students to choose, by the tenth grade, whether they intended to pursue a course to college or to start learning about a particular trade. Another new law entitled all employees who work more than 25 hours per week to be given an unpaid family leave of up to 12 weeks every two years to care for children, ill spouses, or relatives. A health care plan nearly five years in the making involved major changes in Medicaid, the state and federal program that provides health care to the poor. The bill, ultimately rejected by the Bush administration, would have made Oregon the second state in the nation to have universal health care coverage.

In 1992, however, Roberts' relationship with the voters soured, and she found herself the target of an angry and unprecedented recall campaign. Though she was not charged with any crimes or ethical lapses, the movement coalesced voter discontent around a variety of issues. Her opponents included foes of abortion angry at her prochoice position, as well as supporters of the state's powerful timber industry inflamed by her environmentalist stands. The state was also suffering from a wrenching budget crisis brought on by a voter-initiated tax-cutting measure that forced a 20 percent cut in state government for the two-year budget beginning in 1993. As cuts began to be made in areas like school supplies, prison guards, and road repair, Roberts became the most visible target of voter resentments. Opponents charged that she was not doing enough to save a state budget being cut to shreds by the antitax measure.

Defenders, on the other hand, retorted that there was absolutely no justification for the recall from a straight policy point of view. Others suggested that sexism, especially from timber voters, was a crucial factor in the recall drive.

The loosely knit group of recall activists, led by conservative Democrat Herschel Taylor, failed to get enough signatures on petitions to schedule the recall election. Nonetheless, they vowed to begin another recall effort.

While surviving this midterm crisis, Roberts suffered another blow in 1992 when her new tax package was rejected by Oregon lawmakers. Among other things, her proposal would have cut the state income tax and instituted a new 3.5 percent sales tax, the state's first.

Roberts was a vocal and stinging critic of the "quagmire" in Washington during the Reagan-Bush years. Insisting that "the states are where the action is," she has lauded the innovative potential of activist state governors.

Bibliography: Biographical information courtesy of governor's office; *The Chronicle of Higher Education*: 10–31–90; 8–14–91; 7–8–92; Phil Duncan, ed., *Politics in America 1992* (Washington, D.C.: Congressional Quarterly Press, 1991); *The New York Times*: 5–13–90; 11–7–90; 8–22–91; 5–8–92; 5–10–92; 8–14–92; *The Star-Ledger* (Newark, N.J.), 5–16–90; *USA Today*: 2–9–90; 5–16–90; 6–1–90; 11–8–90; 1–23–92.

Robert P. Casey *(Courtesy of Governor's Office)*

PENNSYLVANIA

ROBERT P. CASEY, 1987–

Born in Jackson Heights, New York, on January 9, 1932, Casey is the son of Alphonsus and Marie Casey. A Roman Catholic, he is married to the former Ellen Theresa Harding. The couple has eight children.

Casey grew up in Scranton, Pennsylvania, where he was senior class president and valedictorian of the class of 1949 at Scranton Prep. An accomplished athlete, he was named to the *Scranton Times* 1949 All-Regional Basketball Team. Attending the College of the Holy Cross on an athletic scholarship, he played on nationally ranked Holy Cross basketball teams that included All-Americans Bob Cousey and Tom Heinsohn.

After graduating from Holy Cross with a B.A. in English, cum laude, in 1953, Casey attended George Washington University Law School on a trustees' scholarship. A member of the Order of the Coif and research editor of the law review, he received his J.D. in 1956. After graduation, he worked as an associate with the prestigious Washington, D.C. law firm of Covington and Burlington. Two years later, he returned to Scranton to begin his own law practice.

He began his political career in 1963, winning election as state senator from Lackawanna County. In office, he distinguished himself by authoring landmark environmental legislation that became a model for the Federal Clean Air and Water Act. In 1967, he was elected to serve as a delegate to the state constitutional convention. Serving as first vice-president of the convention, he played a leading role in the writing and ratification of the state's present constitution.

In 1968, Casey was elected to the first of two consecutive terms as state auditor. From 1969 to 1977, he revolutionized the office of auditor general, turning it into a model of professionalism and efficiency. He won praise for putting the office on a professional basis, for fighting corruption, and for avoiding scandal at a time when Democrats in other state offices did not. In the words of one political commentator, Casey took a backwater agency long known as a haven for patronage and turned it into a "rushing current of reform."

In 1977, Casey returned to private law practice, although he continued to remain active in both Scranton civic affairs and national politics.

In 1986, he entered the Democratic gubernatorial primary to succeed retiring Governor Richard Thornburgh, a Republican, who was constitutionally ineligible to serve more than two consecutive terms. Despite losses in three previous Democratic gubernatorial primaries in 1966, 1970, and 1978, he won the nomination in a three-way race, defeating Edward G. Rendell and Steve Douglas. His opponent in the general election was Lieutenant Governor William Scranton III, the son of a former state governor and presidential candidate. The race was seen as a classic contest between political generations. While Casey sought to portray the 39-year-old Scranton as a child of privilege and a product of the 1960s, Scranton countered by calling Casey a political relic, the product of a dead era of patronage politics and smokestack economics, and ill-equipped to lead the state into the postindustrial age. The campaign was marred by negative political attacks, with Scranton's use of drugs as a student becoming a point of controversy. In TV ads, Casey painted Scranton as a laid-back, less-than-diligent lieutenant governor who missed most meetings of groups he was supposed to preside over, such as the state senate and Board of Pardons.

Casey's victory over Scranton with 51 percent of the vote to the Republican's 48 percent was widely credited to his detailed and extensive blueprint for developing the state's economy. With his victory, he became the first Democrat to hold the governorship in eight years and only the second in the last quarter-century.

Seeking reelection in 1990, Casey defeated state Auditor General Barbara Hafer with 68 percent of the vote, the largest victory margin in a Pennsylvania gubernatorial race in half a century. It was a race that drew national attention because of a curious role reversal in party positions—one between an antiabortion, antitax, all-is-well Democrat and a pro-choice, socially activist Republican. Hafer failed to win much support or financing even from within her own party in this largely Democratic state. Although the race initially appeared to be a referendum on abortion, the issue soon receded behind more immediate concerns like education and the economy. Casey campaigned on his 4-year record, citing his programs for clean water, toxic waste disposal, and drug education, as well as the state's selection by a small-business magazine as the fourth-best-managed state in the nation. Casey also heralded his role as the first Pennsylvania governor in 43 years not to raise taxes.

During his years in office, Casey has outlined five key objectives: creating new jobs and economic opportunities, cleaning up the environment, strengthening family life, fighting drug abuse, and improving the quality of education. His second term has been rockier than his first, with economic concerns paramount. A 35-day deadlock over the budget in 1991 resulted in the passage of the largest tax increase in the state's history, a revenue-raising plan necessary to end an impasse that had kept more than 100,000 state employees from receiving any paycheck for almost one month. In 1992, continuing budget woes caused Casey to propose a bitterly controversial plan to cut aid to private colleges, explaining that the state needed to focus its limited resources on public, not private, institutions.

A fiery opposition to abortion has marked Casey's tenure and attracted national attention to him as a highly visible and outspoken anomaly in Democratic ranks. In 1989, Casey signed the nation's most restrictive state abortion law, one that ultimately drew scrutiny by the U.S. Supreme Court in the landmark case of *Planned Parenthood v. Casey*. His anger with the Democratic party establishment brought him to the forefront of national politics during the 1992 campaign. Beginning his attacks on the national party in April 1992, when the Supreme Court hearings on Pennsylvania's restrictive abortion law gave him an extensive forum in the press, he criticized the Democratic presidential primary process, saying that it produces candidates who can't win. Democrats, in his view, had been losing presidential elections because the party's staunch "abortion on demand" stance is in opposition to the views of millions of mainstream Democrats. He took his battle against the party's proabortion position to the National Platform Committee hearings in Cleveland, where he called for a new plank supporting "reasonable regulation" of the procedure, such as parental consent laws and bans on late-term and sex-selection abortions. He also insisted that the party's stand was "wrong in principle" and "out of the mainstream of our party's commitment to protecting the powerless." Republican party strategists tried to make political capital out of the Democratic party's unwillingness to let Casey address its 1992 national convention, portraying it as an example of the party's intransigence and doctrinairism.

Despite Casey's publicly expressed doubts about his electability, Bill Clinton's 1992 presidential victory now raises questions about Casey's own future in Democratic party ranks.

More serious are lingering concerns about Casey's health. In 1991, news reports announced that he suffers from a genetic disorder, a milder form of a rare disease that killed the mayors of Pittsburgh and Erie. Although doctors insisted that his strain of familial amyloidosis should allow him to live ten years or more, the announcement was seen as weakening him politically. Even more serious was an emergency and extremely rare heart and liver transplant required to save Casey's life in June 1993.

Casey's serious health problems raise questions about his political future. With Democratic control of the White House, the Pennsylvania governor had begun to carve out a name for himself as a highly visible spokesman for the prolife movement and as the nation's most prominent antiabortion Democrat. Before his surgery, there had been reports that he was giving serious consideration to challenging President Clinton in the 1996 Democratic presidential primaries. Insisting that he has always been a loyal Democrat with strong liberal, economic, and prounion views, Casey explains that he wants his party to come back to its traditional and long-standing position as the home and voice of the most powerless in society—this time, the unborn.

Bibliography: Michael Barone et al., *The Almanac of American Politics, 1988* (Washington, D.C.: National Journal, 1987); biographical information courtesy of governor's office; *The Chronicle of Higher Education*: 11–12–86; 8–28–91; 5–27–92; *National Review*, 6–8–92; *The New York Post*, 4–24–93; *The New York Times*: 10–20–86; 10–22–86; 11–5–86; 11–6–86; 1–21–87; 6–30–87; 5–16–90; 10–11–90; 11–7–90; 11–11–90; 8–6–91; 4–24–92; 2–26–93; *The Star-Ledger* (Newark, N.J.): 5–16–90; 1–9–92; 6–14–93; 6–15–93; *USA Today*: 5–16–90; 7–30–91; 8–5–91; 5–19–92; 6–14–93; 6–15–93.

RHODE ISLAND

EDWARD DANIEL DiPRETE, 1985–1991

Born in Cranston, Rhode Island, on July 8, 1934, DiPrete is the son of Frank A. DiPrete and Maria Grossi DiPrete. A Roman Catholic, DiPrete married the former Patricia Hines in 1956. The couple has seven children.

A graduate of Cranston public schools, LaSalle Academy, and the College of the Holy Cross, DiPrete is a veteran of the U.S. Navy, released as a lieutenant after serving in the western Pacific from 1955 to 1959. After this navy stint, he worked in a small real estate business started by his father, before entering public service. He was first elected to the Cranston School Committee in 1970. Reelected in 1972, he served as chairman through 1974. In 1974, he was elected as an at-large member of the Cranston City Council, and reelected in 1976. He was elected mayor of Cranston on November 7, 1978, and reelected on November 2, 1982 by the largest majority in the city's history, 83 percent. As mayor, he developed a reputation for getting things done without stirring up controversy.

In 1984, DiPrete sought the governorship upon the retirement of four-term incumbent Joseph Garrahy. He waged an aggressive campaign against state Treasurer Anthony J. Solomon, who suffered from a divided Democratic organization. Solomon had won his party's nomination in one of the most expensive and bitter primaries in state history. His opponent was Joseph Walsh of Warwick, whose allies had seized control of the party from retiring Governor Garrahy. Many political analysts believed that the battle between Solomon and Walsh, who traded charges of lying and fiscal irresponsibility, made it possible for the Republicans to win the governor's office for the first time in 16 years. DiPrete's victory over Solomon, by an impressive margin of 60 percent to 40 percent, was seen as a historic one for the Republican party. Republicans also won five out of nine statewide offices, the first time in 40 years that the party held a majority of statewide posts. Analysts attributed the sweep to a perception by state voters that the old Democratic leadership was tainted by corruption and incompetence.

DiPrete easily won reelection in 1986, defeating political newcomer Bruce Sundlun, a rich businessman who spent liberally on his campaign.

Edward Daniel DiPrete *(Courtesy of Governor's Office)*

DiPrete won 64.7 percent of the vote to his opponent's 32.4 percent. Minor party candidates split the remaining 2.9 percent of the vote.

An avowedly probusiness politician, DiPrete worked for the revival of the state after several decades of decline. Rhode Island had been suffering from the decay of its textile and jewelry industry and from the consequent loss of population, especially among its young. To buttress his economic development program, DiPrete persuaded the Democratic legislature to adopt what he described as an agenda for jobs. He succeeded in getting the legislature to pass a 16 percent cut in the state income tax and a restructuring of the state unemployment compensation system. He also repealed the state gift and estate tax as well as the highly controversial strikers' benefit statute—a provision that enabled union members to collect unemployment benefits while on strike. He also established a state Partnership for Science and Technology and increased funding for education, Head Start, and other children's programs. Using the national media, he ran ads in newspapers across the country saying, "If you want to talk business in Rhode Island, talk to a businessman, the governor." Sensitive to the state's poor image, he used state money to help the University of Rhode Island expand its robotics laboratory in conjunction with private industry and to help Brown University develop pharmaceutical products at its large medical school that could be marketed by commercial concerns. He also called for more research to bolster economic development, and more cooperation between public and private colleges.

With the state's economy growing and the unemployment rate well below the national average, political analysts observed that DiPrete's policies seemed to be working. His second-term program—more money for school textbooks, encouraging small businesses, implementing workfare incentives—met with approval from Democrats as well as Republicans.

Seeking a third term in 1988, DiPrete was locked in a tough battle with Bruce Sundlun, the wealthy broadcasting executive he had defeated in 1986. DiPrete had been considered a sure bet for reelection until the disclosure that his family was involved in a land deal that netted $2 million in profits. Surviving a campaign beset by ethical questions, DiPrete squeaked out a narrow 51 percent victory over his Democratic challenger.

Although he had enjoyed high popularity ratings during the boom years of the 1980s, DiPrete's third term was marked by a rapid fall from grace, attributable to several factors: the serious fiscal and economic problems facing the entire Northeast; the state's worst banking crisis since the depression; and lingering questions about his own ethical standards. With the state's economy in a tailspin and unemployment rising, he was forced to reverse himself on a no-new-taxes pledge. Holding off for more than a year while going through six rounds of budget cuts, he finally proposed a temporary increase in the state sales tax in May 1990. He was also the target of severe criticism for his failure to prevent the collapse of a bank deposit insurance company that was millions short of what it needed to cover failures in its member institutions. Also damaging were a series of political scandals involving himself and members of his family, when questions continued to be raised about the relationship between a highly profitable family real estate transaction in Cranston where he had formerly served as mayor.

For all these reasons, DiPrete was seen as highly vulnerable in his 1990 bid for a fourth term. Facing longtime rival Bruce Sundlun, whom he had already defeated in 1986 and 1988, he went down to defeat by a 4–1 margin, with Sundlun gaining 74 percent of the vote. Of the 36 governors' races in 1990, this was the widest margin of victory for a challenger over an incumbent. Sundlun ran as a political outsider who called his campaign "a civic crusade to return government to the people."

DiPrete's troubles worsened out of office. In 1992 Providence newspapers reported that, as governor, DiPrete had received more than $100,000 in campaign donations from credit union officials and borrowers, some of whom later faced criminal charges for their role in the state's banking crisis. The chairman of a state commission investigating the crisis also raised questions about DiPrete's responsibility for the problem, charging that the state agency charged with monitoring the credit unions had become "dysfunctional" during DiPrete's administration. Others suggested that DiPrete had found it difficult to refuse the largesse of the credit union lobby. In his defense, the former governor called himself a scapegoat in a "politically motivated witchhunt."

Nonetheless, DiPrete's political capital has fallen precipitously. A state grand jury is now probing allegations of kickback rackets in his administration.

Bibliography: Michael Barone et al., *The Almanac of American Politics, 1988* (Washington, D.C.: National Journal, 1987); biographical information courtesy of governor's office; *The Chronicle of Higher Education,* 11–12–86; *The New York Times*: 9–11–84; 9–13–84; 11–6–84; 1–2–85; 9–15–85; 9–11–86; 11–8–88; 11–9–88; 9–11–90; 11–7–90; 11–11–90; *The Star-Ledger* (Newark, N.J.): 11–10–88; 9–2–90; *USA Today*: 10–11–88; 11–8–90; 7–6–92.

BRUCE SUNDLUN, 1991–

Sundlun was born in Providence, Rhode Island, on January 19, 1920. He is a graduate of Williams College (1946), the U.S. Air Force Command and Staff School (1948), and Harvard Law School (1949). In addition, he has been the recipient of honorary degrees from Bryant College (1980) and Roger Williams College (1980).

Sundlun served as a captain in the U.S. Air Force, 1942–1945, and remained an active member of the U.S. Air Force Reserve, 1945 to 1980. Highly decorated for his military service, he has been the recipient of the Distinguished Flying Cross, Purple Heart, Légion d'Honneur (France), and Prime Minister's Medal (Israel).

Sundlun began his career as an assistant U.S. attorney in Washington, D.C. A founder and partner of two different law firms from 1954 to 1976, he went on to become a self-made millionaire through his involvement in numerous business, broadcasting, and communications ventures: Worthington Industries, Columbus, Ohio, 1972–1986; Qintex Entertainment, McLean, Virginia, 1984–1990; Quest Tech, McLean, Virginia, 1972–1990; Communications Satellite Corporation, 1963 to the present; Executive Jet Aviation, Columbus, Ohio, 1970–1976; Outlet Communications, Providence, Rhode Island, 1976–1984; and Sundlun and Co., Providence, Rhode Island, 1988–1991.

A Democrat, Sundlun had made two previous unsuccessful runs for governor in 1986 and 1988 before winning the statehouse in 1990. On all three occasions his opponent was Republican Edward DiPrete, whom he had consistently accused of serious ethical lapses. By 1990, DiPrete's approval ratings were in free-fall due to the state's fiscal problems as well as a credit union crisis. DiPrete had been badly wounded by ethics questions and a sagging economy. Having promised not to raise taxes during his 1988 campaign, he was forced to do so when the state's economy deteriorated.

DiPrete's weakened position was responsible for a hotly contested Democratic primary fight. Sundlun defeated Providence Mayor Joseph R. Paolino, Jr., and Warwick Mayor Francis Flaherty to win the nomination with 40 percent of the vote.

In the general election, he sought to capitalize on antiincumbent sentiment with his "I am not a politician" theme. Seeing his campaign as a "civic crusade to return government to the people," he focused on the perceived need to root out corruption in state government, to correct

Bruce Sundlun *(Courtesy of Governor's Office)*

long-standing abuses, and to deal with a rapidly worsening state economy. Pledging to cut state government, balance the budget, and roll back DiPrete's unpopular sales tax increase, he won voter confidence by boasting that "my whole life's experience is solving financial problems." Sundlun won the election by a 4–1 ratio. Of the 36 governors' races held in 1990, this was the widest victory margin for a challenger over an incumbent.

The most serious crisis Sundlun faced upon taking office was the collapse of a bank deposit insurance company that was millions of dollars short of what it needed to cover failures in its member institutions. One hour after his inauguration, he closed 45 banks and credit unions in the state, thereby freezing over $1 billion in assets. Although he promised depositors that they would be protected up to $100,000 even if the money had to come from the state treasury, the crisis galvanized a political movement led by angry citizens who negotiated for months with Sundlun over the terms of the bailout. Saying that problems in the banking industry reflected widespread corruption in the state, protestors made Sundlun a target of their anger and accused him of prolonging the crisis. The leader of the protest, Joseph Devine, even went so far as to announce as an independent candidate for governor. Despite the protests, Sundlun won praise for his response to the crisis. In the words of the *Providence Journal,* his response demonstrated "his steely decisiveness and willingness to take tough stands carrying political risks."

Recognizing the public perception that widespread corruption was at the root of the banking crisis, Sundlun placed the improvement of ethical standards in government at the top of his list of priorities. He introduced legislation to tighten up campaign spending, to streamline the procedures of the Ethics Commission, and to prohibit officials from representing themselves before agencies on which they serve. He also worked to curb abuses in the state pension system.

The Sundlun administration also won passage of a compulsory automobile insurance bill, a measure that had been proposed unsuccessfully for years. He also proposed the reorganization of the Department of Corrections and sought new state revenue from the introduction of off-track betting on out-of-state horse races simulcast at Rhode Island's existing dog track and jai alai fronton.

Nonetheless, as a bleak economic climate continued to afflict the state, Sundlun was forced to take harsh measures. Although he had pledged not to raise taxes except as a last resort, he proposed a series of tax increases in 1991, including a 20 percent increase in the personal income tax, an 11 percent surcharge on corporate income taxes, and a nickel per gallon increase in the gasoline tax. He also called for sharp cuts in state aid to education, the layoff of 1,000 state employees, and a controversial measure requiring state employees to take one unpaid holiday every two weeks. In making his tax increase proposals, Sundlun cast blame on his predecessor, saying that the DiPrete administration had overestimated revenue and consistently underestimated spending.

Despite such harsh medicine, Sundlun was a strong candidate for re-election, especially since Republicans had great difficulty finding a big-name challenger to oppose him. For a time, party leaders had hoped to entice former Congresswoman Claudine Schneider to enter the race, but their efforts met with no success. Ultimately challenged by Elizabeth Leonard, the owner of a car dealership making her first run for public office, Sundlun won credit for stabilizing the state banking crisis and for running a scandal-free administration—quite a rarity in Rhode Island. Although Leonard tried to cast herself as the "perfect outsider" in an attempt to capitalize on the anti-incumbency mood of the electorate, her lack of political experience apparently hurt her with state voters, and she also had some difficulty formulating policy positions. Sundlun won his reelection bid with 64 percent of the vote.

Sundlun's second term has been sullied somewhat by his admission, under threat of a paternity lawsuit, that he had paid a woman $30,000 over several years to settle a paternity claim involving a teenager who was "very likely his daughter." Political observers believed that Sundlun's admission, while "titillating," would have insignificant political impact. In electing Sundlun—who has been married four times—Rhode Islanders were obviously aware of his "womanizing" past.

Bibliography: Biographical information courtesy of governor's office; *The Chronicle of Higher Education,* 11–11–92; Elmer E. Cornwell, Jr., "Rhode Island: Bruce Sundlun and the State's Crisis," in Thad Beyle, ed., *Governors and Hard Times* (Washington, D.C.: Congressional Quarterly Press, 1992); Phil Duncan, ed., *Politics in America 1992* (Washington, D.C.: Congressional Quarterly Press, 1991); *National Review,* 3–30–92; *The New York Times*: 9–11–90; 9–12–90; 11–7–90; 2–1–91; 8–27–91; 7–6–92; 10–26–92; 11–4–92; 6–11–93; *Providence Journal,* 3–14–91; *USA Today*: 11–8–90; 1–4–91; 5–12–92; 7–6–92; 9–15–92; 11–4–92; 6–9–93.

SOUTH CAROLINA

CARROLL A. CAMPBELL, JR., 1987–

Born in Greenville, South Carolina, on July 24, 1940, Campbell is the son of Carroll Ashmore Campbell and Anne Williams Campbell. An Episcopalian, he married the former Iris Rhodes in 1959. The couple has two children.

Educated in the Greenville public schools, Campbell graduated from the McCallie School in Tennessee. He attended both the University of South Carolina and American University in Washington, D.C. on a part-time basis. At age 19, he was working in the real estate business when he and a partner founded Handy Park Company, a successful chain of parking facilities. In 1967, he was a principal in the formation of Rex Enterprises, which developed a chain of 13 Burger King restaurants before being sold in 1978. Campbell also became active as a breeder of Arabian horses and owned and operated a farm near Fountain Inn, South Carolina, for many years.

Campbell began his political career helping a friend run for public office in 1960 and through the years managed campaigns for others, including the campaign that elected the first Republican mayor of Greenville. He himself first sought political office in 1969 but was defeated in a special election. He ran successfully in 1970, elected to the South Carolina House of Representatives, winning reelection in 1972. In 1973, Campbell served as assistant minority leader and was elected as the first Republican in a century to hold an office on a standing committee. He lost a close race for lieutenant governor in 1974 and in 1975–1976 served as executive assistant to Governor James B. Edwards, the first Republican governor in South Carolina since Reconstruction. He served in the South Carolina State Senate from 1976 to 1978, when he was elected to the U.S. Congress from South Carolina's Fourth Congressional District. The popular congressman served four terms before being elected governor in 1986. In Congress, Campbell served on two powerful committees, the Appropriations and Ways and Means committees. He also served for four years as a member of the Republican Policy Committee of the Textile Caucus. While in Congress, he received the Watchdog of the Treasury Golden Bulldog Award for fiscal responsibility, as well as the National Federation of Independent Business Award for support of the free enterprise system.

Carroll A. Campbell, Jr. *(Courtesy of Governor's Office)*

In 1986, Campbell sought the governorship upon the retirement of popular incumbent Richard Riley. Relinquishing a safe House seat to make the run, he waged an uphill battle to become only the second Republican to hold the statehouse in over a century. His opponent was Lieutenant Governor Michael Daniel, who in 1984 gained national attention for his efforts to cool racial tensions after two white men had burned down three rural black churches in Lancaster County. Daniel waged a defensive campaign, running on Riley's record and seeking to rebut Campbell's charges that the state was not doing well.

Campbell promised to throw out the "good ol' boy" system of entrenched state politicians. Stressing education, economic development, and political ethics, he called for cutting insurance rates, reorganizing state government, and lowering taxes. In the campaign, he seemed to be following a strategy developed in 1985 at a meeting of leading Republican governors, members of Congress, and political consultants. The group, convened by Governor Lamar Alexander of Tennessee, concluded that Republicans could not win state elections by running on the "Washington agenda" of foreign policy and social issues. Although Republicans had won national elections by promising to restrain the role of the federal government, they had to recognize that people expected state government to be active and involved in solving their problems. Political analysts saw Campbell as a model of a new breed of Republican emerging in the modern South, a conservative who was actively seeking black votes. Campbell also benefited from President Reagan's popularity in the state.

Campbell pulled out a narrow victory, 51 percent to 49 percent. His margins came in suburban areas, especially in his home base of Greenville. Profiting from a well-tuned and well-financed party organization, he managed to withstand a vicious smear campaign by some Democratic activists. The controversy, which had been a lingering undercurrent in South Carolina politics for some time, dated back to his 1978 campaign for Congress. Critics suggested that he or his campaign organization was behind an attempt to make his Democratic opponent's Jewish faith an issue in the race, which Campbell won.

Campbell was sworn in on January 14, 1987, as the state's 112th governor. Seeking reelection in 1990, he won handily, drawing 70 percent of the vote. The election drew national attention due to the presence of Democratic candidate Theo Mitchell, a lawyer and state senator hoping to become the first black to win a statewide election in South Carolina since Reconstruction. Race played a role in the election, with Campbell using his good working relationship with white state Democratic leaders to defeat Mitchell. Although Mitchell had vowed to run an all-inclusive campaign, reaching out to voters of all races, some of his comments proved inflammatory and divisive. Democratic leaders never fully embraced Mitchell after he branded black backers of Campbell "black prostitutes."

Campbell is only the second Republican in more than a century to occupy the statehouse. In office, he has stressed education reform and economic development. His emphasis on literacy and the challenges of the global economy prompted him to develop the Governor's Initiative on Work Force Excellence, which has provided basic skills and literacy training at the workplace to thousands of state residents. He was a driving force behind the Cutting Edge, a major package of higher education initiatives, and Target 2000, a revolutionary set of measures granting deregulation and flexibility to the state's best-performing schools.

Campbell's expertise in this area has drawn national attention. Championing the cause of lifelong learning during his stint as cochair of the National Governors Association (NGA) Task Force on Education, he coauthored the set of national education goals championed by President George Bush and the nation's governors. Campbell has also been active in the work of the National Educational Goals Panel, which is devising new methods to measure educational progress. He is cochair of the panel's Interim Council on Standards and Testing.

Campbell has also served as chair of the Southern Technology Council and the Southern Growth Policies Board, as well as cochair of the Appalachian Regional Commission and NGA Budget Task Force. In 1992, he became vice-chair of the National Governors Association.

In the opinion of political observers, Campbell has been instrumental in building an effective Republican party in South Carolina. A past chair of the Republican Governors Association, he was a strong ally of the Bush White House and served as Bush's southern campaign chairman in both 1988 and 1992. His name appeared on a long list of contenders for the vice-presidential spot in 1988, and he is already rumored to be a contender for the Republican presidential nomination in 1996. Unable by state law to seek a third term in the statehouse, he may choose to run for the U.S. Senate upon the retirement of longtime incumbent Strom Thurmond.

Bibliography: Michael Barone et al., *The Almanac of American Politics, 1986, 1988* (Washington, D.C.: National Journal, 1985, 1987); biographical information courtesy of governor's office; *The Chronicle of Higher Education*: 11–12–86; 2–18–87; 2–5–92; *The New York Times*: 8–6–85; 9–4–86; 9–24–86; 11–6–86; 1–15–87; 11–9–88; 11–8–90; 1–28–91; 7–7–92; 8–17–92; *The Star-Ledger* (Newark, N.J.): 11–15–89; 8–5–92; *USA Today*: 6–7–88; 2–26–90; 6–14–90; 11–8–90; 11–18–92.

SOUTH DAKOTA

GEORGE SPEAKER MICKELSON, 1987–1993

Born in Mobridge, South Dakota, on January 31, 1941, Mickelson was the son of George Theodore Mickelson, a former governor of South Dakota (1947–1951) and Madge Ellen Turner Mickelson. In 1963, he married the former Linda McCahren. A Methodist, Mickelson and his wife had three children.

Mickelson was a graduate of Washington High School, Sioux Falls; the University of South Dakota, Vermillion (1963); and the University of South Dakota School of Law (1965). He entered the U.S. Army in 1965, serving tours of duty in Fort Benjamin, Indiana; Fort Knox, Kentucky; Fort Lee, Virginia; and Vietnam. He was honorably discharged in 1967 with a rank of captain.

Working as an attorney in private practice since 1968, he began his public service career in 1970, serving as Brookings County attorney from 1970 to 1974. A member of the South Dakota House of Representatives from 1975 to 1980, he was elected speaker pro tem for two years and speaker of the house for two years. While in the legislature, he served on the Taxation, Judiciary, State Affairs and Intergovernmental Relations committees, as well as on a special committee studying personal property tax replacement. He also served for four years as chairman of the state Board of Pardons and Paroles.

A Republican, Mickelson defeated three other candidates to win his party's gubernatorial nomination in 1986. In the general election, he defeated Democrat Lars Herseth with 52 percent of the vote. He got his winning margin in the state's two biggest cities, Sioux Falls and Rapid City, where the banking programs of outgoing Republican Governor William Janklow had created hundreds of jobs and stronger economies than in other Farm Belt towns.

Seeking reelection in 1990, Mickelson defeated Bob Samuelson, a former state senator and state Democratic party chairman, with an overwhelming 59 percent of the vote.

During his years in office, Mickelson stressed economic development and education improvement. He was responsible for pioneering the state's revolving economic development fund, landmark environmental legisla-

George Speaker Mickelson *(Paul Jones, Photographer)*

tion, and health care reform. He was a strong supporter of higher education, particularly as a means to promote economic development. During his first term, he helped secure greater autonomy for the South Dakota Board of Regents, the governing board for all higher education in the state. He also supported new taxes to benefit colleges and public schools, but his proposal for a half-cent increase in the state sales tax was defeated by the legislature in 1991.

In a state with a long and tragic history of relations with Native Americans, Mickelson announced a statewide reconciliation program that would continue into the next century. In 1991, he joined leaders of nine Sioux tribes in a peace-pipe ceremony at the state capitol in Pierre.

One distinct low point of the Mickelson administration occurred in early 1990, when the parents of a 16-year-old girl claimed that she had been raped by four teenagers during a drinking party at the governor's mansion. The rape allegedly took place in November 1989 while Mickelson and his wife were out of town, but questions were raised about the presence and role of the governor's 17-year-old son. A special prosecutor was appointed to investigate the incident, which drew national attention and resulted in much sympathy for the popular Republican.

On the national level, Mickelson was a former chair of the Western Governors Association and actively involved in the health care agenda of the National Governors Association.

Mickelson's term in office ended abruptly on April 19, 1993, when he and seven others were killed in a tragic plane crash as they returned from a trip to Cincinnati to promote economic development. The twin engine turboprop had been heading for an emergency landing at the Dubuque, Iowa, Airport when it struck a barn about 15 miles away. Federal Aviation Administration investigators looking into the crash of the state-owned jet found a crack in a propeller hub and one missing blade.

Mickelson was succeeded in office by his lieutenant governor, Walter Dale Miller.

Bibliography: Michael Barone et al., *The Almanac of American Politics, 1988* (Washington, D.C.: National Journal, 1987); biographical information courtesy of governor's office; *The Chronicle of Higher Education*: 11–12–86; 2–18–87; 10–31–90; 8–28–91; *Newsweek*, 2–19–90; *The New York Post,* 4–20–93; *The New York Times*: 6–1–86; 6–7–90; 9–19–91; 4–20–93; *The Star-Ledger* (Newark, N.J.), 4–20–93; *USA Today,* 1–24–90; 2–1–93; 4–30–93.

Walter Dale Miller *(Courtesy of Governor's Office)*

WALTER DALE MILLER, 1993–

Miller was born in Viewfield, South Dakota, on October 5, 1925. A widower, he has four children.

A graduate of New Underwood High School, Miller attended South Dakota School of Mines and Technology in Rapid City, South Dakota. He is the owner and operator of a 7,000-acre ranch in Meade County.

A Republican, Miller has held positions in both local government and in party organizations. Serving as a school board member for 20 years, he began his political career in the state house of representatives. In office from 1967 to 1986, he led his colleagues as majority whip, assistant majority leader, majority leader, speaker pro tem, and speaker. A member of the Legislative Research Council's Executive Board, he chaired standing committees on local government, taxation, state affairs, and legislative procedure.

Active in Republican party ranks, he has been a precinct committeeman, state central committeeman, and delegate to Republican National conventions in 1976, 1980, and 1984. State chairman of the 1984 Reagan-Bush campaign, he cochaired the 1988 Bush-Quayle organization in the state. He is presently serving on the Executive Committee of the state Republican party and as a Republican national committeeman from South Dakota.

Elected lieutenant governor in 1986, Miller was reelected in 1990. He holds the distinction of being the first full-time lieutenant governor in state history. As lieutenant governor, he chaired task forces on air service, state employees' health insurance, and telecommunications. He also supervised the work of state commissions on taxation, government cost-effectiveness, and workers' compensation. In 1991, he was appointed an advisory committee member of the Export-Import Bank of the United States and in 1992 became chairman-elect of the National Conference of Lieutenant Governors.

As lieutenant governor, Miller ascended to the statehouse in tragic circumstances. On April 19, 1993, a plane crash took the life of Governor George Mickelson, and Miller was sworn in as the state's 29th governor the next day. In an emotional tribute to his popular predecessor and friend, Miller explained that he hoped he could accomplish all that Mickelson ''wanted to accomplish for us.''

Bibliography: Biographical information courtesy of governor's office; *The Record* (Bergen County, N.J.), 4–21–93.

Ned McWherter *(Courtesy of Governor's Office)*

TENNESSEE

NED McWHERTER, 1987–

Born in Palmersville, Tennessee, on October 15, 1930, McWherter is the son of sharecropper parents Harmon R. McWherter and Lucille Smith McWherter. A Methodist, McWherter was married to the late Bette Jean Beck McWherter. He is the father of two children.

McWherter operated several small businesses and a farm headquartered in Dresden, Tennessee, before entering political life in 1968. He also served 21 years in the Tennessee National Guard, retiring with the rank of captain.

A Democrat, McWherter began his career in state government in 1968 when he won a vacant Tennessee House seat. After just two terms, he was elected speaker of the house, a post he then went on to hold longer than anyone in Tennessee history. As speaker, McWherter fought for improved education, jobs, and economic development; better highways; a cleaner environment; and responsible management of state tax dollars. A pioneer of open government, he authored Tennessee's campaign-financing disclosure law and supported legislation requiring all public officials to disclose their financial holdings. He also backed legislation to open all government meetings and records, as well as all proceedings of the house, to the public and the press. While McWherter was speaker, Tennessee consistently balanced its annual budget, attaining the highest bond rating of any state and keeping its taxes among the lowest in the nation.

Although he had never before been elected by a constituency larger than his state legislative district, McWherter proved successful at winning votes when he ran for the governorship in 1986. He defeated two serious candidates to win the Democratic gubernatorial nomination: Public Service Commissioner Jane Eskind, the Democratic nominee against U.S. Senator Howard Baker in 1978, who spent liberally on her campaign; and Richard Fulton, the longtime mayor of Nashville. McWherter garnered 42 percent of the vote in the three-way race, to his opponents' 30 percent and 26 percent, respectively. Minor candidates shared the remaining 2 percent of the vote.

In the general election, he faced Republican Winfield Dunn, a former governor. Although McWherter ran behind the usual Democratic show-ings in the state's four largest cities, he ran ahead in rural areas and carried the far tip of eastern Tennessee, defeating Dunn with 54 percent of the vote.

On November 6, 1990, McWherter became only the second Tennessee governor ever elected to a second four-year term. His 61 percent margin over Republican State Representative Dwight Henry was the largest any state gubernatorial candidate had enjoyed in 20 years. The voters em-braced McWherter even as Henry accused him of preparing to push for the state's first income tax, a proposal that was ultimately turned back by the legislature.

As governor, McWherter promised to build on the achievements of his Republican predecessor, Lamar Alexander, by building a better educa-tional system and a modern transportation network and providing more well-paying jobs for state citizens. Continuing his commitment to honest and open government, he has established a comprehensive system of public integrity and disclosure requirements for ranking officials in his administration. He has also operated under an unprecedented open door policy to provide access to all citizens.

McWherter has stressed tough financial management, elimination of bureaucratic red tape, and creative solutions to state problems. In 1992, he signed a tax package designed to generate nearly $300 million in new state revenues, with more than half the funding earmarked for the im-provement of public education. Recognizing his inability to impose a state income tax, he raised needed revenue by hiking the state sales tax half a cent, by raising business fees, and by charging lawyers, accountants, and other providers of professional services a $200 annual fee.

Under McWherter's stewardship, Tennessee has enjoyed a period of record economic growth and development. While the state has emerged as a national leader in the creation of well-paying new jobs, a particular challenge has been to spread the state's development equally across all 95 counties. With record road-building budgets, McWherter has pushed aggressively to open up communities for new jobs. He has started the first state-funded program to help depressed communities build the facil-ities they need to attract industry and has focused on the state's com-munity colleges and regional educational institutions to meet the needs of Tennessee businesses for skilled workers.

McWherter is also credited with initiating the first state–financed pro-gram for low–income housing, using community–based "Drug Free Ten-nessee" organizations throughout the state to attack the problems of alcohol and drug abuse, and expanding rural health care programs.

The one taint on McWherter's administration came in early 1990, with a yearlong round of indictments involving bingo operations and official corruption that put state Democrats on the defensive. The case, dubbed

Operation Rocky Top by the Federal Bureau of Investigation (FBI), has left little taint on him, however. In fact, he was praised by the FBI for his cooperation, which began when he was speaker of the Tennessee House of Representatives. He responded to the scandal by issuing executive orders tightening ethics rules for his appointees, suggesting that the legislature enact measures to broaden the state attorney general's powers to prosecute cases involving official corruption.

Hoping to keep education reform as the top priority of his remaining years in office, McWherter has already announced that he will retire at the end of his present term.

Bibliography: Michael Barone et al., *The Almanac of American Politics, 1988* (Washington, D.C.: National Journal 1987); biographical information courtesy of governor's office; *The Chronicle of Higher Education*: 11–12–86; 8–15–90; 10–31–90; 5–17–91; 8–28–91; 3–25–92; *The New York Times*, 1–28– 90; *USA Today*, 11–8–90.

William P. Clements, Jr. *(Courtesy of Governor's Office)*

TEXAS

WILLIAM P. CLEMENTS, JR., 1979–1983, 1987–1991

Clements was born in Dallas, Texas, on April 13, 1917. An Episcopalian, he and his wife Rita have two children.

After attending Southern Methodist University, Clements was a "roughneck" in the oil fields and a driller of oil rigs from 1937 to 1947. He founded Sedco, Inc., in 1947, a firm that manufactures oil drilling equipment. That venture made Clements a multimillionaire. He worked as a deputy secretary at the U.S. Department of Defense from 1973 to 1977, receiving a Distinguished Public Service Award from the Defense Department in 1975. Clements was also awarded the Bronze Palm by President Gerald Ford in 1976.

The spread of prosperity in Texas throughout the 1970s, as well as a population boom and a large in-state migration from rural to urban areas, gradually altered the state's traditional voting patterns and paved the way for Clements' election in 1978 as the state's first Republican governor since Reconstruction. Spending heavily in his first bid for elective office, the conservative Clements portrayed the election as a referendum on the policies of the Carter administration, which was highly unpopular in Texas. He easily defeated Dallas lawyer and former Texas Republican Chairman Ray Hutchinson in the primary, gaining 73 percent of the vote to Hutchinson's 24 percent. (A minor candidate earned the remaining 3 percent.) Clements then turned his attention to incumbent Democrat Dolph Briscoe, whom he attacked for not taking "an active role in Washington for the state." Clements' criticisms of Briscoe were premature, however, for in a startling upset the incumbent lost his own bid for the Democratic nomination in a bitter primary battle with liberal Attorney General John Hill. Hill's victory gave Texans a choice they had never really had before—a contest between a liberal Democrat and a laissez-faire Republican.

Presenting himself as a conservative businessman who believed in less government, Clements campaigned on a platform promising to reduce state spending and taxes and to streamline the state's bureaucracy. Despite a staggering lead by the better-known Hill in early polls, Clements came back to win a narrow victory, gaining 50 percent of the vote to Hill's 49 percent. Aided by his conservative views, the unpopularity of the Democratic administration in Washington, a high turnout in the affluent urban areas of the state, and a $7 million war chest, Clements gained national attention with his narrow victory. Unlike the retiring Governor Briscoe, he seemed a force to be reckoned with in national politics, as he boldly advocated policies to encourage free enterprise and to reduce the size of government at all levels. Clements was the first chief executive to endorse Ronald Reagan in 1980, and during his term in office, he attempted to make the Republican party a major force in state politics.

During his term Clements tried to cut the state payroll by 5 percent a year and vetoed a record $250 million from the $21 billion biennial budget. He streamlined the bureaucracy; encouraged a tough, anticrime stance in state government; and attempted to work out a plan with Mexico to curb the flood of illegal aliens across Texas borders.

Clements alienated many voters, however, with his outspoken views. For example, when during the campaign he was asked to express his opinion on the problems of Mexican-Americans, he replied gruffly that he was not running for governor of Mexico. In his campaign for reelection in 1982, much was made of this so-called meanness issue and of Clements' personal style. Although he easily overcame the challenge of Duke Embs, a San Antonio insurance broker, to win the Republican nomination with more than 90 percent of the vote, he was not as fortunate in the general election. Clements' opponent was moderate Attorney General Mark White, a Democrat with strong name recognition around the state. In 1978, White had defeated James A. Baker, President Reagan's Chief of Staff, to become attorney general, and in that office, he gained widespread publicity as a champion of law and order and as a protector of consumers.

The 1982 gubernatorial campaign was a rancorous one, with Clements attempting to portray White as a "bumbling incompetent" and White hoping to capitalize on the meanness issue, a charge revived when a Clements campaign tabloid ran a story about White's arrest for drunken driving almost 20 years earlier. Polls indicated that voters were dissatisfied not only with Clements' style but also with his handling of the state's economy. Although the Texas economy had been healthy during most of his administration, and unemployment, at 6.7 percent, was lower than in any other large state, the recession was beginning to hit Texas hard. Rising unemployment rates that set records by Texas standards soon put Clements on the defensive. With worldwide petroleum prices depressed, drilling for new gas and oil wells slowed dramatically, and nearly every state business depending on the oil industry was affected. The Democratic platform attacked Clements' lack of leadership. White also criticized high utility rates, low teacher salaries, looming water shortages, prison crowding, and rising interest rates. Adopting a neopopulist stance, he attempted to link Clements to the wealthy and privileged with the issue of soaring utility rates.

Although Clements raised and spent nearly $12 million in his reelection bid, possibly the largest campaign fund ever devoted to an American gubernatorial election, he lost to White by a rather large margin, 46 percent to 54 percent. The Democrats took more than 85 percent of the Hispanic vote, an increasingly important factor in Texas elections. This, said the neopopulist White, "was a victory of the people."

The election was closely watched by political observers because of the important role that Texas plays in national politics. Although Clements lost by 200,000 votes, most of the Republican strongholds in the state stayed that way, and in most areas, he managed to poll as many votes as he had four years earlier. His defeat was attributed to a surprisingly high voter turnout, which has always favored the Democrats in Texas.

After he left office, Clements returned to his oil drilling equipment business. He was also asked by President Reagan to serve on two national commissions, one on America's policy in Central America and the other on strategic forces.

Clements was encouraged by a grass-roots movement to seek the Republican nomination for governor again in 1986. Incumbent Mark White, who had thwarted Clements' reelection bid in 1982, had himself fallen on hard times, having had the misfortune of holding office during four of the most trying years in Texas history. The plunge in world oil prices had left the state's once-booming energy industry in ruins, and White went into the election with unemployment at 9 percent, well above the national average and as high as 30 percent in some areas. He was forced twice to call for higher taxes and fees to keep up state services and had sought a rise in the sales tax to overcome a $2.8 billion state deficit, the largest ever. Clements made the economy the focus of his campaign, charging that White had failed to provide the leadership to help Texas out of its troubles, and that he had allowed spending and taxes to run "out of control." Putting forth his own six-point employment plan, he contended that White, as a Democrat, was unable to deal with the Republican administration in Washington to help the state's economy recover.

White also gambled heavily with his highly touted program for the reform of Texas public schools. Pushing through measures that, among other things, barred failing students from playing sports and required competency testing of teachers, he alienated teachers and parents alike, as well as rural Texas constituents who were offended when star athletes were unable to perform.

The bitter race provided a measure of personal vindication for Clements, who relished in his 53 percent to 46 percent victory over the man who had defeated him four years earlier. Clements' victory drew national attention as a barometer of growing Republican strength in this once solidly Democratic state.

In office, Clements faced what many observers felt was one of the most painful eras in the state's history. Obstacles confronting him included a state budget deficit approaching $1 billion, high unemployment, an over-crowded prison system under federal court order to improve conditions, an outdated tax system, and legislative leaders who were determined to force him to break his promise not to raise taxes.

Battered by troubles in the oil industry, in 1987 he had no alternative but to endorse a compromise state budget that included new taxes. His antitax stand had been widely regarded as unrealistic, especially in a state whose already low levels of funding for social services left little room for budget cuts to stave off an expected budget deficit.

Clements was also badly hurt by a scandal that rocked his administration in the early months of his second term. As chairman of the Southern Methodist University Board of Governors from 1967 to 1973 and again from 1983 to 1987, Clements admitted that he and other board members had approved improper payments to student athletes, a practice that con-tinued even after the National Collegiate Athletic Association (NCAA) had placed the school on probation in 1985. Attempting to profit from the governor's troubles, state Democrats seized the opportunity to scuttle Clements' plans to cut state spending on education and welfare as an answer to the budget crisis. Some Texas lawmakers even called for his impeachment as efforts to resolve the budget crisis became mired in the college football scandal and resulting political infighting.

In 1990, Clements had no alternative but to raise taxes again. Although long opposed to an increase in the sales tax, he agreed reluctantly after a tumultuous three-month standoff with state lawmakers over how to revise the state's $13.5 billion system of school financing. Like several other states, Texas was under court order to overhaul its methods of school financing in order to ensure that aid was equitable among school districts.

Clements also disappointed opponents of abortion by not fighting more aggressively for increased restrictions on abortion, despite his oft-expressed personal opposition to existing abortion laws.

Extremely unpopular as his second term progressed, Clements an-nounced his intention not to seek reelection more than two years before the completion of his term. Political analysts believed that he almost certainly would have been defeated, had he not chosen to step aside.

Bibliography: Biographical information courtesy of governor's office; *The Chronicle of Higher Education*: 11–12–86; 7–1–87; *The Dallas Morning News, 8–1–87; Newsweek*: 10–4–82; 11–15–82; 3–16–87; *The New York Times*: 3–26–78; 5–4–78;8–18–78;11–8–78;1–17–79;9–23–79;6–29–80;9–9–81;9–22–81;4–29–82;5–

3–82; 5–28–82; 6–16–82; 9–13–82; 10–12–82; 10–14–82; 10–31–82; 11–3–82; 1–19–83; 9–29–86; 10–8–86; 11–1–86; 11–5–86; 11–6–86; 1–21–87; 2–4–87; 3–5–87; 3–6–87; 3–11–87; 4–6–87; 4–22–87; 5–15–87; 6–2–87; 6–24–87; 7–17–87; 10–22–89; 6–2–90; 9–20–90; *U.S. News & World Report,* 9–24–79.

Ann Willis Richards *(Courtesy of Governor's Office)*

ANN WILLIS RICHARDS, 1991–

Richards was born on September 1, 1933, the only child of Cecil and Ona Willis. She graduated from Waco High School in 1950 and Baylor University in 1954 with a major in speech and a minor in political science. She later earned a teaching certificate at the University of Texas and worked as a social studies and history teacher at Fulmore Junior High School in Austin from 1955 to 1956.

She married Dave Richards, a lawyer, in 1953. The couple had four children before divorcing in 1984.

Richards first entered state politics in the 1970s. A Democrat, she earned her party credentials stuffing envelopes and doing grass-roots campaigning in the 1972 state legislative race of Sarah Weddington, the lawyer in the U.S. Supreme Court's celebrated *Roe v. Wade* abortion case. She won her first bid for public office when she was elected a Travis County commissioner in 1976, defeating a three-term incumbent for the post. Serving in that office for 6 years, she went on to win election as Texas state treasurer in 1982, winning with more votes than any other statewide candidate on the ballot and becoming the first woman elected to statewide office in Texas in more than 50 years. In 1986, she was reelected without opposition.

Establishing herself as a fiscal conservative, she overhauled the methods of the treasurer's office, pioneered new banking and investment practices, and made the department a model in the hiring and promotion of women and minorities. While serving as state treasurer, she catapulted to fame and national prominence as a result of her keynote address to the 1988 Democratic National Convention. Witty, energetic, and somewhat brash, she excoriated then Vice-President George Bush as a man "born with a silver foot in his mouth." An overnight celebrity as a result, she went on to publish a campaign autobiography in 1990, *Straight from the Heart: My Life in Politics and Other Places* (Simon & Shuster), and entered the Texas gubernatorial race that year.

The battle for the Democratic nomination was brutal and bitter, pitting Richards against former Governor Mark White, who had been ousted by voters in 1986 when he broke a promise and raised taxes, and Attorney General Jim Mattox, a onetime political ally. The three-way March 13, 1990, primary put Richards on top with 39.4 percent of the vote but forced her into a runoff with second-place finisher Mattox. Since their positions on issues were nearly identical, both pinned their hopes for the April 10 runoff on securing the votes of former White supporters. White, for his part, however, denounced Richards, underscoring the divisions among state Democrats with a bitter attack on his former rival. Saying that he would never endorse her, never support her, and never vote for her, he charged that her tactics in the primary campaign would "make [Nazi SS and Gestapo leader Heinrich] Himmler blush."

Richards faced two serious problems in her quest for the nomination— the difficulties of being a woman in the man's world of Texas politics and the troubling new realities of the politics of drugs and alcoholism. As an admitted recovering alcoholic, she was asked during a televised debate in Dallas whether she had ever used illegal drugs. Refusing to answer the question, she announced that she had already disclosed all that she intended to disclose about her private life. In the mean-spirited runoff, Mattox sought to make political capital out of the issue, alleging that Richards had used illegal drugs, including cocaine, and challenging her to release her medical records. Richards countered by accusing Mattox of profiting from public service and daring him to release his income tax returns. According to political analysts, even hardened Texas voters were shocked by the tenor of the campaign, dubbed "Muddlemania II" by the *Fort Worth Star-Telegram*. Some political professionals speculated that Mattox pushed his attacks so hard that they backfired on him. Richards emerged victorious with 57 percent of the vote, the first woman nominated for governor of Texas since Miriam ("Ma") Ferguson won the Democratic nod and later the office in 1932. Although feminists nationally hailed her victory, coming as it did in the rough and tumble world of Texas politics, other analysts worried that the bitterness and nastiness of the two Democratic contests had served only to dramatically increase GOP chances in the fall campaign.

Republican candidate Clayton Williams, a West Texas businessman making his political debut, held an early lead. At the heart of his campaign was a call for the restoration of the values of "old Texas." Combining a populist appeal and homespun charm with tough stands on drug abuse and government spending, he portrayed Richards as out of the Texas mainstream, sympathetic to death row inmates, in favor of gun control and higher taxes, associated with gay rights activists, and allied politically with Jane Fonda.

Williams, however, squandered both his early lead and millions of dollars of his private fortune with an inept campaign marked by a series of embarrassing gaffes. He stumbled badly when asked on TV about the only proposed constitutional amendment on the ballot, then acknowledged having paid no income taxes in 1986 when the oil industry collapsed. His refusal to shake hands with Richards at a joint appearance in Dallas alienated many. Even worse were several crude and insensitive remarks, in the most notorious of which he compared rape to bad weather: "If it's inevitable, relax and enjoy it."

Richards' narrow, come-from-behind victory was attributed to a savvy ability both to exploit her opponent's missteps and to get her own message across. Charging that Williams had no knowledge of government and was unfit to be governor, she presented herself as a skilled and experienced tactician with a progressive vision for Texas. She campaigned for a "new Texas," with improvements in education, the economy, and the environment as her top priorities. Taking a no-new-taxes pledge, she pointed to her record as state treasurer and said she had the skills to find the revenues needed for proposed expenditures. Using populist themes, she repeatedly invited voters to help her "take back the government," unveiling a tough attack on the state's insurance industry and what she charged was little or lax regulation by the departing Republican administration of Bill Clements.

A colorful talker, Richards was aided by the rising celebrity status she enjoyed in national Democratic ranks, as well as by feminist-sponsored fund-raisers featuring Lily Tomlin and Marlo Thomas. She went on to defeat Williams with 49.6 percent of the vote, a margin of barely 100,000 votes out of 3.7 million cast. It was an important win for Texas Democrats, who would now preside over the distribution of a bonanza of new congressional seats following the 1990 census.

Nonetheless, Richards' victory was somewhat tarnished by the "scurrilous" nature of the campaign itself. Voters seemed turned off to both candidates, christened "The Doper vs. Dopey" by one popular campaign T-shirt.

Richards continued her populist crusade and its attendant symbolism right into the statehouse. On inauguration day, January 15, 1991, she and a crowd of 15,000 led a one-mile "people's march" to her swearing-in on the steps of the Texas capitol, where she exuberantly proclaimed, "Welcome to the first day of the New Texas."

Richards has drawn high marks during her gubernatorial tenure, and her popularity remains high. Since Texas governors have few formal powers and the office itself is constitutionally weak, their power stems from style, ability to persuade, and popular appeal—all strategies that Richards appears to have mastered. Appointing women and minorities to state jobs has been one of her major preoccupations. She has also pressed for legislation tightening regulation of the insurance industry and disposal of hazardous waste, and she has promoted a new government ethics law. Insisting during the campaign that an improving economy, belt tightening, and a state lottery would enable the state to avoid new taxes, she has been unable to make good on her no-new-taxes pledge. Although she was able to win narrow approval for her lottery proposal despite serious and sustained opposition by religious groups, a $2.7 billion tax increase was necessary in the face of a $4.5 billion deficit in the 1992–1993 biennial budget. Another key concern of her tenure has been a court-mandated struggle to produce a new funding formula for public schools, aimed at ending a disparity in wealth and per pupil spending between school districts.

Political analysts believe that Richards, who chaired the 1992 Democratic National Convention, has national political ambitions. Although she disappointed supporters by her refusal to run for the U.S. Senate seat vacated by Lloyd Bentsen, Bill Clinton's treasury secretary, there is strong speculation that she will one day make a presidential bid.

Bibliography: Biographical information courtesy of governor's office; *The Chronicle of Higher Education,* 8–28–91; Alison Cook, "Lone Star," *New York Times Magazine* (Feb. 7, 1993): 22–27, 38, 42, 47; Phil Duncan, ed., *Politics in America 1992* (Washington, D.C.: Congressional Quarterly Press, 1991); Celia Morris, *Storming the Statehouse: Running for Governor with Ann Richards and Dianne Feinstein* (New York: Scribner's, 1992); Richard Murray and Gregory R. Weiher, "Texas: Ann Richards, Taking on the Challenge," in Thad Beyle, ed., *Governors and Hard Times* (Washington, D.C.: Congressional Quarterly Press, 1992); *The New York Times:* 12–10–89; 3–1–90; 3–5–90; 3–15–90; 4–9–90; 4–11–90; 4–12–90; 4–15–90; 5–6–90; 8–4–90; 9–21–90; 10–29–90; 11–3–90; 11–5–90; 11–6–90; 11–8–90; 11–11–90; 1–20–91; 4–28–91; 5–29–91; 7–19–91; 1–19–92; 1–3–93; *The Record* (Bergen County, N.J.), 11–7–90; *The Star-Ledger* (Newark, N.J.): 8–13–89; 4–11–90; 10–28–90; 3–11–91; 8–28–91; 10–31–91; *USA Today:* 9–28–89; 1–3–90; 4–4–90; 4–6–90; 7–2–90; 10–15–90; 1–14–91; 1–17–91; 3–6–91; 3–29–91; 7–16–91; 7–19–91; 8–5–91; 6–26–92; 7–13–92; 1–11–93.

UTAH

NORMAN H. BANGERTER, 1985–1993

Bangerter was born in Granger, Utah, on January 4, 1933. Married to the former Colleen Monson, he and his wife have six children, one foster son, and nine grandchildren.

After graduating from Brigham Young University, Bangerter began a career as a builder that has continued to the present. A building contractor and longtime participant in Utah's home-building and real estate development industries, he is past president of NHB Construction. A Korean War veteran, he has given his time and talents to various business and labor-oriented activities. He has been a past member of the advisory board of Utah Technical College, Salt Lake; a member of the State Constitutional Revision Commission; and former chairman of the advisory board for Latter Day Saints Social Services in Utah. He has also served on Utah's Job Training Council, the task force formed to recommend the proper distribution of Utah's federal oil lease money, and as Utah chairman of the apprenticeship program for the Home Builders of America.

A Republican, Bangerter made his first run for public office in 1974 when he won a seat in the Utah House of Representatives from the burgeoning middle-class suburbs west of Salt Lake City. Four years later he was elected majority leader by house Republicans and two years later ascended to the speakership. As a prominent Mormon, however, Bangerter was familiar with public life even before his first political campaign. The Mormons, who believe in the priesthood of all male members, quickly promote church activists to positions that require public speaking and public administration of the church's extensive social and political activities. Bangerter had been a ward bishop of the church, equivalent to the head of a congregation, and stake president, head of a parish.

As a state legislator, Bangerter was recognized by President Reagan for his leadership. He is listed in *Who's Who in Politics* and *Who's Who in the West*. In 1983 he was named as one of the top ten legislators in America by the National Republican party.

Bangerter entered the race for governor in 1984, a race that had suddenly been thrown wide open by the surprise retirement of longtime incumbent Scott Matheson. He was an upset winner in his party's August primary,

Norman H. Bangerter *(Courtesy of Governor's Office)*

defeating Congressman Dan Marriott with 56 percent of the vote. Marriott, a four-term incumbent, had given up a safe seat in the U.S. House of Representatives to make the run.

In the general election, Bangerter faced Democrat Wayne Owens, a former congressman. Although Owens repeated a campaign tactic that he had used successfully before—walking the breadth of the state—he faced formidable obstacles in the race: his reputation as a liberal in this conservative state and the opposition of the Democratic leadership. He was forced to campaign without the endorsement of a majority of party leaders, whom he had alienated through a series of political maneuvers years ago, when he was a freshman congressman.

During the campaign, Bangerter promised to limit the role of his administration to helping Utahans help themselves—a characteristic message of self-reliance and governmental restraint from the conservative Republican. He pledged the following: to help make the state's public school students "understand that they are ultimately responsible for their own learning and destiny"; to redouble efforts to foster a strong probusiness climate; and to streamline the state bureaucracy. He also promised to hold the line on taxes for at least two years—a pledge made possible by a budget surplus of almost $100 million left by outgoing Governor Matheson.

The sharpest point of difference between the two candidates was over the state's response to federal exploration of a southern Utah site as a dump for high-level radioactive waste from nuclear power plants. Although Bangerter had taken a wait-and-see attitude during the race, after his victory he declared his opposition to the nuclear depository.

Bangerter won the election with 56 percent of the vote. The victory was an important one for Republicans, since Democrats had held the governorship for 20 years, 12 under Calvin L. Rampton (1965–1977) and 8 under Matheson (1977–1985).

Democrats sought revenge in 1988 when Bangerter campaigned for reelection. Stigmatized by a record $166 million tax increase enacted during his third year in office, Bangerter won narrowly. Staving off an aggressive challenge from former Salt Lake City Mayor Ted Wilson, he won 40 percent of the vote in a three-way race, with Wilson gaining 38 percent and antitax third-party candidate Merrill Cook drawing 21 percent. Minor party candidates split the remaining 1 percent of the vote.

Bangerter faced tremendous challenges and opportunities during his eight years in office. He took as his governmental priorities: education, economic development, efficiency in government, and the environment. Political analysts gave him a mixed review when assessing the extent to which he accomplished his objectives.

Yet, the successes of his administration were many. Public education received more money as a proportion of the annual state budget during each year of his term. Test scores of elementary school students rose consistently and, in some schools, nearly doubled. Personal income of state residents grew by 58 percent, and more than 167,000 new jobs were created. Despite the tax hikes that so infuriated his former supporters, tax burdens for sales and personal income tax, as a percentage of personal income, actually declined during his tenure, while the state's budget, growing in actual dollars, decreased after considering inflation and population growth.

Yet Bangerter also had his critics, especially those who believed that health care deserved more attention than the governor was willing to give it. Democrats also challenged him for his proposal to construct a $1.1 million "Literacy Lab" at the state prison to help rehabilitate inmates. Opponents charged that the money would be better spent in the state's public schools.

Two constitutional issues also drew national attention to Utah during Bangerter's second term: the first, a legal controversy over saying prayer at public school graduation exercises; and the second, his signing into law one of the toughest antiabortion measures in any of the 50 states.

Despite his critics' charge that he failed to provide effective leadership on key issues, the Bangerter administration received much positive acclaim in the national print media. *Financial World Magazine* ranked Utah as the top financially managed state in the country, while *Time, U.S. News & World Report,* the *Economist, The New York Times,* and the *Boston Globe* all highlighted the quality of life in the state. In October 1990, *Fortune* magazine ranked Salt Lake City as the nation's number-one city in which to do business.

After almost 20 years in public life, Bangerter announced that he would retire to private life after the completion of his second term. He was succeeded in office by Republican Mike Leavitt, a former aide to U.S. Senator Jake Garn.

Bibliography: Michael Barone et al., *The Almanac of American Politics, 1986, 1988, 1992* (Washington, D.C.: National Journal, 1985, 1987, 1991); biographical information courtesy of governor's office; *The Chronicle of Higher Education,* 2–18–87; *Desert News* (Salt Lake City, Utah), 1–14–92; *The New York Times*: 5–6–84; 8–22–84; 8–23–84; 11–8–84; 1–6–85; 1–8–85; 11–8–88; 1–26–91; *The Star-Ledger* (Newark, N.J.): 11–10–88; 8–27–90; 9–9–92; *USA Today,* 10–11–88.

MICHAEL OKERLUND LEAVITT, 1993–

Born in Cedar City, Utah, on February 11, 1951, Leavitt is the son of Anne and Dixie Leavitt, ranchers from Loa, Utah. Married to the former Jacalyn Smith of Newton, Utah, he has five children.

A graduate of Cedar City High School, Leavitt earned a degree in business and economics from Southern Utah University. He then began his career in the family business, the Leavitt Group, a regional insurance firm and one of the top brokerages in America. Eventually becoming president and chief executive officer, Leavitt was also appointed to the boards of directors of Pacificorp, Utah Power and Light, and Great Western Thrift and Loan.

Prior to his embarking on a political career, Leavitt displayed a keen interest in education. A member and chair of the Utah State Board of Regents, he has also chaired the Southern Utah University Board of Trustees and the Education Subcommittee of the Utah Commission for Efficiency and Economy in Government. He also served as a member of the Strategic Planning Committee for Public Education, aiming to develop a long-range plan for the state's public education system.

A Republican, Leavitt sought the governorship in 1992 upon the retirement of incumbent Norman Bangerter. Although he had never before held a public office, he was a longtime political activist, having run campaigns for U.S. Senators Jake Garn and Orrin Hatch, as well as for the retiring Bangerter himself. In the campaign, Leavitt faced perennial independent candidate Merrill Cook and Democrat Stewart Hanson, a lawyer and former state district judge also making his first bid for elective office. Hanson's liberal views, especially his prochoice position on abortion, hurt him in this conservative state, and Leavitt pulled out a 43 percent plurality over his two opponents. Cook drew 34 percent and Hanson the remaining 23 percent.

Leavitt was inaugurated as the 14th governor of Utah on January 4, 1993. His running mate, Olene S. Walker, had the distinction of becoming the first female lieutenant governor in the state's history.

In office, Leavitt has set five objectives for his administration: strengthening and improving education; achieving a stronger, more diversified economy; protecting the state's high quality of life; making government more efficient and effective; and caring for the needy while developing principles of self-reliance and personal responsibility.

Michael Okerlund Leavitt *(Courtesy of Governor's Office)*

Bibliography: Biographical information courtesy of governor's office; *The Chronicle of Higher Education,* 11–11–92; *The New York Times*: 10–26–92; 11–5–92; *USA Today,* 11–4–92.

Madeleine May Kunin *(Courtesy of Governor's Office)*

VERMONT

MADELEINE MAY KUNIN, 1985–1991

Born in Zurich, Switzerland, on September 28, 1933, Kunin is the daughter of Ferdinand May and Renee Bloch May. As a Jew, she fled Zurich with her widowed mother and brother in 1940. The Nazis later killed five other members of her family. The family settled in Forest Hills, New York, and later moved to Pittsfield, Massachusetts. Working her way through the University of Massachusetts as a waitress, she earned a B.A. in history in 1957. She also holds an M.A. in journalism from Columbia University and an M.A. in English literature from the University of Vermont. Turned down for a reporting job at the *Washington Post,* apparently for reasons of sex discrimination, she took a job instead at the *Burlington [Vt.] Free Press.* In Burlington she met her husband, Dr. Arthur Kunin, a kidney specialist and professor of medicine. The couple has four children.

A Democrat, Kunin began her political career in 1972 with election to the state house of representatives. She served three two-year terms and chaired the Appropriations Committee, 1977 to 1978. In the legislature, she developed a reputation as a liberal concerned with issues of poverty, environment, and education. She was elected the state's lieutenant governor in 1978 and reelected in 1980.

Making her first run for the governorship in 1982, she was defeated by popular incumbent Richard Snelling. She then spent some time as a fellow at the Institute of Politics of the Kennedy School of Government at Harvard.

Her unsuccessful 1982 campaign, however, had given her the stature to head a list of potential candidates upon Snelling's retirement in 1984. More aggressive as a campaigner that year, she forcefully promoted her experience as lieutenant governor and as a state legislator. She proposed a toxic waste cleanup fund, as well as stronger rules for reviewing the impact of ski area development. Her Republican opponent, Attorney General John J. Easton, Jr., was best known outside the state for directing a raid on a religious community in Island Pond, responding to charges of child abuse there. The election was the closest state gubernatorial contest in 22 years, with Kunin escaping a legislative runoff by only 60 votes. With her victory, Kunin became the first woman ever to govern Vermont and only the third Democrat to hold the office in 130 years. She was the fourth woman in U.S. history to be elected governor in her own right, following Dixy Lee Ray of Washington, Ella Grasso of Connecticut, and Martha Layne Collins of Kentucky.

Kunin was subsequently reelected to office in 1986 and 1988, becoming the first female chief executive in the nation ever to win a third term. In 1986, she drew 47 percent of the vote in a three-way race against Republican Peter P. Smith, the lieutenant governor, and independent Bernard Sanders, the socialist mayor of Burlington. In 1988, she easily defeated Michael Bernhardt, house minority leader, with 56 percent of the vote.

During her three terms in office, Kunin closed a budget deficit she had inherited from the previous administration and increased state aid to education and child care. A liberal Democrat who was often called "a symbol of the new Vermont," she built a national reputation as one of the nation's most outspoken governors in the areas of abortion rights and environmental protection.

Things began to unravel during her third term, however, as Vermont came to be affected by the widening recession overtaking the troubled economy of the Northeast. A surging economy in the 1980s had yielded surpluses allowing spending initiatives, but the economic downturn prompted cutbacks and tax increases. In Vermont, sagging state revenues necessitated sharp budget reductions and a proposed 12 percent increase in personal income taxes for fiscal year 1991. Kunin's popularity plummeted as she faced these fiscal challenges. She also suffered a popular backlash against a tough environmental planning law that critics charged would diminish the power of communities to control their own growth.

Beset by such difficulties, Kunin announced that she would not seek a fourth term in 1990. She insisted, however, that her decision was not a result of any "disillusionment with politics" but motivated by a reluctance to tackle the rigors of another biennial statewide campaign. Nonetheless, analysts noted that Kunin would have faced a brutal and costly campaign due to her mounting unpopularity. Twice during the month preceding her announcement she had been booed by audiences at public events, and her prospective opponent, former Governor Richard Snelling, posed a formidable challenge.

Despite her decision, Kunin was confident of her place in the record books. "We have made history here in Vermont," she noted. "We have shown that women are strong and capable leaders."

Retiring from the governorship in 1991, Kunin began a stint as a visiting fellow at the Mary Ingraham Bunting Institute at Radcliffe. Researching a book on women in politics, she also gave lectures on the environment and the development of leadership roles among women.

A strong supporter of Arkansas Governor Bill Clinton's 1992 presidential bid, she was rumored to have been among his choices for the vice–

presidential slot on the ticket. After his victory, she emerged as an important adviser on his transition team and on general public policy issues. She presently holds the position of deputy secretary of education in the Clinton administration. In that role, she is an advocate of increased education spending and new initiatives in the area of early childhood education.

Bibliography: Michael Barone et al., *The Almanac of American Politics, 1984, 1986, 1988* (Washington, D.C.: National Journal, 1983, 1985, 1987); biographical information courtesy of governor's office; *The Chronicle of Higher Education,* 11–12–86; James Howard Kunstler, "The Selling of Vermont," *New York Times Magazine* (Apr. 10, 1988):53–54, 66–67, 71; *National Review,* 6–8–92; *The New York Times*: 3–6–84; 9–3–84; 9–9–84; 11–8–84; 11–14–84; 12–11–84; 1–11–85; 11–4–86; 11–6–86; 1–13–88; 4–4–90; 6–21–91; 12–7– 92; 4–7–93; *The Star-Ledger* (Newark, N.J.), 4–4–90; *Time,* 11–21–88; *USA Today*: 10–11–88; 3–7–90; 4–4–90; 11–10–92.

Richard Arkwright Snelling *(Courtesy of Governor's Office)*

RICHARD ARKWRIGHT SNELLING,
1977–1985, 1991

Born in Allentown, Pennsylvania, on February 18, 1927, Snelling was the son of Walter Otheman and Marjorie Gharing Snelling. A Unitarian, he married Barbara Weil in 1947. He was the father of four children.

Snelling attended Lehigh University and the University of Havana, Cuba. He received an A.B. cum laude from Harvard University in 1948. After entering the U.S. Army as a private in 1944, he served in the infantry in the European theater of operations from 1945 until his discharge in 1946. Snelling served as a member of the Vermont Development Commission from 1959 to 1961 and became active in Republican politics by serving as a delegate to Republican national conventions in the 1960s. The president of Shelburne Industries of Shelburne, Vermont, he was also president and chairman of the Executive Committee of the Greater Burlington Industrial Corporation from 1961 to 1964. Snelling was a member of the State Republican Executive Committee from 1963 to 1966 and a longtime member of the Vermont State Republican Committee beginning in 1970.

Although he was an unsuccessful candidate for lieutenant governor of Vermont in 1964 and for governor in 1966, Snelling did serve as a member of the Vermont House of Representatives between 1973 and 1977. He served as house majority leader from 1975 to 1976.

Snelling was first elected as Vermont's chief executive in 1976, the first governor in modern state history to serve four consecutive terms. Defeating William G. Craig to win the Republican nomination for governor that year, he defeated Democrat Stella B. Hackell to win the statehouse by a vote of 99,268 to 75,262. He was inaugurated in January 1977. Snelling's first term was marred by a dispute over the selection of a lieutenant governor, after the Vermont legislature was required to consider the matter because no candidate had received a majority in the general election.

In the 1978 gubernatorial contest Snelling overcame light opposition in the primary and defeated Edwin C. Granani, a state legislator, by a vote of 78,181 to 42,482. By virtue of his victory, Snelling became the only Republican to win a governor's seat in New England that year. Snelling's second term was marked by a serious secession movement involving residents of the islands located in Lake Champlain, who had become bitter over the elimination of a state attorney's office in the county that held jurisdiction over the island. In 1980, Snelling suggested to Canadian officials that they speed up construction of Canada's hydroelectric projects and sell any surplus electricity to New England.

Seeking a third term in 1980, Snelling overwhelmed Clifford Thompson in the Republican primary and then went on to defeat state Attorney General Jerome Diamond, an old political foe, by 123,229 votes to 77,363 votes. During this term in office, Snelling became chairman of the National Governors Association. He established a five–year transportation plan to cope with the loss of federal funds incurred during the Reagan administration and vetoed a bill that would have raised the drinking age to 19.

In his race for a fourth term in 1982, Snelling reneged on an earlier decision not to seek reelection and went on to defeat Lieutenant Governor Madeleine Kunin by a vote of 93,111 to 74,394. Kunin, who had promised to raise the drinking age to 19, contended that the governor had ignored the safety of Vermonters by permitting certain nuclear waste shipments to pass through the state. Snelling responded by pointing to the influx of jobs and businesses into Vermont. During his fourth term, Snelling rose to prominence in the National Governors Association, using that forum and others to make his case that the individual states could not provide services lost through federal budget cuts. An expert on federalism, he became a national spokesman on that issue and a stern critic of Reagan administration proposals.

In January 1984, Snelling surprised the legislature by announcing that he had chosen not to seek reelection to a fifth term. He planned instead to devote himself to finding a solution to the state's fiscal problems.

The legacy of Snelling's first four terms in office was a positive one. The number of jobs in Vermont climbed almost 20 percent, and the state's unemployment rate dipped to one of the lowest in the nation. Snelling was instrumental in securing landmark hydroelectric contracts for long-term electrical power and for initiating major New England–wide contracts with Hydro–Québec. Admirers praised his record of attracting industry to the state. He remained popular, despite his willingness to take tough policy stands on issues and his courage in challenging the Republican White House.

Snelling's retirement from public life proved short-lived. He sought to make a political comeback in 1986 by challenging incumbent Democrat Patrick J. Leahy for the U.S. Senate. Both men were popular among voters who, in the words of one political observer, were being asked to choose "the better of two goods."

Snelling tried to charge Leahy with being a big spender and with not showing up at hearings of the Senate Committee on Agriculture, Nutrition, and Forestry, of which he was a member. The moderate Snelling also tried to portray Leahy as being too liberal for state voters. Political observers felt that Snelling's negative campaign backfired. In his defense, Leahy was able to counter that he would become chairman of the Senate

Agricultural Committee if the Democrats regained control of the Senate. In a race where voters had begun with positive feelings about both candidates, the tide of public opinion turned in favor of Leahy, and he won by 63 percent of the vote, carrying all the state's counties and all but ten of Vermont's towns.

In the wake of Snelling's defeat, the state Republican party strove to recast its image in a new, more liberal light. The need to do so was brought home not only by Leahy's overwhelming victory but also by Democratic Governor Madeleine Kunin's reelection to a second term.

In 1990, after incumbent Madeleine Kunin chose not to seek reelection, Snelling sought once again to return to his old post as governor. Seeing the state's red ink mounting and considering its economy to be in a "shambles," the fiscally conservative Snelling threw his hat in the ring for an unprecedented fifth term. In announcing his bid, he denounced the policies of the outgoing administration. Criticizing its pattern of lavish spending during good times, he insisted that surplus state revenues should have been saved for the lean years to come. Although critics derided Snelling as a "has been," analysts immediately saw him as the frontrunner in the race. Snelling himself was so confident of victory that he put his 46-foot sailboat up for sale months before the election, saying that he wouldn't have time to use it as governor.

Running as a no-nonsense manager, Snelling faced a difficult challenge from Peter F. Welch, the first Democratic president pro tem of the Republican-controlled state senate. Welch sought to undermine Snelling's campaign with negative ads that portrayed his opponent as a wealthy businessman out of touch with the concerns of most Vermonters. Snelling, by contrast, projected the image of a prudent statesman, especially competent in fiscal affairs. He won handily over Welch and two minor party candidates, drawing 52 percent of the vote.

Snelling immediately set about restoring Vermont's fiscal health, paying off a $58 million deficit by pushing through the largest tax increase in state history—more than $90 million—and by imposing deep cuts in spending programs. Despite the tax increases, Snelling proved popular, with public opinion polls registering 65 percent approval ratings.

In the words of former Governor Thomas Salmon, Snelling's current governorship was beginning to take on "heroic proportions" when he died of an apparent heart attack on August 13, 1991, just months into his fifth term. His unexpected death thrust a Democrat, Lieutenant Governor Howard Dean, into the state's highest office. Dean was to serve out the remainder of Snelling's term, set to expire in January 1993.

Snelling served as Vermont's governor for eight and a half years, longer than any other chief executive since 1820. He was the first Vermont governor to die in office since 1870, and the first of the nation's governors to die in office since 1982, when New Hampshire's Hugh Gallen suffered kidney and liver failure. President George Bush called Snelling's death "a real shocker. He was a good man, a good governor."

Snelling's widow, Barbara, a former director of development at the University of Vermont, was under pressure to continue her husband's legacy by seeking the Republican nomination for governor. She declined, however, saying she should start her political career at a lower level. She was elected the state's lieutenant governor in 1992.

Bibliography: Michael Barone et al., *The Almanac of American Politics, 1986, 1988* (Washington, D.C.: National Journal, 1985, 1987); biographical information courtesy of governor's office; *The Chronicle of Higher Education*: 10–31–90; 9–18–91; Phil Duncan, ed., *Politics in America 1992* (Washington, D.C.: Congressional Quarterly Press, 1991); *The Miami Herald,* 8–15–91; *The New York Times*: 11–3–76; 1–4–77; 1–14–79; 1–6–84; 11–8–84; 9–9–86; 11–15–87; 4–4–90; 9–12–90; 11–7–90; 8–15–91; *The Star-Ledger* (Newark, N.J.), 8–15–91; *USA Today*: 11–8–90; 8–15–91.

HOWARD DEAN, 1991–

Born in New York City on November 17, 1948, Dean grew up in East Hampton, New York, and became a resident of Vermont in 1978. He was educated at Yale University (B.A., 1971) and Albert Einstein College of Medicine (M.D., 1978). In 1988, he was awarded an honorary doctor of law degree by Southern Vermont College. He is married to Judith Steinberg, M.D., and has two children. He is the nation's only sitting governor who is also a physician.

A Democrat, Dean first became interested in politics while working for Jimmy Carter's presidential campaign. He was a delegate to the Democratic National Convention in 1976. As a member of the Vermont House of Representatives from 1983 to 1986, Dean served on three committees: Education, Municipal Corporations and Elections, and Rules. He held a leadership position as assistant minority leader from 1985 to 1986.

Concurrently serving as a clinical professor of medicine at the University of Vermont, Dean recognized that doctors seldom run for public office. However, he had been urging the medical profession to seek more of a leadership role in helping to stem soaring health care costs and provide care to more Americans. In order for doctors to get their views across, he insisted on the necessity of political involvement through medical societies, the community, and elected office.

Acting upon that philosophy, he sought the lieutenant governorship in 1986. Subsequently reelected in 1988 and 1990, he involved himself in several areas of concern: creating partnerships between business and government; studying Vermont's liability insurance problems; promoting the availability of affordable, high-quality child care; and seeking solutions to the problem of youth suicide. In 1991, he was named to chair the Task Force on Health and Human Services of the National Conference of Lieutenant Governors.

As lieutenant governor, Dean acceded to the governorship suddenly and in tragic circumstances, upon the untimely death of incumbent Richard Snelling. Dean was sworn in as his successor on August 14, 1991. Moving into the statehouse was not a goal that he had ever sought. Although in 1990 he had been mentioned as a possible Democratic successor to retiring Governor Madeleine Kunin, he had decided against the run because of the toll he feared it might take on his young children. Even as Dean assumed the governorship, he was not a household name, despite three statewide electoral victories. In a 1991 poll, he outpaced all other

Howard Dean *(Courtesy of Governor's Office)*

Vermont politicians in the percentage of those surveyed who had never heard of him.

Serving out Snelling's unexpired term to January 1993, he enjoyed a political honeymoon within the state, retaining Snelling's staff and moderate policies. He was overwhelmingly elected to his own term as governor in November 1992, winning 75 percent of the vote against Republican John McClaughry, a state legislator and former White House aide. In his race against the staunchly conservative Republican, Dean drew bipartisan support from moderates in both parties who liked his social liberalism and fiscal conservatism.

In office, Dean has been especially interested in health care issues, paying particular attention to national health insurance. He drew considerable national notice in 1992 when he signed into law a plan to give Vermont universal health care by 1995. The law created a state agency, the Vermont Health Care Authority, with power to negotiate lower rates with doctors and hospitals in the state. Using what Dean called "enormous leverage," it should have the ability to gain better insurance coverage at lower rates. The law was seen as one of the more ambitious in a series of recent efforts by states to tackle problems of runaway medical costs and increasing numbers of uninsured.

On the national level, Dean currently serves as cochair of the National Governors Association's Health Care Task Force.

Bibliography: Biographical information courtesy of governor's office; *The Chronicle of Higher Education,* 9–18–91; *The New York Times:* 4–4–90; 8–15–91; 9–3–91; 5–12–92; 10–26–92; 11–4–92; 11–5–92; *USA Today:* 8–16–91; 5–13–92; 11–4–92.

Gerald L. Baliles *(Courtesy of Governor's Office)*

VIRGINIA

GERALD L. BALILES, 1986–1990

Baliles was born on July 8, 1940, in a mountain farming community in Patrick County, Virginia. Married to the former Jean Patterson, he and his wife have two children.

Graduating as the leader of the Cadet Corps from Fishburne Military School in Waynesboro, Virginia, 1959, he went on to earn his undergraduate degree at Connecticut's Wesleyan University in 1963. He received a J.D. from the University of Virginia in 1967. From 1967 to 1975, he worked in the state attorney general's office as an assistant attorney general and then deputy attorney general, where he developed a reputation as an expert in environmental law. Joining a private law firm in 1975, he also began his political career that year. Defeating the incumbent in an upset, he won a seat in the state House of Delegates, where he served from 1976 until 1982. During his first term in office, he was voted one of the most effective members of the legislature in a survey by the *Virginian-Pilot*.

In 1981, Baliles was elected state attorney general, part of a Democratic sweep that year of the offices of governor, lieutenant governor, and attorney general. As attorney general, he served as chairman of the Southern Association of Attorneys General. In 1985, he was selected as the most outstanding attorney general in the nation by his peers in the National Association of Attorneys General.

Baliles sought the governorship in 1985, looking to succeed his friend and political mentor Charles Robb, constitutionally barred from succeeding himself. Forging a coalition of blacks and whites, he defeated Lieutenant Governor Richard Davis in the state party convention to win the Democratic gubernatorial nomination. In the general election, he faced Richmond lawyer Wyatt B. Durrette, a former state legislator who had lost races for lieutenant governor in 1977 and attorney general in 1981.

In the campaign, Baliles worked hard to establish an identity for himself separate from that of the Robb administration of which he had been a part, and whose policies of fiscal conservatism and social moderation he pledged to continue. Because the ideological differences between the two candidates were not great, Baliles emphasized that he had more state government service and leadership experience than his opponent.

Baliles' victory, with 55 percent of the vote, was a historic sweep in a state long considered to be a conservative stronghold. The race drew national attention because of the nature of the Democratic ticket: Baliles' successful running mates included a black candidate for lieutenant governor, L. Douglas Wilder, and a female candidate for attorney general, Mary Sue Terry.

In office, Baliles was regarded by political observers as a tough, intelligent, and shrewd politician and viewed as one of the brightest stars in the nation's gubernatorial corps. Highly successful in working his programs through the legislature, he led a historic statewide program to modernize the state's infrastructure with a $12 billion transportation package for the improvement of roads, seaports, airports, and mass transit. He established Virginia's first cabinet-level post for economic development and directed the expansion of world trade promotion initiatives. As Virginia's chief advocate for economic development and improved trading relationships, he led eight trade and business development missions overseas, including trips to China, Denmark, Hong Kong, Israel, Italy, Japan, Korea, Sweden, Taiwan, and Turkey. As a result of these efforts, exports of Virginia products increased to record levels: Within two years, exported products accounted for over 25 percent of the state's economic growth. In addition, foreign investment in Virginia by the United Kingdom, the Netherlands, Germany, and Japan increased significantly.

In line with these efforts, Baliles spearheaded a vigorous program of education reform aimed especially at preparation for work in an international marketplace. He initiated several new programs designed both to improve the image of the state and to strengthen the effectiveness of its high-technology training. Most notable in this area were the Governor's Language Academies, the Japanese Language and Culture initiatives at several Virginia colleges and universities, and the introduction and enhancement of the study of foreign languages and geography in the public schools.

Active in cooperative efforts and programs with his fellow governors, Baliles served as chairman of the International Trade Committee of the National Governors Association, chairman of the Southern States Energy Board, and chairman of the Advisory Council for International Education in the Southern Governors Association. While chairman of the Southern Growth Policies Board (1987–1988), Baliles introduced awareness of the international economy to southern regional economic development efforts. The historic annual meeting of the board focused the attention of the 14 member states on trade potential with developing countries and emerging trading partners, including India, Latin America, and the then–Soviet Union.

Vice-chairman of the National Governors Association from 1987 to 1988, he succeeded New Hampshire's John Sununu to the chairmanship in 1988. During his year in that post, he directed the attention of his fellow governors to international economic development, publishing his agenda in a policy paper, "America in Transition: The International Frontier." Concurrent with these objectives, he led a delegation of governors to Brussels for meetings with officials of the European Economic Community and the North Atlantic Treaty Organization (NATO).

Prevented by state law from seeking a second consecutive term, Baliles retired from the governorship in 1990. Among his last actions as chief executive were numerous cost-cutting efforts to ensure that the proposed 1990–1992 biennial budget of $26 billion would be balanced, as mandated by the state constitution. These included reducing spending by state agencies from 1 to 5 percent, limiting teacher salary increases, and reclaiming lottery profits designated for construction projects.

Upon retiring from the governorship, Baliles became a partner in the Richmond law firm of Hunton and Williams, where he specializes in trade issues. He has also worked as a lobbyist seeking to lure businesses to Virginia. Although there was some speculation that he might challenge Republican incumbent John W. Warner for the U.S. Senate in 1990, the run never materialized.

With the accession of his friend and fellow governor Bill Clinton to the White House, Baliles' name has surfaced as a potential appointee to a number of national posts, including the Justice Department and the Supreme Court. He is presently chairing a 26-member U.S. Airline Commission appointed by Clinton to give recommendations on how to help the nation's troubled airline industry.

Bibliography: Michael Barone et al., *The Almanac of American Politics, 1986, 1988* (Washington, D.C.: National Journal, 1985, 1987); biographical information courtesy of governor's office; *The New York Times*: 11–5–85; 11–6–85; 1–12–86; 7–29–87; 3–22–88; 7–30–89; 1–14–90; 11–7–90; 4–21–92; *The Star-Ledger* (Newark, N.J.), 2–6–93; *USA Today,* 5–25–93.

Lawrence Douglas Wilder *(Courtesy of Governor's Office)*

LAWRENCE DOUGLAS ("DOUG") WILDER, 1990–1994

Wilder was born on January 17, 1931, in Richmond, Virginia, the grandson of slaves. His namesakes include abolitionist-orator Frederick Douglass and poet Paul Lawrence Dunbar. Making his home in Richmond's segregated Church Hill neighborhood, he grew up in a large, deeply religious Baptist family. His father Robert was an insurance salesman and his mother Beulah worked as a maid. Wilder is a 1951 graduate of Virginia Union University and a 1959 graduate of Howard University School of Law. While in law school, he met and married Eunice Montgomery. Before divorcing in 1978, the couple had three children. Wilder served in the Korean War, 1952 to 1953, during which he received the Bronze Star for heroism in ground combat.

A Democrat, Wilder founded a private law practice in Richmond—Wilder, Gregory, and Martin—before his 1969 election to the Virginia Senate. The first black to serve in that chamber since Reconstruction, he served five terms in office, 1969 to 1985. He began his senate career as a confrontational liberal. Sporting a bushy Afro and calling himself a "maverick firebrand," he called for fair housing legislation, more minority hiring in business, and the abolition of the death penalty. In his maiden speech, he condemned the state as racist to the core and demanded the dropping of its official song, "Carry Me Back to Old Virginia." Because the song was a nostalgic recollection of plantation life and included the words *massah* and *darkie,* he charged that it was insulting to blacks. The call marked him as a radical in the eyes of the Virginia establishment.

Over the years, however, his career changed course. Moderating his position on key issues such as the death penalty, he became known as one of the legislature's great compromisers and ultimately became a respected political insider, assuming the chairmanship of key committees: Transportation; Rehabilitation and Social Services; Privileges and Elections; the Advisory Legislative Council; and the Democratic Steering Committee. Consistently named one of the state's most effective leaders in annual surveys conducted by the Norfolk *Virginian-Pilot,* he sponsored legislation that toughened penalties for capital murderers and prison escapees, mandated investigation of discriminatory housing practices by real estate agents, regulated drug paraphernalia, and established a state holiday for Dr. Martin Luther King, Jr.

Elected lieutenant governor of Virginia in 1985 in an election that was the first sign of a new kind of politics emerging in the state, he served as chairman of the National Democratic Lieutenant Governors Association and of the Drug Interdiction Task Force of the National Conference of Lieutenant Governors. Political observers feel that he used his four years in Virginia's number-two post to expand and strengthen his contacts throughout the state.

As part of the administration of Governor Gerald Baliles, who along with his Democratic predecessor Chuck Robb altered the liberal image that plagued the Democratic party throughout the late 1960s and 1970s, Wilder established his reputation as a pragmatic and able black politician able to win white votes. He depicted himself as the logical heir to this moderate model, one that had enabled Virginia Democrats to buck the winning Republican trends of the 1980s. Already the highest-ranking black elected official in the country as lieutenant governor, Wilder was nominated for governor without opposition at the 1989 state Democratic convention, itself a striking development in a state that is 81 percent white and was once the centerpiece of the old Confederacy.

His opponent in the general election was former state Attorney General J. Marshall Coleman, a conservative who had lost a previous bid for governor in 1981. Coleman entered the race already badly damaged by a bruising primary fight, the GOP's first in 40 years, and one of the state's most acrimonious and hard fought.

In the campaign, Wilder posed as a fiscal conservative with a social conscience. His "Three for Virginia" plan called for permanent tax relief, a fight against drugs and drug-related crime, and the creation of jobs and housing for rural Virginians. Focusing on the booming prosperity of the state under its string of Democratic governors, he took pains to present himself not so much as something new but as a "traditional Virginian" in his stands on taxes, crime, and labor. To emphasize his tough, no-new-taxes position, he even broke with his own party on the issue of increasing the state sales tax to fund transportation aid.

No great ideological gulf separated the candidates. Each opposed any tax increase, favored the death penalty and right to work laws, and stressed his commitment to education and the fight against drugs and crime. Coleman tried to suggest, however, that Wilder was hiding his real ideology, and painted him as a poor manager of his personal and professional affairs. He criticized Wilder for accepting honoraria for speeches given in Virginia and accused him of being in effect a "slumlord" in the Church Hill section of Richmond where he had grown up.

The issue that gave Wilder the edge in this hard-fought and narrowly decided race was the increasingly volatile one of abortion rights. Wilder built his campaign around the prochoice position to an extent that no major candidate for governor in any state had ever done before. As such, the Virginia race seemed an important bellwether of the burgeoning politics of abortion, a controversy that was to have such an impact on national politics over the years ahead.

While both candidates were careful to avoid openly raising the issue of race, Wilder supporters charged that Coleman's TV ads tried to stir racial fears with suggestive images. Political analysts concluded that race was indeed a factor in the campaign both in making the turnout on both sides far higher than it had ever been before and in the tightness of the final results. It was apparent from a study of vote tallies that a significant number of white voters clearly supported other white Democrats on the ticket while shunning Wilder, since his victory margin was significantly less than that of his running mates for attorney general and lieutenant governor. Wilder's victory margin was the closest in state gubernatorial history: only 6,854 votes, or about three-eighths of 1 percent. Charging unspecified irregularities in the election, Coleman even demanded a recount, although this resulted in only an insignificant change in the final tally.

Despite his razor-thin victory margin, Wilder's win made history. Sworn into office on January 13, 1990, he changed the face of American politics, becoming the nation's highest-ranking black elected official and a political figure to be reckoned with nationally. The first American black ever elected governor of a state, he was hailed as a symbol not just of a changing Virginia but of a changing South and of a changing nation. He inspired other politicians, notably Atlanta Mayor Andrew Young, to make subsequent gubernatorial runs elsewhere, and he provided a new model for a successful black politician—pragmatic, able, and nonthreatening. Able to attract white voters, he preached a gospel of fiscal responsibility, back-to-basics values, and economic growth.

Once in office, Wilder promised no wholesale shakeups and chose his appointees from the state's political mainstream. He followed the trend set by recent Virginia governors and appointed women and members of ethnic minorities to government posts, boards, and commissions. The most serious issue he faced was a pressing budget deficit, brought on by a falloff in the state's economy and by a steadily increasing demand for state services. Adamant from his first day in office that he would not resort to tax increases, he focused instead on cutting spending, deferring the construction of public works, canceling pay raises, and laying off state workers. In his most publicized move, he ordered state agencies and schools to divest themselves of stocks held in companies doing business with South Africa.

He did, however, have his critics. Black liberals, especially Jesse Jackson, publicly debated him, suggesting that what Wilder called "mainstream politics" was leaving the poor and needy in a social and economic "backwater." Others felt that his national stature and frequent out-of-state engagements caused him to pay too little attention to state affairs.

There was also widespread grousing among state educators and editorialists about his appointment of Patricia Kluge, the estranged wife of one of the world's wealthiest men, to the board of the University of Virginia. Critics contended that she had little experience in education matters and pointed out that she and her husband John had been major contributors both to the university and to Wilder's own campaign. Others focused on Wilder's personal faults and foibles: his penchant for political vindictiveness and opportunism, and his tendency to be a kind of political chameleon, moved not by principle but by political expediency.

By far the two most serious questions were raised in the summer of 1991. In the wake of Clarence Thomas' nomination to the U.S. Supreme Court, Wilder suggested that Thomas should face sharp questioning about his views on abortion because of his long-standing affiliation with the Catholic church. He ultimately had to apologize for questioning whether Thomas would allow his "allegiance to the Pope" to interfere with his duties as a Supreme Court justice. Also that summer, he was damaged by the public unmasking of his nasty, bitter, and long-running feud with U.S. Senator Charles Robb, his longtime rival and one of the state's leading Democrats. In an ugly affair christened Virginia's Watergate, Robb asserted that Wilder had ordered the state police to investigate his private life, while Wilder countered that the senator had obtained tapes of his private phone conversations. Wilder later had to issue two apologies for misleading reporters by denying he had ordered a state police investigation into rumors of drug use and sexual escapades by Robb.

Wilder had attained such prominence as the nation's first black governor that it came as no surprise when he announced his intention to seek the presidency in the election of 1992. Calling himself the "longest of longshots" when he entered the race in September of 1991, he attacked the divisive economic and social policies of the Bush administration. His "Put America First" crusade hoped to attract middle-class voters, black and white, with a call for an immediate $50 billion cut in federal spending. The savings were to be used to cut taxes and to send needed dollars to cities and states to handle social problems like drug abuse and homelessness. Wilder boasted of his success in balancing Virginia's budget in the face of revenue shortfalls and without raising taxes, while supporters contended he could bridge the ideological split that had denied Democrats the presidency in recent elections.

Despite such high expectations, however, Wilder's candidacy never crystallized. He faced huge fund-raising obstacles and was never able to put together a credible and effective organization. With polls indicating that he was making little headway, he became the first candidate to drop out of the Democratic field, less than one month before the first primary of the 1992 campaign season. Never before in more than 20 years of political involvement had Wilder suffered a campaign defeat.

In pulling out of the race, Wilder explained that he didn't have the time to seek the nomination and also to run his state, which was facing its worst budget crisis in half a century. Polls in Virginia were showing his popularity steadily dropping, and his political future there seemed more and more in doubt. The 1991 statewide elections registered a Republican sweep. The general assembly that convened in January 1992 saw the Republicans as a major legislative force for the first time since Reconstruction. The most telling sign of voter discontent with incumbent Democrats was the overwhelming victory of Republican George Allen in the 1993 gubernatorial race to succeed Wilder himself.

Given the one-term limitations on Virginia governors and his sinking approval ratings, Wilder's political future is somewhat in doubt. After much speculation, he announced his intention to challenge rival Chuck Robb for the U.S. Senate in 1994, a race that promises to be especially bitter and nasty considering the rancor between the two men. Wilder has even gone so far as to say he might run as an independent if he doesn't get the Democratic nod. Regardless of the outcome, history will credit Wilder with causing a major revolution in racial politics by becoming the first black ever to be elected chief executive of any state and then going on to seek the presidency. He remains among the most conservative of the nation's major black political figures and a force to be reckoned with in national Democratic politics.

Bibliography: B. Drummond Ayres, Jr., "Wilder's Flier," *New York Times Magazine* (Jan. 12, 1992): 30–33, 48; biographical information courtesy of governor's office; *The Chronicle of Higher Education*: 4–10–91; 8–28–91; Phil Duncan, ed., *Politics in America 1992* (Washington, D.C.: Congressional Quarterly Press, 1991); Thomas R. Morris, "Virginia: L. D. Wilder: Governing and Campaigning," in Thad Beyle, ed., *Governors and Hard Times* (Washington, D.C.: Congressional Quarterly Press, 1992); *Newsweek*: 5–14–90; 5–13–91; 7–15–91; *The New York Times*: 6–10–89; 6–15–89; 9–18–89; 10–15–89; 11–6–89; 11–9–89; 11–26–89; 11–28–89; 12–22–89; 1–10–90; 1–14–90; 5–13–90; 10–14–90; 11–11–90; 3–6–91; 4–4–91; 6–14–91; 6–27–91; 7–8–91; 8–28–91; 9–14–91; 10–15–91; 11–8–91; 11–19–91; 12–25–91; 12–30–91; 1–9–92; 1–11–92; 5–23–92; *The Star-Ledger* (Newark, N.J.): 6–11–89; 10–8–89; 1–9–92; *USA Today*: 6–14–89; 9–21–89; 11–28–89; 12–10–89; 2–22–91; 6–10–91; 7–15–91; 8–30–91; 9–16–91; 5–27–92; 1–28–93; 3–19–93; 6–25–93; *The Washington Post*, 1–6–91.

George F. Allen *(Courtesy of George Allen Governor Campaign)*

GEORGE F. ALLEN, 1994–

Born in Whittier, California, on March 8, 1952, Allen is the son of George H. Allen, a former coach of the Washington Redskins, and Henrietta Lumbroso Allen. He and his wife, the former Susan Brown, have two children, Tyler and Forrest. He is a Presbyterian.

A graduate of the University of Virginia, Allen earned his B.A. in history in 1974 and his J.D. in 1977. Following his graduation, he clerked for U.S. District Court Judge Glen Williams before opening a private law practice in Charlottesville.

A Republican, Allen served nine years in the Virginia House of Delegates, where he rose to the rank of Assistant Minority Leader. In office, he led a successful seven-year effort to adopt a constitutional amendment that directed proceeds from the sale of confiscated drug dealer assets to local law enforcement agencies. In 1991, he moved to Washington after victory in a special congressional election. Serving one term before his 7th district seat fell victim to re-districting, he supported Republican cost-cutting initiatives, backing a balanced budget amendment, the line item veto, and limits on tax increases.

In June 1993 Allen received a record-breaking 64.1 percent of the vote at the Republican state convention to win his party's nomination for governor in the race to succeed outgoing incumbent Douglas Wilder. That convention, as well as the gubernatorial race that ensued, was noteworthy for the involvement of the religious right, which mobilized voters through registration drives and the distribution of over one million voter guides in church bulletins. These highlighted candidate stands on hot button issues like abortion, taxes, education, welfare, and social policy. The Republican candidate for lieutenant governor—elected in a separate ballot from the gubernatorial nominee—was Michael P. Farris, an outspoken fundamentalist linked to the now-defunct Moral Majority of the Reverend Jerry Falwell.

Early polls showed Allen trailing his better-known Democratic opponent by as much as 30 points. Mary Sue Terry, striving to become the first female governor in state history, had been a state legislator and two-term attorney general and was a long-time associate of the Virginia Democratic dynasty that had produced former governors Chuck Robb, Gerald Baliles, and outgoing incumbent Doug Wilder. Once considered a shoo-in for the state's highest office, Terry, however, stumbled badly in her quest for the statehouse. Struggling to distance herself from a Clinton administration that registered only 30 percent approval ratings in the state, she suffered, too, from her image as the consummate political insider. Virginia voters seemed in the mood for a change after a 12-year Democratic lock on the statehouse. Polls showed that the bitter public feuding and nasty rivalry between Robb and Wilder, the state's top two Democrats, had seriously alienated voters. Terry was further weakened by Virginia's worsening economy, fueled in part by Clinton-era defense cutbacks in a state heavily dependent on defense spending. Despite name recognition and a substantial warchest, Terry watched her once substantial lead in the polls evaporate, and she came to be known by the stinging sobriquet "Mary Souffle."

Allen, by contrast, waged an effective campaign despite never before having sought statewide office. Benefiting from a folksy, down-home appeal (he is partial to cowboy boots and chewing tobacco), Allen focused his campaign on the crime issue. While Terry championed gun control with a call for a five-day waiting period on handgun purchases, Allen called for more police, stronger crime laws, and the denial of parole to serious offenders. Winning the support of the Fraternal Order of Police, he presented himself as an agent of change and championed a conservative agenda: pledging to veto any sales or income tax increases; calling for "workfare not welfare," and presenting a "Champion Schools Initiative" to improve the public schools. In a campaign noteworthy for the involvement of the religious right, Allen gained further support with his call for a voucher system to facilitate school choice, providing tax credits for children attending private or religious schools.

Although Terry strove to distance herself from the unpopular Clinton administration—denouncing his tax increases and proposal to lift the ban on gays in the military—Allen persisted in painting the election as a referendum on Clintonomics.

At times, the tactics of both candidates sparked controversy. Terry's attempts to link Allen with the "radical religious right" were denounced as religious bigotry, while Allen surrogates raised eyebrows with their suggestions that the unmarried and childless Terry was somehow less suited for the statehouse than was Allen, the Republican family man.

In the end, Allen triumphed with a remarkable come-from-behind victory. His 58-percent win over Terry was one of the largest in recent state history, and he became Virginia's first Republican governor since John N. Dalton's term expired in 1982. Allen's victory encouraged and enheartened Virginia Republicans seeking to upset incumbent U.S. Senator Chuck Robb in 1994.

Allen has presented himself as a new-generation Republican "who trusts people as opposed to trusting the government." As one of his first actions in office, he has promised to appoint a Blue Ribbon Strike Force made up of business and community leaders to identify wasteful spending practices and inefficiencies in all levels of state government.

Bibliography: Biographical information courtesy of the George Allen Governor campaign; *The New York Times:* 6–6–93; 6–7–93; 10–31–93; 11–3–93; *The Record* (Bergen County, N.J.), 10–22–93; *The Star-Ledger* (Newark, N.J.), 10–24–93; *USA Today:* 6–7–93; 8–2–93; 8–27–93; 9–15–93; 10–19–93; 11–3–93.

Booth Gardner *(Courtesy of Governor's Office)*

WASHINGTON

BOOTH GARDNER, 1985–1993

Booth Gardner was born in Tacoma, Washington, on August 21, 1936, the son of Bryson Gardner and Evelyn Booth Gardner. Married to the former Jean Forstrom, he has two children.

Gardner received a B.A. in business from the University of Washington in 1958 and an M.B.A. from Harvard University in 1963. Prior to beginning his political career, he served as assistant to the dean at the Harvard Business School from 1966 to 1967 and as director of the School of Business and Economics at the University of Puget Sound from 1967 to 1972. A Democrat, he was first elected to public office in 1970 when he became a state senator from the 26th District. Serving one term, he chaired the Education Committee in addition to serving on committees dealing with manufacturing, development, commerce, and regulatory agencies.

He left the legislature in 1973 to devote time to his posts as president of the Laird Norton Company, a national building supply firm, and as a member of the board of directors of the Weyerhauser Company, the timber giant to which he is family heir. Before returning to public life, he also taught economics and held an administrative job at Pacific Lutheran University in Tacoma.

In 1980, Gardner was elected as the first county executive of Pierce County, the state's second most populous. As county executive, he was credited with turning a $4.7 million county deficit into a $4 million surplus by the time of his accession to the governorship.

Seeking the governorship in 1984, he upset state Senator Jim McDermott to win his party's nomination. McDermott had been defeated four years earlier by Republican John Spellman, the incumbent whom Gardner sought to unseat.

In the campaign, Gardner presented himself as an outsider with a fresh approach to government. As a business executive himself, he promised to bring better management to government and to deal effectively with the state's economic problems. As a political moderate, he drew considerable support from conservatives and independents. He also enjoyed the benefits of his vast personal fortune, which he tapped to help finance his campaign. Gardner defeated the incumbent with 53 percent of the vote.

Spellman's unexpected loss was attributed to several factors, notably a lingering recession in the logging and lumber industries.

A strong candidate for reelection in 1988, Gardner won by a landslide over archconservative Republican Bob Williams, a state representative and evangelical Christian. With his convincing victory, Gardner bucked a trend in the state, which had not reelected a governor since 1972.

Political observers viewed Gardner as an extremely effective governor, the first, in the opinion of some, to establish real command over state government since Daniel Evans retired in 1976. His communication skills caused him to be compared with Ronald Reagan, another "Great Communicator." Indeed, Democratic state legislator Joanne Brekke once christened Gardner "the Ronald Reagan of the state of Washington."

Highlights of Gardner's two administrations were his efforts to reform the education and welfare systems, to make health care accessible and affordable, and to clean and protect the environment. He oversaw Washington's economic recovery and elevated the state's role in international trade, stressing the need for Washington to compete economically with other portions of the Pacific Rim. In sharp contrast to other states suffering from the economic decline of the early 1990s, Gardner could announce with pride in mid-1991 that his state was "one of the most economically healthy states in the nation."

Bucking a longtime historical tradition, Gardner proposed a 3.9 percent income tax in 1989, at the same time that he proposed a significant reduction in the state sales tax. His motive, he explained, was tax relief for low- and moderate-income citizens, since an income tax was more equitable than the regressive sales tax.

In the area of education, Gardner was an activist governor, providing new funds to accommodate enrollment growth in the state's colleges and universities and to add nursing and engineering programs at some branch campuses. His drive to improve the state's work force focused even more attention on two-year institutions, while four-year institutions, inspired by his example, devoted increased efforts to improving elementary and secondary education.

Gardner drew national attention in 1992 by signing a measure that outlawed the sale to minors of any music deemed obscene. In signing the bill, he said he wanted "to send a warning shot across the bow of the recording industry." He also hoped the law would "give parents some needed assistance" in limiting their children's access to certain kinds of music. The controversial new law made record store retailers and their employees criminally liable for selling such music to anyone under 18.

After serving as vice-chair of the Western Governors Association and of the Committee on Foreign Trade of the National Governors Association, Gardner became chair of the National Governors Association in 1991. He devoted his year as chair to promoting health care reform, mapping a strategy for the nation's governors that would ensure every American had adequate and affordable health care by the year 2000.

Gardner surprised and disappointed admirers with his October 1991 announcement that he would retire from the governorship at the end of his second term. He insisted that his decision was unrelated to a 1992 ballot measure, ultimately successful, that limited future governors to two terms. He also ruled out a future challenge to incumbent U.S. Senator Brock Adams, a fellow Democrat. Friends suggested that Gardner was interested in a college presidency or a return to private business. There had also been some speculation that Gardner might be named secretary of health and human services in the Clinton administration, a move that never materialized.

Bibliography: Michael Barone et al., *The Almanac of American Politics, 1986, 1988* (Washington, D.C.: National Journal, 1985, 1987); biographical information courtesy of governor's office; *The Chronicle of Higher Education,* 8–28–91; *The Miami Herald,* 8–13–91; *The New York Times:* 9–16–84; 11–8–84; 1–17–85; 11–9–88; 2–3–91; 3–21–92; *The Star-Ledger* (Newark, N.J.): 8–16–91; 11–6–92; *USA Today:* 10–11–88; 11–10–88; 1–12–89; 8–16–91; 10–23–91.

Michael Lowry *(Courtesy of Governor's Office)*

MICHAEL LOWRY, 1993–

Lowry was born on March 8, 1939, in St. John, Washington, where his family had first homesteaded in 1882. A graduate of Endicott High School and Washington State University, he and his wife Mary have one daughter.

A Democrat, Lowry began his public service career as a staff director of the Ways and Means Committee of the Washington State Senate. From there, he went on to hold a wide variety of positions in state and local government. Public affairs director for Group Health Cooperative of Puget Sound from 1974 to 1975, he was elected to the King County Council in 1975. Becoming chairman of the council in 1977, he was elected president of the Washington Association of Counties in 1978.

Lowry made his first bid for higher office in 1978, when he won election to the U.S. House of Representatives. Representing Washington's Seventh Congressional District, he was reelected four times, serving a total of ten years in Congress. Considered to be among the most liberal members of the House during his tenure, Lowry served on the House Budget Committee, the House Banking and Urban Affairs Committee, and the House Merchant Marine and Fisheries Committee. Among his noteworthy legislative achievements were the creation of two new marine sanctuaries for his home state, passage of the Homeless Person Assistance Act, and securing the first federal appropriations for AIDS research.

Lowry also experienced two political setbacks early in his political career. Attempting to move on to the Senate after the death of Scoop Jackson in 1983, he lost a special election to former Governor Dan Evans. This defeat was followed by the loss of his congressional seat. After serving five terms in the House, he was defeated by Republican Slade Gorton in 1988. His narrow 51 percent to 49 percent loss was attributed by analysts to a failure to attract traditional blue-collar Democrats.

Out of office, Lowry continued his political involvement, teaching public administration at Seattle University's Institute for Public Service. He also joined with former Governor and U.S. Senator Dan Evans to chair the Washington Wildlife and Recreation Coalition, a nonprofit organization dedicated to preserving the environment, natural wildlife habitats, and scenic beauty of his home state.

In 1992, the retirement of popular two-term Governor Booth Gardner threw the race for the statehouse wide open. Lowry's contest with state Attorney General Ken Eikenberry was described by analysts as a classic liberal-conservative confrontation. Eikenberry, a former Federal Bureau of Investigation (FBI) agent, promoted a strong antitax message, warning state voters that Washington could not afford to fall into the economic morass plaguing neighboring California. Lowry, by contrast, did not shirk from admitting that higher taxes might be needed to balance the state budget. Long associated with the party's liberal wing, Lowry was able to pull out an upset victory in the race by broadening his appeal to moderate Republicans. Successful in his attempt to attract business-minded supporters to his campaign, he also benefited from pledges to avoid negative advertising and to spurn any campaign contributions above $1,500. In his appeal for ethics in government, Lowry was helped considerably by an emerging scandal in the Eikenberry camp. According to press reports, an Eikenberry supporter had tried to solicit a $50,000 contribution from a University of Washington regent in return for a promise of reappointment. Although Eikenberry dismissed the story as a lie, it seemed nonetheless to lend credence to Lowry's populist call for a new citizen involvement in government. He won the election with 53 percent of the vote, the first governor in state history to succeed a governor of the same party.

In office, Lowry has made balancing the state budget and health care reform his top priorities. In May 1993, he signed a state health care package that included basic elements common to Bill Clinton's heralded national reform program. The centerpiece of the Lowry plan is the requirement that employers contribute at least half of their workers' premiums.

Lowry has also promised to support job training programs and to increase spending on public education.

Bibliography: Michael Barone and Grant Ujifusa, *The Almanac of American Politics, 1992* (Washington, D.C.: National Journal, 1991); biographical information courtesy of governor's office; *The Chronicle of Higher Education,* 11-11-92; *The New York Times:* 10-26-92; 11-5-92; 5-19-93; *USA Today,* 11-4-92.

WEST VIRGINIA

ARCH A. MOORE, JR., 1969–1977, 1985–1989

Born in Moundsville, West Virginia, on April 16, 1923, Moore is the son of Arch A. Moore and Genevieve Jones Moore. A Methodist, he married Shelley S. Riley in 1949. The couple has three children.

Moore was educated in the public schools of Marshall County. He enrolled at Lafayette College in 1941 but left to join the U.S. Infantry during World War II, going on to win several combat decorations. He completed his education after the war, graduating from West Virginia University with an A.B. in political science and from the West Virginia University College of Law with a J.D. in 1951.

A dominant figure in West Virginia public life for more than three decades, Moore was the first governor in the state's modern history to be reelected to a four-year term and the first governor in state history to be elected to three four-year terms. His victories were all the more impressive since he is a Republican in a state where Democrats dominate by more than 2–1.

Moore began his political career in 1952, winning a seat in the West Virginia House of Delegates. In 1956, he was elected to the U.S. House of Representatives, winning reelection by impressive margins in 1958, 1960, 1962, 1964, and 1966. He chose to leave his safe congressional seat to seek the governorship in 1968, winning the statehouse by a narrow margin in a year when his party's candidate for president failed to carry the state. A popular governor, he won a change in the state constitution that allowed him to run for—and ultimately win—a second consecutive term in 1972. Four years later, he made plans to seek a third term, contending that since the constitution had been revised while he was in office, his second term could be counted as his first. The state supreme court, however, rejected this argument, and he was forced to step down after the completion of his second term in 1977.

A self-made man with a booming voice and a no-nonsense manner, Moore was a popular governor. In fact, his career was so successful that one faction of the dominant party became known as "Arch Moore Democrats," those who stuck with the Democratic ticket unless Moore was running for office. Even Democrats conceded that Moore had a unique

Arch A. Moore, Jr. *(Courtesy of Governor's Office)*

talent for winning compromises from union members and management whose differences seemed irreconcilable. In his first two terms in office, he also became a prominent leader among the nation's governors. In 1971, he became the first and only West Virginia governor to be elected chairman of the National Governors Association. He also served as cochairman of the Appalachian Regional Commission in 1971, president of the Council of State Governments in 1972–1973, and national chairman of the Republican Governors Association in 1976. An educationally oriented governor, he served as president of the Education Commission of the States from 1974 to 1976. He also made an impact in the international arena. In 1974, he was one of the first governors to be invited to visit the People's Republic of China. In 1976, he served as the special representative of President Gerald Ford and formally opened the Bicentennial Exposition of the "World of Franklin and Jefferson" in Warsaw, Poland.

Despite these successes, Moore's future seemed uncertain after he was indicted on extortion charges in 1976, the final year of his second term. Although acquitted of charges that he had extorted $25,000 from a financier seeking a state bank charter, the indictment seemed to affect the voters' attitude. He lost races for the U.S. Senate and for the governorship in 1980, the first defeats in his political career.

In 1984, Moore struggled with a decision to seek either the governorship or the U.S. Senate seat being vacated by retiring incumbent Jennings Randolph. Reluctant to face his old nemesis Jay Rockefeller—the man who had defeated him for the governorship in 1980—Moore decided to seek a third term as governor rather than run for the Senate against Rockefeller. Unopposed in the Republican primary, he defeated Democrat Clyde M. See, Jr., speaker of the House of Delegates, with 53 percent of the vote to win an unprecedented third term in the statehouse. In the campaign, he pledged to enact the "most revolutionary economic development program ever put before a legislative body." He also promised not to raise taxes.

Moore faced serious economic challenges during his third term and entered office with state voters in a bleak mood. The state suffered from the highest unemployment rate in the nation and, dependent as it was on basic industries, had yet to show solid progress toward recovery from the recession of the early 1980s. As his term drew to a close, however, Moore was claiming credit for $1 billion worth of new jobs, for tax cuts, and for placing new emphasis on higher education, an area where West Virginia has traditionally trailed behind most southern states.

In 1988, Moore officially announced that he would be seeking an unprecedented fourth term as governor, ending months of speculation that he would challenge incumbent Robert Byrd for the U.S. Senate. He won renomination only after a bitter primary fight with businessman John Raese. His opponent in the November 1988 general election was Democrat

Gaston Caperton, an insurance executive whose primary victory in a seven-candidate field left the party bitter and divided. Depicting Moore as an old-style politician and blaming him for the state's high unemployment rate, Caperton framed the race as a referendum on Moore and the state's stagnant economy. The campaign was also noteworthy for the vast sums of money spent on both sides, causing critics to focus on the contrast between the state's suffering economy and its free-spending gubernatorial candidates. The citizens' lobbying group Common Cause estimated that campaign spending topped $8 million.

In the end, analysts believed that the electorate was in the mood for a change, as voters handed Caperton a 59 percent victory over the long-serving Moore, the only incumbent unseated in the 1988 elections. Caperton called the outcome "a great victory for those of us who want change."

Moore's troubles mounted after the election. Caught in a three-year probe of public corruption in West Virginia, he was indicted by a federal grand jury on charges of extortion, mail and tax fraud, and obstruction of justice. The leading charge against Moore was that he had used his position to extort funds from the Maben Energy Corporation, a coal company based in the town of Beckley. He was also charged with filing false federal income tax returns, illegally funneling campaign funds, and taking illegal payments to finance his unsuccessful 1988 campaign. Later, he also admitted efforts during 1989 to thwart the grand jury's investigation by falsifying documents and trying to persuade witnesses to lie.

In the face of the charges made against him, Moore agreed to a plea bargain arrangement with the federal government. In July 1990 he was sentenced to a five-year, ten-month prison term at the Maxwell Air Force Base prison camp in Montgomery, Alabama. The sentencing and imprisonment of West Virginia's longest-serving governor was the most devastating of a series of blows to state government, which had been rocked by a number of political corruption scandals in recent years.

Bibliography: Michael Barone et al., *The Almanac of American Politics, 1986, 1988, 1990* (Washington, D.C.: National Journal, 1985, 1987, 1989); biographical information courtesy of governor's office; *The New York Times*: 3–25–84; 4–29–84; 11–6–84; 1–15–85; 4–1–87; 4–8–87; 12–3–87; 1–12–88; 5–10–88; 5–12–88; 11–8–88; 4–13–90; 7–1–90; 7–11–90; *The Star-Ledger* (Newark, N.J.), 11–10–88; *USA Today*: 1–3–89; 8–8–90.

GASTON CAPERTON, 1989–

Born on February 21, 1940, in Charleston, West Virginia, Caperton is a 1963 graduate of the University of North Carolina, where he earned a B.A. in business. Having no previous political experience prior to his election as governor in 1988, the millionaire Democrat served as president and chief executive officer of the McDonough-Caperton Insurance Group. An Episcopalian, he is married to Maestra Rachael Worby, conductor of the Wheeling Symphony Orchestra, and has two sons.

Caperton's business savvy and image as a political neophyte served him well in his first bid for office in November 1988. Painting long-term incumbent Arch Moore as an old-style politician and blaming him for the state's high unemployment rate, Caperton ousted the legendary Moore from office, winning with 59 percent of the vote. His campaign had promised to restore fiscal and ethical integrity to a state on the brink of bankruptcy, shackled with a $500 million deficit and suffering from serious problems in education and employment. Caperton called the outcome "a great victory for those of us who want change." Critics, however, condemned the vast amounts of money spent by both candidates in the race, estimated by Common Cause to have topped $8 million.

Early in his administration, Caperton drew high marks as a take-charge leader and business-minded governor. Claiming that "a state is no different than a business," he argued that the state could not move forward unless placed on a firm financial footing. He acted quickly with a comprehensive package of fiscal reforms that included huge tax hikes and a $100 million cut in public spending. This tough medicine moved the state from a $500 million deficit to a balanced budget. By 1991, West Virginia was one of a handful of states to boast a surplus in a tough recessionary climate.

In addition to his fiscal programs, Caperton exercised leadership in other areas as well. Shortly after taking office, he gained passage of one of the nation's toughest ethics laws and reorganized 131 government agencies into seven major departments. He launched a massive education reform package that included a $200 million school construction and renovation program; a three-year, $5,000 pay raise for teachers; and a ten-year, $70 million basic skills computer initiative designed to put a computer in every elementary classroom in the state.

Economic development has also been a focus of his agenda. His Partnership for Progress initiative was designed to bring together business,

Gaston Caperton *(Courtesy of Governor's Office)*

labor, education, and government in a combined effort to capitalize on regional strengths and to prepare workers for the high-technology jobs of the future. Under his leadership, more than 30,000 new jobs have been created, and tourism revenues have increased by more than 13 percent. Caperton reformed the state's economic development program by creating a Council for Community and Economic Development and a $10 million Jobs Investment Trust. In 1991, West Virginia became the first state to open a trade office in the Japanese industrial city of Nagoya.

Initiatives in environmental protection and health care rounded out Caperton's program for his first term. In 1991, he led the fight for landmark legislation strictly limiting the size of landfills and requiring community recycling programs. He also achieved new legislation protecting the state's groundwater supply. A 1991 grant from the Kellogg Foundation enabled Caperton to establish a model program for rural health care delivery and to further improve access to basic health care in the state.

Caperton's reforms, however, were not accomplished without controversy and criticism. Just four months after he took office, he and his wife Dee announced that they were divorcing after a 23-year marriage. The messy court battle that followed exposed the extent of Caperton's personal fortune—with his former wife reportedly receiving a $10 million settlement. The saga of his personal life remained in the forefront of public attention when his ex-wife, a former one-term state legislator, later ran for state treasurer. The race turned into a kind of soap opera attracting national attention and raising questions about how the divorced couple could possibly work together to conduct state business.

More serious was Caperton's resort to tax hikes to heal the state's fiscal ills. Reneging on his 1988 election promise not to raise taxes, he responded with $465 million in business and sales tax hikes, the largest tax increase in state history. His approval rating plummeted to 14 percent, the worst ever recorded by a West Virginia governor, and he registered barely a 35 percent approval rating in polls of his own party. His most unpopular tax hike hit the poor hard—raising the sales tax from 5 to 6 percent and extending it to food. His spending cuts included eliminating three state mental institutions and cutting state employment 5.9 percent. A plan to reduce the amount of money spent on medical education in the state by consolidating the state's three medical schools drew more opposition, and the sale of state liquor stores further weakened his popularity by eliminating many political patronage jobs. Analysts believed that voter displeasure over Caperton's tax hikes was behind the overwhelming defeat of three constitutional amendments that he said were necessary to complete his reorganization of state government.

The year 1990 found Caperton embroiled in West Virginia's first statewide teacher strike, as teachers protested his failure to provide them with a raise in his proposed 1990–1991 budget. Adding further fuel to the fire were the criticisms of prolife forces, who condemned Caperton for switching from abortion foe to abortion rights backer.

With his popularity plummeting, Caperton faced a reelection challenge from within his own party. Four Democratic opponents attacked him for breaking his no-new-taxes vow of 1988, for dropping his opposition to abortion rights, and for "throwing money at the schools." The most serious threat came from state Senator Charlotte Pritt, who capped her campaign for lower taxes and more government services by calling herself a "coal miner's daughter." It was a powerful image to use against the millionaire Caperton.

In the end, voters seemed to agree with Caperton that he had done a good job in a tough situation. "Nobody likes taxes," he explained. "But we made the investments we needed to make." Winning the Democratic nomination against Pritt, he went on to face state Agricultural Commissioner Cleve Benedict in the general election. In a state where Democrats outnumber Republicans by 2–1, the match against the Republican was an easy contest for Caperton, who went on to win reelection with 56 percent of the vote. Although Benedict had promised to roll back the unpopular sales tax from 6 to 3 percent, he was apparently hurt by his ties to former Governor Arch Moore, then in prison on a variety of corruption charges. A write-in campaign by Charlotte Pritt drew 7 percent of the vote.

Bibliography: Biographical information courtesy of governor's office; *The Chronicle of Higher Education*: 5–22–91; 9–18–91; Phil Duncan, ed., *Politics in America 1992* (Washington, D.C.: Congressional Quarterly Press, 1991); *The New York Times*: 11–8–88; 9–11–89; 3–13–90; 10–26–92; *The Star-Ledger* (Newark, N.J.): 11–10–88; 7–2–89; *USA Today*: 1–3–89; 4–7–89; 1–29–90; 5–2–90; 6–28–91; 5–11–92; 5–12–92; 5–13–92; 11–4–92; 11–5–92.

WISCONSIN

TOMMY G. THOMPSON, 1987–

Born in Elroy, Wisconsin, on November 19, 1941, Thompson is the son of Allan Thompson and Julie Dutton Thompson. A Catholic, he is married to the former Sue Ann Mashak and has three children.

Thompson graduated from the University of Wisconsin–Madison in 1963 with a degree in history and political science. In 1966, he received a law degree from the same university. A Republican, he became interested in politics early. In 1964, he was vice-chairman of Wisconsin Collegians for Goldwater, and from 1964 to 1966, he was a legislative messenger in the Wisconsin State Senate. Elected to the state assembly in 1966, he served as assistant minority leader from 1972 to 1981 and as Republican floor leader from 1981 until his accession to the governorship. In the assembly, he served on numerous committees: Assembly Organization, Legislative Council, Rules, the Strategic Development Commission, the Select Committee on the Future of the University System, and joint legislative commissions on Employment Relations and Legislative Organization. During his years in the legislature, he also worked as an attorney in private practice with the firm of Elroy and Mauston and as a real estate broker.

In 1986, Thompson challenged Democratic incumbent Anthony Earl for the statehouse. Since Earl had a reputation as one of the most liberal governors in America, and Wisconsin had long been known as a liberal state, political observers were surprised by the Thompson win. As a conservative Republican, Thompson's victory was even more surprising because most incumbent governors did fairly well in the 1986 elections. Despite his record of competence, Earl's loss was attributed to an inability to get his message out and to his reliance on an overly tight-knit campaign staff. The electorate also seemed concerned that the state's high tax policies—which Earl defended—were stifling economic growth. Thompson, on the other hand, based his campaign on a ringing call to cut both taxes and welfare. He defeated Earl by 100,000 votes, garnering 53 percent of the vote to the incumbent's 47 percent. Of all the gubernatorial contestants in 1986, Thompson was the only Republican candidate to defeat an incumbent Democrat.

Tommy G. Thompson *(Courtesy of Governor's Office)*

After a successful first term, Thompson was returned to office in 1990, defeating Democratic Assembly Speaker Tom Loftus with 58 percent of the vote. He won all but 5 of Wisconsin's 72 counties, including the traditional Democratic strongholds of Kenosha, Milwaukee, and Racine. Loftus was unable to mount much of a challenge, despite campaign stands that would seem to have appealed to much of the state's normally liberal electorate.

In office, Thompson has acquired a national reputation as a pragmatic innovator and conservative activist. Moved by a commitment to revitalize the state economy and to run state government like a successful business, he has focused on reducing state spending, cutting taxes, and investing in economic development. Probably his most renowned and controversial proposals have involved the overhaul of the state welfare system, an approach that has turned Wisconsin into a laboratory for conservative social ideas and brought national attention to him.

Thompson has made efforts to cut welfare costs a centerpiece of his administration. After the federal Family Support Act of 1988 invited states to experiment with welfare reform, Thompson responded with a series of initiatives, the ultimate aim of which has been to move people from public assistance to self-sufficiency. He began with a 5 percent cut in Aid to Families with Dependent Children (AFDC) payments, then pushed through Learnfare, which pares family benefits if children don't attend school. Another program aimed to reward teenage mothers who marry and penalize those who don't. Thompson has also unveiled a pilot program to cap welfare payments to unwed teenage mothers regardless of how many children they have and to pay larger grants to those who marry. Recipients would also have to finish high school or get job training in order to continue benefits. Thompson has bolstered the state's child support program by automatically withholding funds from parents' paychecks. He got the federal government to waive rules limiting two-parent welfare families from working more than 100 hours a month, and he has channeled more than $18 million shaved from other programs into the state's child care budget, which has more than doubled.

In another highly controversial move, Thompson proposed a two-tiered public aid system that reduces benefits for newcomers to the state. Declaring that Wisconsin had become a welfare magnet, Thompson sought to deal with the problems caused by the influx of thousands of poor residents, mostly from inner-city neighborhoods in Chicago, who were drawn to Wisconsin because its welfare benefits were higher than those of Illinois. Under the three-year experiment due to begin in July 1994, Wisconsin would pay welfare recipients moving in from other states the same amount in AFDC benefits that they would have received in the state they left. Only after living in Wisconsin for six months would new residents receive Wisconsin's level of benefits. The proposal survived a constitutional challenge in the state supreme court, which rejected the argument that the law unconstitutionally frustrated the right of poor people to settle where they chose.

Thompson's proposals have touched off a national debate on welfare reform. Although Wisconsin has long been associated with innovative approaches to social policy, and boasts a long history of activist chief executives, all, however, had been Democrats. Thompson is the first conservative Republican activist in state history. Supporters defend his programs as "tough love," saying he aims to help the poor by breaking a dangerous cycle of welfare dependency. They insist his efforts are working. Fifty thousand fewer people are currently getting welfare than when he became governor in 1987, a 19 percent drop in the AFDC caseload. In 1990, Wisconsin was the only state whose AFDC caseload didn't increase. Critics, on the other hand, say he is a mean-spirited bully who is only after publicity and votes. They accuse him of pursuing a callous, soak-the-poor agenda that has left some of the state's 238,000 welfare poor even poorer. Learnfare has caused an even bigger furor, after audits uncovered numerous cases of unfair sanctions due to sloppy record keeping by public schools. Nonetheless, Thompson's programs have made him popular among voters and a rising star among GOP governors.

Thompson has also been the first prominent political leader in the country to come face to face with the new politics of biotechnology. He has made attracting and supporting biotechnology businesses a cornerstone of his program to stabilize Wisconsin's struggling rural economy, and the state is home to several leading agricultural biotechnology companies. In 1990, however, Thompson faced a serious contest with the legislature over approval of the first economically important farm product of the young biotechnology industry to come to market—a genetically engineered drug intended to increase milk production in cows. Critics had many complaints. They charged that the new drug would be an economic disaster for farmers; that it was being forced on the state dairy industry by big companies; that it would result in a huge milk surplus; and that consumer fears about the health effects of residues in milk might lead some people to stop buying dairy products.

Besides his interests in welfare reform and biotechnology, Thompson has also been a strong advocate of international trade. His overseas trade missions to Japan, Belgium, Germany, Canada, and Mexico have created new markets for Wisconsin products. Due to his efforts, Wisconsin is one of only eight states to enjoy a foreign trade surplus.

Thompson has frequently been mentioned as a future Republican presidential candidate, and his name is already surfacing on a longshot list of contenders for 1996. For now, however, he must decide whether to seek an unprecedented third gubernatorial term in 1994. An impressive victory then would give him the necessary springboard from which to launch a presidential bid.

Bibliography: Michael Barone et al., *The Almanac of American Politics, 1988* (Washington, D.C.: National Journal, 1987); biographical information courtesy of governor's office; *The Chronicle of Higher Education*: 11–12–86; 12–17–86; 3–11–87; 8–12–92; *Newsweek,* 10–15–90; *The New York Times*: 1–6–87; 3–31–88; 3–15–89; 4–21–90; 11–7–90; 2–12–91; 6–4–92; 6–19–92; 8–17–92; *The Record* (Bergen County, N.J.), 4–11–92; *The Star-Ledger* (Newark, N.J.), 11–28–91; *USA Today*: 9–10–90; 1–8–91; 11–16–92; 11–18–92.

Mike Sullivan *(Courtesy of Governor's Office)*

WYOMING

MIKE SULLIVAN, 1987–

Born in Omaha, Nebraska, on September 22, 1939, Sullivan is the son of
J. B. Sullivan and Margaret E. Sullivan. He was raised in Douglas, Wyoming, where he graduated from Converse County High School in 1957.
He followed both his parents to the University of Wyoming, where he
received a B.S. in petroleum engineering in 1961 and a J.D. in 1964. After
his graduation from law school, he practiced law in Casper, specializing
in trial work. He and his wife, the former Jane Metzler of Powell, Wyoming, have three children.

A life long Democrat, Sullivan rode a distinguished career in law and
years of varied civic activities to the state's highest office. Over the years,
he served in many civic organizations, including the Casper Rotary Club
(of which he was president), Natrona County United Fund, board of
directors of the Shepherd of the Valley Nursing Home, board of directors
of the University of Wyoming Alumni Association, board of trustees of
Natrona County Memorial Hospital (of which he was chairman), board
of trustees of St. Joseph's Children's Home in Torrington, and board of
directors of Norwest Bank, West Casper. In 1986, he served as cochairman of the "We Are Wyoming" fund, which raised money throughout
central Wyoming for victims of Cheyenne's 1985 flood.

The 1986 race for governor was wide open due to the unexpected retirement of three-term incumbent Ed Herschler. Most political observers
predicted victory for Republican Pete Simpson, brother of U.S. Senator
Alan K. Simpson and winner of a divisive party primary. The Republican
candidate, however, proved less than adept as a campaigner, paving the
way for Sullivan's 54 percent to 46 percent victory. During the race,
Sullivan called for more economic diversification and impressed voters
with his optimistic attitude and record of competent achievement.

He was reelected to a second term in November 1990 by a record
margin, defeating rancher Mary Mead with 65 percent of the vote and
winning 21 of the state's 23 counties.

In office, Sullivan has demonstrated strong commitment to education,
energy, and rural development issues. As vice-chair and later chair of the
Western Governors Association, he moved the group of 18 state and 3

territorial governors to pursue improved relations with the federal government. Under his leadership, the group has worked in the areas of rural development, tourism, Indian water rights, and waste disposal.

Sullivan also serves on the executive committee of the National Governors Association (NGA) and chairs an NGA action team on education reform. He is past chairman of the Interstate Oil Compact Commission, an organization of oil-producing states, and cochairs the Alliance for Acid Rain Control.

As governor, Sullivan has favored expanding the University of Wyoming's economic development efforts and has opposed the creation of any new four-year colleges. He has strongly supported the efforts of community college officials to raise faculty salaries. In 1992, Sullivan signed a controversial bill designed to curtail welfare spending on college students and their families. The bill ordered the State Department of Family Services to ask the federal government for the right to cut off welfare benefits to clients who are pursuing education beyond an initial bachelor's degree. It also called for cutting benefits to recipients who took more than four years to complete an associate's degree or more than six years to complete a bachelor's degree.

Bibliography: Michael Barone et al., *The Almanac of American Politics, 1988* (Washington, D.C.: National Journal, 1987); biographical information courtesy of governor's office; *The Chronicle of Higher Education*: 11–12–86; 8–28–91; 6–23–92; *The New York Times*: 1–6–87; 8–23–90; 11–8–90; *USA Today*: 3–7–90; 8–20–90; 11–8–90.

INDEX

Complete biographical entries of governors included in this volume appear in **bold** print.

About the Author

MARIE MARMO MULLANEY is Professor of History and Political Science at Caldwell College. Among her earlier publications are *Biographical Directory of the Governors of the United States 1983–1988* (Greenwood Press, 1989), and *American Governors and Gubernatorial Elections 1979–1987* (Greenwood Press, 1988).